The Complete Diaries
of Theodor Herzl

The Complete Diaries of
THEODOR HERZL

Edited by
Raphael Patai

Translated by
HARRY ZOHN

VOLUME I

HERZL PRESS
AND
THOMAS YOSELOFF

New York *London*

© 1960 by The Theodor Herzl Foundation, Inc.

Library of Congress Catalog Card Number: 60-8594

Thomas Yoseloff, *Publisher*
11 East 36th Street
New York 16, N. Y.

Thomas Yoseloff Ltd.
123 New Bond Street
London W. 1, England

Printed in the United States of America

Preface

A hundred years after his birth, fifty-six years after his death, and twelve years after the realization of his dream in the State of Israel, Theodor Herzl is universally recognized in Jewish history, and, in fact, in world history, as the founder of political Zionism and the father of the Jewish state. His *Diaries*, published here in full for the first time, contain the fascinating record of the eight last years of his life during which, practically single-handed and at the sacrifice of his fortune, his career, his family and his very life, he created a world movement among the Jews and made the rulers and governments of his day accept the idea that the Jewish people must have a homeland of its own.

When Herzl began keeping his *Diaries* in 1895, he was a leading Viennese feuilletonist and playwright. He was celebrated in his home town, and had achieved some fame abroad as well. He was a recognized master of the pen who clad his philosophical ideas, social criticism, and subtle satire in a sensitive, refined, and polished style. In the *Diaries*, however, he consciously forewent any stylistic sparkle. In them his language is generally simple, direct and straightforward, but sometimes obscure. The entries were often written hastily, and occasionally even carelessly. They were intended to be not literature but a frank account of his day-to-day struggle for the movement, of his meetings, plans, and actions, and of the ideas and ideals that motivated him. Herzl put his ideas down as they came to him, often using expressions in French, English, Yiddish, Hebrew, Italian, Hungarian, Latin, Greek, and Turkish, or falling back on the Viennese idiom.

To translate such a document into English was certainly not an easy undertaking. In Professor Harry Zohn we found a translator fully equal to the task. Professor Zohn achieved that happy medium between too close an adherence to the original and too free a rendering which makes his translation read as if Herzl had written in English instead of German.

The *Diaries* represent merely a part of Herzl's literary output. He wrote many feuilletons, short stories, sketches (some of them collected and edited in separate volumes), some thirty plays, a book on the Jewish State, a novel (*Altneuland*), Zionist addresses and other writings, and a great number of letters addressed to hundreds of writers—artists, statesmen, scholars, Zionist leaders, etc.—scattered in more than a dozen countries. While creating the Zionist movement, this writing activity went on unceasingly, as did his work as literary editor of the *Neue Freie Presse*.

There can be no doubt as to Herzl's exceptional talents in many fields and his complete dedication to the Jewish cause. Yet his success among both the simple people and in the courts of the high and mighty sprang from yet a third source. This was his tremendous personal magnetism which made its impact on everyone and which added weight to his arguments and power to his convictions. The *Diaries* contain only occasional reflections of this unique personality, filled as they are with details of his unceasing efforts to convince and convert, to motivate and activate people as dissimilar as the mighty German Kaiser, the timid Chief Rabbi

v

of Vienna, the shrewd Oriental expert Arminius Vámbéry, and the hardheaded scions of the Rothschild dynasty. Therefore it is recommended that these *Diaries* be read together with at least one biography of Herzl, several of which are now available in English.

Prior to the present edition, less than one third of the text of the *Diaries* was published in English. Even the German edition, printed in the early 1920's in Berlin, did not contain the entire text. Hundreds of passages, a number covering several pages, were omitted because of political or personal considerations. Today, more than half a century after the last entry was made, it is felt that everything contained in the original manuscript of Herzl's *Diaries* belongs to history and not only *can*, but *should*, be made public. Thus the present edition—published at the initiative of Dr. Emanuel Neumann, president of the Theodor Herzl Foundation Inc.—contains for the first time every word Herzl entered in the eighteen copybooks he filled.

The editor has attempted to annotate this edition as fully as possible. The first four volumes contain the text of the *Diaries,* the fifth the notes and the Index. The notes are arranged alphabetically and cover practically all the names of persons, places, institutions, organizations mentioned by Herzl as well as supplying additional details on many subjects. A special prefatory note to the fifth volume will contain information on the nature of the annotations and their use, as well as the acknowledgments to the dozens of individuals and institutions who helped the editor in assembling them. Mention however must be made here of the Zionist Central Archives of Jerusalem in whose safekeeping the original manuscript of Herzl's *Diaries* is deposited and whose director Dr. Alex Bein and staff filled untiringly the innumerable requests called forth by this work.

New York RAPHAEL PATAI
March 16, 1960

Translator's Foreword

It is a rare privilege to be associated with the first complete and unabridged publication in any language of the Herzl Diaries, surely one of the most significant works of its kind in world literature.

It has been my aim to produce a very faithful translation and to beware of the "translator's itch" to dress up the material and endow it with a stylistic gloss which the original, so striking in its immediacy and directness, does not possess.

It would never have been possible to finish this lengthy and arduous task in a comparatively short period of time without the encouragement and cooperation of a number of people. In particular I wish to express my gratitude to the associates of the Theodor Herzl Institute, especially to Drs. Emanuel Neumann and Emil Lehman, for their confidence in me. My warmest thanks also go to the Institute's Director of Research, Dr. Raphael Patai, who has proved the ideal editor, and to his secretary, Pearl Silver. My Brandeis colleague Dr. John B. Wight has given me invaluable stylistic advice, and Barbara Wight has assisted me with the translations from the French.

I should like to dedicate this translation to the memory of Ludwig Lewisohn—dynamic Jewish leader, brilliant man of letters, master translator from the German, and fatherly friend.

Brandeis University HARRY ZOHN
Waltham, Massachusetts
March, 1960

Contents

Volume I

Book One

*Of the Jewish Cause
Begun in Paris
Around Pentecost, 1895*

For some time past I have been occupied with a work of infinite grandeur. At the moment I do not know whether I shall carry it through. It looks like a mighty dream. But for days and weeks it has possessed me beyond the limits of consciousness; it accompanies me wherever I go, hovers behind my ordinary talk, looks over my shoulder at my comically trivial journalistic work, disturbs me and intoxicates me.

It is still too early to surmise what will come of it. But my experience tells me that even as a dream it is something remarkable, and that I ought to write it down—if not as a reminder to mankind, then at least for my own delight or reflection in later years. And perhaps as something between these two possibilities—that is, as literature. If my conception is not translated into reality, at least out of my activity can come a novel.

Title: The Promised Land!

To tell the truth, I am no longer sure that it was not actually the novel that I first had in mind—although not as something "literary" for its own sake, but only as something that would serve a purpose.

And the fact that after such a short time I am no longer sure of it is the best proof of how necessary this written record is. How much I have regretted that on the day of my arrival in Paris I didn't start a diary to preserve the experiences, the impressions and visions which cannot get into the newspaper because they have an odd way of disappearing too fast. In this way a lot has escaped me.

But what are the experiences of a newspaper correspondent compared with what I am now working on! What dreams, thoughts, letters, meetings, actions I shall have to live through—

3

disappointments if nothing comes of it, terrible struggles if things work out. All that must be recorded.

Stanley interested the world with his little travel book *How I Found Livingstone*. And when he made his way across the Dark Continent, the world was enthralled—the entire civilized world. Yet how petty are such exploits when compared to mine. Today I must still say: compared to my dream.

When did I actually begin to concern myself with the Jewish Question? Probably ever since it arose; certainly from the time that I read Dühring's book. In one of my old notebooks, now packed away somewhere in Vienna, are my first observations on Dühring's book and on the Question. At that time I still had no newspaper as an outlet for my writings—it was, I believe, in 1881 or 1882; but I know that even today I repeatedly say some of the things that I wrote down then. As the years went on, the Jewish Question bored into me and gnawed at me, tormented me and made me very miserable. In fact, I kept coming back to it whenever my own personal experiences—joys and sorrows—permitted me to rise to broader considerations.

Naturally, each passing year brought a change in my thinking, something I was consciously aware of. In the same way, a different man now looks out at me from a mirror than formerly. But despite the altered features, the person is the same. By these signs of age I recognize my maturity.

At first, the Jewish Question grieved me bitterly. There might have been a time when I would have liked to get away from it—into the Christian fold, anywhere. But in any case, these were only vague desires born of youthful weakness. For I can say to myself with the honesty inherent in this diary—which would be completely worthless if I played the hypocrite with myself—that I never seriously thought of becoming baptized or changing my name. This latter point is even attested to by an incident. When as a green young writer I took a manuscript to the Vienna *Deutsche Wochenschrift,* Dr. Friedjung advised me to adopt a pen-name less Jewish than my own. I flatly refused, saying that I wanted to continue to bear the name of my father, and I offered to withdraw the manuscript. Friedjung accepted it anyway.

I then became a writer of sorts, with little ambition and petty vanities.

The Jewish Question naturally lurked for me around every turn and corner. I sighed over it and made fun of it; I felt unhappy, but still it never really took hold of me, although even before I came here I wanted to write a Jewish novel. I was going to write it during my travels in Spain on which I set out in the summer of 1891. At that time it was my next literary project. The hero was to have been my dear friend Heinrich Kana, who had shot himself that February in Berlin. I believe that through the novel I wanted to write myself free of his ghost. In its first draft the novel was entitled *Samuel Kohn,* and among my loose notes there must be many which have reference to it. I wanted in particular to contrast the suffering, despised, and decent mass of poor Jews with the rich ones. The latter experience nothing of anti-Semitism which they are actually and mainly responsible for. The milieu in which Kana lived was to be set off against that of his rich relatives.

The *Neue Freie Presse* sent me to Paris as its correspondent. I took the job because I sensed at once how much I would see and learn of the world in that post; but I still regretted the abandoned plan of the novel.

In Paris I was in the midst of politics—at least as an observer. I saw how the world is run. I also stood amazed at the phenomenon of the crowd—for a long time without comprehending it. Here too I reached a higher, more disinterested view of anti-Semitism, from which at least I did not have to suffer directly. In Austria or in Germany I must constantly fear that someone will shout "Hep, hep!" after me. But here I pass through the crowd unrecognized.

In this word "unrecognized" lies a terrible reproach against the anti-Semites.

Up to now I have heard that cry of "Hep, hep!" with my own ears only twice. The first time was when I passed through

Mainz in 1888. One evening I entered a cheap nightclub and had a beer. When I got up to leave and made my way to the door through the noise and the smoke, a fellow called "Hep, hep!" after me. A chorus of horse-laughs arose around him.

The second time was at Baden near Vienna. Someone shouted "Dirty Jew" at me as I was riding by in a carriage, coming from Speidel's home at Hinterbrühl. This shout went deeper, because it came as a memorable epilogue to the conversation I had had in Hinterbrühl and because it resounded on my "home" soil.

In Paris, then, I gained a freer attitude toward anti-Semitism which I now began to understand historically and make allowances for.

Above all, I recognized the emptiness and futility of efforts to "combat anti-Semitism." Declamations made in writing or in closed circles do no good whatever; they even have a comical effect. It is true that in addition to careerists and simpletons there may be very stalwart people serving on such "relief committees." These resemble the "relief committees" formed after—and before!—floods, and they accomplish about as much. The noble Bertha von Suttner is in error—an error, to be sure, which does her great honor—when she believes that such a committee can be of help. Exactly the case of the peace societies. A man who invents a terrible explosive does more for peace than a thousand gentle apostles.

This is roughly what I answered Baron Leitenberger when he asked me three years ago what I thought of the *Freies Blatt* as an organ to "combat etc." I said I thought nothing of it. However, something *could* be done through the medium of the press, I said, and then I unfolded to him a plan for a popular paper for combatting Jew-hatred—a paper to be directed by a simon-pure Gentile. However, the Baron thought my plan too complicated, or too costly. He wanted to fight only on a small scale—against anti-Semitism!

Today, of course, I am of the opinion that what seemed adequate to me at that time would be a feeble, foolish gesture.

Anti-Semitism has grown and continues to grow—and so do I.

I can still recall two different conceptions of the Question and its solution which I had in the course of those years. About two years ago I wanted to solve the Jewish Question, at least in Austria, with the help of the Catholic Church. I wished to gain access to the Pope (not without first assuring myself of the support of the Austrian church dignitaries) and say to him: Help us against the anti-Semites and I will start a great movement for the free and honorable conversion of Jews to Christianity.

Free and honorable by virtue of the fact that the leaders of this movement—myself in particular—would remain Jews and as such would propagate conversion to the faith of the majority. The conversion was to take place in broad daylight, Sundays at noon, in Saint Stephen's Cathedral, with festive processions and amidst the pealing of bells. Not in shame, as individuals have converted up to now, but with proud gestures. And because the Jewish leaders would remain Jews, escorting the people only to the threshold of the church and themselves staying outside, the whole performance was to be elevated by a touch of great candor.

We, the steadfast men, would have constituted the last generation. We would still have adhered to the faith of our fathers. But we would have made Christians of our young sons before they reached the age of independent decision, after which conversion looks like an act of cowardice or careerism. As is my custom, I had thought out the entire plan down to all its minute details. I could see myself dealing with the Archbishop of Vienna; in imagination I stood before the Pope—both of them were very sorry that I wished to do no more than remain part of the last generation of Jews—and sent this slogan of mingling of the races flying across the world.

As soon as I had an opportunity to discuss the matter with them, I intended to win over to this plan the publishers of the *Neue Freie Presse*. From Paris I had previously given them some advice which, to the detriment of the Liberal Party in Austria, they did not follow. About a year before the Socialists' drive for electoral reform became acute, I recommended that the Christmas editorial should suddenly demand universal suffrage. In this way the Liberals could regain the solid ground they had lost among the people and the intelligent elements in the working-class. Subsequently, the agitation for electoral reform reached my publishers from the outside, and their stand on it was not a felicitous one.

It is true that I had no real authority with the editorial writers; they regarded me only as a talker and a writer of *feuilletons*.

Thus Benedikt, too, rejected my idea about the Pope when I spoke with him about it here in Paris, as Bacher had earlier rejected my idea concerning universal suffrage.

But one thing in Benedikt's response struck me as being true. He said: For a hundred generations your line has preserved itself within the fold of Judaism. Now you are proposing to set yourself up as the terminal point in this process. This you cannot do and have no right to do. Besides, the Pope would never receive you.

This, however, did not prevent the *Neue Freie Presse* and the Austrian liberals from seeking the Pope's intervention against the anti-Semites later. This happened last winter, a year and a half after my conversation with Benedikt, though under circumstances that were unfavorable and even ran counter to the principles involved—that is to say, when Cardinal Schönborn went to Rome in order to ask the Pope to come out against that element among the anti-Semites which the clergy and the government were beginning to find troublesome. By such irrevocable actions the Liberals recognized what they had always denied previously: the right of the Pope to meddle in the internal affairs of Austria. The result of this abdication equalled zero.

I had meant something entirely different: a diplomatic peace treaty concluded behind closed doors.

Naturally I could not do anything without my newspaper. Where would I have got any authority from? What would I have been able to offer in exchange? The services of the leading liberal paper might have induced the clever Pope to do something, issue a declaration or drop a hint. On a later occasion, incidentally, I heard a remark which Leo XIII made about the paper: Too bad that the *Neue Freie Presse* is so well done.

After this plan had been abandoned, there ripened in my unconscious, in that obscure way, another idea, one not so political but more contemplative. I first formulated it clearly in a conversation with Speidel last summer when I came from Baden to visit him at Hinterbrühl. We were walking over the green meadows, philosophizing, and got on the Jewish Question.

I said: "I understand what anti-Semitism is about. We Jews have maintained ourselves, even if through no fault of our own, as a foreign body among the various nations. In the ghetto we have taken on a number of anti-social qualities. Our character has been corrupted by oppression, and it must be restored through some other kind of pressure. Actually, anti-Semitism is a consequence of the emancipation of the Jews. However, the peoples who lack historical understanding—that is, all of them—do not see us as an historical product, as the victims of earlier, crueler, and still more narrow-minded times. They do not realize that we are what we are because they have made us that way amidst tortures, because the Church made usury dishonorable for Christians, and because the rulers forced us to deal in money. We cling to money because they flung us onto money. Moreover, we always had to be prepared to flee or to conceal our possessions from plunderers. This is how our relationship to money arose. Then, too, as *Kammerknechte* of the Emperor we constituted a kind of indirect taxation. We extracted money from the people which later was stolen or confiscated from us. All these sufferings rendered us ugly and transformed our character which had in earlier times been proud and magnificent. After all, we once were men who knew how to defend the state in time of war, and we must have been a highly gifted people to have endured two thousand years of carnage without being destroyed.

"Now, it was erroneous on the part of the doctrinaire libertarians to believe that men can be made equal by publishing an edict in the Imperial Gazette. When we emerged from the ghetto, we were, and for the time being remained, Ghetto Jews. We should have been given time to get accustomed to freedom. But the peoples around us have neither the magnanimity nor the patience. They see only the bad and conspicuous characteristics of a liberated people and have no idea that these released men have been unjustly punished. Added to this is the prevalent Socialist opposition to mobile private capital, the kind with which Jews have been forced to occupy themselves exclusively for centuries past.

"But if the Jews turn from money to professions that were previously barred to them, they cause a terrible pressure on the area in which the middle classes earn their living, a pressure under which the Jews actually suffer most of all.

"However, anti-Semitism, which is a strong and unconscious force among the masses, will not harm the Jews. I consider it to be a movement useful to the Jewish character. It represents the education of a group by the masses, and will perhaps lead to its being absorbed. Education is accomplished only through hard knocks. A Darwinian mimicry will set in. The Jews will adapt themselves. They are like the seals, which an act of nature cast into the water. These animals assume the appearance and habits of fish, which they certainly are not. Once they return to dry land again and are allowed to remain there for a few generations, they will turn their fins into feet again.

"The traces of one kind of pressure can be effaced only by another kind."

Speidel said: "This is a universal historical conception."

Then I drove out into the falling darkness, in the direction of Baden.

As my fiacre sped through the tunnel behind the Cholera

Chapel, two young fellows, one of them in cadet uniform, were passing by. I believe I was sitting huddled in thought. At that point I distinctly heard a cry from behind the carriage: "Dirty Jew!"

I started up in anger and, incensed, turned around in the direction of the two youths, but they were already far behind. A moment later my brief impulse to scuffle with street urchins had vanished. Besides, the insult had not been directed at me personally, for I was unknown to them, but at my Jewish nose and Jewish beard, which they had glimpsed in the semi-darkness behind the carriage lanterns.

But what a curious echo to my "universal historical" conception! World history is of no use in such a situation.

A few months later I was sitting for the sculptor Beer who was doing my bust. Our conversation resulted in the insight that it does a Jew no good to become an artist and free himself from the taint of money. The curse still clings. We cannot get out of the Ghetto. I became quite heated as I talked, and when I left, my excitement still glowed in me. With the swiftness of that dream involving a pitcher of water in the Arabian fairy-tale, the outline of the play came into being. I believe I hadn't gone from the Rue Descombes to the Place Péreire when the whole thing was already finished in my mind.

The next day I set to work. Three blessed weeks of ardor and labor.

I had thought that through this eruption of playwriting I had written myself free of the matter. On the contrary; I got more and more deeply involved with it. The thought grew stronger in me that I must do something for the Jews.

For the first time I went to the synagogue in the Rue de la Victoire and once again found the services festive and moving. Many things reminded me of my youth and the Tabak Street temple at Pest. I took a look at the Paris Jews and saw a family likeness in their faces: bold, misshapen noses; furtive and cunning eyes.

Was it then that I conceived the plan of writing on "The Situation of the Jews," or had I conceived it earlier?

Now I remember that it was earlier. I had already talked about it in Vienna the previous fall. I wanted to visit the localities where the vagaries of history had strewn Jewish communities: particularly Russia, Galicia, Hungary, Bohemia; later, the Orient, the new Zion colonies; finally, Western Europe again. All my faithful reports were to bring out the undeserved misfortune of the Jews and to show that they are human beings whom people revile without knowing them. For here in Paris I have acquired a reporter's eyes which are needed for such perceptions.

Some time before Easter I came into contact with Daudet. During one conversation we got on the subject of the Jews. He confessed himself an anti-Semite. I explained to him my own standpoint and once again warmed to my subject (which might be proof that, basically, I think best while talking). When I told him that I wanted to write a book for and about the Jews, he asked: A novel?—No, I said, preferably a man's book!—Whereupon he said: A novel reaches farther. Think of *Uncle Tom's Cabin*.

I then orated some more and moved even him to such an extent that he finally said: *"Comme c'est beau, comme c'est beau* [How beautiful this is]!"

That again put doubts in my mind about "The Situation of the Jews," and I thought of the novel once more. However, Samuel Kohn—Heinrich Kana was no longer the central figure. In the first draft, the final chapter dealt with the moods that preceded Samuel's suicide. One evening he strolled along Unter den Linden, feeling superior to everybody because of his imminent death. Mockingly he looked at the officers of the guard, anyone of whom he could take with him into death. When the thought of doing something useful with his suicide occurred to him, he became a commander. He walked in such a proud and lordly manner that instinctively everyone got out of his way. This placated him; he went home quietly and shot himself.

In the present form of the novel, Samuel still was the weaker but dearly beloved friend of the hero whom the fortunes of his life bring to the point where he discovers, or, rather, founds, the Promised Land.

Shortly before the sailing of the boat which is to take him to new shores, together with a staff of officers expert in exploration, he receives Samuel's farewell letter. Samuel writes: "My dear, dear boy, when you read this letter, I shall be dead."

At this point the hero moves his fist, in which he is crumbling the paper, to his heart. But the next instant there is only rage in him.

He gives the command for departure. Then he stands at the bow of the boat and stares fixedly into the distance where the Promised Land lies.

And he takes the letter, in which there is so much touching love and loyalty, and cries into the wind: "You fool, you scoundrel, you wretch! Oh, for the life that belonged to us and is lost!

*   *   *

How I proceeded from the idea of writing a novel to a practical program is already a mystery to me, although it happened within the last few weeks. It is in the realm of the Unconscious.

Perhaps these ideas are not practical ones at all and I am only making myself the laughing-stock of the people to whom I talk about it seriously. Could I be only a figure in my novel?

But even then it would be worth writing down what I have thought about during this period and am continuing to think about.

One day I suddenly wrote a letter to Baron Hirsch who has taken such a striking millionaire's interest in the Jews. After I had finished this letter, I left it lying there and slept on it for fourteen days and nights. When even after this interval the letter did not seem devoid of sense to me, I mailed it. This letter reads as follows:

Dear Sir:

When may I have the honor of calling on you? I should like to discuss the Jewish Question. I do not want to interview you nor to talk about a disguised or undisguised financial matter. It seems that the claims on you are so manifold that one cannot guard against the suspicion of unsavory designs soon enough. I simply wish to have a discussion with you about Jewish political matters, a discussion that may have an effect on times that neither you nor I will live to see.

For this reason I should like you to arrange our meeting on a day when you can devote an uninterrupted hour or two to the matter. Because of my regular occupation, a Sunday would be best for me. It does not have to be this coming Sunday, but any date you please.

What I have in mind will interest you. But even though I am not telling you much by saying this, I should not want you to show this letter to the people around you—secretaries and others. Kindly treat it confidentially.

Perhaps my name is not unknown to you. In any case, you are acquainted with the newspaper which I represent here.

> Respectfully yours,
> Dr. Herzl,
> Correspondent of the *Neue Freie Presse*

*   *   *

This is a rough draft of the letter, still in my possession. I may have made some changes in the clean copy; at that time I did not yet think of saving all these things as documents.

My main concern was that this letter might be regarded as the beginning of a journalist's feat of extortion. After all, I did not want to meet the man on account of his money, but because he is a very useful force for the cause.

Several days passed. Then I received a reply from London W., 82 Piccadilly.

London, May 20, 1895

Dr. Théodore Herzl, Paris.*

I received your letter here where I am going to be for two months. I am sorry to be unable, with the best will in the world, to arrange the meeting you asked me for. Perhaps you could tell me in a letter what you were going to say to me in person, putting "Personal" on the envelope.

I beg your pardon for replying to you in the handwriting of my secretary, and in French, but as the result of an old hunting injury to my right hand I am unable to hold a pen for any length of time.

Very truly yours,
M. de Hirsch

*   *   *

To this letter I replied:

37 rue Cambon, May 24, 1895

Dear Sir:

I am deeply sorry that we were not able to meet here.

It is not easy to write down what I wanted to tell you. I shall not dwell on the mishaps that a letter may be subject to. My intentions, which are at the service of an important cause, could be desecrated by idle curiosity, or spoiled by the lack of understanding of a chance reader. Furthermore, my letter could come into your hands at a moment when you are distracted by other things and cannot give it your undivided attention. If then you had your secretary answer me with some polite formula about the matter being "under consideration," I would be through with you forever. And in the general interest that might be regrettable.

Nevertheless I am going to write to you. Only, at the moment I am too busy to be brief, as the old saying goes. But in point of fact, I do not want to bore you with a grandiloquent presentation. As soon as I find the time, I shall submit to you a plan for a new Jewish policy.

* The letter is in French in the original.

16 THE COMPLETE DIARIES OF THEODOR HERZL

What you have undertaken till now has been as magnanimous as it has been misapplied, as costly as it has been pointless. You have hitherto been only a philanthropist, a Peabody; I want to show you the way to become something more.

Do not get the idea, however, that I am a maker of projects or some new species of fool, even though the way in which I am writing to you deviates somewhat from the ordinary. Right from the start I admit the possibility that I am mistaken and I shall accept objections.

I certainly do not expect to convince you right away, for you will have to re-think a number of your present attitudes. Although I am presumably only an unknown to you, all I desire is your fullest attention. In conversation I would probably have gained it for myself, but it is harder to do this by correspondence. My letter lies on your desk among many others, and I can imagine that you get plenty of letters every day from beggars, parasites, fakers, and the professionals of charity. That is why my letter will come in a second envelope marked: Letter from Dr. Herzl. I ask you to lay this second envelope aside and not to open it until you have a completely rested and unoccupied mind. That is what I desired for our conversation which did not take place.

Respectfully yours,
Dr. Herzl.

* * *

In this case, too, my rough draft is not reliable. It now seems to me that in copying the letter I changed a few phrases. But in substance, those were its contents, and again the only fear I had was that Hirsch or some third party looking over his shoulder might take me for a money-seeker.

During the following days I prepared a memorandum. I filled a great number of slips of paper with my notes. I wrote while walking, in the Chamber of Deputies, in the restaurant, in the theater.

A wealth of details was quickly added.

In the midst of these preparations Hirsch surprised me with another letter:

London, May 26

Monsieur Herzl, 37 rue Cambon, Paris.*

I received your letter of the day before yesterday. If you have not already prepared a long report, you can save yourself the trouble. In a few days I shall be in Paris for forty-eight hours, and on next Sunday, June 2, at 10:30 a.m., you will find me at your disposal at 2 rue de l'Elysée.

Yours very truly,
M. de Hirsch.

This letter gave me satisfaction, because I saw that I had judged the man correctly and had hit him at the *locus minoris resistentiae* [place of least resistance]. Apparently my statement that he could become more than a Peabody had had an effect on him.

Now I began to make notes in earnest, and by the Saturday before Pentecost they had grown into a thick bundle. Then I divided them into three groups according to their contents: Introduction, Elevation of the Jewish Race, Emigration.

I made a clean copy of them thus arranged. They added up to 22 closely written pages, although I had only used catchwords, aids to my memory during the interview. I always was, and still am, compelled to make allowance for my initial shyness.

When dealing with famous or well-known people here in Paris, I have often made myself ridiculous by my self-consciousness.

Spuller, who is certainly no great light (although he did originate the *esprit nouveau*), once overawed me to the point of denseness when I called on him during his term as a Minister.

On Whitsunday morning I dressed myself with discreet care. The day before I had purposely broken in a new pair of gloves

* In French in the original.

so that they might still look new but not fresh from the shop. One must not show rich people too much deference.

I drove up to the Rue de L'Elysée. A palace. The grand courtyard, the noble side-stairway—to say nothing of the main staircase—made a strong impression on me. Wealth affects me only in the guise of beauty. And there everything was of genuine beauty. Old pictures, marble, muted gobelins. *Donnerwetter!* One of our sort never thinks of these corollaries of wealth when he disparages it. Everything had truly great style, and, a bit dazed, I let myself be handed from one attendant to another.

I was scarcely in the billiard-room when Hirsch stepped out of his study, shook hands with me quickly and absently, as though I were an acquaintance, asked me to wait a little while, and disappeared again.

I sat down and examined the exquisite Tanagra figurines in a glass case. The Baron, I thought to myself, must have hired someone to be in charge of good taste.

Then I heard voices from the adjoining room and recognized that of one of his philanthropic functionaries with whom I had exchanged a few words in Vienna once, and on two occasions here.

I did not like the idea of his seeing me here on his way out. Perhaps Hirsch had arranged it that way on purpose. This thought made me smile again, for I was not minded to become at all dependent on him. Either I would bend him to my will or I would leave with my mission unaccomplished. I was even ready with an answer if, during our conversation, he should offer me a position with the *Jewish Association:** "Enter your service? No. That of the Jews? Yes!"

Then the two officials came out. I shook hands with the one I knew. To the Baron I said: "Can you spare me an hour? If it is not at least an hour, I'd rather not start at all. I need that amount of time merely to indicate how much I have to say."

He smiled: "Just go ahead."

* In English in the original.

I pulled out my notes. "In order to present the matter lucidly I have prepared a few things in advance."

I had hardly spoken five minutes when the telephone rang. I think it was prearranged. I had even meant to tell him in advance that he need not have himself called away on imaginary business, that he had only to say right out whether he was unoccupied. However, he said over the telephone that he was not at home to anybody. By this I knew that I had made an impression on him; he had let his guard down.

I developed my plan as follows:

"In what I have to say you will find some things too simple and others too fantastic. But men are ruled by the simple and the fantastic. It is astonishing—and common knowledge—with what little intelligence the world is governed.

"I by no means set out deliberately to occupy myself with the Jewish question. You too originally did not plan to become a patron of the Jews. You were a banker and made big business deals; you ended up devoting your time and your fortune to the cause of the Jews. Similarly, at the beginning I was a writer and a journalist, with no thought of the Jews. But my experiences and observations, the growing pressure of anti-Semitism compelled me to interest myself in the problem.

"All right. So much for my credentials.

"I won't go into the history of the Jews, although I intended to start with it. It is well known. There is only one point I must emphasize. Throughout our two thousand years of dispersion, we have been without unified political leadership. I regard this as our chief misfortune. It has done us more harm than all the persecutions. This is why we have inwardly gone to rack and ruin. For there has been no one to train us to become real men, even if only out of imperial selfishness. On the contrary, we were pushed into all the inferior occupations, we were locked up in ghettos where we caused one another's degeneration. And when they let us out, they suddenly expected us to have all the attributes of a people used to freedom.

"Now, if we had a united political leadership, the necessity for which I need not demonstrate further and which should by no means constitute a secret society—if we had such leadership, we could tackle the solution of the Jewish question—from above, from below, from all sides.

"The aim that we will pursue once we have a center, a head, will determine the means.

"There are two possible aims: either we stay where we are or we emigrate somewhere else.

"For either course we need certain identical measures for the education of our people. For even if we emigrate, it will be a long time before we arrive in the Promised Land. It took Moses forty years. We may require twenty or thirty. At any rate, in the meantime new generations will arise whom we must educate for our purposes.

"Now, with regard to education, I propose to employ, from the outset, methods quite different from those which you are using.

"First of all, there is the principle of philanthropy, which I consider completely erroneous. You are breeding shnorrers [beggars]. It is symptomatic that no other people shows such a great incidence of philanthropy and beggary as the Jews. It strikes one that there must be a correlation between these two phenomena, meaning that philanthropy debases our national character."

He interrupted me: "You are quite right."

I continued:

"Years ago I heard that your attempts to settle Jews in Argentina had had poor results, or none."

"Would you like me to reply to you as you go along whenever I have an objection?"

"No, I would prefer that you permit me to give you the whole substance of my presentation. I know that some of the things I say will not be in accordance with the facts, because I have never collected facts and figures. Just let me formulate my principles."

From that point on Hirsch jotted down his objections on a writing pad.

I said: "Your Argentinian Jews behave in a disorderly fashion, I am told. One item rather shocked me; the house built first was one of—ill repute."

Hirsch interjected: "Not true. That house was not built by my colonists."

"Very well. But in any case, the whole thing should not have been started the way you did it. You drag these would-be Jewish farmers overseas. They are bound to believe that they have a right to be supported in the future, too, and the last thing in the world that will be promoted by this is their eagerness to work. Whatever such an exported Jew may cost you, he isn't worth it. And how many specimens can you transport over there anyway? Fifteen to twenty thousand! More Jews than that live on one street in the Leopoldstadt. No, direct means are altogether unsuitable for moving masses of people. You can be effective only through indirect means.

"To attract Jews to rural areas you would have to tell them some fairy-tale about how they may strike gold there. In imaginative terms it might be put like this: Whoever plows, sows, and reaps will find gold in every sheaf. After all, it's almost true. The only thing is, the Jews know that it will be a tiny little lump. That is why you would be able to tell them, more rationally: the man who manages best will receive a bonus, one that might be very substantial.

"However, I do not believe that it is possible to settle the Jews in the rural areas of the countries which they now inhabit. The peasants would kill them with their flails. One of the strongholds of German anti-Semitism is Hesse, where Jews engage in small-scale farming.

"With twenty thousand of your Argentinian Jews you will prove nothing, even if those people do well. But if the experiment fails, you will have furnished a dreadful bit of evidence against the Jews.

"Enough of criticism. What is to be done?

"Whether the Jews stay put or whether they emigrate, the race must first be improved right on the spot. It must be made strong as for war, eager to work, and virtuous. Afterwards, let them emigrate—if necessary.

"To effect this improvement, you can employ your resources better than you have done up to now.

"Instead of buying up the Jews one by one, you could offer huge prizes in the chief anti-Semitic countries for *actions d'éclat* [striking deeds], for deeds of great moral beauty, for courage, self-sacrifice, ethical conduct, great achievements in art and science, for physicians during epidemics, for military men, for discoverers of remedies and inventors of other products contributing to the public welfare, no matter what—in short, for anything great.

"Such prizes will accomplish two things: the improvement of everyone, and publicity. You see, because the prize-winning feat will be unusual and glorious, it will be talked about everywhere. Thus people will learn that there are good Jews too, and many of them.

"But the first result is more important: a general improvement. The individual annual prize-winners do not really matter; I am more interested in all the others who try to outdo themselves in order to win a prize. In this way the moral level will be raised—"

At this point he interrupted me impatiently:

"No, no, no! I don't want to raise the general level at all. All our misfortune comes from the fact that the Jews want to climb too high. We have too many intellectuals. My intention is to keep the Jews from pushing ahead. They should not make such great strides. All Jew-hatred comes from this. As for my plans in Argentina, you are misinformed on that, too. It is true that in the beginning some dissolute fellows were sent over, and I would just as soon have thrown them into the water. But now I have many decent people there. And it is my intention, if the colony prospers, to charter a fine English vessel, invite a hundred newspaper correspondents—consider yourself already invited— and take them across to Argentina. Of course, it all depends upon the harvests. After a few good years I could show the world that the Jews make good farmers after all. As a result of this, maybe they will be allowed to till the soil in Russia as well."

Now I said: "I didn't interrupt you although I hadn't finished. I was interested to hear just what you have in mind. But I realize that it would be pointless to go on presenting my ideas to you."

He then remarked in a benevolent tone, much as if I had asked him for a position in his banking house: "I do see that you are an intelligent man."

I merely smiled to myself. Such things as my undertaking are above personal vanity. I am going to see and hear many more things of this sort.

Hirsch now qualified his praise: "But you have such fantastic ideas."

I got up. "Well, didn't I tell you that it would seem either too simple or too fantastic to you? You don't know what the fantastic really is and that the great motives of men can be surveyed only from the heights."

"Emigration would be the only solution," he said. "There are lands enough for sale."

I almost shouted: "Well, who told you that I don't want to emigrate? It is all there in these notes. I shall go to the German Kaiser; he will understand me, for he has been brought up to be a judge of great things . . ."

At these words Hirsch blinked perceptibly. Was he impressed by my rudeness, or by my intention to speak with the Kaiser? Perhaps both. I put my notes in my pocket and concluded.

"To the Kaiser I shall say: Let our people go! We are strangers here; we are not permitted to assimilate with the people, nor are we able to do so. Let us go! I will tell you the ways and the means which I want to use for our exodus, so that no economic crisis or vacuum may follow our departure."

Hirsch said: "Where will you get the money? Rothschild will subscribe five hundred francs."

"The money?" I said with a defiant laugh. "I shall raise a Jewish National Loan Fund of ten million marks."

"A fantasy!" smiled the Baron. "The rich Jews will give nothing. Wealthy people are mean and care nothing about the sufferings of the poor."

"You talk like a Socialist, Baron Hirsch!"

"I *am* one. I am quite ready to hand over everything, provided the others have to do likewise."

I did not take his charming notion any more seriously than it was meant and took my leave. His final words were:

"This has not been our last conversation. As soon as I come over from London again I shall let you hear from me."

"Whenever you wish."

Again I passed over the beautiful staircase and the noble courtyard. I was not disappointed, but stimulated. All in all, a pleasant, intelligent, natural sort of man—vain *par exemple!*—but I could have worked with him. He gives the impression of being reliable, despite all his wilfulness.

Once home I immediately rushed to my writing desk.

*   *   *

Vienna, April 16, 1896

This is where I interrupted the connected presentation at that time, for there followed several weeks of unexampled productivity, during which I no longer had the peace to make a clean copy of my ideas. I wrote walking, standing, lying down, in the street, at table, at night when I started up from sleep.

The slips with my notes are dated. I no longer find the time to transcribe them. I began a second book in order to enter the noteworthy events each day. Thus the slips remained untouched. Now I am asking my good Dad to enter them for me in the present book, in the order in which they were written. I know now, and knew throughout that whole tempestuous period of production, that much of what I wrote down was wild and fantastic. But I made no self-criticism of any sort, so as not to cripple the sweep of these inspirations. There would be time later, I thought, for clarifying criticism.

In these notes the Jewish State is imagined now as something real, now as material for a novel, because at the time I had not made up my mind whether I should dare to publish it as a serious proposal.

This is the rational explanation for the abrupt transitions in these notes; what mattered most to me in this respect was to let no idea escape. Even in the second notebook the novelistic form is reverted to in a few instances.

Even what is fantastic in these disconnected ideas will one day be of interest—certainly to myself and possibly to others as well. Today I am giving them to my dear father to be entered, though with such necessary reservations as are dictated by reason. For today my project has come a step closer to realization, one that may be historically memorable. Reverend Hechler, who has gone tō Karlsruhe to win the Grand Duke and through him the Kaiser for the idea, has wired me to be ready to come to Karlsruhe.

*   *   *

3rd letter to Baron Hirsch, Paris.

Whit-Monday, June 3, 1895

Dear Sir:

In order to forestall the *esprit de l'escalier*,* I had made notes before I went to see you.

On returning home I found that I had stopped on page 6, and yet I had 22 pages. Due to your impatience you heard only the beginning; where and how my idea begins to blossom you did not get to hear.

No matter. In the first place, I didn't expect an immediate conversion. Furthermore, my plan certainly does not depend on you alone.

True, for the sake of speed I would have liked to use you as an available force and a known quantity. But you would have been only the power I would have started with. There are others.

* Translator's Note: Literally, "the spirit of the staircase," that is, the bright ideas that come too late, while descending the stairs, after a meeting.

There are, ultimately and above all, the Jewish masses, and I shall know how to get across to them.

This pen is a power. You will be convinced of it if I stay alive and healthy—a reservation which you too must make with regard to your own activities.

You are the big Jew of money, I am the Jew of the spirit. Hence the divergence between our means and methods. Note that you could not have heard of my attempts as yet, because the first one just took place in your house, on you. I am on my way.

Naturally, your attitude toward me was one of gentle irony. That's what I expected. I told you so in my opening remarks. That is the reception new ideas get. Moreover, you didn't even have the patience to hear me out. Nevertheless, I shall say what is on my mind. I hope you will live to see the magnificent growth of my ideas. You will then recall that Whit-Sunday morning, for despite all your irony I believe you to be open-minded and a man receptive to great plans. And you have tried to do a great deal for the Jews—in your own fashion. But will you understand me if I tell you that the entire process of mankind's development gives the lie to your methods? What! you want to hold a large group of people on a certain level, in fact, press them down? *Allons donc!* [Come, come!] We know, don't we, what phases the human race has passed through, from its primitive to its civilized state. The progression is ever upwards, despite everything and anything, higher and higher, always and ever higher! There are setbacks, it is true. This is not a mere phrase. Our grandfathers would be dumbfounded if they came back to life; but who would want to produce a setback by artificial means— quite apart from the fact that it cannot be done. If it were possible, don't you think that the Monarchy, the Church, would bring it about? And what influence these forces have over the bodies and souls of men! What are your resources by comparison? No, at the very most you can impede progress for a little while, and then you will be swept away by the great whirlwind.

Do you realize that you are pursuing a terribly reactionary

policy—worse than that of the most absolute autocracy? Fortunately your resources are insufficient for it. Your intentions are good, *parbleu, je le sais bien* [Heavens, I know it well]. That is why I should like to give them direction. Do not let the fact that I am a rather young man prejudice you against me. In France, at my thirty-five years of age, men are Ministers of State, and Napoleon was Emperor.

You cut me short with your polite derision. It is still possible to disconcert me in a conversation. I still lack the aplomb which will increase in me with time, because it is necessary to someone who wants to break down opposition, stir the indifferent, comfort the distressed, inspire a craven, demoralized people, and associate with the lords of the world.

I spoke of an army, and you already interrupted me when I began to speak of the (moral) training necessary for its march. I let myself be interrupted. And yet I have already drawn up the further details, the entire plan. I know all the things it involves: Money, money, and more money; means of transportation; the provisioning of great multitudes (which does not mean just food and drink, as in the simple days of Moses); the maintenance of manly discipline; the organization of departments; emigration treaties with the heads of some states, transit treaties with others, formal guarantees from all of them; the construction of new, splendid dwelling places. Beforehand, tremendous propaganda, the popularization of the idea through newspapers, books, pamphlets, talks by travelling lecturers, pictures, songs. Everything directed from one center with sureness of purpose and with vision. But I would have had to tell you eventually what flag I will unfurl and how. And then you would have asked mockingly: A flag, what is that? A stick with a rag on it?—No, sir, a flag is more than that. With a flag one can lead men wherever one wants to, even into the Promised Land.

For a flag men will live and die; it is indeed the only thing for which they are ready to die in masses, if one trains them for it; believe me, the policy of an entire people—particularly when it is scattered all over the earth—can be carried out only with imponderables that float in thin air. Do you know what went into the making of the German Empire? Dreams, songs, fantasies, and black-red-and-gold ribbons—and in short order. Bismarck merely shook the tree which the visionaries had planted.

What! You do not understand the imponderable? And what is religion? Consider, if you will, what the Jews have endured for the sake of this vision over a period of two thousand years. Yes, visions alone grip the souls of men. And anyone who has no use for them may be an excellent, worthy, sober-minded person, even a philanthropist on a large scale; but he will not be a leader of men, and no trace of him will remain.

Nevertheless, a people's visions must have firm ground underneath. How do you know that I do not have eminently practical ideas for individual details? Details which, to be sure, are themselves of gigantic dimensions.

The exodus to the Promised Land constitutes in practical terms an enormous job of transportation, unprecedented in the modern world. Did I say "transportation"? It is a complex of all kinds of human enterprise which will be geared one into the other like cog-wheels. And this undertaking will even in its first stages provide employment for an aspiring multitude of our young people: all the engineers, architects, technologists, chemists, physicians, lawyers, who have emerged from the ghetto during the last thirty years and who thought that they would gain their livelihood and their bit of honor outside the higgling and haggling Jewish trades. They must now be getting desperate and are beginning to constitute a frightful proletariat of intellectuals. But all my love belongs to them, and I want to increase their numbers even as you wish to decrease them. In them I see the future, as yet dormant strength of the Jews. In a word, my kind of people.

Out of this proletariat of intellectuals I shall form the general staff and the cadres of the army which is to seek, discover, and take over the land.

Their very departure will create some breathing space for

the middle classes in anti-Semitic countries and ease the pressure.

Don't you see that at one stroke I shall get both Jewish capital and Jewish labor for our purposes, and their enthusiasm as well, once they understand what it is all about?

These, of course, are only rough outlines. But how do you know that I have not already worked out the details involved? Did you let me finish?

It is true the hour was late; perhaps you were being expected somewhere else, or had work to do, or whatever. But the progress of such a weighty matter must not be made to depend on such petty contingencies. Have no fear, it really does not.

You will wish to continue our conversation, and—without waiting for you—I shall always be ready to furnish you with the further details.

If the stimuli I have given you are still active within you and you wish to talk with me, then write me: *"Venez me voir* [Come to see me]." That will suffice, and I shall come to London for a day. And if on that day I don't convince you any more than I did yesterday, I shall go away just as undismayed and cheerful as I went away the first time. Would you like to make a bet with me? I am going to raise a national Jewish Loan Fund. Will you pledge yourself to contribute fifty million marks when I have raised the first hundred million?

In return, I shall make you the head man.

What are ten billion marks to the Jews? They are certainly richer than the French were in 1871, and how many Jews were among them! As a matter of fact, if need be, we could get under way even with one billion. For this will be working capital, the foundation for our future railroads, emigration fleet, and navy. With it we shall build houses, palaces, workers' dwellings, schools, theaters, museums, government buildings, prisons, hospitals, insane asylums—in short, cities—and make the new land so fruitful as to turn it into the Promised Land.

The loan will itself become the main channel for the emigration of capital. This is the heart of the matter as far as state finances are concerned. It may not be superfluous to remark at this point that I am presenting all this as a man of politics. *I am no businessman and never want to be one.*

Jewish money is available in huge quantities for a Chinese loan, for Negro railroads in Africa, for the most exotic undertakings—and would none be found for the deepest, the most immediate, the direst need of the Jews themselves?

I shall stay in Paris until the middle of July. Then I shall go away for some length of time. It concerns the cause. I beg you, however, to maintain complete silence on this point as well as all the others I have touched upon. At present, my actions may not seem important to you as yet; this is precisely why I am drawing your attention to the value that I attach to absolute secrecy.

For the rest, I assure you in all sincerity that our discussion, even in its fragmentary state, has proved interesting to me and that you have been no disappointment.

With a respectful greeting, I am

Yours sincerely,
Dr. Herzl

Here follow fragmentary thoughts, all of which relate to the Jewish State and are utilized in my political treatise, *The Jewish State.*

June 5, 1895

Central Employment Office

There records will be kept on the fluctuations of the labor market, the way that a bank keeps track of bills of exchange.

A large-scale farmer telegraphs: Request 1000 hands tomorrow. (Sent by train, military style.) A tailor needs assistants. An apprentice shoemaker seeks training. Every enterprise, the largest and the smallest, converges in this department. A reservoir of labor. Unions, employment agencies to be nationalized —like railroads, insurance, etc.

Secretary Goldschmidt.

Similarly, an advisory center for capital. Money is needed in such-and-such a place. In one place there is no sugar factory; in another, there is petroleum. And this office will be a clearing house for the applications of prospective borrowers and investors. This might take the form of an official publication. Forestall profiteering everywhere.

*   *   *

Principle: well-tried enterprises, such as banking, railroads, insurance, shipping, etc. will be taken charge of by the state where there is no doubt that they will prosper. (In return, remission of taxes!)

Risk will be left to private capital, with the inducement of large profits. Successful enterprises later will pay taxes graded in direct proportion to the growth of their returns. Clearly draw the line where private enterprise is not strangled.

When eveything is underway over there, the task of the Director-General will begin in earnest. The emigration must take place *respectably*. The Jewish Company will make good on any fraudulent dealings before emigration and then indemnify itself from the swindler over there.

In this way we shall avoid major crises and prosecutions in later phases of the emigration and lay the foundation for respect in the eyes of the world.

We shall also show our gratitude to benevolent governments by setting ourselves up as large taxpayers in places where we could evade taxes (that is, everywhere, due to the legal sovereignty of foreign countries) and by offering a broad base.

What we lose in this way and through the devaluation of the immovables that are taken over from us we shall amply make up for by our enormous earnings through our planned improvement of the cheap land over there.

*   *   *

Tentative principle for construction: At first decorative, with light materials (designed for 10-20 years, with the exception of monuments), *cela attire l'oeil* [that attracts the eye], exposition style. This will provide for subsequent new construction, thus opportunities for employment indefinitely. Then, durable and handsome.

*   *   *

The *Society of Jews** will proceed in a substantial, financially sound, reliable manner. It is, among other things, also a big shipping agency (take Leinkauf) and will arrange for special passenger and freight rates from the railroads.

This will also be a sort of appeasement for our exodus. For, subsequently people will be sorry and want to follow us, as did Pharaoh. But we shall leave no dirty dealings behind. Jewish honor begins.

*   *   *

Woe to the swindlers who may try to enrich themselves through the Jewish cause. We shall set up the most severe punishments for them, involving the loss of civil rights and of the right to acquire real estate.

*   *   *

For the *Society* must not become a Panama.

*   *   *

We shall unite all Zionists.

*   *   *

Health measures prior to departure. Infectious diseases to be cured on this side. We shall have embarcation hospitals (quarantines), baths, clothing centers before departure.

*   *   *

To breed a peasantry like that of bygone times would be like equipping a modern army with bows and arrows.

*   *   *

* In English in the original.

The idea now absorbs me to such an extent that I relate everything to it, as a lover to his beloved.

Today I went to see Floquet's secretary about Nemec, a member of the Foreign Legion, who was recruited under false pretenses. While the secretary read me the War Minister's Official Report—obviously an irregular procedure as far as the hierarchy is concerned—all I could think about was our own troops; how I could create discipline and yet prevent such inhuman acts.

In the evening, *Tannhäuser* at the Opera. We too will have such splendid auditoriums—the gentlemen in full dress, the ladies dressed as lavishly as possible. Yes, I want to make use of the Jewish love of luxury, in addition to all other resources.

This again made me think of the phenomenon of the crowd.

There they sat for hours, tightly packed, motionless, in physical discomfort—and for what? For something imponderable, the kind that Hirsch does not understand: for sounds! for music and pictures!

I shall also cultivate majestic processional marches for great festive occasions.

June 6, 1895

We shall have to go through bitter struggles: with a reluctant Pharaoh, with enemies, and especially with ourselves. The Golden Calf!

*   *   *

But we shall carry it through, earnest and far-sighted, as long as the people always sense and know the loftiness of our aims.

*   *   *

Keep the army well in hand!

*   *   *

All officials in uniform, trim, with military bearing, but not ludicrously so.

*   *   *

Gigantic *assistance par le travail* [public works].

* * *

On the transport we work out the passage of the destitute. But they do not get it free. Over there they will pay by working, which is part of their training.

* * *

Prizes of all kinds for virtues.

* * *

Tobacco plantations, silk factories.

* * *

The Wonder Rabbi of Sadagora to be brought over and installed as something like the bishop of a province. In fact, win over the entire clergy.

You must convert the algebraic to the numerical. There are people who do not understand that $(a + b)^2 = a^2 + 2ab + b^2$. For them you must calculate it in familiar terms.

* * *

I fully realize that the most immediate in my outline is as sound as the most remote. But precisely in the most immediate (which everyone can see) there must be no errors, otherwise people will take the whole thing for a fantasy.

* * *

Order of procedure:
1. Money-raising (syndicate).
2. Start of publicity (which will cost nothing, for the anti-Semites will rejoice, and I shall break down the liberal opposition by threats of competition).
3. Enrollment of land-seekers.

4. More publicity, on the largest scale. Make Europe laugh at it, swear at it—in short, talk about it.

5. Negotiations with Zion.

6. Agreements on the purchase of land.

7. Issuing of land priorities (one billion).

8. Purchase and building of ships.

9. Continuous enlistment of *all* who come forward; recruitment, assignment, training.

10. Begin to publicize the big subscription.

11. Sailing of the expedition to take possession of the land, with news service for the entire press.

12. Selection and demarcation of the land and the sites for the main cities.

13. Workers from Russia, etc. will have been building embarcation barracks (on Italian or Dutch coast, first for themselves, then for subsequent contingents).

14. Fare and freight contracts with railroads. We must make a big profit on transportation.

15. Exchange of old items for new ones begins.

16. The wheels already in motion will, of course, be kept turning; gradually all the other elements in my program will be added until the entire machine is running!

17. To the German Kaiser (request privileges! from him).

*   *   *

On our part, we guarantee good order and provide a base for taxation (possibly in return for permission for a public subscription to a lottery loan).

June 7, 1895

Hirsch—a week ago he still was the cornerstone of my plans; today he has declined to a *quantité absolument négligeable* [completely negligible quantity], toward which I even feel magnanimous—in thoughts.

*   *   *

Read *Daniel Deronda*. Teweles talks about it. I don't know it yet.

* * *

To the Family Council. I start with you, because at the beginning, until my cadres are set up, I cannot use a *grand fracas* [big row], and can more safely lead out the life and property of the masses. On the other hand, if I stir up the masses first, I endanger the rich.

* * *

Thus I can proceed more cautiously.

* * *

I am the man who makes aniline dyes out of refuse. I must use analogies of different kinds, for this thing is something unparalleled.

* * *

One can put it simply and say that I am having a pair of boots made.

* * *

I have been to Hirsch, I am going to Rothschild, as Moltke went from Denmark to Prussia.

* * *

Let the cowardly, assimilated, baptized Jews remain. We shall benefit even them—they will boast of their kinship with us of which they are now ashamed. We faithful Jews, however, will once again become great.

At the same time, if I win over the R's, I do not want to cast off poor Baron Hirsch.

I shall give him some vice-presidency (in recognition of his past services, and because he is acquainted with my plan).

For the rest, I am not afraid of his divulging my three letters.

But if he does, I shall smash him, incite popular fanaticism against him, and demolish him in print (as I shall inform him in due course).

But I would much prefer to unite him and all the other big Jews under one banner.

First, the administrative council of the Society shall comprise *les plus "upper"* [the uppermost] (for authority's sake). Then I shall install the Camondos and Mendelssohns as heads of the daughter institutions.

I bring to the R's and the big Jews their historical mission. *J'accueillerai toutes les bonnes volontés* [I shall gather all men of good will]—we *must* be united—*et écraserai les mauvaises* [and shall crush all those of ill will] (this I shall say threateningly to the Family Council).

A letter to Teweles (courage is not enough). I must write Beer that I can use his Beerite.

*   *   *

My moving from Vienna to Paris and back was historically necessary, so that I might learn what emigration is.

Güdemann: I will make you the first bishop of the capital. I called you to Glion to offer you visible proof of what we are already capable of in Nature.

If the R's are not willing, I shall take the matter before the entire community of Jews. Apart from the delay, this would have the additional disadvantage of forcing me to divulge my most carefully guarded plans and deliver them to public discussion, including that of the anti-Semites.

The disadvantage to the R's is the fact that the cause would become public knowledge and produce storms of rage (the Jews want to move away!); this could lead to serious unrest in the streets and to repressive legislation.

I either safeguard or endanger their property. And I accomplish this because my pen has remained clean and will continue to be not for sale.

Second Sheet from the *Bois*

I present the solution of the Jewish Question through safeguarding the R. property, and vice versa.

But I am not dependent on the R's—I should merely prefer to use them as a focal point, because I could raise the whole money in one afternoon, by a *simple passage d'écriture* [stroke of the pen].

They should induce Albert R. to present the matter to the Family Council and invite me to address the Council (but not in Paris, because the setting might overawe me).

June 7. In the Palais Royal gardens

Build something on the order of the Palais Royal or the Square of St. Mark.

*   *   *

No Jew to be sent away. Everyone to be used according to his ability or lack of it, e.g., to be taught the breeding of horses.

Introduction at Glion before the clergyman and the layman.

History. Things cannot improve, but are bound to get worse —to the point of massacres.

Governments can't prevent it any longer, even if they want to. Also, there is Socialism behind it.

In the twenty years "before it becomes known," I must train the boys to be soldiers. But only a professional army. Strength: one-tenth of the male population; less would not suffice internally.

In fact, I shall educate one and all to be free, strong men, ready to serve as volunteers in case of need. Education by means of patriotic songs, the Maccabees, religion, heroic stage-plays, honor, etc.

June 7

The Exodus under Moses bears the same relation to this project as a Shrovetide Play by Hans Sachs does to a Wagner opera.

*   *   *

June 7

I am prepared for anything: lamenting for the flesh-pots of Egypt, the dance around the Golden Calf—also the ingratitude of those who are most indebted to us.

Popular hymns (a *Marseillaise* of the Jews) to be commissioned from Goldmark, Brüll, and other Jewish composers (including Mandl). A prize contest unnecessary and ludicrous. The best one will become universal.

We shall probably model the Constitution after that of Venice, but profit by her bad experiences by preventing them. If the Rothschilds join with us, the first *Doge* is to be a Rothschild. I will not and never shall be a *Doge,* for I wish to secure the state beyond the term of my own life.

For Glion.—I have asked you to meet here in order to demonstrate to you how independent of Nature men have already become.

1st main point: I solve the question by either safeguarding the R. fortune or the reverse.

2nd main point: If I cannot do it together with the R's, I shall do it in opposition to them.

Young people (as well as the poor) will get English games: cricket, tennis, etc.; schools in the mountains.

By offering prizes I shall raise the moral level of *our* group, not of those who stay behind! (viz., prizes that are valuable but do not cost us anything, such as landed property, decorations, etc.)

Principle: Every one of my former acquaintances who comes will get a job, near or far.

At first I shall speak with them cordially and examine them; but the moment their employment starts, this geniality will stop as a matter of principle; I shall tell them this right at the outset, for reasons of discipline.

*   *   *

In the Tuileries, before Gambetta's statue. I hope the Jews will put up a more artistic one of me.

* * *

After a hundred years, universal military service should be introduced; but who knows how far civilization will have progressed by then.

We shall give up the Jewish jargons, Judeo-German, which had sense and justification only as the stealthy tongue of prisoners.

I think of the seven-hour working day as an international publicity scheme, to begin with; perhaps it can even be made a permanent feature. If not, the *jeu naturel* [natural course of things] will straighten things out again.

To everyone, high and low, I say: No narrow-mindedness! In a new world there is room for all . . .

With important people one must be gruff if one wants something from them; they see too many smiles.

It took at least thirteen years for me to conceive this simple idea. Only now do I realize how often I went right past it.

The "public works" system has been very important to me.

* * *

Circenses [entertainments] as soon as possible:

German theatre, international theatre, operas, operettas, circuses, café-concerts, Café *Champs Elysées*.

* * *

Send wonderful display material for the Exposition of 1900.

* * *

The High Priests will wear impressive robes; our cuirassiers, yellow trousers and white tunics; the officers, silver breast-plates.

* * *

As soon as we have decided on the land and concluded a preliminary treaty with its present sovereign, we shall start diplomatic negotiations with all the great powers for guarantees. Then, issuance of the Jewish loan.

*   *   *

Rousseau believed that there was such a thing as a *contrat social*. There is not. In the state there is only a *negotiorum gestio*.

Thus I conduct the affairs of the Jews without their mandate, but I become responsible to them for what I do.

To the Family Council: For you that is *un simple passage d'écriture* [a stroke of the pen].

And yet this safeguarding of your property will yield you the biggest profit you have ever made.

That is why I want the great masses of the Jews to get some of it, whether through a second issue for which only the original subscribers are eligible or through shares for the first takers of land (the latter procedure would be better and more social-minded). We shall easily find the proper form.

That is in your interest as well; otherwise the Jews will bear you a great deal of ill-will later.

June 8, 1895

Dig out the centers and take them across. Transplant whole environments in which the Jews feel *comfortable*.

*   *   *

Seek out and hire anyone who at any time may have done me an injury and therefore hesitates to approach me. Because I must be the first to set an example of supreme magnanimity.

The solution of the Jewish Question must be a mighty final chord of reconciliation. We part as friends from our foes—this should be the beginning of Jewish honor.

To the men at Glion and, later, to the Family Council:

Note that I am not letting my imagination run riot, but working with nothing but facts which you can examine for yourselves; the imagination is inherent only in their combination.

*   *   *

I firmly believe that I shall win the people over. Only petty people take revenge.

*　　*　　*

The Company will make restitution for dishonest dealings that our emigrants leave behind—of course, only what can be proven beyond doubt. We shall make up for it over there. That is manly discipline.

*　　*　　*

Let the German Kaiser say to me: I shall be grateful to you if you lead these unassimilable people out. (This will lend me authority and make a big impression on the Jews.)

Keep a file of my personal correspondence. Start a file for each person with whom I have any dealings.

To bring the Jews all under one hat will be a miserable job, although, or, rather, because, they each have a head.

The first Senator will be my father.

The Senate will include all the prominent Jews who go with us.

Among scraps of paper I today found a slip I wrote in San Sebastian on the eve of my departure for Paris. It says: "I shall have galoshes like a businessman's."

At that time, as usual, I foresaw the whole development—except its duration and its end.

Today I say: I shall associate with the mighty of this earth as their equal.

*　　*　　*

To the men at Glion.

I am now elaborating for you only on the moral-political and the financial aspects, i.e., the goal which I see just as clearly as the point of departure.

The project has many other aspects: technical, military, diplomatic, administrative, economic, artistic, etc.

For the moment you must believe me that I know how to

proceed in these directions as well and have made plans for them.

A department of inventions, with correspondents in Paris, London, Berlin, etc., who immediately report on all novelties which are then tested for their usability.

The department head must be replaced frequently, lest he turn into a routine official.

*   *   *

Popular festivals of an artistic nature, scattered throughout the country, in such a manner that masses do not always converge on one point. For that way crowds only feel unhappy at festivals.

Of course, there will also be national festivals with gigantic spectacles, colorful processions, etc.—e.g., on the foundation day of the State. Perhaps also on the anniversary of Glion.

Baron Hirsch (who will appear as the great rebel immediately after I have made an agreement with the Rothschilds) I must handle with sovereign amiability. Flatter him (all right for me to do, because I no longer need him): "You are a clever and good person; I liked you extremely well from the start; we must reach an understanding. I shall make it up between you and Rothschild. We have to stick together now."

Then, the *sursum corda* [lift up your hearts]: Responsibility before people and history.

Finally, threaten him with fanatics to whom I shall denounce him.

This exodus is to the earlier one as the present-day scientific exploration of the Witwatersrand gold fields is to the adventurous exploration of Bret Harte's Californians.

Guard against an overestimation of myself, arrogance, and folly, if the project succeeds. If it does not, writing will help me get it off my chest.

There are details which I cannot tell you yet, because at this moment I do not know if you are going to be my friends. You

see, you can only be my friends or my foes. There can no longer
be anything in between.

* * *

1st stage: The Rothschilds.
2nd stage: The midget millionaires.
3rd stage: The little people (i.e., wide publicity!) If it comes
to this stage, the first two will rue the day.

* * *

I shall take along all beggars, all peddlers. The devil can have
those who want to stay behind, i.e., refuse to work.

Once I have pulled out the poor, there will be a sigh of relief.

Jewish splendor will not be a bother in Europe any more
either. Because all those who are well advised will build their
palaces over there.

Not until later will the relief give way to a sense of loss; but
by that time we shall be established over there and have our
army and our diplomatic corps.

Diplomats will be the hardest to recruit, because in the
captivity we have lost our style.

To the men of Glion:

The Rothschilds have no idea of how endangered their
property already is. They live in a phony circle of courtiers,
servants, employees, paupers, and aristocratic spongers.

It is a solution because I satisfy all:

Poor men, rich men, workers, intellectuals, governments, and
anti-Semitic peoples.

* * *

To the Family Council:

You give a poor man 100 francs. I give him work, even if
I have none; at worst I lose 100 francs on it. But I shall have
created a useful existence, and you—a pauper. *Avec ça* [thereby],
I create a *market* along with the job! And therefore must make

what entrepreneurs make—*je gagne tout ce que je vieux* [I earn whatever I want].

*   *   *

Your property is an increasing calamity. We shall let ourselves be cheated in the exchange of old immovables for new ones, but shall create a privileged, legal mortgage for dirty dealings left behind.

Study shipping rates with Leinkauf. We must be able to transport persons at the parcel rate. We shall have our own trains, like Cook and Schrökl. I shall study Cook's system as well, in order to figure out what concessions he gets.

*   *   *

Jewish capital must make no new undertakings.

Jewish labor must not compete any more.

Equal rights are still on the law books, but have actually been rescinded.

We produce too much intellect and no longer have a market for it.

To the Family Council: My view is that socialism is a purely technological problem. The distribution of Nature's forces through electricity will eliminate it. Meanwhile our model state will have come into being.

*   *   *

City construction: First canals, water, gas, etc., then wood blocks on top.

June 8

We must not only copy Paris, Florence, etc., but seek a Jewish style expressive of a sense of relief and liberty.

Bright, airy halls, supported by pillars.

Create breathing spaces between towns. Every town like a big house located in the middle of a garden.

In the free areas between the towns there must be only cultivated fields, forests, etc. By this I shall prevent hypertrophic
cities, and the towns will look inhabited sooner.

In the evening I dined with the Schiffs. Their in-laws from
Vienna were visiting them. Well-to-do, educated, depressed
people. They moaned softly about anti-Semitism, to which I
continually steered the conversation.

The husband expects a new St. Bartholomew's Night. The
wife believes that conditions could hardly get any worse. They
argued about whether it was good or bad that Lueger's election
as mayor of Vienna had not been ratified.

Their faintheartedness completely dismayed me. They do
not suspect it, but they are Ghetto types, quiet, decent, timorous.

Most of our people are like that. Will they understand the
call to be free and become human beings?

When I left I was in a very bad humor. My plan again seemed
crazy to me.

But in the middle of my *défaillance* [feeling of depression]
I said to myself: I've started it and now I'll go through with it.

The main thing is for me to show determination—at Glion
and on future occasions.

A thing like that is only a matter of suggestion. The moment
I doubt, I am grotesque.

June 9, 1895

Salo and Güdemann shall each bring along a memorandum.
Güdemann's should deal with the number and distribution of
persecutions that come to his attention, signs as to whether
anti-Semitism is increasing (and if so, at what rate) or decreasing,
with official and officious anti-Semitism, anti-Semitism in schools
and offices, to the extent of his knowledge, etc.—in short, everything that he knows about the moral and political situation.

Salo should cover the conditions under which Jews earn a
living, the interest rate, the distribution of property (the number
of large properties, an estimate of the small ones), the state of

the Jewish entrepreneurial spirit (whether it is growing, and if so, at what rate, or declining), the temper in business circles.

In the morning: Today I am again as hard as iron. The faintheartedness of the people yesterday is one more reason for taking action. Gentiles in their circumstances would be cheerful and enjoy life. Jews are sad.

The provisioning of the population will probably not be handled by the State.

To avoid being called a *"manager"* in England, which sounds too commercial, I shall perhaps have the title of "Chancellor" or something like that.

The subordinate titles would for the time being remain those of regular joint-stock companies. Their conversion into state titles will later be regarded as a reward.

The principle on salaries: grant everyone a noticeable increment of from one fourth to one half of his present income. But retain a margin for advancement, in titles as well as salaries.

In the beginning, the founding officials would not have a proper appreciation of titles; they would even seem ridiculous to them. So let them just regard themselves as employees of a wealthy joint-stock company.

Let a newspaper reader (Schiff) every day keep an eye open for new charitable institutions, hospitals, etc., and submit extracts to me.

In fact, all department heads have instructions to advise me of every important manifestation of progress that the spirit of the times produces in their fields and to give me special reports on major developments.

I myself shall not read any newspapers (following Freycinet's principle—words that he told me about Casimir Périer), and shall give orders not to tell me about anything that concerns me, be it praise or censure.

Henceforth I have the right and the duty to disregard personal attacks of any kind.

Only if a *courant d'opinion* [current of opinion] against the undertaking is about to be created, I must be informed of it immediately, so that I may break down the opposition.

I shall completely ignore the attacks of anti-Semites, as long as they do not want to impede us (which will happen yet).

My personal security will be the concern of a well-run Secret Police.

*   *   *

June 9

It is a military campaign.—

Adopt immediately the principle of the Caravan of Arcueil (*La XIX. Caravane d'Arcueil par Lhermite,* obtainable from the Dominicans in Paris, Ecole Lacordaire).

The Leader (perhaps Bachrach) shall profitably read the book by the Dominican Priest Lhermite and give me a report on it. The very first year we shall send over a caravan (Raoul will go along), and then there will be similar contingents at regular intervals.

To establish stock exchanges, brokerages will be auctioned off, for one year to begin with.

But anyone who, while he is still a free agent, commits actions which will be proscribed later will be disqualified (and he will be warned about this in advance).

On the other hand, anyone who behaves properly will receive priority for the following year without having to bid for it. He can retain his position at the highest price offered for an additional year. This is how it will go until the fifth or the tenth year (we shall determine this according to the circumstances), and then the auctioning will cease and the brokers will become a closed corporation.

Through the grand institution of this stock-exchange monopoly I shall also get an astonished Europe to imitate us. This will crowd the Jews out of the European stock exchanges, because the existing governments certainly will not give these sinecures to Jews. That will yield me fresh emigrants.

I shall insure the alertness and justice of the traveling complaint commissars by holding them responsible. They will be subject to disciplinary measures like salary deductions, transfers, etc. if they disregard just complaints or give a bad or biased judgment.

There will be secret chief inspectors, i.e., legates who will be traveling about in the area anyway and will have to record their observations.

Local self-assessments could lead to swindling. Therefore the emigrants will remain collectively liable until what has been left behind has been realized, and the liability will reside in a privileged mortgage on their new properties.

A stock-exchange monopoly of the state seems a brilliant solution to me now.

Brokerage does not require any previous knowledge; it is *unskilled labor!**

I shall have the licensed brokers in my hand completely and use them for state purposes; I shall direct them according to the requirements of my policy and be able to prevent abuses. I shall tolerate no stock-exchange bucket shops. I want a sound money market. Any broker who promotes speculating will be removed. Removal involves not only the loss of a fat sinecure, but also of civil rights for a graduated period of time.

A broker will become a person of trust like a notary public. I shall combine the brokers in chambers with a tribunal of honor.

A hierarchy of offenses is to be devised and a special code to be established.

It is a broker's duty to take a close look at his clients. He can do what I cannot do: tell a speculator from a would-be investor.

Brokers who have caused someone's economic ruin with demonstrable *culpa* [blame] (even *levis* [slight]) will be removed. But I can also grade the punishments: e.g., temporary suspension

---

* In English in the original.

(which does not involve loss of political rights and can be graduated, from a week to two years; after all, sometimes it is hard to establish a broker's guilt).

I may relieve the tribunal of honor of making decisions about suspension and removal and charge my State Stock-Exchange Commission with it.

Perhaps I shall make this commission only an appellate court, because I want to forestall the machinations of professional jealousy.

June 9

The same organization as for the Stock Exchange also for grain, cattle, and merchandise exchanges as well as everything that is subject to speculation.

*   *   *

The income from this monopoly will give me a substantial contribution to the needs of the state.

*   *   *

Brokerages will at first be granted provisionally on the basis of *redevance* [dues] and will gradually be used for pensions for deserving officials. Later they can also be divided into quarters and eighths (like the *agents* system in Paris).

*   *   *

The brokerships are not inheritable or saleable.—

Thus I can safely make the capital city the headquarters of the world money-market.

Certain posts (military, diplomatic, juridical, administrative, etc.) will never be compensated out of income from the broker-ages, but pensioned directly by the State. That will be only a matter of bookkeeping for us, but it will contribute to the elevation and honoring of these professions.

To the Family Council (June 6):

If I can work with you, I shall have all the advantages of initial secrecy.

As soon as the first cadres are set up, the land is fixed, etc., I can go to governments and tell them: R's are making this sacrifice (a kind of indirect self-taxation) to remove your surplus Jews.

We must use the word "surplus," otherwise they will not let us make propaganda and move away.

In the beginning it must appear that we want to perform the governments a service. We are sacrificing a billion for the "solution of the Jewish Question."

In return for this we receive the favors that we need: release from military service, and the like.

Above all, toleration of our propaganda and occasionally (upon our request) an ungracious word, but with the maintenance of order.

After ten years the movement will be irresistible, and the Jews will come running to us barefoot through fog and darkness. Nothing will be able to stop them, at least not in the countries in which they are free to move.

If there should then be attempts to impede the free passage of the Jews, we shall know how to mobilize the public opinion of the world (liberals, socialists, anti-Semites) against the imprisonment of the Jews.

Then, too, our diplomats will be at work (we shall make financial concessions in the form of loans and special gifts).

Once we are outside, we shall put our trust in our army, our purchased friendships, and a Europe weakened and divided by militarism and socialism.

This is Jewish emancipation.

To the Family Council:

You are accustomed to transacting worldwide deals. Perhaps you will understand me.

I may issue the Jewish National Loan from our capital city.

First I shall negotiate with the Czar (to whom our patron, the Prince of Wales, will introduce me) regarding permission for the Russian Jews to leave the country.

He is to give me his imperial word and have it published in the official gazette (he will believe that I am able to lead away only a few hundred thousand).

Then I shall negotiate with the German Kaiser. Then with Austria. Then with France, regarding the Algerian Jews. Then, as need dictates.

In order to be in high esteem at the European courts, I must secure the highest decorations. The English first.

*　　*　　*

June 9

I shall frequently make surprise spot inspections. (Highly important, so as to prevent *gaspillage* [waste] and officials lying down on the job).

Also get reports on malpractices from a secret Administrative Police.

June 9

At the head of the Jewish paper:

Complaints about malpractices and arbitrary acts of officials are to bear the notation "Complaint to the Director-General" on the envelope.

*　　*　　*

For such complaints I shall establish traveling commissions of investigation (which will also appear unannounced).

Punishment for officials: dismissal only in extreme cases. For minor offenses, transfer to more remote areas, more arduous duties.

But by consistently good conduct such official blemishes will be wiped out and will no longer prevent advancement.

Of course, every official will have his record of conduct in the department and a file in the London headquarters (*en attendant que cela soit dans notre capitale* [until we have one in our capital]).

* * *

The acceptance of gifts will be followed by dismissal in all cases, but the dismissed official will be allowed to settle in the country and live as a free man. Also, his blameless family will be guarded against privation.

One form of buying our release from the states is a double fee for the transfer of immovable properties which are sold by their present owners to the Society, and by the Society to others.

To be sure, we shall not admit this in advance, but shall at first have the Society only act as an agent.

Only when public opinion begins to calm down regarding the removal of property, we shall "after careful deliberation and to show our good will" find the expedient of this double transfer, pledging ourselves to deprive the tax swindlers over there of certain benefits enjoyed by the honest emigrants, e.g., to give reduced rates of transportation and shipping only to those who can produce an official statement from their former place of residence certifying that they have "moved away in good order."

We shall of course recognize the validity of any legal claims made by the previous places of residence (even when our own laws are already in force). Such suits shall be decided with all possible speed and all conceivable expedition and according to the law of the original place of residence.

In return for that, they will have to let us take the Jewish deserters (something that I shall settle in a form not offensive to us). Because of the fact that we shall have a homeland of our own, we shall no longer be obligated to serve in the armed forces of our erstwhile host nations (here I accept the viewpoint of the anti-Semites).

Make the leader of the Youth Caravans (after the pattern

of the Dominicans of Arcueil) responsible for moral discipline, seriousness, and studies of the young men. These are not pleasure tours, but study and work trips, an ambulatory school with daily lessons and lectures, a botanical field trip through the world. I shall get special reports on this each time. Very important.

Once we are over there, the dancers around the Golden Calf will be furious at my barring them from the Stock Exchange. I shall have them dispersed in the street and tell the Parliament:

"That was all right in the time of our captivity. Now we have the duties of freedom. We must be a people of inventors, warriors, artists, scholars, honest merchants, up-and-coming workmen, etc."

In the old days there was an excuse for stock-market gambling. Our intellects were shackled, and we had to traffic in money. Now we are free. Now any Jew can get any office in the state, in our State. Anyone can become a general, a minister, a chief justice, a scholar—in short, anything.

Now only the idlers want freedom to gamble on the stock-market, and this is something that we must overcome, otherwise we shall again be ruined and pitifully dispersed throughout the world.

Far be it from me to say a word against the old-time stock traders. My dear father, after his lumber business had gone to ruin, was obliged to earn his bread as a stock agent, in order not to starve and to give me a decent education. But that was in the days gone by. In those days a Jew had no other way out. Now this is no longer necessary and therefore will no longer be tolerated.

I too could have made a fortune while directing this vast enterprise, just as I made millionaires of men around me. It was I who determined the location of our cities—what real estate deals I could have made in the process!

No! I have only my salary, which I need to keep up a decent front, and the house which I built out of my savings. I know that the nation will never let my posterity suffer want.

June 9

When this book is published, the prescriptions for the organization of the government will be omitted. The people must be guided to the good according to principles unknown to them.

Therefore the editors of the book—if I am no longer alive—shall extract the administrative maxims and keep them in the secret State Archives.

Only the Doge and the Chancellor may read them. To be omitted are also those remarks which could annoy foreign governments.

But the course the negotiations took shall be retained, so that our people may see how I led the Jews home.

June 9

When someone comes to ask for a job:

Am I going to take you? I take everyone who has some ability and wants to work—your brother, your friends, your relatives and acquaintances, all of them, all, all! Got that? And now, go.

June 9

A crop of professional politicans must be prevented in any way possible.

I must study this problem with the utmost care when the time comes.

*   *   *

The Senators will in any case get a salary which will at the same time constitute an honorary pension for our great minds.

*   *   *

June 9

As stipends for my brave warriors, ambitious artists, and loyal, gifted officials I shall use the dowries of our wealthy girls.

I must carry on marriage politics.

*   *   *

To the big bankers, who will look up to me, I shall say: I should like to see you give your daughters to up-and-coming, vigorous young men.

I need this for the State.

It is the self-fertilization of the nation.

June 9

In Palestine's disfavor is its proximity to Russia and Europe, its lack of room for expansion as well as its climate, which we are no longer accustomed to.

In its favor is the mighty legend.

In the beginning we shall be supported by anti-Semites through a *recrudescence** of persecution (for I am convinced that they do not expect success and will want to exploit their "conquest.")

*   *   *

June 9

A possible further concession for the removal of property.

The states concerned shall acquire the immovable property of the Jews.

The price, regardless of what has been paid by us, will be set by a regulatory commission on which we shall also be represented.

*   *   *

June 9

Language will present no obstacle. Switzerland too is a federal state of various nationalities.

We recognize ourselves as a nation by our faith.

Actually, German is, *par la force des choses* [of necessity], likely to become the official language. *Judendeutsch* [the German spoken by Jews]! As the yellow badge is to become our blue ribbon!

I have nothing against French or English, either! I shall steer

---

* In French in the original.

the *jeunesse dorée* [gilded youth] toward English sports and in this way prepare them for the army.

*   *   *

June 9

On the trip to the Grand Prix—outside and on the way back, the main features of the Doge's coronation and of duelling occurred to me.

When I thought that someday I might crown Hans as Doge and address him in the Temple in front of the country's great men as "Your Highness! My beloved son!" I had tears in my eyes.

The procession, which starts from the Doge's palace, will be opened by Herzl Cuirassiers. Then come the artillery and the infantry.

The officials of all ministries, deputations from the cities, the clergy, finally the High Priest of the capital city. The flag with a guard of honor composed of generals. The Doge! And here the procession attains its symbolic splendor.

For, while all are marching in gold-studded gala dress, the high priests under canopies, the Doge will wear the garb of shame of a medieval Jew, the pointed Jew's hat and the yellow badge! (The procession might move through the Ghetto which will in any case be constructed as a reminder and a memorial.)

Behind the Doge there will be the Chancellor, the potentates representing foreign countries, the ministers, generals, etc., the diplomatic corps (provided one already exists), the Council of Ancients (Senate), the Parliament, freely-chosen deputations from the professions, the chambers of commerce, the attorneys, the physicians, etc. The artillery and infantry will bring up the rear.

June 9

My punishments for suicide: for an unsuccessful attempt, permanent confinement in an insane asylum; for accomplished suicide, refusal of an honorable burial.

I need duelling in order to have real officers and to impart a tone of French refinement to good society.

Duelling with sabres is permitted and will not be punished, no matter what the outcome, provided that the seconds have done their share toward an honorable settlement.

Every sabre duel will be investigated by the duelling tribunal only afterwards.

A *matamore,* a braggart who seeks an easy mark and picks out weaker opponents, may be declared as ineligible for further duelling by the tribunal if it can be proved that he was the offender; if he has inflicted serious injury, he may be referred to the regular criminal courts and sentenced according to the common criminal code.

* * *

Pistol duelling (or the American type, if it really exists) must be taken to the tribunal before the duel by the witnesses on both sides; otherwise those concerned will be punished and forfeit the right ever again to appear before the duelling tribunal.

The duelling tribunal may decide on a sabre duel; or, if one party is physically inferior, on no duel at all; or, finally, it may give a secret verdict. Such a verdict is heard only by the two duellers; the seconds have to withdraw. The secret verdict (for which I shall compose secret instructions) decrees a duel in a form no less dangerous, but useful to the state. Since only men of honor can fight a duel, the loser in any case would be the state, and for a long time to come it will need every able-bodied man.

Therefore these duellers will be sent out on dangerous missions which the state happens to require. It may be cholera vaccination, or at other times the fighting of a national enemy. In this way the risk of death of the duel will be retained, and we shall derive wonderful benefit from it.

City construction:

The difficulty: a margin for expansion, and yet with an appearance of being inhabited. May be solved by the construction of garden cities.

* * *

In all local groups, plans and pictures of the *homes** which we have drawn up by our young architects (prizes).

Selection, methods of payment, scales of rates.

* * *

Prizes for fertility and good patriarchal education of children.

* * *

We immediately have *unskilled labor** for hundreds of thousands, namely streets, highways.

A Bois de Boulogne near the capital city, or, rather, the other way around.—

To the Family Council and, earlier, at Glion: The R. fortune. That is what I am talking about. What business of yours is it, the R's will interpose. After all, we do not worry about the Herzl property.

Just a minute! It *is* my business. Every politician must regard its increase as a public menace.

But I worry about it because it is the most frightful menace to the Jews and because I am setting myself up as the *gestor* of the Jews.

More gently, before the Family Council:

In the course of the discussion I shall have to speak about your fortune. Will you concede me this right or shall I first explain that, too?

* In English in the original.

The cryptogam is the plant of Jewry; it has both sexes: capital and labor. (One sees only the capital.)

June 9

Since I want to establish garden cities, I face a dilemma: either to build the cities in forest clearings (possibly quicker, but the experts will tell me the objections to that), or plant trees between the houses, whereby I would lose the advertising appeal, the magic quality, but then I can develop the cities the way I want to; to be sure, they would look as if they were attending a tree nursery.

*   *   *

In any case, take landscape gardeners, horticultural experts along on my expedition to take possession of the land.

*   *   *

On the boat and in all places, work must be done, gentlemen of the General Staff.

*   *   *

June 9

Schiff's brother-in-law, after only two weeks, is home-sick for the Vienna coffee-houses. Consequently, I shall faithfully transplant Viennese cafés to the other side. With such little expedients I shall achieve the desired illusion of the old environment.

Have an ear for such small needs. They are very important.

To the Family Council:
There are two categories of Jews: those with and those without locomotion.

The latter I shall dig up and transport across—they will hardly notice it. The others, those able to move about, such as you and I, will continue to be mobile and will be respected.

*   *   *

Our belonging together! Do you want me to give you an example of it?

Eh bien [all right]: Today I, a stranger, come to you and tell you in confidence my most secret intentions.

It is possible that we shall wind up fighting each other—but like hostile brothers—; that way it is quite possible that we shall kill each other.

* * *

June 9

I am talking about your fortune—not because your name has become synonymous with money, for I have no feeling for it. I am not a money man. Haven't got a nose for it!

* * *

The man who pointed to the cover of a teakettle lifted by steam and said, "This is how I shall move people, animals, and freight, and give the world a new appearance," was derided as a lunatic.

* * *

Well, I shall not only demonstrate the principle to you with a teakettle, but show you the entire finished locomotive.

* * *

My analogies are too dazzling, disconcert you.

Now just imagine: if I dazzle you, from whom I want 1000 million—albeit not for myself—how I shall dazzle those whom I am going to make wealthy, free, and happy.

June 9

For Glion: The R's are to make an immediate decision, Yes or No. I have no time to lose. It has taken me thirteen years.

Family Council: I choose an aristocracy because I need an

elastic form of government for the future. A monarchy would lead to a revolution.

For a republic we are not virtuous enough, Montesquieu.

* * *

Family Council:

If not *with* you, then *in opposition* to you! What do I mean by that? I am not going to call your fortune an ill-gotten one. It would be a lie to say that.

I am not an extortioner and not a pamphleteer (but a statesman, and a Jewish one at that).

All I shall say is: it is too big! And injurious to the people, because private property increases faster than national prosperity. Coming from an unprejudiced Jew, this will create a stir.

June 10

To the German Kaiser:

If Jews emigrate, this must result in a decrease in emigration to America. You thereby gain, or, rather, preserve, genuine German citizens, forestall a revolution which might be hard to contain, weaken socialism which the oppressed Jews must flock to because they are cast out by other parties, and gain time for the solution of social problems.

* * *

My first secretary (E. Schiff) will recruit the naturalist investigators—geographers, geologists, chemists, technologists, botanists, zoologists, etc.

* * *

June 10

Political agitation which can lead to the downfall of the State is punishable by exile or, if the individual could do harm there, by death.

But even exile from the enchanting homeland will be a terrible punishment.

June 10

My constant concern must be the soundness of the economy.
No dissipation, no waste. It is not a *curée* [quarry] for the covetous and the idle. It shall not become a Panama, but a Suez.

*   *   *

June 10

Amnesty!
All crimes committed in captivity, including those involving
property, will be forgiven politically and will not affect civil
rights (of course, the sound common sense of the population will
bar notorious swindlers from positions of honor, *et au besoin j'y
veillerai* [and if necessary I shall see to it]). A new life shall
begin for Jews. But severe punishments for fresh crimes committed over there! Crimes on the eve of departure (dirty dealings
left behind) I shall deal with only *civiliter* [under civil law],
through the above-mentioned privileged mortgage.

June 10

As long as possible no taxes, or at most indirect ones which do
not affect the belongings of the little man.

*   *   *

No luxury tax either, for I need luxury items for the market.
I shall gladly take French officers (Jews), but they must not
be Gallic chauvinists.

*   *   *

From the army of *unskilled laborers** it will be possible to
rise through industry, intelligence, efficiency, as in the Napo-
leonic army.
Anyone can become a marshal of labor. I shall frequently tell
them so, or have them told, in popular addresses.

*   *   *

* In English in the original.

For special accomplishments which I notice, I shall immediately promote the worker and increase his salary. This bit of drama will have an effect on the masses.

As soon as *actions d'éclat* [striking deeds], which will be watched for according to my special instructions, are reported to me, I shall immediately reward them.

*   *   *

Organize the labor battalions along military lines, as far as possible.

*   *   *

Service in the labor battalions leads to a pension, as in the Army.

*   *   *

I must save only the badges of honor for those who risk their lives.

Through bestowing patents of nobility I shall draw great personal sacrifices from people.

Neither patents of nobility nor decorations must be obtainable for money. I shall validate those acquired elsewhere prior to the founding of the State, regardless of how they were obtained.

Later even foreign ones will be recognized only if they were acquired in a truly meritorious manner. A Jew will not be able to buy the title of a Portuguese Marquis and have it recognized by us. But if he is made a nobleman by Portugal for shining deeds (which, after all, will reflect glory on us as well), I shall recognize him at home.

All this will have to be closely examined by the Office of Nobility on an individual basis.

June 10

To the Family Council:
I am taking up once again the torn thread of the tradition of our people. I am leading it to the Promised Land. Do not think

this is a fantasy. I am not an architect of castles in the air. I am building a real house, with materials that you can see, touch, examine. Here are the blue-prints.

*   *   *

Note that the next European war cannot harm our enterprise, but only benefit it, because all Jews will transport all their belongings across, to safety.

Cowards will want to shirk military duty in our State if it comes to war. But just as I want to favor desertion to our side in peacetime, I shall impede it in wartime, on account of Jewish honor.

Let anyone who has delayed his adherence until then do his old duty and fight, and when the war is over we shall receive him with all honors, much greater ones than his former fatherland accorded him. In this way our fighting forces will get experienced warriors who have faced death and will enhance the prestige of our Army.

*   *   *

Incidentally, when peace is concluded we shall already have a say as money-givers and achieve advantages of recognition through diplomatic channels.

June 10

Draw limits of freedom of the press wisely. The pillory for slanderers, and substantial fines.

*   *   *

A House of Lords for the aristocracy, but not inheritable. First there must be an examination as to merit.

I must give more thought to ways of guarding against the absurd heirs of other countries.

*   *   *

Today is Hansi's birthday. He is four years old. I sent him a telegram to Vienna: "Love and kisses to my father-king." That is what my mother calls him. And I think of my dream.

* * *

The House of Lords will perhaps consist of three groups: one chosen by the aristocracy; one named by the government (Doges); the third elected indirectly, as in France. I have the same feeling as I did once in the Protestant *Gymnasium* [high school] at Pest in the senior grade: that I should soon leave school. At that time the death of my poor sister made it happen even sooner than I had thought!

Now I have a presentiment that I am going to leave the school of journalism.

* * *

By amnesty I mean only the restoration of honor after the crimes have been atoned for. Fugitives from justice (Jews) we shall extradite on a reciprocal basis.

* * *

Extradition treaties to exclude deserters in peacetime.

* * *

Literary copyright agreements! At first we shall pay, afterward receive payment, because we shall be a nation of thinkers and artists.

* * *

To the Family Council: The loan will perhaps not even have to be publicly floated; this would save concessions to governments in return for their permission.

Movable property will flock to us if we so much as pass the word in confidence. We shall simply start an account book and enter loans with no limit; and with this we shall acquire land, make foreign loans, etc.

* * *

In addition to transportation, industry, etc., it is also a huge financial transaction.

*   *   *

Come to think of it, in all this I am still the dramatist. I pick poor people in rags off the streets, put gorgeous costumes on them, and have them perform for the world a wonderful pageant of my composition.

I no longer operate with individuals, but with masses: the clergy, the army, the administration, the academy, etc., all of them mass units to me.

*   *   *

To the Family Council: I must call a spade a spade. This should not make you think that I am a rude person. But at the moment I do not know whether I shall proceed with you or in opposition to you. That is why the flourishes of courtesy might compromise me and give my later actions the appearance of revenge.

June 11, 1895

Labor units will march off to work like an army amidst the sounds of a fanfare and return home the same way.

*   *   *

June 11, 1895

No women or children shall work in our factories. We need a sturdy race. Needy women and children will be taken care of by the State.

"Old maids" will be employed in kindergartens and as nurses for the orphans of the working class, etc.

I shall organize these girls who have been passed over by suitors into a corps of governesses for the poor. They will be given housing by the State, enjoy due honors (just as every gentleman treats a governess courteously), and eventually will be pensioned. But they can rise in the ranks in the same way that men can.

Moral conduct is a prerequisite. This makes the head of the Personnel Department an important person. For this position I must select a gentle, just, worldly-wise, elderly man and supervise him constantly, for any mistakes he might make could do a lot of harm and arouse dissatisfaction and bitterness.

But I want a happy nation.

A lot of toasts will be drunk to me. On important occasions I shall accept them and say: I like to see a leader being honored. That is necessary for his work and shows him that he enjoys the confidence of the people (unless self-seeking is part of it). But too much of it might do me harm. I want to be honored, but not flattered, otherwise I shall lose the naturalness and simplicity of my make-up.

The ship on which my parents, wife, and children make the crossing will also bring over all our relatives, near and distant. No one will feel violently uprooted, for the entire soil will go along.

A company of actors, singers, and musicians will help while away the passage; in fact, provision will be made on every ship for entertainment as well as instruction.

But games of chance will not be tolerated.

My officials will not be allowed to gamble at all. Such diversion of the intellect is no longer necessary. We need, and can use, all our intellectual resources. The love of adventure, which finds an outlet in gambling, shall now fertilize the soil of our new homeland.

As a young man I myself was a gambler—like Lessing, Laube, and many others who later became respectable men after all—but only because my craving for action had no other outlet.

This I shall at first tell the gamblers as a gentle warning. However, anyone who does not obey I shall dismiss from my service.

Only children and old people will be allowed to play. However, the games of the children must serve their physical development: Running and ball games, cricket for boys, tennis for girls.

The inactive games must be designed to prepare the future development of the intellect. Drawing, painting, reading significant fairy-tales, games of construction for increasing the pleasure in synthesis, and the like.

Old men may play cards, but *not* for money, because this might tempt the onlookers and is unseemly for patriarchs. I want to have a patriarchal spirit in families.

However, I shall permit refined card-clubs, but with no members under forty years of age and with a stiff tax on playing cards for State revenue.

June 11

The Jews who have hitherto been in the consular service of various powers can be taken over into our diplomatic service. Of course, each individual will be tested for his qualifications.

There may be among them capable men who have acquired the polish and the forms of diplomacy. But no one has an *a priori* right to be appointed; the decisive factor is his usefulness to us.

But since for the time being we shall not be able to afford them any protection, we shall not give them any ringing titles, but call them agents, something that they can combine with their current consular assignments. Thus they will be covered by the respect they have at present.

We must not let our diplomatic titles, which will later attain high prestige, be made ridiculous at the outset.

*   *   *

Yacht owners can become our professional seamen and prepare to take command of our future Navy.

*   *   *

Should we go to South America, which would have a lot in its favor on account of its distance from militarized and seedy Europe, our first state treaties will have to be with South American republics.

We shall grant them loans in return for territorial privileges and guarantees. One of the most important concessions they will have to make to us is to allow us to have defensive troops.

In the beginning we shall need their permission. Gradually we shall get strong, grant ourselves everything that we need, and be able to defy everyone.

For the time being we must get protection from the troops of the state that receives us. Later we shall make an independent alliance with it.

We must have a South American and a European policy.

If we are in South America, the establishment of our State will not come to Europe's notice for a considerable period of time.

In South America we could at first live according to the laws, extradition treaties, etc. of the receiving state (vis-à-vis Europe).

Our defensive troops will always comprise ten percent of the male emigrants. In this way we shall get an Army together unobserved, but will for a long time proceed cautiously, exploiting the enmities of the republics and preserving their friendship through presents, bribes, loans, etc.

The crossing is to take place by local groups and social units. There will be first-class, second-class, and third-class ships, each with instruction and entertainment appropriate to it.

In this way the inciting example of class differences (observed at close proximity over many days) will be avoided.

Everyone will pay for his passage himself. I want luxury, but not fruitless envy.

*   *   *

I want luxury as a patron of the arts, as goal and prize. To see the enjoyments of the earth and to know that they are attainable through honest labor is a spur to great effort.

If I do not succeed in winning over the R's or the midget millionaires, I shall publish the entire plan in book form: *The Solution of the Jewish Question,* Duncker and Humblot, publishers, to whom I shall give only the first five editions under the same conditions as my *Palais Bourbon*. They will only get an option on subsequent editions.

In my book *The Solution* etc., I shall tell about all my steps, from Hirsch via Rothschild to the midget millionaires.

Preface: They came to Rothschild with the electric light, too. He did not understand what it was all about.

I must eliminate all Venetian political elements from the book.

*　　*　　*

The danger of the R. fortune will, of course, not be presented in the manner of a pamphleteer, but with my own customary seriousness.

All polemics will be omitted. After all, I am concerned with the cause. And it will be of enormous benefit to the Jews that this will be said by a Jew who is above doubt, who has never made any deals, least of all with his pen.

June 11

S. C.'s answer was due yesterday and is not here even today. This directs my thoughts to the book. I am getting accustomed to the idea that it will not materialize.

June 11

In the Palais Royal (while standing up):

We are bad soldiers, because we are devoid of honor, because there is nothing for us beyond death. And yet there is no lack of examples to show that we know how to die well (Naquet's speech). But we cannot become leaders, and in this the states are right; otherwise we would be brigadier-generals everywhere within two generations, especially since war has become an intellectual affair. And certainly the nations cannot admit defeat by making the members of an unassimilated and unassimilable group the leaders of their armies.

*　　*　　*

The worth of my plan obviously lies in the facts that I am using only available resources, making unutilized or unutilizable things fruitful by combining them, that I have regard for all suffering (certainly including the hurts inflicted by Jews on Gentiles), protect all acquired rights, take all human impulses into account, balance world supply and world demand, use the progress of technology, and hold tradition sacred.

Make this correction above: The prudent immediately recognize the safe cobble-stones.

*   *   *

Yes, we have become a scourge for the peoples which once tormented us. The sins of their fathers are now visited on them. Europe is being punished for the ghettos now. To be sure, we are suffering under the sufferings that we are causing. It is a scourging with scorpions, live scorpions which are not to blame that they did not become lions, tigers, or sheep. After all, in the scourging the scorpions suffer most of all.

I could accept a mass request from the little Jews to lead them out only if all the governments concerned asked me to, promised me their sympathetic cooperation, and gave me guarantees for the peaceful completion of the enormous task, just as I would give them guarantees for an exodus without economic ill-effects. (I don't know whether I should have this printed in Roman type).

*   *   *

(Addendum to Teweles' letter): I must read *Daniel Deronda*. Perhaps it contains ideas similar to mine. They cannot be identical ones, because it took a concatenation of many specific circumstances to bring my plan into being.

If we have not yet emigrated by the outbreak of the next war, all Jews of quality must go to the front, regardless of whether they were "fit for active service" when they reached the draft age, whether they are still of military age, whether they are healthy or sick. They must drag themselves to the army of their present fatherland, and if they are on opposite sides, they must shoot at one another.

Some may regard this as paying a debt of honor, others as a down-payment on our future honor. But all will have to do it.

* * *

June 11

Schiff came to see me today. I asked him to substitute for me for a few days. Was I starting a newspaper? he asked when I dropped a few vague hints.

A newspaper! *Il y a belle lurette que je n'y pense plus* [I haven't thought of that for a long time].

True enough, I first sought the practical ideas with the founding of the "Neue Zeitung" in mind.

Like Saul, who went forth. . . !

* * *

June 11

Schiff's brother-in-law said the other day: Emigrate? Yes, I'd like to, all right. But where to? Switzerland? The first country to make laws against the Jews!

Where to? This question made me inwardly very happy.

* * *

June 11

About the *assistance par le travail* [public works] I had some correspondence with Chlumecky two years ago. He did not get the idea.

* * *

Today I dined at a *brasserie* [small restaurant] near the Châtelet. I am shunning all my acquaintances. They tread on my toes, having no idea of the world I come from; this makes daily living terribly irritating.

*　　*　　*

Tard au danger, tard aux honneurs [late to danger, late to honors].

Anyone who has not joined us during the first twenty years of our existence (although he has turned thirty or more during this period), cannot hold office nor be eligible for it.

But he can be naturalized.

*　　*　　*

A museum of technical trades.

*　　*　　*

The R's did not understand Jablochkow's "candles," but they did understand the Guttmanns' coal proposals. Thus they may not comprehend the luminous side of my idea, but they will understand the coal side of the matter.

To the Family Council: Every day you grant financial favors for minimal gestures of tolerance or even to governments that do nothing for you.

Put *that* under your own management—and in twenty years' time we shall be recognized by the whole world!

June 11

Hungarians will be the hussars of Judea; they could make splendid cavalry generals.

June 11

Every worker who makes a complaint will be transferred to another company, so that the foreman cannot take revenge. Or the foreman will be transferred.

*　　*　　*

Daudet asked me whether I wanted to carry on my Jewish campaign in a novel. He reminded me of *Uncle Tom's Cabin.*

I told him then and there that I desired a more manly form of announcement. At that time I was still thinking of the *Enquête* [treatise] to be entitled *The Situation of the Jews.*

Today, the more I think about it the more it seems to me that it would really be beneath my dignity to make my plan palatable to the masses through love affairs and little jests, as Bellamy did in his utopian novel.

It would be easy for me, because I am an experienced writer of *belles-lettres.* Yet I must take care not to let the book become unreadable. After all, it is to make a deep impression on the people, on the nations.

Let it have a bit of literary fascination, then. It consists in the free-flowing sequence of ideas as they moved through my mind during these sunny days of the world dream in serene profusion, with all their *accidents* [imperfections], as the sculptors put it ("finger marks in the clay").

This will also prevent leafing through this book in search of chapter headings. Whoever wants to know what is in it will have to read it.

*   *   *

The *assistance par le travail,* which has been so important to me, I am going to insert somewhere—namely, in my article in the *Neue Freie Presse.*

The book will be "dedicated to my parents, Herr Jacob and Frau Jeanette Herzl."

*   *   *

The ship of coffins! We shall also take our dead along with us.

*   *   *

Much in these notes will seem ludicrous, exaggerated, crazy. But if I had exercised self-criticism, as I do in my literary work, my ideas would have been stunted. However, the gigantic serves the purpose better than the dwarfed, because anyone can do the trimming easily enough.

Artists will understand why I, otherwise of rather clear intelligence, have let exaggerations and dreams proliferate among my practical, political, and legislative ideas, as green grass sprouts among cobble-stones. I could not permit myself to be forced into the straitjacket of sober facts. This mild intoxication has been necessary.

Yes, artists will understand this fully. But there are so few artists.

June 11

In the book I may bring out typographically the distinction between the two intermingling dream worlds, by having the fantasy printed in a different type. That way the initiates will immediately see where and how the grass grows—others will hear it grow—and the rest will recognize the solid cobble-stones.

*   *   *

The little parallel folds of the epidermis of an artist in bronze.

*   *   *

Letter to Güdemann of June 11, 1895.

Dear Doctor Güdemann:
This letter will be a surprise to you in every respect: both in what it says and what it does not say.

I have decided to take the lead in an action on behalf of the Jews and am asking you whether you would like to be of assistance to me.

Your first task would be to draw up an accurate report of everything that you know about the present moral and political situation of the Jews, not only in Vienna and Austria-Hungary, but also in Germany, Russia, Rumania, etc. I don't think it should be a report with certified statistics, because that would take too much of your time and the report would have to be finished in two or three days. The exact figures and documentation we can obtain at a later date. As a start I want only a general and faithful presentation from you. The loftier the vantage point that you choose, the fewer the details you go into, the more suitable it will be. Naturally you will use your own judgment in selecting illustrations for your assertions. These, then, are the things to be covered: vital statistics of the Jews in the above-mentioned countries (births, marriages, deaths, listed by occupation); observable trends in change of residence (e.g., from Galicia to Lower Austria); whether and to what extent these changes of locality were caused or impeded by anti-Semitism; a brief survey of typical major and minor persecutions of Jews that have come to your attention (persecution in parliaments, newspapers, at rallies, on the street); signs of the increase or decrease of anti-Semitism, and in what proportion; official and unofficial anti-Semitism; hostility toward Jews in schools, offices, closed and open professions.

This looks as though I were asking a very exhaustive memorandum of you. On the contrary, please put down only what is known to you about all these matters at the moment.

It cannot be difficult for a man as skilled in words and with the pen as you are and who has surely given this matter so much deep thought to write this down or dictate it in a few hours. But if you dictate it, your secretary must not find out for what purpose it is being done.

Let me right at this point request you most earnestly to keep our correspondence as well as all succeeding steps a complete secret. The matter is an infinitely serious one. You can see this from the fact that I am not telling a word even to my parents and closest relatives. I am relying on your discretion.

Please bring me the report detailed above to Caux, overlooking Territet on Lake Geneva. If I may have your kind assistance, that is where we shall meet in a week, i.e., on Tuesday, June 18th. Why that place was chosen you will learn there. In case you are unable to finish the entire report, you can complete it verbally

then and there. However, you will not want to come all by yourself, but with a capable, serious-minded man who can supplement
your statements from other aspects. You see, at Caux I shall need
one spiritual and one worldly Jew. My first choice was Herr Salo
Cohn who, I believe, is well known to you. I wrote him last
Thursday, June 6. His reply was due yesterday. It has not arrived
today. I cannot wait any longer.

I first wanted to make sure of his cooperation, but did not
tell him that I wanted to approach you as well—afterwards, because (and I hope I was not mistaken) your assistance seemed
assured from the outset. You probably know me better from my
newspaper work than from personal acquaintance; and I imagine
that you take me as seriously as I really am.

And I may receive an answer from S. C. after I mail this letter
and before you receive it. In that case I shall ask you by telegram to get in touch with him.

In return I ask you to be so kind as to send me one of two
telegrams as soon as you have made your decision, if possible on
the same day you receive this letter: "Agreed" or "Sorry, impossible." Also include your present address (probably Baden?), so
that I could send you a telegram.

If S. C. does not take on the serious and great assignment with
which I wanted to honor him, we shall have to look for another
man. I leave the choice to you. I don't want any of my relatives,
otherwise I should have asked my father, first of all. The second
gentleman should be a businessman. He, too, must take a report
to Caux, to cover the following: an approximate description of
how Jews earn a living in the above-mentioned countries; the
distribution of property (an estimate of the number of large,
medium-sized, and small fortunes—I know that this can only
be a very vague estimate, but even that will do); in what countries do the Jews own a lot of immovable property; the state of
the Jewish enterprising spirit (is it increasing—and if so, at what
rate—or decreasing); the mood in business circles; the situation
of Jewish small businessmen and manufacturers (on the Franz-
Josefs-Quai, etc.)

This report, too, should not be timidly statistical, but should, as far as possible, be rather free, lively, unconstrained, and idiomatic. It will gain by being dictated.

From the foregoing you will see what sort of man we need— a calm, superior, unaffected man, not too young; he must, in any case, be a respected man of self-assured bearing, because of the tasks which he will face later on. Unfortunately I must add that I should prefer a well-to-do man, for our propertyless Jews are rather put-upon and lack bearing. But the aim which you will find out about at Caux requires, too, the second man to have a dignified, independent comportment. The person you select will presumably know me by name and will perhaps give me his confidence. For I know well that a certain amount of confidence is required in face of the presumptuous request to take a major trip the purpose of which is not clearly enough stated.

Since it is absolutely impossible for me to express myself any more clearly than this in writing, I can only pledge myself to pay a fine if I should trifle. If you two gentlemen should find at Caux that I have troubled you to no purpose, I shall hand you there one thousand francs which you will be good enough to give to your favorite charities.

And now, dear doctor, I ask you to come. A great project for our poor, unfortunate brethren is at stake. You are a spiritual adviser. At Caux a duty awaits you. That is all I can tell you.

With expressions of my cordial esteem, I am

Yours sincerely,
Theodor Herzl,
37, rue Cambon.

*   *   *

June 11

In my letter to Hirsch I wrote: "In France, at my age of thirty-five, men are Ministers of State, and Napoleon was Emperor."

I now find that in my haste I formulated my meaning badly.

As it stands, it smacks of megalomania. I merely meant that I too have a right to ponder political affairs and that at my age it is possible to have the maturity associated with a statesman.

June 11

The idea of having a meeting with those two Jews at Caux on Lake Geneva is a good one in many respects.

There they will be lifted out of their everyday, narrow, restricted concepts.

They will see a victory of mind over matter. And I shall be thinking of Rousseau, who saw a social contract where I discovered the *negotiorum gestio*.

*   *   *

June 11

The little Jews will perhaps band together in local groups and raise the money that the R's did not want to give. But will I be able to take it after I have disclosed my entire program to the world?

The big Jews will have frustrated the project through their refusal; of course, they will probably be the first to suffer for it.

*   *   *

Yet the publication will be of indirect benefit to the Jews.— Many of my thoughts, such as those about duelling, suicide, support of inventors, a stock exchange monopoly, traveling complaint commissions, are good for all nations. Therefore people may treat the Jews more gently because these suggestions were born of their sufferings and their spirit.

June 12, 1895

It is not enough for me to run a work project, but I must have it conducted by a permanent commission. The head of this commission must have a systematic mind.

*   *   *

June 12

Short-sighted people will refuse when I ask them to transplant their pension institutes, etc. The good example must carry the day here. There are three kinds of pension institutes that I have in mind:

1) those with an all-Jewish membership (*Hevras* and the like); they are the easiest to transplant, for they can be dug up with all their roots.

2) those with a majority of Jewish members (an example is the Vienna *Concordia*): There a general meeting may decide to divide up the property, or the minority can be given a cash settlement and the rest can be transplanted as above. A very effective move would also be to leave the immovables to the minority (which would cost less than it appears, because this would save a twofold transfer).

3) those with only a scattering of Jews (like an association of civil servants). In such cases we must either waive our claims to the sums due us (after all, we compensate all our people who have sustained any losses, on the principle of solidarity), or, if the statutes permit it, the pension can be made over to somebody else, or we may request that the income be forwarded abroad.

*   *   *

June 12

The boat sailing to occupy the land can carry, in addition to the officers of the Company, representatives of the Local Groups (possibly as non-paying passengers) who may occupy sites for their establishments over there. These representatives must have the authorization to enter into agreements binding on their Local Groups; and they, rather than the Company, will be responsible to their groups for the choice of sites and the like.

*   *   *

The distribution of this new world will be handled equitably!

*   *   *

I shall determine the time of my tour of the Local Groups later.

This tour will take place about two months before the sailing of the land-taking expedition, one month before it at the latest.

Of course, I shall be able to visit only the largest cities.

The method of this centralization is something still to be considered. Shall I send my missionaries out into districts? For this the two Schiffs would be quite suitable; this could be completed in two months if Europe were divided into two or four districts. Or shall I give lectures to a group of traveling scholars and then spread the fellows out over the countries? Perhaps the first plan should be adopted at the beginning, when everything still has to be done cautiously and secretly, and the second one later.

*   *   *

On my main tour I shall everywhere invite a small number of the most respectable (not the wealthiest) men to come to see me, make them take an oath of secrecy, and reveal to them the plan which I am going to announce to the Family Council. Then will follow a second, bigger meeting, the composition of which will be suggested to me by the first group. To this meeting I shall announce the "outflow" plan—there is no mention in it as yet of the State—, telling them only that we are seeking security for our capital and new soil for our labor. But I must take care in every country not to get involved in any "secret society" business. Perhaps I shall call in the first confidants one by one and have them take oaths individually.

Carefully avoid the danger of "secret societies" everywhere. That is why our official propaganda must be made by the most circumspect people. We shall cover ourselves by submitting our "secret instructions" to the governments for their approval.

After all, we want to proceed with the consent of the governments, but undisturbed by the mobs of parliament and press.

*   *   *

June 12

It will, incidentally, spread like wildfire. One of my dreams during the period of uncertainty was to force Alois Lichtenstein, Schönerer or Lueger to a duel. If I had been shot, a letter left behind by me would have told the world that I fell a victim to this most unjust movement. Thus my death might at least have improved the heads and hearts of men. But if I had shot my opponent, I wanted to make a magnificent speech before the assize court, first expressing my regrets at "the death of an honorable man," like Morès who had stabbed Captain Mayer to death. Then I would have gone into the Jewish Question, making a powerful, Lassalle-like speech which would have shaken and moved the jury and inspired respect from the court, leading to my acquittal. Thereupon the Jews would have offered to make me a member of parliament. But I would have been obliged to decline that, because I did not want to become a representative of the people over the dead body of a human being.—And now! I find that the anti-Semites are fully within their rights.

*   *   *

It would be an excellent idea to call in respectable, accredited anti-Semites as liquidators of property.

To the people they would vouch for the fact that we do not wish to bring about the impoverishment of the countries that we leave.

At first they must not be given large fees for this; otherwise we shall spoil our instruments and make them despicable as "stooges of the Jews."

Later their fees will increase, and in the end we shall have only Gentile officials in the countries from which we have emigrated.

The anti-Semites will become our most dependable friends, the anti-Semitic countries our allies.

We want to emigrate as respected people.

June 12

No Jewish paper!

Jewish papers! I will induce the publishers of the biggest Jewish papers (*Neue Freie Presse, Berliner Tageblatt, Frankfurter Zeitung,* etc.) to publish editions over there, as the *New York Herald* does in Paris.

The transplantation of habits includes one's favorite paper at breakfast.

The newspapers will keep their readers, satisfy the needs (which will soon be enormous) of those who have stayed behind, and exchange news by telegraph. At first the overseas editions will be the smaller ones. Then the old editions will shrink and the new ones become big.

The Gentile editors will stay here and feel liberated and comfortable; the Jewish ones will go overseas and become rich and respected, taking an active part in politics; in fact, at present the journalists are the only Jews who know anything about politics.

I am the best proof of this.

Amnesty for moral misdemeanors of the press, too. All shall start a new life. But let everyone be respectable over there from the outset! Tribunals of honor, like those of the lawyers. The press must be free, but let it have and preserve the priestly honor of its opinions. In this way we shall also have the most decent press in the world.

*   *   *

The insurance business!

It will become a big department, probably requiring a ministry of its own. We shall start with a Director of Insurance.

The capital is contained in the State (at first in the *Society**).

* In English in the original.

We shall make use of all Jewish officials of private insurance companies (that Viennese named P. who was sentenced will get a good position); they will be State officials, of course, and can advance to high positions.

Insurance is a tested, well-known enterprise in all its branches, like banking, railroads, telephone, etc. Private capital no longer has any right to make profits here, because there is no risk any more.

The determining factor for the promotion or impediment of a private enterprise is the element of risk. Where there is no risk, there must be no entrepreneurial profit. On the other hand, we shall magnanimously tolerate any untried enterprise.

*   *   *

Induce the Hirsch brothers to build a "Louvre" over there.

*   *   *

June 12

My Russian Jews, who constitute the great reservoir of *unskilled labourers*,* will be organized into labor batallions.

They will be given labor ranks, as in the army, perhaps even badges to indicate them, and advance according to their efficiency and seniority. Everyone has a marshal's baton in his pack. I do not want a horde of helots who eternally remain in misery. For workers' pensions I shall gradually use all institutions similar to the *Tabaktrafik;* these permit grading, according to local differences.

June 12

Should there be a tobacco monopoly?

Probably yes. It is the most bearable form of indirect taxation; it is known to most people from their present countries; it makes bigger claims on the big consumers than on the small ones; it will give me the opportunity to start tobacco plantations (on a

* In English in the original.

franchise basis, with the penalty of cancellation in case of tax fraud) and to give business to tobacco factories, and I shall have state-licensed tobacco shops to give to workers as a pension.

* * *

June 12

Induce all big Jewish-owned factories, businesses, etc. to establish branches over there (analogous to the overseas editions of the newspapers). In this way they will be able gradually to transfer their plant and inventory as well as their business experience to the other side.

This is the transplanting of businesses; it will immediately produce employment, commerce, etc., and meet needs in the usual manner.

In the transplanting of businesses, too, those left behind will gradually pass over into the hands of Gentiles. Crises will be prevented.

A lot of people will become wealthy in the countries that we leave.

At our departure, people will gratefully and cordially shake the hands of the Jews whose business acumen has arranged everything so ingeniously. Here, too, the beginning of Jewish honor!

* * *

Quite generally, I should like to pay all pensions in the form of such easy occupations, if possible.

Homes for the aged and infirm are places of cruelty to the human soul. Old people are cut off from life there, buried before their time. A man's old age becomes his prison, and that is considered the reward for a good life. Through my tobacco-shop pensions I shall preserve freedom for old people, too, as well as their participation in life, giving them the comforting illusion of usefulness, an easy occupation which will keep them from brooding. And when such an old person gets little treats for himself, he need not look about timidly.

The tobacco-shops will at the same time be the exclusive outlets for the sale of newspapers. This will increase the pensioners' income. It will be welcome to the newspapers—and should they ever endanger the external or internal security of the state, they can be confiscated at these central points.

No state stamp for newspapers. But a bond for safeguarding against wantonness, malice, baseness, irresponsibility, and profiteering manoeuvres.

Those newspaper owners who are known to be ethical may be exempted from this bond. The money can later be returned when a newspaper has proved itself to be clean. But it can be imposed again or even increased if the newspaper concerned is found guilty of abusing the power of the press.

But I should like to submit this abuse of power of the press (a new offense) to the verdict of a jury. Under no circumstances must a paper be prosecuted on account of a hostile attitude, as long as it does not use reprehensible methods. The question of how to preserve a healthy freedom of the press and prevent insolence is worthy of very serious consideration. Possibly through courts of delegated jurors?

*   *   *

June 12

A monopoly on hard liquor, in any event.

Some privileges, similar to those of the tobacco monopoly, manufacture, and state-licensed shops. The latter will also serve to fight drunkenness, just as brokerages fight the gambling mania. For it will be possible to impose graded fines, culminating in the revocation of the license, for encouraging drinking by giving credit, etc.

*   *   *

June 12

The transition from *Society** to State is a complicated problem.

* In English in the original, here and *passim*.

This will have to be recognized conclusively in the drawing up of the Company contract and the statutes. For the *Society* will have enormous profits with which the stockholders will be reluctant to part.

From the moment at which the State comes into being the *Society* will be placed under public ownership—probably in such a way that the State acquires all shares at a stipulated price, but leaves the *Society* in its present legal status, subject to British law; for it will be some time before we ourselves shall have the power to push through the claims of our citizens or of the State itself.

June 12

When we occupy the land, we shall bring immediate benefits to the state that receives us. We must expropriate gently the private property on the estates assigned to us.

We shall try to spirit the penniless population across the border by procuring employment for it in the transit countries, while denying it any employment in our own country.

The property-owners will come over to our side. Both the process of expropriation and the removal of the poor must be carried out discreetly and circumspectly.

Let the owners of immovable property believe that they are cheating us, selling us things for more than they are worth.

But we are not going to sell them anything back.

*   *   *

June 12

It goes without saying that we shall respectfully tolerate persons of other faiths and protect their property, their honor, and their freedom with the harshest means of coercion. This is another area in which we shall set the entire old world a wonderful example.

At first, incidentally, people will avoid us. We are in bad odor. By the time the reshaping of world opinion in our favor has been completed, we shall be firmly established in our country, no longer fearing the influx of foreigners, and receiving our visitors with aristocratic benevolence and proud amiability.

* * *

June 12

The voluntary expropriation will be accomplished through our secret agents. The Company would pay excessive prices.

We shall then sell only to Jews, and all real estate will be traded only among Jews. To be sure, we shall not be able to do this by declaring other sales invalid. Even if this did not run counter to the modern world's sense of justice, our power would not suffice to force it through.

Therefore we must safeguard each of our sales of immovables through an option of re-purchase on the part of the Company. That is, if the owner wants to sell the property, we shall have the right to buy it back at our original sale price. However, we shall add a compensation, to be fixed by a board of experts, for any improvements that have been made. The owner will name an expert and we shall name one of our own. If these two cannot agree, they will choose a disinterested third to make a decision.

This option of re-purchase will be a special privilege that cannot be revoked by a mortgage.

* * *

The *Society* will have a department for the granting of mortgage credit. This will be a branch bank, nationalized, of course, like all other subsidiary institutions "over there."

The employees of private banks on this side will gradually become state employees on the other side, with bigger salaries, honors, etc.

For the voluntary expropriation we shall have to use local sub-agents who must not know that their employer is himself a secret agent who takes instructions from the centralized "Commission for Property Purchases."

These secret purchases must be carried out *simultaneously*, as upon the pressing of an electric button. Our secret agents, who will appear over there as purchasers on their own account, will receive the signal: *Marchez* [go ahead]!

Within a week all sales must have been completed. Otherwise the prices will increase exorbitantly.

Of course, this will have to be preceded by painstaking preliminary research in land registers (where they exist), through discreet inquiries and investigation of specific situations, etc.

Estate owners who are attached to their soil because of old age, habit, etc., will be offered a complete transplantation—to any place they wish, like our own people. This offer will be made only when all others have been rejected.

If this offer is not accepted either, no harm will be done. Such close attachment to the soil is found only with small properties. Big ones are to be had for a price.

Should there be many such immovable owners in individual areas, we shall simply leave them there and develop our commerce in the direction of other areas which belong to us.

*   *   *

The secret land buyers will not be free agents, but our employees.

They will be told in advance that any attempt to engage directly or indirectly in land speculation on this particular occasion will bring about their immediate dismissal with permanent loss of honor.

But, like all our employees, they will have special privileges in the choice of location of their houses which we shall build for them inexpensively, making deductions from their salaries on the principle of amortization.

June 12

Special note:

If I have to do it in book form, everything that looks like a prospectus must be avoided.

I must suggest to the little Jews and the governments to

request it from me; but if I don't do it *d'un air absolument détaché* [with an air of absolute detachment], I shall become ludicrous and an instrument unfit for the magnificent purpose.

June 12, 1895

As soon as we sight the new shores from the pioneering ship, the flag of the *Society* (which will later become the national flag) will be hoisted.

All will bare their heads. Let us salute our flag!

The first man ashore will carry a cheap, shoddy flag in his hand. It will later be preserved in the National Museum.

June 12

For the future legend, have a distinctive cap designed, *à la* Stanley. Wear the yellow badge while occupying the land, and all pioneers are to receive a little yellow ribbon.

June 12

The novel. Its hero:

One of his table talks on the boat will be on the subject of Jewish Honor.

Afterwards the little yellow ribbons will be passed out to all those present. At that moment he may not be able to tell as yet that it will become a decoration.

He is only distributing it as a souvenir. He has had a list made in advance. Everyone acknowledges receipt of the little silver mark on the yellow ribbon.

This list is preserved. It contains the first knights of Jewish honor.

*   *   *

Over there the ribbon is worn from the beginning. He does not prescribe it—"simply looks upon it with favor." Unauthorized persons are not allowed to wear it.

*   *   *

A juridical difficulty presents itself: how is the State, as yet non-existent, to secure for itself the purchase of the *Society*'s shares? Incidentally, the change-over can perhaps take place only under moral guarantees.

June 12

Those South American republics must be obtainable for money. We can give them annual subsidies. But only for about twenty years, i.e., until we are strong enough to protect ourselves; otherwise this would become a tribute which would be incompatible with our future dignity and the stoppage of which could lead to war.

The duration of these subsidies should be determined by the length of time indicated by our military head as sufficient for us to become a match for all these republics together.

But at the start, before they even know that we are coming over, we could get big concessions in return for the mere prospect of loaning them money at one percent less!

June 12

Discreet, delicate investigations should first be carried on regarding the financial needs, the internal political situation, and currents in these South American republics.

On the whole, it will be a voluntary parting with the land.

*   *   *

But especially for these things do I need the Rothschilds.
And what if they refuse?
Well, then they will simply take the consequences.

*   *   *

Since my plan is now dependent on the Rothschilds, I naturally think about them a lot. I only know a few of them by sight. I know something about only two. Albert in Vienna seems to be an industrious banker and a clear thinker. At the same time, a court snob. I am told that someone came to him with the idea of a Palais de Glace [Ice Palace]. He said: "Vienna has no patronage for that," and gave intelligent reasons for it.

I frequently see Alphonse, the Parisian, in the street, also saw him at court in the Burdeau-Drumont trial, where he had a modest, trembling appearance. He cringes in a refined way. I last saw him at the Grand Prix and had a peculiar feeling then. For this sorry, wobbly figure of a man possesses the means to turn an enormous stream of happiness on humanity —if he goes along with my plan. I followed him through the crowd for a while and looked at him with my thoughts.

June 12

I shall write Bacher a very cordial letter of farewell. He has been my friend; that I have felt.

*   *   *

Julius Bauer, the director of the National Theater, crosses over on the same boat with my family, in order to entertain my parents during the voyage . . . (Oh Heavens, this would be a pretty chapter for the novel—but if it becomes reality, who of the passengers I am now dreaming of will still be alive?)

June 12

For me these notes are not work, but only relief. I am writing myself free of the ideas which rise like bubbles in a retort and would finally burst the container if they found no outlet.

My God, after this confession Lombroso might consider me mad. And my friend Nordau will conceal from me the apprehension I cause him. But they are wrong. I know that two and two is four.

June 12

These notes prevent me from putting earlier things in my book.

In my clean copy I am still on my conversation with Hirsch. But the growth of the new ideas is more important. Who knows how soon it is going to stop?

Through it all I have the fear described by Heyse in that wonderful little poem about the artist:

> *Ich bebe:*
> *Dass ich hinfahren könnte über Nacht,*
> *Hinfahren, ehe ich dies Werk vollbracht.*

[I shudder to think that I could depart over night, depart before I have completed this work.]

Ah, once I have things in order and have deposited my papers with the local Academy under lock and key, while I have the book copied, the property will be secured and will be an imperishable treasure of mankind.

Of all mankind, not merely of the Jews.

* * *

On the basis of these candid notes, some people will think me a megalomaniac. Others will say or believe that I want to do some business or advertise myself.

But my peers, the artists and philosophers, will understand how genuine all this is, and they will stand up for me.

* * *

June 12

To the architects:

Typical designs of workshops for shoemakers, tailors, carpenters, etc.; these can be printed in large quantities and distributed everywhere.

This will be publicity for emigration!

It will be a joy to work. Everyone to attain a little house of his own, wherever possible.

* * *

A conference of architects to discuss workers' dwellings; I shall preside, as with the jurists' conference.

Other mass designs for the "own house" of the middle class, "Cottage" system. Distribute this also as advertising.

* * *

Rental and amortization for these houses. In the construction industry (whether for housing, railways, roads, etc.) we will greatly favor private enterprise by granting it *sound* construction credits (which must be given careful study).

The *Society* will profit only through the increase in land values. Construction is to be inexpensive, because building increases the general value of the land.

* * *

June 12

Pawnbroker's Office:

Name and address must be given when something is pawned. The pawner will not be told the reason for this. The names of those who have pawned beds, tools, items of utter necessity will be turned in directly to the Central Welfare Office. This office makes equally discreet investigations and then takes whatever action it wishes. By keeping alphabetical lists it will soon recognize habitual pawners and swindlers.

* * *

June 12

At the present time we are stepchildren in all countries. I am even today filled with unshakable confidence that I shall succeed.

If I had any thought of making some profit on this, I should get a loan today with no qualms.

* * *

June 12

Am I working it out?

No! It is working itself out in me.

It would be an obsession if it were not so rational from beginning to end.

An earlier term for such a condition was "inspiration."

June 12

Today the thought arises in me that I may be solving much more than the Jewish Question.

Namely, *tout bonnement* [very neatly], the social question! I don't know, I doubt it, because in all these matters I have the creation of new conditions in mind; and the difficulty in the social question is precisely that everywhere men are bogged down in ancient abuses, lengthy stagnation, and inherited or acquired wrong. Whereas I presuppose a virginal soil. But if it turns out to be true, what a gift of God to the Jews!

*   *   *

When I say "God" I do not mean to offend the free-thinkers. As far as I am concerned, they can use "World Spirit" or some other term in place of this dear old wonderful abbreviation by means of which I get across to the simple intelligences. In our academic battle of words, we still mean one and the same thing. In fact, in belief as well as in doubt we mean the very same thing: that it is inexplicable!

*   *   *

June 12

Send a circumspect man over as housing officer even before the sailing of the pioneering expedition. The pioneers, especially the representatives of the Local Groups, must find things comfortable.

The Housing Officer will later have bigger and bigger tasks and head a department when workers arrive.

June 12

Prostitution:

There is not likely to be any immediate solution. (In any case, a conference of politicians will have to be convened on this.

Poets will be called in because of their continual preoccupation with love.) Long-range solutions are the following:

Patriarchal families; the encouragement of early marriages, which, incidentally, will come about *par la force des choses* [by itself], because we shall give employment to great numbers of young men, pay them well, and thus give them an early opportunity to establish households of their own. Then, too, in the early stages of our settlement they will want to have a house, because there will as yet be no big-city entertainments, no easy attractions, and no market of females.

*   *   *

Also, we shall give salary allowances to married men and mass-produce inexpensive wedding outfits for different classes "as premiums for industry, efficiency, etc." Our purpose in this will be the encouragement of marriage.

*   *   *

Allowances for children.

*   *   *

June 12

We Jews are a vain people. We supply the biggest quota of the snobs of "good" society. An aristocratic sponger can get whatever he wants from the bankers if he dines at their homes where others can see him.

But I believe we are vain only because we have no access to honor. Once we have regained our honor, we shall not be vain, but ambitious. Good, clever Montesquieu with his *ressorts* [competences].

*   *   *

I shall probably make enemies of the big Jews. Well, this is going to be apparent from the attacks or the silence of the servile part of the press.

*   *   *

June 12

If we move into a region where there are wild animals to which the Jews are not accustomed—big snakes, etc.—I shall use the natives, prior to giving them employment in the transit countries, for the extermination of these animals. High premiums for snake skins, etc., as well as their spawn.

* * *

June 12

I shall inform my *unskilled** laborers from Russia that they can advance and later at least get tobacco shops and the like (if they are not fitted to become officers of the labor batallions).

Therefore they will properly use the rest of the seven-hour day for self-improvement in workers' and trade schools.

For this, again, I shall need a new corps of educators: the trade instructors. A workman can become such an instructor, too.

* * *

The Seven-Hour Day!

Of course, work will be carried on not just during seven hours of a day, but during fourteen.

Two shifts or four? This will depend on the proximity of homes and schools. For if I make the workers travel long distances twice a day, I shall do them great harm.

* * *

June 12

In the *Palais Royal*, amidst the strains of military music, to my subordinates who want to flatter me:

One must not praise me because one must not censure me either. For I am the Leader. I am saying this not only on account of discipline, but also because my mind must remain sound

* In English in the original.

and simple if I am to carry it through. I shall recognize by the quality of your obedience and the warmth of your enthusiasm to what extent I can count on you.

*   *   *

What an example I am to the poor, aspiring Jews, such as I used to be myself!

If my object had been money, I should never have been able to come face to face with the biggest financial power on earth, the Rothschilds, the way I am going to do.

*   *   *

Even if Güdemann fails me, I shall send Baron Jacobs to the Palestine Rothschild—Edmond, I think—and have him arrange an interview for me.

*   *   *

I shall be reproached with practising state socialism—no reproach, even if it were true, provided the State aims at the right things. That is, not the advantage of one group or caste, but the gradual ascent of everyone to the distant lofty goals of mankind.

But only the narrow-minded and the malevolent can overlook the fact that I want to make the individual free, great, rich, and happy.

*   *   *

I merely eliminate the entrepreneur's profit on safe undertakings.

*   *   *

I owe to Drumont a great deal of the present freedom of my concepts, because he is an artist.

*   *   *

I did not want to write another utopian novel. All this is true, reasonable, possible.

Why should I not tell it straightforwardly?

*   *   *

Should not the dowries of wealthy girls be taxed?

The proceeds could be used to provide for penniless "old maids," just as there must always be a moral adjustment between the joys of some and the sorrows of others, by means of taxation. (A good thing in France is the amusement tax which benefits the *assistance publique* [public welfare]. We shall have one too.)

Actually, the Jews are already observing this principle, on a small scale and in the haphazard, fatuous manner of all "philanthropy" up to now. At big weddings a lot of money is donated to the poor.

But I want not only to bring this under firm, sound regulations, but also to call on the hard-hearted people who do not remember the needy.—Certainly I don't have to spare the matrimonial fortune-hunters. (In this connection it is a droll thought that the tax can also be slapped on the father-in-law.)

I shall prevent or punish tax fraud by invalidating fake contracts, giving big rewards to informers, imposing heavy fines, and making the swindler permanently ineligible to be elected to office, to receive a decoration, or to be raised to the nobility.

*   *   *

June 14, 1895

Today a severe headache.—In order to divert the blood from my head, today I will start learning to ride a bicycle. Otherwise I shall not be able to carry the task through.

*   *   *

June 14

The moral blessings and physical bliss of labor.

*   *   *

Yesterday I dined with a wealthy Viennese bachelor, a useless playboy. He groaned about the anti-Semites, about the blood-libel. I got him to talk. That way I confirmed my opinion of the temper of the rich. For a moment I even took this man seriously. I asked him if he was prepared to do something for the Jewish cause. He seemed to suspect a financial sacrifice and drawled, "Naw!" I hastened to rectify this misconception and said: "For instance, a journey to Constantinople?" "No," he said, "I am no good at such things. I am too lazy." Yes indeed! It will be a long time before I arouse, before I shake, the Jews out of the indolence of their prison life.

June 14

The Promised Land, where it is all right for us to have hooked noses, black or red beards, and bandy legs without being despised for these things alone. Where at last we can live as free men on our own soil and die in peace in our own homeland. Where we, too, can expect honor as a reward for great deeds; where we shall live at peace with all the world, which we shall have freed through our own freedom, enriched by our wealth, and made greater by our greatness.

So that the derisive cry "Jew!" may become an honorable appellation, like "German," "Englishman," "Frenchman"—in short, like that of all civilized peoples. So that by means of our State we can educate our people for tasks which still lie beyond our horizon. For God would not have preserved our people for so long if we did not have another role to play in the history of mankind.

* * *

The flag occurs to me. Perhaps a white flag with seven gold stars. And the white field will signify our new, clean life. Just as the stars are the working hours. Under the banner of labor we shall enter the Promised Land.

* * *

It is a great good fortune for me and will gild my parents' old age and be to the lasting honor of my descendants that I have devised this great project.

* * *

June 14

Güdemann telegraphs me today:

"Unable to make trip. Salo at North Cape. Letter follows. Going to Baden Sunday afternoon. Güdemann."

Oh yes, it will be hard to get the Jews interested in it. But get them I shall. I feel a gigantic strength for the glorious task gathering in me. A man grows with greater purposes!*

* * *

To the Family Council:

I should gain greater glory if I moved to the Promised Land only with the poor and the wretched and made a proud and respected people out of them. But I shall renounce this glory, just as I should be ready to recede into the background entirely. The only thing is that a master builder must, as long as he is alive, supervise the building himself, no matter how great the worry, the toil, and the responsibility.

* * *

Our entire youth, all those who are now between twenty and thirty years of age, will abandon their vague socialistic leanings and turn to me. They will go forth as itinerant preachers to their own families and into the world—without my having to urge them.

For the land is to be theirs!

June 15, 1895

The non-Jewish expropriates over there will, after the purchase has been made, be given the choice between payment

* Translator's Note: This is a line, slightly misquoted, from Friedrich Schiller's Prologue to his *Wallensteins Lager*.

in cash or in shares (according to the face value). No outwitting, only self-protection.

After all, through us the world shall be acquainted with something that has not been considered possible in 2000 years: Jewish honor.

* * *

To the Family Council:

Your older men will assist us with their advice as to finances, banking, railroads, and politics, perform diplomatic services for us, etc.

Your sons, and I would want you to have as many of them as possible, will be in positions of leadership in the army, the diplomatic corps, etc., according to their abilities—but strictly according to their abilities—, govern provinces, etc.!

With your daughters you will reward our best officers, our finest artists and most brilliant officials. Or continue to marry them off in Europe, as the Americans do, something that I consider rather useful. The main thing is that your money be scattered far and wide.

June 15

Today I am an isolated and lonely man, tomorrow perhaps the intellectual leader of hundreds of thousands—in any case, the discoverer and proclaimer of a mighty idea.

* * *

To the midget millionaires I shall send my representatives: Schiff, Goldmann, Wolf Schulmann.

I shall ask the millionaires who still have Jewishness in their hearts to meet with a rabbi who will read my address to them.

The rabbis who do not want to come along will be shunted aside. There is no stopping the procession.

* * *

But the rabbis will be pillars of my organization and I shall honor them for it. They will arouse the people, instruct them on the boats, and enlighten them on the other side. As a reward they will be formed into a fine, proud hierarchy which, to be sure, will always remain subordinated to the State.

*   *   *

While I have been writing, and especially when I have seen in my mind's eye the solemn, festive mood on the boats and the arrival, the gala reception on the other side, I have often wept over the misfortunes of my people.

But if I am to lead my people, I must not show any tears. The leader must have an impassive face.

June 15

I do not believe there is a mania for speculation among our people. These people are good providers. And a solicitous *pater familias* [family man] approaches the stock exchange with trepidation.

But what other place is there for him to go under present conditions?

*   *   *

June 16, 1895

During these days I have more than once been afraid I was losing my mind. This is how tempestuously the trains of thought have raced through my soul.

A lifetime will not suffice to carry it all out.

But I shall leave behind a spiritual legacy. To whom? To all men.

I believe I shall be named among the greatest benefactors of mankind.

Or is this belief already megalomania?

*   *   *

June 16

I must, above all, keep myself under control.

As Kant noted down for himself: No more thoughts about Johann.

My Johann is the Jewish Question. I must be able to summon it and dismiss it.

*　　*　　*

June 16

No one ever thought of looking for the Promised Land where it actually is—and yet it lies so near.

This is where it is: within ourselves!

I am not misleading anyone. Everyone can satisfy himself that I am telling the truth. For everyone will take across, in himself, a piece of the Promised Land—one in his head, another one in his hands, a third in his savings. The Promised Land is where we carry it!

*　　*　　*

I believe that for me life has ended and world history has begun.

*　　*　　*

June 16

At first we shall only work on and for ourselves in all secrecy.

But the Jewish State will become something remarkable. The land of the seven-hour working day will be not only a model country for social experiments and a treasure-house for works of art, but a miracle country in all civilization. It will be a destination for the civilized world which will come to visit us the way it now visits Lourdes, Mecca, Sadagora. Do you at last understand me? But I shall be at my strongest in the third stage. There I shall have the whole world on my side—Jews, Christians, the common people, the middle class, aristocrats, the clergy of all denominations, kings and emperors!

*　　*　　*

Sadagora.

No pressure will be exerted on anyone's conscience; the subtle suasions of civilization will have an effect on all.

* * *

I shall take in the *pieds crottés* [men with filth on their shoes] outside the stock exchange, all lost and wrecked existences, and give them a new life! These will be our best co-workers.

* * *

June 16

Goethe, Goethe!

For three hours I tramped around the Bois in order to walk off the pangs of new trains of thought. It grew worse and worse. Now I am sitting at Pousset's, writing them down and feeling relieved. It is true that I am also drinking beer.

The Jewish State is a world necessity.

They will pray for me in the synagogues. But in the churches as well.

If you force me into opposition to you, I shall in the second stage—which I do not quite believe in, although it is certainly possible—gather about me all medium and smaller millionaires. A second formidable Jewish financial force will march up. For in the initial period, when I have no use as yet for the fully deposited billion, I shall have to engage in banking transactions.

I have no more aversion to banking, if the cause requires it, than I have to transportation, construction, etc.

But will Europe bear both you and us?

The earth is already trembling here.

* *

One of the major battles I shall have to fight will be against the self-mockery of the Jews.

This readiness to scoff represents, at bottom, the feeble

attempt of prisoners to look like free men. That is why this mockery actually touches me.

*   *   *

June 16

As soon as we have established ourselves and all diplomatic moves and land purchases have been completed, I shall give my speech (with the changes desired by the R's) to the *Neue Freie Presse,* because I discovered this thing as their correspondent.

I want the *Neue Freie Presse* to make extracts available to the other papers, including the anti-Semitic ones. To the *Berliner Tageblatt* as well.

*   *   *

June 16

A more beautiful Sadagora!

One of the things, perhaps the main thing, that we shall have learned from the civilized nations will be tolerance.

They did have the good will to emancipate us. It no longer worked, in the old surroundings.

*   *   *

The Stock-Exchange Monopoly will probably be the first thing in which Europe will imitate us. And that will push the vacillating, cowardly Jews my way. They will follow us a bit late.

In this, too, the procession will ride over the reluctant.

*   *   *

June 15

Family Council:

You see that we are not hoodwinking anybody. Nor are we doing violence to anyone—except to ourselves, our habits, our evil inclinations, and our faults. But he who wants to do great things must first conquer himself.

*   *   *

June 15

Anyone who cares to wear a *kaftan* may continue to do so unmolested.

We shall only observe the principles of modern hygiene, for the well-being of all.

Insert: To the Family Council:

Through amicable expropriation the State will be able to acquire factories, etc., which Ministers of Finance never dared to think about.

*   *   *

Insert:

Shares for the expropriated. Right of repurchase on the part of the *Society*.

*   *   *

June 16

Schiff was here today and teased me, saying that I looked as if I had invented the dirigible airship.

—Hm, perhaps I did! I thought to myself, and kept silent.

June 16, 1895

Second letter to Güdemann.

Dear Doctor Güdemann:

Your letter made amends for the impression which your telegram gave me. It had made me think, a bit angrily: Just try to help the Jews! Which, to be sure, did not stop me from proceeding vigorously with the project itself, just as I shall, heedless of everything, march on to my goal! Anyone who wants to help me is most welcome; he will be doing nothing for me, everything for himself. I shall pass over those who are recalcitrant or indifferent.

Thus even the first impact of your telegram did not dismay

me, but only annoyed me. The next moment I said to myself: I probably did not make it sufficiently clear to him how desperately serious things are. My plan is actually as serious as the situation of the Jews itself, and I feel that the Jews in their torpor do not realize this seriousness clearly enough.

I further said to myself: the man does not know me, that is, knows me only very slightly; we have exchanged a few unimportant phrases or jokes, and in the newspaper he reads articles of the lightest kind from my pen. But your letter appeased me. It is written in a tone that pleases me, the kind that I need for my purpose. I can see that you will be the right kind of helper to me, one of my helpers, for I shall need many.

You are surprised at my warm interest in "our cause." At the moment you cannot even suspect the degree of heat which this interest has reached. Of course, I did not have it before. I was indifferent to my Jewishness; let us say that it was beneath the level of my awareness. But just as anti-Semitism forces the half-hearted, cowardly, and self-seeking Jews into the arms of Christianity, it powerfully forced my Jewishness to the surface. This has nothing to do with affected religiosity. Despite all my piety for the faith of our fathers I am not a bigot and shall never be one.

That I am not planning anything contrary to religion, but just the opposite, is shown by the fact that I want to work with the rabbis, with *all* rabbis.

I called you and the businessman to Caux for two reasons. First, because I wanted to take both of you out of your accustomed surroundings and place you in the lofty freedom of the mountains where everyday life fades away, where a glacier railway would offer you visible proof of the extent to which the human inventive faculty has already conquered Nature, and this would have put you in a sufficiently serious and yet unconstrained mood for my unusual message.

The second reason was that for weeks I have toiled over written work and shall have to continue to toil for an indefinite period of time, and thus desired a respite of two or three days from the enormous work which I would not have abandoned thereby, because I must not abandon it any longer.

I should have given you a verbal explanation of everything, observed the impression it made on you, dispelled your doubts, and constantly appealed from one to the other. For on those points, spiritual or secular, where one of you might not have understood me, the other disinterested man would have certified that I was proceeding constantly on the basis of solid fact.

Your companion need not have been a wealthy man or a philanthropist, for my project is dependent neither on the rich nor on the charitable. It would really be bad if it were. The only requirement was that he be an independent Jew.

You two were intended to be my first helpers. Since I cannot have you right away, I do not need the other man either.

I should immediately have approached other men if, as I have already said, I had not recognized from the contents of your letter that you are the right helper after all. I should have found others; and if not, I should simply have gone by myself. For I have the solution of the Jewish Question. I know it sounds mad; but in the initial period people will often think me mad until they realize with deep emotion the truth of all I have been saying. I have found the solution, and it no longer belongs to me; it belongs to the world.

As I have said, you two would have been my first assistants, or, more correctly, my messengers, for the time being. Your first joint mission would have been to Albert Rothschild to whom you would have given my message, and again the spiritual man would have been supported by the worldly man in the clarification of questionable points. Albert Rothschild would have taken the matter before his family council, and they would have asked me to appear there and give them a talk about my project.

Let me hasten to clear up a misconception that may arise in your mind. I am as little dependent on the Rothschilds' cooperation as I am on that of the other wealthy Jews. But the special character of my plan involves the necessity of notifying the Rothschilds.

Once you know the plan, you will see why.

Today I cannot tell you what it consists of. I would mutilate my thoughts if I sought to crowd them into a letter.

For weeks I have been writing from morning to midnight just to get the main features down on paper. It would be torture if it were not such bliss. I am the first one to be made happy by the solution. That is my reward, and it shall be my only reward.

How did I discover it? I do not know. Probably because I pondered it all the time and felt so unhappy about anti-Semitism. Thirteen years is my estimate of the period during which this idea took shape in my mind. For my first notes date from 1882, the year in which I read Dühring's book. Now that everything is so clear in my mind I marvel at how close to it I frequently was and how often I passed by the solution. I consider it a great good fortune that I have found it. It will gild the old age of my parents and be the lasting honor of my descendants.

I confess to you that I have tears in my eyes as I write this; but I shall carry it through with all rigor.

Perhaps you still believe that I am daydreaming. You will change your mind when you know everything. For my solution is a strictly scientific one, and this you must not take for academic socialism or congressional twaddle.

Enough of this! I am going to write down the address which I was going to make here before the Rothschild Family Council. It is a very long speech and yet it contains only the main features.

On this stationery and with this close handwriting it amounts to sixty-eight pages so far, and I am not nearly finished yet. It will take you a few hours to read it off. For your first mission, dear Doctor Güdemann, will be to read this speech to Albert Rothschild. Don't give it to him to read; you read it to him.

I believe that he will, as a matter of course, have enough respect for you and confidence in you to listen to you for as long as you deem necessary. You will, of course, have read the speech beforehand and will tell him in advance what decision his family will be faced with.

According to a newspaper report I have read, Albert Rothschild is on his country estate at Gaming-Waidhofen. Let me know by telegram if you are ready to go there.

Since you were going to come to Caux if I had given you an indication of what it was all about, you will certainly make that short trip to Gaming. Then I request you to ask Albert Rothschild by letter when he can receive you without interruption. He must make himself free for a whole day. He will be just as deeply moved and just as happy as you are, because I have been told that he is a serious, good Jew. He will immediately come to Paris to see me. You see, for the time being I have to stay here because of the discussion with all the Rothschilds.

After receipt of my letter, you send me a telegram and write him immediately. I hope to finish my address the day after tomorrow. Then it will take me at least three days to make a clean copy.

So the speech will be sent off from here on Saturday and be in your hands on Monday. You can have your meeting with Rothschild at Gaming on Tuesday, the 25th, or Wednesday, the 26th.

All the rest is contained in the speech. But even now you can indicate to Albert Rothschild in the same serious tone which you, as a Bible expert, surely sense in my letter that a most important matter of Jewish life is involved. I shall make the greatest effort to finish it quickly. I shall not put up with a genteelly dilatory treatment of the matter. The Jews are waiting.

Everything must be done immediately! That, too, is part of my program.

I could probably have saved myself the delay of this correspondence, etc., if I had procured an introduction to some member of the Rothschild family here, which would have been an easy matter. But I have valid reasons, which you will learn, for not entering into any personal contact with the Rothschilds before they have voiced their agreement in principle. And they will not have much time to deliberate, either.

Now I greet you in trusting admiration as my first associate.

Yours,

Th. Herzl.

Third letter to Güdemann.

June 17, 1895

Dear Doctor Güdemann:

I sent you a registered letter today. It is possible that it will be delivered in Baden at a time when you are out walking in the fields toward Soos where in my youth I also used to take philosophical walks by myself, or across the meadow to the *Kramerhütte* where it must be such a lovely early summer now. When you come home you might learn that someone attempted to deliver a registered letter to you. You are expecting the letter which I told you of in my telegram and you are a bit impatient, though not very much as yet, because, after all, you do not know yet. Perhaps you will go to the Weikersdorf post office or even the one in Baden. I don't know whether I have already aroused your interest, nor do I know from which post office registered letters are delivered there. Perhaps you will sit down and wait for the postman to return. Or you haven't been out at all and received my first letter promptly; in that case this one will strike you as superfluous, peculiar, long-winded.

Why do I write you a separate letter, then?

Because in the main letter there is, as yet without further details, the sentence: "I have the solution of the Jewish Question." And I can see the worried expression with which you are muttering into your fine patriarch's beard: "Completely cracked! His poor family!"

No, I am not cracked, neither completely nor partially, not cracked at all.

And that is why I am sending you these lines in addition to

that letter, as a sign that I never lose sight of the actual situation and take into account the smallest things just as accurately as the biggest ones.

Oh yes, even in my most exalted expositions I shall, here and there, have to mention casually, as though accidentally, that two times two is four, two times three is six, and $17 \times 7 = 119$. And I shall say that I quite distinctly remember what you or somebody else said to me, or must have thought about me, at some earlier point in my life—just so people will see that I still have my wits about me rather nicely.

A task in which things of this sort have to be faced is not a comfortable one—but great things are not done with comfort.

Again, my most cordial greetings.

Sincerely yours,
Th. Herzl
37 rue Cambon.

* * *

June 17, 1895

Schiff says: It is something that a man tried to do in the last century. Sabbatai!

Well, in the last century it was impossible. Now it is possible —because we have machines.

* * *

Telegram to Doctor Güdemann, Baden near Vienna.

"Must request you return unopened my non-registered letter sent yesterday. One of friends involved whose consent had likewise been presupposed raises absolute objections. Must comply."

June 18, 1895

Gardens of the Tuileries:

I was overstrained with thought. So I came here and recuperated by looking at the statues.

Outdoor art is the source of much happiness. The bowl-shaped green lawn with the charming "Runners" of Coustou (1712) should be copied without delay.

* * *

June 18, 1895

Have been to the same place again with Schiff. He "cured" me. For I accept the negative part of his observations, namely, that through this undertaking I would make myself "either ridiculous or tragic." It's that business of Jewish mockery. The negative part I do accept—and thereby differ from Don Quixote. The positive side (talk about socialism, face slapping, etc.) I reject—and herein differ from Sancho Panza.

* * *

Fourth letter to Baron Hirsch.

June 18

Dear Sir:

My last letter requires a postscript. Here it is: I have given the matter up. Why? My plan would be more likely to be wrecked by the opposition of the poor Jews than that of the rich.

You told me as much on that Pentecost morning, it is true. But I was in no position to believe you, for you had not let me finish what I had to say.

But recently I expounded my entire plan to a sensible friend (who is not a financier). I softened him completely, he swam in tears; I convinced his reason and wrung his heart.

Then he slowly got control of himself and said to me: "Through this undertaking you will make yourself either ridiculous or tragic." Becoming a tragic figure would not scare me; as for ridicule, it would ruin not me but the cause. The worst that people could say about me is that I am a poet. This is why I am giving the matter up.

For the present there is no helping the Jews yet. If someone were to show them the Promised Land, they would scoff at him. For they are demoralized.

Still, I know where that land lies; within ourselves! In our capital, in our labor, and in the peculiar combination of the two which I have devised. But we shall have to sink still lower, we shall have to be even more insulted, spat upon, mocked, whipped, plundered, and slain before we are ripe for this idea.

For the time being we shall have to endure *affronts* in high society where we try to push our way, an economic squeeze among the middle classes, and the most frightful misery in the lower classes.

We are still not desperate enough. That is why a rescuer would be greeted with laughter. Laughter? No, only with smiles; people no longer have the strength to laugh.

There is a wall—namely, the demoralization of the Jews. I know that beyond it lie freedom and greatness.

But I cannot break through this wall, not with my head alone. Therefore I am giving it up.

I merely repeat once more: the only way out is to weld all the smaller Jewish bankers into a second formidable financial power, fight the Rothschilds, pull them with us or pull them down—and then over and across.

If we meet again sometime, soon or late, and you ask me how this can be done without plunging Europe into the most horrible stock-market crisis, how anti-Semitism everywhere can, by this very expedient, be brought to an immediate standstill, I shall give you the explanation.

As a practical proposition, I am done with the matter. But I hold on to the theory of it and cherish it. Maybe this goes to show that I too am only a demoralized Jew. A Gentile would go through thick and thin for an idea of such power.

What would you have me do? I don't care to look like a Don Quixote.

But the petty solutions—your 20,000 Argentinians, or the conversion of the Jews to socialism—I will not accept. For I am no Sancho Panza either, but

Yours respectfully,
Dr. Th. Herzl

June 19, 1895

Schiff was here today, brought me the *reçus* [receipts], and then we did some figuring. It was a great relief to me to find that I was doing addition more rapidly and more accurately than he was. It took him a long time and he kept making fresh mistakes. So badly had he upset me yesterday!

* * *

June 19

I found an escape from the mental torment into which Schiff's anguished opposition had plunged me.

I am turning to Bismarck.

He is big enough to understand me or cure me.

* * *

Letter to Bismarck.   June 19, 1895
Your Highness: (Highness everywhere!)

Perhaps one or another of my writings has had the good fortune to come to Your Highness' attention, possibly my essays about French parliamentarianism which appeared in the literary section of the *Neue Freie Presse* under the titles "Election Sketches from France" and "The Palais Bourbon."

On the basis of this questionable and meagre authority I am asking Your Highness to receive me for a political discourse.

I am not trying to obtain an interview by cunning in this manner. Your Highness has occasionally granted such a favor to a journalist, and an editor of my paper in Vienna has been among those who have received the distinction of being admitted to you. But I have nothing of the sort in mind. If desired, I shall pledge my word of honor that I shall not publish anything about this discussion in newspapers, precious though it may be for my memory.

And about what subject do I want to make the political discourse? About the Jewish Question. I am a Jew and therefore qualified *ad causam* [on the subject].

I may remind Your Highness that you once spoke with another Jew also without mandatory authority, a man named Lassalle, about matters not exclusively Jewish.

What do I have to say on the Jewish Question? Actually it is very hard for me to utter the word. For if I do, the first impulse of every rational human being must be to send me to the observation room—Department for Inventors of Dirigible Balloons.

Well, how shall I preface it? Perhaps this way: two times two is four, two times three is six, $17 \times 7 = 119$, unless I am mistaken. I have five fingers on each hand. And I am writing with violet ink. And now I shall finally risk it:

I believe I have found the solution to the Jewish Question. Not *a* solution, but *the* solution, the only one.

It is a very voluminous, complicated plan. After completing it, I have told it to two Jews here, one very wealthy and one poor; the latter is a cultured person.

I can truthfully say that the rich man did not think me crazy. Or was it only out of tact that he treated me as if I still seemed sane to him? At any rate, he went into the theoretical possibility and finally said only, "You won't get the rich Jews for it; they are no good." (I implore Your Highness not to reveal this family secret.)

But on the poor Jew it had a different effect. He sobbed bitterly. At first I thought, without being astonished at it, that I had overwhelmed his reason and wrung his heart. No! His sobs were not those of a Jew, but of a friend. He was worried about me. I had to cheer him up, swear to him that I was firmly convinced that two times two was still four and that I did not foresee the time when two parallel lines could converge.

He said, "By this proposal you will make yourself ridiculous —or tragic!"

I finally promised him everything he asked: that I would use the plan only for a novel in which the tragic or comic hero is only on paper. In this way I succeeded in raising my shattered friend up again.

Being a tragic figure would not daunt me, nor would even the most terrible ridicule frighten me. But even though I have the right to stake my person for my idea, be it crazy or sound, I still have to limit the sacrifice to my person; and if I got the reputation of being insane, that would no longer be the case. I have parents and a wife who would grieve profoundly, as well as children whose entire future could be spoiled if people considered me a crazy do-gooder.

In this quandary—whose morality is clear, I believe—I am turning to Your Highness. Allow me to present my plan to you! If worst comes to worst, it will be a utopian novel of a kind of which many have been written from Thomas More to Bellamy. A Utopia is the more amusing the farther it strays from the rational world.

I dare to promise that in any case I shall bring with me a new Utopia and therefore an entertaining one. I am enclosing with this letter a leading article on "Public Works" which I published in the *Neue Freie Presse* two years ago. I am sending it to you not as a noteworthy literary achievement, but because the principle of public works is one of the many pillars on which my edifice rests.

When I studied all these institutions here two years ago and wrote about them, I did not know that later they would serve me for the solution of the Jewish Question. Yet I should have to preface my talk with this essay. Therefore I ask you to take note of it for the time being. After all, it will reflect the fact that I am not a Social Democrat.

It will be an easy matter for Your Highness to make inquiries in Hamburg, Berlin, or Vienna whether I have hitherto been considered a sensible man and whether it would be all right to admit me to a room—*bien que ça n'engagerait pas l'avenir* [that would not commit the future]. But the way I imagine Prince Bismarck, you will not need to make any inquiries after you have finished reading this letter. Anyone who reads the faces and the guts of men the way you do will also understand the soul of something written.

I can really not turn to a lesser person. Shall I go to a psychiatrist and say to him: "Tell me frankly, is this still the reasoning of a sane person?" In order to judge this he would have to have sociological, juridical, and commercial information of all kinds, which a medical man does not have even in the land of the *sous-vétérinaires* [assistant veterinarians].

Shall I ask individuals, Christians or Jews? Such an inquiry would gradually produce the very thing that I want to avoid.

No, it must be the last court of appeal right away. Only the man who has stitched a torn Germany together with his iron needle in such a wonderful way that it no longer looks patched up, only he is big enough to tell me once and for all whether my plan is a truly saving idea or an ingenious fantasy.

If it is but a novel, I shall have enjoyed the favor of providing some diversion for Your Highness and at the same time gratifying my old longing to commune with you for a moment—a longing which I should never have dared to express without such a momentous occasion.

But if it is true, if I am right, then the day on which I come to Friedrichsruh will go down in history. Who will still dare to call my plan a pretty dream after the greatest living empire builder has stamped his approval on it? And for you, Your Highness, it will be a participation in the solution of a question which is tormenting not merely the Jews, but all of Europe—a participation which is in moral, national, and political harmony with all the proud accomplishments of your glorious life.

The Jewish Question is a dragged-out piece of the Middle Ages with which the civilized nations cannot cope, even with the best will in the world, in a manner different from that planned by me. They have tried it through emancipation, but it came too late. It does no good to declare abruptly in the Legal Gazette: "Starting tomorrow, all men will be equal."

This sort of thing is believed only by beerhall politicians and their higher colleagues, the classroom theorists and drivelling fools in Clubs. And the last-named lack even the best part of those less learned exercises, the beer!

Would it not have been better to let the Jews rise to emancipation gradually and during this ascent assimilate them, gently or vigorously, depending on circumstances? Perhaps! How? One could have passed them through the filter of mixed marriages and ensured a new generation of Christians. But it would have been necessary to put emancipation after assimilation, not the other way around; that was bad thinking. But in any case, it is too late for this, too.

Just try to rescind the legal equality of the Jews. (Only their *legal* equality exists, anyway. What a misunderstood doctrine for the men from the beerhall!) What would be the consequences of that? Immediately all Jews, not only the poor ones as hitherto, but the rich ones as well, would join the Socialist Party with all their resources. They would plunge to their moneybags the way a Roman plunged unto his sword.

Crowd the Jews out of the country by force and you will have the most serious economic upheavals. In fact, even a revolution directed exclusively against the Jews—if such a thing were conceivable—would bring no relief to the lower strata even if it were successful. Movable property has become more intangible than ever. It immediately sinks into the ground, and into the ground of foreign countries at that.

But I do not want to talk of things that are impossible or for which it is too late, but of timely ones. At worst it might be too early for them—for I won't believe in the fantastic nature of my ideas before I hear it from your mouth.

If my plan is only premature, I shall put it at the disposal of the German government. It will be used if it is considered sound.

As a planner I must reckon with all eventualities, including the one that Your Highness will not answer my letter or will decline my visit.

Then my plan *will* be a fantasy. For I cannot demonstrate the feasibility of my solution any more clearly than, in this letter, I have demonstrated the justification for my desire to present the solution to Your Highness.

In that case, too, my mind will be at ease. Then I shall simply have dreamed, like the Utopians from Chancellor Thomas More to Bellamy.

I beg Your Highness to accept this assurance of my profound reverence and admiration.

Dr. Theodor Herzl
Paris Correspondent of the *Neue Freie Presse*

June 20, 1895

A hat parable (a kind of "Tale of the Three Rings"), or Belief, Doubt, Philosophy resolved in "the Inexplicable."

I take my headgear from my head and show it to people. What is it?

"A *chapeau*," says one.

"No, a *hat*," yells another.

"He's wrong! It's a *capello*," says a third.

"You fools, it's a *sombrero*," cries the fourth.

"A *kalap*," the fifth.

"Scoundrels! *Es ist ein Hut!*"

And so everyone uses a different word—there are countless ones; and yet these are only the general words, which in turn break down into generic terms like "cap," "helmet," "bonnet," etc.

And people are irritated at one another because they use different words for the same thing.

I agree with everyone, and everyone is indeed right. It *is* a hat, a *chapeau*, a *capello*. I tell everyone in his own language; otherwise he would not understand me. But I want to be understood, now and in the future, and I make my greatest concessions in the terms that I use.

I don't fight over words. I have no time for that.

What do you mean to say by your "faith"? And you, by your "doubt"? Is it not simply that it cannot be explained by reason?

Nous sommes d'accord [We are in agreement]. You may squabble among yourselves—but not with me.

I do say—that it cannot be explained rationally!

Let everyone get from this what he will. Do I appear to be evasive? Not at all.

For after I have talked to everyone in his own language, I take the floor for a general, clear explanation, and say, "Is this an object which serves to protect my head against drafts, rain, and sunshine?"

They all cry, "It is!"

"Does it serve me to greet my friends, and do I also take it off before a flag?"

"Yes, yes!"

And I can close with a pleasantry: "Do I also take it off when I join a social gathering?" As a matter of politeness—that is, because we have agreed to consider this polite. Everyone has his own specific hat and should not annoy others because its shape is different.

I can thus conciliate people by explaining to them the meaning and purpose of a thing.

June 20

What if Bismarck had felt constrained to say, in his Frankfurt period: I will unite these states, which are incapable of small sacrifices, by forcing them to make great ones. I will make them brothers through the bloodiest brawls with one another. And since I cannot get them to agree upon a Kaiser within the country, I shall take them out of the country.

And because I cannot find a German city in which all would convene without objection, I shall take them to a small French provincial town where long-forgotten French kings once erected a castle.

What would people have said to that? In the 1860's, 70's, 80's, and 90's! That is, if he had not carried it through!

June 20

Taverne Royale, over a *cassoulet* [stew].

I believe that if an acquaintance of mine were to invent a dirigible airship, I would box his ears. It would really be an awful insult to me. Why was it he and not I? If it were a stranger, I wouldn't mind.

With things that are above personal considerations, their connection with a person is offensive.

*   *   *

June 20

Faults of Democracy:

One gets only the disadvantages of its insistence on publicity. This publicity brings about the loss of that respect which is necessary for government. All the world finds out that the men who govern us are merely human beings too—and in so many cases laughable, narrow persons. Thus I lost my "respect" in Paris. On the other hand, only average types should be allowed to run the government. The geniuses and prodigies are necessary for the creation of things, but harmful to existing things, whether they replace them by something greater or expand them to the point of madness. They cannot leave the world the way they found it; they would be their own ruin if they were not able to destroy something, no matter whether bad or good.

The existing order, one that is to be preserved, must be governed only by mediocre people. The geniuses understand the past, they divine the future—but they are in a hurry to abolish the present, which the healthy ones among them also understand perfectly.

Something impels them to leave their mark. They are afraid of passing on before anyone notices that they have been here.

For government, however, we need ordinary men because they alone appreciate all the ordinary needs of mankind: food, drink, sleep, etc.

A prodigy pays no attention to these needs—in himself or in others.

And this is the difference between a healthy and an unhealthy genius. The unhealthy genius ignores ordinary needs because he does not understand them. The healthy genius ignores them despite the fact that he understands them!

*   *   *

Moreover, the light of publicity which Democracy offers is only something false and fictitious. Behind its glare things do take place which later emerge as scandals, such as the Panama affair and the like.

June 20

Taverne Royale.

After my *déjeuner* the two Marmoreks came to my table. I got them to talk. Without suspecting it, they confirmed what I wanted. The architect described the virulent state of anti-Semitism in Vienna. Things were getting worse and worse. He thought there was some relief in the fact that the City Council had been suspended. I explained to him the nature of such a suspension: it was a suspension of the Constitution. And after that? Either the Constitution is allowed to function normally again—in which case the common variety of anti-Semites will return with a lot of noise; and stronger than ever! Or the Constitution is suspended "for good." This would be done with a furtive loving glance in the direction of the anti-Semites, and they will get the point, or it will be explained to them if necessary. The Constitution will be abolished, equal rights for the Jews will be chucked out—and afterwards a special Constitutional Assembly will be magnanimously granted.

* * *

Marmorek, the medical scientist, said: There will be no other course left but to assign us a state of our own! (This is the clever fellow who does research to find a serum and kills streptococci.)

I was inwardly delighted.

I need such supporters at this point. This is how greatly Schiff demoralized me with his agitation and his tears.

I see now that he lacks understanding, for all his integrity and loyalty. Yet I owe him a great debt of gratitude. First, for his unmistakably great friendship; secondly, for dissuading me from the insufficient Güdemann, and thus making me hit upon the Bismarck idea—without his being aware of it.

Bismarck is now the touchstone and cornerstone of the project.

*   *   *

June 21, 1895

Democracy is political nonsense which can only be decided upon by a mob in the excitement of a revolution.

*   *   *

June 22, 1895

I must introduce educational considerations into the census. The franchise can be qualified as follows: literacy required to vote for delegates to the Constitutional Assembly, advanced education for the election of higher representatives, etc. Thus I can make levels of representation out of educational levels. To be eligible for election by one level, a candidate must himself hold the franchise of the next higher level.

*   *   *

The community defrays expenditures out of direct assessments (autonomy). A grievance court for the protection of individuals against the community.

The community is liable through assessments for obligations incurred in the auctioning of land.

*   *   *

Institutions of learning will be established in provincial cities, on the pattern of the German universities. A student may not be an active member of a uniformed association for more than one year. Students have no business in the capital city.

*   *   *

June 22

Being asleep on the job will disqualify a judge; habitual rudeness, an official. (An *accès de mauvaise humeur* [a touch of ill humor] in people must be viewed leniently.)

June 22

How can I make suicide something dishonorable? It will be easy with attempted suicide: insane asylum, involving loss of all civil and personal rights. Harder if death results. Burial in a separate place, after the body has been used for scientific purposes, will not suffice. There must be legal consequences as well. The last will and testament of the suicide (provided it can be established that he made it with suicide in mind) will be declared invalid as the work of a lunatic. His letters and posthumous writings must not be published.

His funeral must take place at night.

*　　*　　*

June 22

Sometimes one hears it said: this man has been driven mad by the Jewish Question; another by Jewish exploitation; a third, by socialism; a fourth, by religion; a fifth, by doubt, and so on.

No, these people were *already* mad. The only thing is that their hitherto imperceptible madness or colorless wandering wits have taken on the hue of some fashionable trend, just as jets of steam in a stage production may be tinted red, yellow, blue, etc.

Such a *couleur à la mode* [fashionable color] for suicide is anarchism. I can no longer arrest the anarchist idea. So I must seize suicide by the throat.

Who was greater, Napoleon or Bismarck? Napoleon.

But his greatness was an inharmonious one. Napoleon was the sick superman, Bismarck is the healthy one.

June 22

After completing my letter to Bismarck I thought of a funny story that I could have used regarding precedents for an interview.

One day I asked an Austrian diplomat to get me an interview with Casimir-Périer—*en ces temps éloignés président de la République* [in those illustrious times president of the Republic]. The diplomat groaned: That will not be possible. There is no precedent for it!

That man would have been extremely embarrassed if someone had asked him to invent gunpowder. There was no precedent for it.

But I beg of you, Your Highness, never to tell this to an Austrian diplomat. No matter which one you tell it to, there is a chance that he will feel offended.

* * *

June 22

But will Bismarck understand me?

Napoleon did not understand the steamboat—and he was younger and thus more accessible to new ideas.

* * *

June 22

Today, incidentally, I have regained my spiritual equilibrium which I lost when Schiff had rocked the boat.*

In this respect I am really like the errand boy who has drawn the grand prize in the lottery and an hour later says cold-bloodedly: "Pooh! What are a hundred thousand guilders?"

An inventor need not inevitably go mad. A man loses his mind only while questing or through the tremendous shock of discovery—as when gold first flashes before the alchemist's eyes,

* Translator's Note: Herzl uses the word *Schiffsstoss*, a pun on the name of his friend. (*Schiff* means boat.)

when a steam engine begins to work, or a balloon suddenly shows itself to be dirigible.

Inventions that are *trouvailles* [finds] are more conducive to madness than systematic discoveries, because they are so fortuitous, especially in the final, decisive leap. A Pasteur does not go mad, and his successors, who may make quite original discoveries, may be plain jackasses.

Right now I even believe that the implementation of my plan will find me tranquil. I used to be afraid of it.

Provided that I convince Bismarck. If I do not, or if he won't even see me—well, then the whole thing will have been a novel. Oh, an immortal one!

That too is something.

*   *   *

[The following notes, which form the conclusion of Book I, are entitled "Address to the Rothschilds" in the copy prepared by Herzl's father.]

June 13

To the Family Council.

I should first like to enlighten you on the special character of our conversation. It will create a permanent relationship between you and me. Henceforth I must be your friend or your foe forever. The force of an idea resides in the fact that there is no escape from it.

You will think: we have invited a bad visitor.

But it would not have changed anything in the situation if you had not sent for me. In that case I merely would not have had the personal *égards* [consideration] to which I feel obliged now.

At first, to be sure, I thought that I could carry on my project only in opposition to you. That is why I first went to Baron Hirsch. Oh! I did not tell him that I was an adversary of the Rothschilds. It may well be that this would have been a more powerful inducement to him than anything else. But I conduct things on an impersonal plane. All I said to him was: *tous les juifs ont plus* [all the Jews have more]. For I wanted to . . . (there follows an account). Hirsch did not let me finish.

Actually, he does not know my plan. In the end he said only: we shall talk some more. I am ready, I replied, but I am not going to wait for you. Perhaps he will come to me, like so many others, when my plan is a living reality. For one has many friends when one does not need them.

I shall go on. It occurred to me: Wait! What makes you think that you cannot do it with the Rothschilds? And that is why I am here. For the moment, it is *de bonne politique* [good policy] and perhaps it will be *de bonne guerre* [good military strategy].

Now I must beg your permission to speak about your fortune. If it were small, like mine, I should have no right to do so. But its size has made it a matter of public concern.

I don't know whether it is underestimated or overestimated. With a fortune of this size it is no longer a matter of what is visible or tangible in the way of gold, silver, securities, houses, estates, factories, and concerns of all kinds. It is no longer a matter of the material resources, even much less in your case than with a state bank. Because, if a bank can secure coverage with two-thirds, one-half, even one-third, perhaps one-tenth or less will suffice for you. Your credit is enormous, monstrous, amounts to many billions. I do not say ten, twenty, or fifty billions. Incalculable amounts are involved, and they cannot be expressed in figures.

And *that* is where the danger lies! The danger for you, for the countries in which you are established, for the entire world.

Your fortune—and by this I mean resources plus credit—is like a tower. This tower continues to grow; you continue to build, you must continue—and that is the sinister part of it. And because you cannot change the laws of nature, because you remain subject to them, either the tower must one day collapse by itself, destroying everything around it, or it will be demolished by force. In any event, an enormous convulsion, a world crisis.

I bring you your salvation—not by razing the tower, but by

giving it a broader foundation, one designed to last, as well as a harmonious conclusion. For a tower must have a limit. At the top I will place a light which will cast a wide beam. I shall make it into the highest and safest tower, an Eiffel Tower with a magnificent electric lantern.

It goes without saying that it has not been my purpose to meddle with your interests. Your private affairs are none of my business. I don't want to make any business deals with you, I am not in your service and never will be.

But I want to place myself at the service of all Jews.

After all, every person, and most of all, every Jew, is entitled to take an interest in the jeopardized Jewish cause, provided that he does it as an honest man with the best of intentions and conscience. The future will then bring him either approval of his actions or condemnation for the harm he may have done.

Improvement is out of the question because of the aforementioned cogent reasons. If someone were to ask me how I know this, I should tell him that I also know where a stone rolling down an incline finally arrives—namely, at the very bottom. Only ignoramuses or madmen do not take the laws of nature into account.

Therefore we must finally end up at the bottom, rock bottom. What appearance this will have, what form this will take, I cannot surmise. Will it be a revolutionary expropriation from below or a reactionary confiscation from above? Will they chase us away? Will they kill us?

I have a fair idea that it will take all these forms, and others. In one of the countries, probably France, there will come a social revolution whose first victims will needs be the big bankers and the Jews.

Anyone who has, like myself, lived in this country for a few years as a disinterested and detached observer can no longer have any doubts about this.

In Russia there will simply be a confiscation from above. In Germany they will make emergency laws as soon as the Kaiser can no longer manage the *Reichstag*. In Austria people will let themselves be intimidated by the Viennese rabble and deliver up the Jews. There, you see, the mob can achieve anything once it rears up. It does not know this yet, but the leaders will teach it.

So they will chase us out of these countries, and in the countries where we take refuge they will kill us.

Is there no salvation?

Oh yes, gentlemen, there is one, one that has existed before. It will be necessary to repeat a very old, very famous, very proven maneuver, albeit in a different, modern, more refined form. All the resources of the present may be used for this simple, easily understood purpose.

This simple old maneuver is the exodus from *Mitzraim* [Egypt].

I have intentionally prefaced my address with this brief critical part, although everything in it was already known to you, and at the risk of boring you. My main aim was to convince you that I am thinking along the same rational lines as you do, that I view things with the same calm eyes as you. I may have delineated rather sharply a few dangers and complexities with which you do not concern yourselves frequently or willingly. But in any case, everything has been true, simple, and sensible.

Do not, then, consider me a visionary. I shall now proceed to develop the business aspects of the matter which will give you a chance to observe closely whether I am talking sense or nonsense.

The only possible, final, and successful solution of the Jewish Question requires a billion francs. This billion will be worth three in twenty years—three billion exactly, as you will see later.

But before I present my plan to you, I will tell you in two sentences the principle that it is based upon. This will help you understand everything more easily. 1. We shall solve the Jewish Question by either safeguarding or liquidating the fortune of the wealthy Jews. 2. If we cannot do it with the help of the wealthy Jews, we shall do it in spite of them.

This is not a threat. We do not threaten any more than we beg. This will become clear to you at a later point.

The plan is as follows:

As soon as the *Society of Jews** has constituted itself, we shall call a conference of a number of Jewish geographers to determine, with the help of these scholars, who as Jews are loyally devoted to us, where we are going to emigrate. For I shall now tell you everything about the "Promised Land" except its location. That is a purely scientific question. We must have regard for geological, climatic, in short, natural factors of all kinds with full circumspection and with consideration of the latest research.

Once we have agreed on the continent and the country, we shall begin to take diplomatic steps with the utmost delicacy. So as not to operate with wholly vague concepts, I shall take Argentina as an example. For a time I had Palestine in mind. This would have in its favor the facts that it is the unforgotten ancestral seat of our people, that its very name would constitute a program, and that it would powerfully attract the lower masses. But most Jews are no longer Orientals and have become accustomed to very different regions; also, it would be hard to carry out there my system of transportation, which will follow later. Then, too, Europe would still be too close to it, and in the first quarter-century of our existence we shall have to have peace from Europe and its martial and social entanglements, if we are to prosper.

But on principle I am neither against Palestine nor for Argentina. We merely have to have a varied climate for the Jews who are used to colder or to warmer regions. On account of our future world trade we have to be located on the sea, and for our large-scale mechanized agriculture we must have wide areas at our disposal. The scientists will be given a chance to provide us with information. The decision will be made by our Administrative Council.

I can tell you right now that due to technical progress we shall

* In English in the original, here and *passim*.

be able to occupy a country, build cities, and found a civilization much more successfully than could be done in antiquity—indeed, as recently as a hundred years ago. The railroads have made us independent of the course of the rivers, and thanks to electricity we can settle in the mountains. At the outset, factories will be located in the mountains where cheap water power is available, the accumulation of masses of workers is impossible, and the working population can live and thrive more happily in the health-giving air. In this way, too, we shall prepare for the obviously coming development which will divide the forces of nature for small-scale industry and make them available to the individual.

As soon as we have determined the country that is to be occupied, we shall send out trusted and skillful negotiators who are to conclude treaties with the present authorities and the neighboring states covering our reception, transit, and guarantees for internal and external peace.

I am assuming that we shall go to Argentina. In that case we shall negotiate with the South American republics.

I shall now tell you the main features of our policy. Our goal must be to acquire the country we occupy as an independent one immediately after we declare ourselves a State. For this reason we shall probably grant financial advantages to the receiving country, although they must not take the form of a tribute. This would be incompatible with our future dignity. The subsequent cessation of payments could embroil us in an unnecessary war. In any case, it would damage our good reputation in the eyes of the world. We want to proceed legally and be good neighbors to everyone, if we are left in peace.

The financial emoluments that we give the South Americans need not be in cash, of course. Even the procuring of loans on favorable terms would make them grateful and disposed to make major concessions. It would be a good investment for the reason that we would divert streams of wealth to South America. For the neighboring states will have enormous indirect advantages in addition to the direct ones. Through us and with us, an unprecedented commercial prosperity will come to South America. The countries adjacent to ours cannot help becoming rich. This will, of course, be adequately explained to them during the negotiations.

While we are establishing these diplomatic connections over there, we shall have other tasks in Europe. A great deal of what I am here presenting successively will take place simultaneously.

The *Society of Jews* will start operations by making treaties of removal with the governments. Only with Russia will there be a specific treaty of this kind; in the other countries involved, free movement is guaranteed by law. But we want to work hand in hand with the governments everywhere. We wish to, and shall, part as good friends. Great things are accomplished not with hatred and vengefulness, but only with Olympian friendliness.

Russia will undoubtedly allow our people to move away. Baron Hirsch is permitted to recruit even men subject to military service; when they come back, to be sure, they are treated as deserters. That will be all right with us. Surely we shall be granted at least the same concessions. After all, we shall take not only young and vigorous people, but the old, the sick, women and children as well (I shall tell you later what I shall do with these categories).

The moment may conceivably come in which the Russian government begins to view the departure of so many people with displeasure. At that point your credit policy will have to come to the rescue. How often in recent times have you put your financial power at Russia's disposal?! And I ask you: what for? Just consider what unused political power lies dormant in your granting of credit. In short, if we proceed purposefully, it will be an easy matter to keep the Russian government in a good mood, until our last man has gone.

The treaties of removal will take a different form in other countries. The individuals' freedom to move about is of no use to us. Here, too, we shall of course have to strive to procure the release of men liable for military duty, and under the same harsh conditions as in Russia. In Germany, they don't like to have Jews in the army, anyway; and the people who want to remove the Jews from the army are certainly right from their point of view.

But what about the free removal of property? In its present form, movable property is easier to get out than ever. But what about immovables?

In the beginning, before our movement becomes a universal one, the first Jews who go with us will find it easy to sell their immovables. Gradually various contrarieties will appear. At first these emigrants will force one another's prices down. Without our aid, all sorts of business crises would occur in the countries affected by the departure of the Jews, crises whose form and extent could not even be calculated. Finally the population would be disconcerted and enraged, and it would hold the remaining Jews responsible. They might resort to legal chicanery, but certainly to the administrative kind.

The Jews who don't go with us could fare badly. We could, to be sure, leave them to their fate, since they were too cowardly or too mean to join us.

But what we have in mind is a project of justice and charity. We want to have mercy even on the contemptible. For are we not offering the solution? And a solution is only what satisfies all.

Now, gentlemen, we come to a commercial key point of the plan.

You have already suspected that the *Society* will be piloting us to our State. But we are still a long way from that point.

(This is the point at which to make an interpolation; for, as I have already said, many activities which I have described in succession will in reality take place simultaneously.)

We left our diplomatic negotiators in South America where they were concluding treaties of occupation with the states. These treaties are now completed, and we are assured of the land that we are going to occupy.

There can be no doubting that this operation is a legal one.

But it is not scrupulous. We know about the increase in value which the seller does not suspect. For that reason we shall, after the transaction has been completed, give him a choice between a cash payment and a compensation in shares at the nominal value. If he thinks the whole thing a fraud—*tant pis pour lui* [so much the worse for him]. In any case, we shall have nothing to reproach ourselves for.

The building material will have been taken care of by our geologists when they were looking for sites for our cities.

Our principle of construction will be that we ourselves shall undertake the building of workers' dwellings (and by this I mean the dwellings of all manual laborers). I am certainly not thinking of the sad-looking workers' barracks in European cities, nor of the paltry shacks which are lined up around factories. Our workmen's houses must have a uniform appearance too, to be sure—because we can build cheaply only if we mass-produce uniform building materials—, but these individual houses with their little gardens shall everywhere be combined into beautiful collective units.

A normal working day will consist of seven hours. This does not mean that only for seven hours each day will trees be felled, earth dug, rocks carted—in short, a hundred chores done. No, work will be going on for fourteen hours. But the workers will relieve one another after shifts of three and a half hours each. The organization will be quite military, with ranks, advancement, and retirement. You will hear later where I shall get the pensions from.

A healthy man can do a lot of concentrated work in three and a half hours. After resting for an equal period of time, a period which he will devote to his relaxation, his family, his guided self-improvement, he will be quite alert again. Such laborers can work wonders.

The seven-hour working day! I choose the number seven because it is connected with age-old associations of the Jewish people and because it makes possible fourteen general working hours; you can't get more into a day. Moreover, it is my conviction that the seven-hour day is something entirely feasible (Jules Guesde speaks of five hours). In this, the *Society* will gather a store of new experiences from which the other peoples of the earth will benefit as well.

(Widows, too, are taken care of in my somewhat complicated welfare system.)

We shall raise the children right from the start the way we need them. I shan't go into this now.

As for *assistance par le travail* [public works]:

This *assistance* consists in every needy person being given *unskilled labor*,* some light, non-specialized work, as, e.g., splitting wood, making *magotins* [kindling wood] such as is used to start the fire in kitchen stoves in Paris households. It is a sort of prison labor *before* the crime, i.e., one that is not dishonorable.

No one will have to resort to crime from necessity any longer, if he is willing to work. No more suicides must be committed out of hunger. As it is, suicides are one of the worst stigmata of a civilization in which tidbits are thrown to the dogs from the tables of the rich.

The public-works system thus gives employment to everyone. Does it have a market for its products? It does not, at least not an adequate one. This is a flaw in the existing structure.

This *assistance* always operates at a loss. It is prepared for one, of course. After all, it is a charitable institution. The alms constitutes the difference between the cost of production and the selling price. Instead of giving a beggar two sous, the *assistance* gives him work on which it loses two sous.

But a beggar who has become a skilled worker will make 1 franc 50 centimes. Instead of 10 centimes, 150! Do you know what this means? It means increasing the benefaction fifteen-fold, making 15 billion out of 1 billion. The *assistance*, to be sure, loses the 10 centimes. However, you will not lose the billion, but triple it.

---

* In English in the original.

All this will be done according to a big plan which is set from the start.

I left the main theme of this presentation at the construction of workers' dwellings under State auspices.

Now I go back to other categories of homes. We shall have the architects of the *Society* build homes for the petty bourgeois, too, either for barter or for money. We shall have the architects make drafts of about 100 types of houses and reproduce them. These pretty designs will also serve as part of our publicity. Every house will have its fixed price; the quality of the execution will be guaranteed by the *Society,* which does not wish to make a profit on the construction of homes. And where will the houses be constructed? I shall tell you this when I speak of the Local Groups and the pioneering expedition.

Since we will not make a profit on construction work, but only on the land, we shall welcome it if many free-lance architects build on private commissions. This will enhance the value of our other land-holdings, and bring luxury into the land, and we need luxury for various purposes, especially art, industry, and, finally, to make up for the decline of the large fortunes.

Yes, the rich Jews who at present must timidly conceal their treasures and give their uneasy parties behind drawn curtains will be able to enjoy them freely over there.

If our emigration is accomplished with your participation, capital will be rehabilitated among us on the other side, for it will have shown its usefulness in an unparalleled project.

In this area of my plan, too, you could do us great services with your credit.

In this instance, it is drawing-room credit. If you begin to build your castles, at which people in Europe are already looking askance, *over there* and if you stimulate your syndicate members to do likewise, it will soon become fashionable among the wealthy Jews to settle in sumptuous houses on the other side. *Il y a là un mouvement à créer* [there is a movement to be created]. And that is such an easy matter. You simply tell good friends who will pass the word on: "Want some good advice? Build over there." You see, this really *is* good advice.

In this manner the art treasures of the Jews will gradually find their way across. You know best how great these treasures already are. Perhaps this will be the point at which the governments will first interfere, if we do not have your help in this project, that is, the benefit of diplomatic assistance, and must establish contact with the Jewish people through publicity. The kind of action that the governments would have to take has already been shown in Italy. May I remind you of the prohibition to export works of art.

However, it would be very injurious to the movement if the governments hit upon the idea of extending this ingenious prohibition to other pieces of tangible property as well. The little Jews would be least affected by this—*et pour cause* [and with reason]; the bigger ones would be hit harder and harder, and you, gentlemen, would be hit the latest and the hardest. Do not overlook the legal nature of this export prohibition. It is the partial deprivation of the right to dispose of an object; one quality of the object, its exportability, is confiscated.

To me even this seems like a bad thing. And once confiscation starts, where is it going to stop?

Let us not provoke this; but can we prevent it if it occurs in the course of our movement? You will see from our entire proposal that we are not bent on harming you—on the contrary! We are showing you the way, making you suggestions as to how this huge movement can be led gently, without upsets. It will come into being—you probably surmise that much, gentlemen; and it will be to your advantage to go along with *us*. If you do not, we could not bother about the liquidation of your European business interests. We liquidate only the fixed assets and businesses of the people who have gone with us by a certain date—let us say, within the first decade. For we shall have to withdraw from Europe. We can stay here no longer. And we shall be allowed to leave without molestation only if we don't do much shilly-shallying.

We can and will liquidate all those who desire it as quickly as possible. All except you, because it will be utterly impossible. For after the Jews have emigrated, Europe could not stand the additional shock of your liquidation.

June 14

Address to the Family:

The movement will be born the moment I impart my idea to the world. You are rich enough, gentlemen, to further this plan; you are not rich enough to prevent it. The reason is remarkably simple: I cannot be bought.

Yes, I would be sincerely sorry if you did not go along with me and thus suffered harm. For your refusal would not be due to wickedness or narrow-mindedness—you are known to be loyal adherents of despised Judaism; you would be refusing because you did not see the correctness of my assertions, or because I did a bad job of explaining my plan. In that case I shall go to the depths with my solicitation. If the *Society of Jews* cannot be formed through aristocrats of money, it will be formed through democrats of money. Among them, as I told you in the beginning, the anxiety is greater; consequently their desire to draw a free breath will be greater. If then a few Jews and their possessions perish in the movement, I shall have no further responsibility. I have given a clear enough warning: The procession is under way!

But is this not in contradiction to my earlier statement that the peaceful exodus of all Jews should be secured? It is not, for we can protect only those Jews who go along with us, who entrust themselves to us. Those in the procession will not be stepped on. In regard to them we can assume guarantees vis-à-vis the governments and nations and receive in return their protection by the states and by public opinion.

You, gentlemen, are too big for us to take you under our protection at a later date. This is not due to *rancune* [rancor], nor because we shall in the meantime have arrived at opposite ends and shall have to have it out in many areas; on the contrary, we shall give you a brotherly reception over there if one day you come in search of protection and peace. To be sure, we shall have to take some safety measures against your dangerous wealth.

If you do not give me your support, you will inflict great damage on my plan. For the most delicate, the most secret, the diplomatic aspects become impossible if I have to conduct things in public.

I could not deal then with the South American republics the way I am planning to, could not expropriate things so inexpensively, would have a thousand difficulties attendant upon publicity.

With your aid it will be a splendid business (oh, but not for me); with the help of the midget millionaires a doubtful one; with that of the small Jews a bad one which could possibly not be brought to fruition and could end with a scandal (as in Panama).

"I hold you responsible for it"—this might be something you would smile at.

No, I shall say: You will suffer for it if the project, as a popular one, fails. And if it succeeds we shall let in all the Jews except the Rothschilds.

And that is not such a matter of indifference to you as it may seem today. For even after our departure your fortune will continue to grow in an alarming manner, and all the hatred which hitherto has been spread over countless Jewish heads will be concentrated on just a few—namely, yours.

These few heads will not be firmly attached, least of all in France.

Gentlemen! The only conceivable form the voluntary liquidation of the Rothschild fortune could take is the one about which I have been talking to you for so long: the emigration of the Jews.

Well, in what form will the *Society of Jews* (whether it has an aristocratic or a democratic complexion) give guarantees that there will be no impoverishment or economic crises in the countries we have left?

I have already told you that we want to let respectable anti-Semites participate in our project, respecting their independence which is valuable to us—as a sort of people's control authority. But the state, too, has fiscal interests which could be damaged. It loses a class of tax payers which enjoys little civic respect, but is highly valued financially. We must offer the state some compensation for this. We are giving it an indirect one by leaving behind our businesses which Jewish astuteness and diligence have fashioned, by letting our Gentile fellow citizens move into the positions that we have abandoned, thus making it possible for masses to rise to prosperity in a manner unprecedented in such scope and peacefulness. On a smaller scale, the French Revolution produced something similar, but there the blood had to flow in streams under the guillotine, in all provinces of the country and on the battlefields of Europe, and inherited and acquired rights had to be violated into the bargain. And this only served to feather the nests of the shrewd buyers of national property.

Another indirect advantage the states will have is the tremendous growth of their export trade. Since over there we shall be dependent on European products for a long time to come, it will be essential for us to import them. And in this, too, my system of Local Groups (more about which soon) will create an equitable adjustment. The customary requirements will be met by the customary places for a long time. But the greatest indirect advantage, one that may not immediately be appreciated in its full import, is the social alleviation. Social discontent will be put at rest for some time, perhaps twenty years, possibly even longer. As for the social question, gentlemen, I consider it a merely technological question. Steam power has gathered men around the machines in factories where they are squeezed together and make one another unhappy. Production is enormous, indiscriminate, unplanned, and every moment brings about serious crises which ruin the workers along with the management. Steam, then, has crowded people together; I believe that the exploitation of electricity will disperse them again to happier places of work. That is something I cannot predict. But in any case, the technical inventors, the true benefactors of mankind, will go on working in those twenty years, and, I hope, invent such wonderful things as before—no, ever more wonderful ones.

As for us, we shall utilize and improve upon all innovations over there; and just as we shall institute the seven-hour working day as an experiment for the good of all mankind, we shall lead the way in all philanthropic pursuits and be a new country of experimentation, a model country.

But the states will hardly content themselves with indirect benefits. They will want direct payments. In this we must lend the governments and parliaments a helping hand. It is perhaps one of the noblest aims of this plan that the modern civilized nations are to be spared the shame of making special laws against a people that is already unfortunate. In order to spare the governments an emigration tax on the Jews, the *Society* will assume all responsibility. Our headquarters will be in London, because in matters of civil law we must be under the protection of a great nation which is not anti-Semitic at present. But if we receive official and semi-official support we shall everywhere provide a broad base for taxation, what is called *surface* in France. We shall everywhere found taxable subsidiary and branch institutions. Moreover, we shall provide the advantage of a double transfer of fixed property, which means double fees. Even where it acts only as an agent for immovables, the *Society* will assume the temporary appearance of a buyer. Thus, even when we do not wish to be the owners, we shall for a moment be entered as buyers in the land register.

This, of course, is purely a matter of bookkeeping. In each individual place it will have to be investigated and decided how far we can go in this without endangering the existence of our undertaking. We shall have to have frank discussions with the

Ministers of Finance about it. They will clearly see our good intentions and will everywhere grant us those special considerations which we demonstrably need for the successful completion of our historic project.

Another direct contribution which we shall make is in the field of freight and passenger transportation. In the case of state railroads this is immediately obvious. In the case of private railroads we shall get special rates, like every major shipping agent. We must, of course, transport our people and their belongings as cheaply as possible, because everybody pays his own way across. For middle-class people we shall have the Cook System, and for the poor classes, travel at special reduced rates. For the freight we have our experienced agents. We could make a big profit on passenger and freight discounts. But in this area, too, our principle must be merely to break even. We must not make any more profits in Europe. Therefore we shall divide the discount between our emigrants (fare reduction) and the states (providing *surface* through the establishment of shipping agencies and freight-insurance companies).

It will not be necessary to establish new moving agencies everywhere. In many places the moving business is in the hands of Jews. These companies will be the first we will need and the first we will liquidate. Their present owners will either enter our service or freely establish themselves over there. After all, receiving agents will be needed at the point of debarkation; and since this is an excellent business and people not only may, but should, immediately make money on the other side, it is evident that there will be no shortage of enterprising spirits in this field.

We ourselves will undertake the management of the boats, and at the same time we shall encourage Jewish ship-owners. At first we shall buy the boats (and through secret and simultaneous purchases, similar to the centralized system of land purchase which will have been developed earlier, we shall prevent price increases); later, and as soon as possible, we shall build our own ships over there. We shall encourage the shipbuilding of free-lance entrepreneurs through various benefits (inexpensive material from our forests and blast furnaces). The labor supply will be handled by our Central Employment Office.

In the beginning we shall have little or rather unrewarding cargo on the return trips of our boats (except, perhaps, from Chile, Argentina, and Brazil). Our scientific assistants, who will be the first to go across on the pioneering ship, will have to give their immediate attention to this point as well. We shall look for raw materials and take them to Europe; this will be the beginning of our export trade. Gradually we shall produce industrial goods, at first for the poor among our emigrants. Clothes, underwear, shoes, etc., will be mass-produced, for in the European ports of embarkation our poor people will be given new clothes. This will not be a gift to them, because we have no intention of humiliating them. Their old things will merely be exchanged for new ones. We do not care if we lose anything on this; we shall put it down as a business loss. The completely destitute will be our debtors for their clothes, and over there they will pay by working overtime; we shall exempt them from this for good conduct.

There shall be something symbolic about these very clothes: You are starting a new life now! And we shall see to it that on the boats a serious and festive mood is maintained through prayers, popular lectures, information regarding the purpose of the undertaking, hygienic advice for the new places of residence, and directions for their future labors. For the Promised Land is the land of labor. On the other side, each ship will be given a festive reception by the heads of our government. Without fatuous jubilation, for the Promised Land will yet have to be won. But right from the outset these poor people shall see that they are at home there.

As you can imagine, our clothing industry for emigrants will not be aimless in its production. Through a centralized network of agencies—which constitute our political administration, as opposed to the autonomous Local Groups—we shall always know in time the number of emigrants, their day of arrival, and their requirements, and we shall make provision for them. In this systematic management of an industry there are the faint beginnings of an attempt to avoid production crises. This is how we shall proceed in all areas where the *Society* appears as an industrialist. But on no account do we want to crush private enterprise with our superior power. We shall be collectivists only in those instances where the enormous difficulties of the task require it. In general, we want to cherish and protect the individual and his rights. Private property as the economic basis of independence shall have free and respected development among us. After all, we shall allow our very first unskilled laborers to acquire private property. Moreover, you have already seen in several examples (the free building contractor, the free shipowner, the free shipping agent) how we want to encourage the enterprising spirit. In industry we shall favor the entrepreneur in various ways. Protective tariff or free trade are not principles, but matters of usefulness. At first we shall, in any case, be free-traders. Later the requirements of our policy will decide.

But there are other ways in which we can aid industry, and we shall use them. We have the allotment of cheap raw materials under our control and can regulate their supply through sluices, like the flow of water. This will become important later for the prevention of crises. And then we shall establish an institution of permanent and increasing value: an Office of Industrial Statistics, with public announcements.

Thus the enterprising spirit will be stimulated in a salutary way. Risky desultoriness will be avoided. The establishment of new industries will be announced promptly, so that any entrepreneurs who six months later might have the idea of going into a certain industry will not build their way into a crisis, into misery. Since the purpose of a new establishment will have to be reported to our Industrial Police, the outlook for new ventures will be available to anyone at any time, just as the land registers make available information about the property situation.

Finally, we are offering entrepreneurs a centralized labor pool. An employer applies to the Central Employment Office which charges him only a fee required for its operating expenses (office rent, salaries, postage, and telegram charges). The employer sends a telegram: Require tomorrow 500 unskilled laborers for three days (or three weeks or three months). The next day the 500 men requested arrive at his agricultural or industrial establishment. Our Central Employment Office collects them from various places where they may happen to become available. The migration of laborers in search of work* will be improved along military lines and changed from a crude procedure into a meaningful institution. We shall, of course, supply no slave labor, but only seven-hour laborers who will keep their—that is, our—organization and retain their seniority as regards rank, advancement, and pensions even when they change their location. A free entrepreneur may get his workers from somewhere else if he wants to; but I doubt if he will be able to.

We shall thwart the importation of non-Jewish slave labor through some sort of boycott of uncooperative industrialists, through making their commercial activity more difficult, denying them raw materials, and the like. So people will have to take our seven-hour-a-day workers. You see, gentlemen, how we are almost painlessly approaching the regular seven-hour working day.

It is evident that what applies to the unskilled laborers will be even easier to accomplish with more skilled labor. The part-time workers in the factories may be brought under the same regulations. There is no need for me to go into detail on this.

As for the independent artisans, the small master craftsmen, we want to foster them with a view to the future progress of technology, give them technological information even if they are no longer young, and make water power and electricity available to them. These independent workers, too, shall be

---

* Translator's Note: Herzl uses the term *Sachsengängerei*, referring to laborers from the eastern part of Prussia who tried to find work in the Saxon lands.

sought out by our Central Employment Office. A Local Group will apply to this office: we need so-and-so-many carpenters, locksmiths, glaziers, etc. The Central Office will make this public and the people will come forward. They and their families will move to the place where they are needed and remain there, not crushed by random competition. A permanent, good home will have come into being for them.

This brings me to the Local Groups. So far I have only shown how the emigration may be accomplished without an economic upheaval. But in such a mass migration many strong emotions are involved. There are old customs and memories which bind all of us to certain places. We have cradles and we have graves, and you know what graves mean to Jewish hearts. The cradles we shall take along; in them there slumbers our future, rosy and smiling. Our beloved graves we must leave behind. I think this is what we covetous people will find it hardest to part with, but it will have to be.

Even now, economic distress, political pressure, and social hatred frequently remove us from our places of residence and our graves. Even at present the Jews constantly move from one country to another. There is even a strong overseas movement, to the United States, where we are not liked either. Where will people want us so long as we have no homeland of our own? But we will give the Jews a homeland—not by uprooting them forcibly from their earth, but by carefully digging them up with all their roots and transplanting them into a better soil. Just as we want to create new economic and political conditions, we intend to keep sacred all the emotional attachments to the past.

I am only touching on this briefly. On this point, more than on any other part of my plan, there is great danger that you will consider it overly romantic. And yet even this is as clear in my mind as everything else.

Our people are to emigrate in groups of families and friends. But no one will be forced to join any group departing from his present locality. Everyone may go the way he wants to. After all, everyone is paying his own way, in whatever class of railroad and ship he chooses. But I should always like to use trains and boats that have only one class. On such long trips the poor are bothered by differences in wealth. And even though we are not taking our people across for entertainment, we still do not wish to spoil their good humor on the way. No one will travel under conditions of hardship; everything in the way of elegant comfort will be available. People will make arrangements far in advance; after all, it will be years before the movement by homogeneous property classes gets rolling. The well-to-do will form traveling parties. All personal connections will be taken along. As you know, with the exception of the wealthiest, Jews have almost no social relations with Gentiles. A Jew who does not happen to support a few dinner-table parasites, spongers, and Gentile flunkeys does not know any Gentiles at all.

Therefore, those of average means will make prolonged and careful preparations for departure. Every locality will form a group. In the large cities there will be several district groups which will communicate by means of elected representatives. There is nothing obligatory about this division into districts; it is actually intended only as an aid to those less well-to-do, so that no discomfort or homesickness will arise during the trip. Everyone is free to travel alone or to attach himself to whatever Local Group he prefers. The conditions will be the same for all members of each class. If a traveling party is large enough, the *Society* will give it a special train and thereafter a special boat. In transit and on the other side, the Central Housing Office, headed by the Director of Housing, will have provided suitable housing (Cook System). On the boats, entertainment and instruction will be provided, this time not according to property classes, but according to educational levels. Jewish actors, singers, and musicians, as well as Jewish professors and teachers will, after all, go along too. They will all be given assignments, which they will soon have guessed anyway. We shall make a special appeal for the participation of our clergymen. Each group will have its Rabbi who is traveling with his congregation. You can see how naturally all these groups fall into place. A Local Group will have a Rabbi as its nucleus; there will be as many such groups as there are Rabbis. The Rabbis will be the first to understand us and become enthusiastic over our cause, and they will impart their enthusiasm to the others from their pulpits. Imagine with what fervor our old saying "Next year in the Promised Land!" will be spoken henceforth. There is no need to call any special assemblies with a lot of blather. This propaganda will be included in the religious service, and properly so. We recognize our historic identity only by the faith of our fathers, because we have long since inextinguishably absorbed the languages of various nationalities. I shall return to this point later when I speak of the Constitution of our State.

The Rabbis will then regularly receive the advices of the *Society* and announce and interpret them to their congregations. Israel will pray for us and for itself.

The Local Groups will appoint small committees of representatives under the chairmanship of the Rabbis. These committees will discuss and decide all practical issues in accordance with local needs. What will be done with the charitable institutions I shall explain later.

The Local Groups will elect their representatives who will go across with the pioneer ship in order to select sites for towns. In all our activities we shall aim at a gentle transplantation, and the preservation of all legitimate claims.

Later the Local Groups will have plans of the towns. Our people will know beforehand where they are going, in what towns and in what houses they will live. I have already mentioned the building plans and clear illustrations which will be distributed among the Local Groups.

Just as strict centralization will be the principle of our administration, the principle for the Local Groups will be full autonomy. Only in this way can the transplanting be accomplished painlessly.

I am not imagining all this to be easier than it actually is; on the other hand, you must not imagine it to be harder.

The middle classes will automatically be drawn along by our movement. Some will have their sons on the other side, as officials of the *Society*, judges, lawyers, physicians, architects, railroad engineers, bridge-builders, etc. Others will have daughters married to our workers. These will all be good matches, for those who come with us will rise high, especially the pioneers who will be rewarded for their devotion, and also because the positions which do not lend themselves to any *actions d'éclat* [striking deeds] will be governed strictly according to seniority rather than influence.

Then one of our unmarried people will send for his fiancée, another for his parents, brothers, and sisters. In a new civilization, people marry young. This can only benefit general morality, and we shall have sturdy offspring—not those delicate children of fathers who have married late, having already spent their energies in life's struggles. It is evident that especially the poorest will go with us. The already existing Emigrants' Committees in various cities will accept our leadership. Since they were founded by well-meaning men who have a heart for their poor brethren, there is no doubt that they will readily submit to our higher purpose, our higher institutions. If they do not, we shall forget about the envious ones. But I don't think there will be any such people. It would be pitiful; and they would incur disgrace as surely as we shall gladly honor them if they join forces with us.

June 15

Address to the Family:

Any person of discernment must see the development clearly even now. But no great exertion will be necessary to stimulate the migration movement. The anti-Semites are already taking care of this for us. As soon as our institution becomes known, the anti-Semites will agitate for the *Society* in the government, in parliament, at rallies, and in the papers. Good for the Jews who

are going with us! Woe to them who will let themselves be forced
out only by brutal arguments.

But our exodus must and will be a voluntary one. Anyone who
appreciates the phenomena of acquisition and entertainment—
panem et circenses [bread and circuses]—must also realize how
right I am.

Let me explain to you these phenomena which I learned to
understand myself only in Paris.

How can I direct a multitude to a particular spot without
giving them a command? Baron Hirsch, a man who is concerned
about Jewry, but whose attempts I consider a failure, says: "I
shall pay these people to go there." That is dead wrong, and all
the money in the world cannot pay for it.

By contrast, I say: I am not going to pay them; I am going
to make them pay. Only, I shall offer them something.

Let us say that Hirsch and I want to assemble a crowd of
people on the plain of Longchamps on a hot Sunday afternoon.
By promising them 10 francs each, Hirsch will, for 200,000
francs, bring out 20,000 perspiring, miserable people, who will
curse him for having inflicted this drudgery on them. I, on the
other hand, shall offer the 200,000 francs as a prize for the swiftest
race horse; and then I shall put up barriers to keep the people off
the Longchamp course. Those who want to get in have to pay:
1 franc, 5 francs, 20 francs.

The upshot will be that I get half a million people out there;
the President of the Republic will drive up *à la Daumont;* and
the people will have a good time entertaining one another. Most
of them will find the exercise in the open air a pleasure in spite of
the heat and the dust. And for my 200,000 francs I shall have
taken in a million in admissions and betting taxes.

I can get those same people out there again any time I want to,
but Hirsch cannot, not at any price.

Let me show you the same phenomenon in an economic situation. Try to get someone to shout this out in the streets of a city:
Whoever is willing to stand all day long, in the bitter cold of

winter or the burning heat of summer, in an iron hall exposed on all sides and there to accost every passer-by and offer him junk, or fish, or fruit, will receive two florins, or four francs, or anything you please.

How many people would you get to go to that hall? If hunger drove them there, how many days would they stand it? And if they did hold out, how much eagerness would they display in trying to persuade the passers-by to purchase fruit, fish, or junk?

I shall go about it in a different way. In places where trade is active—and these places I shall discover all the more easily because I myself shall channel trade in any direction I please—there I shall build large halls and call them markets. I could make these halls worse, more unhealthy than those I have mentioned, and yet people would flock to them. But I shall make them better and more beautiful, put my whole good will into them. And the people, to whom I have promised nothing, because I cannot promise them anything without deceiving them, these good, enterprising people will create an atmosphere of fun and do a thriving business. They will tirelessly harangue the buyers. They will stand on their feet and hardly notice their fatigue. Every day they will not only rush to be the first on the job, but will form unions, combines, all sorts of things, just so they can continue this gainful employment undisturbed. And even if it turns out at the end of the day that all their honest work has netted them only a guilder-and-a-half, or three francs, or whatever, they will still look hopefully to the next day which may be better for them. I shall have given them hope.

You would like to know where I am going to get the demand which I need for the markets. Do I really need to tell you that? Did I not demonstrate that the *assistance par le travail* will produce a fifteenfold return? One million will produce 15 millions and one billion, 15 billions.

Well, you may wonder if this is just as true on a large scale as it is on a small one. After all, capital yields a return diminishing in inverse ratio to its own growth. That is true of inactive capital, capital that has gone into hiding, but not of the active kind.

In fact, that kind of capital yields a tremendously increasing return in large amounts. The social question is contained in this. Is what I am saying true? You be your own witnesses, gentlemen. Why are you managing so many industries? Why do you send men to work underground and bring up coal amidst terrible dangers and for meager wages? I cannot imagine this to be pleasant, even for the mine owners. For I do not believe, and do not pretend to believe, that capitalists are heartless. I am not an agitator, but a peacemaker.

Do I need to illustrate the phenomenon of masses and the ways of attracting them to any desired spot by discussing religious pilgrimages, too?

This speech may have to be published, and I do not wish to offend anyone's religious sensibilities by words which could be misinterpreted.

Let me just mention in passing what the pilgrimage to Mecca means in the Mohammedan world, Lourdes and the Holy Mantle at Treves to the Catholics, and so many other places from which people return home comforted by their faith.

So, over there we will build a more beautiful Sadagora for the Wonder Rabbi. After all, our clergymen will be the first to understand us and go with us.

We shall let everyone find salvation over there in his own way. That includes, and very particularly, our beloved freethinkers, our immortal army which is conquering more and more new territory for mankind.

No more force will be applied against anyone than is necessary for the preservation of the State and public order. And the force necessary will not be arbitrarily determined by whatever person or persons happen to be in authority at a given time, but will reside in iron-clad laws.

I have mentioned commerce and the markets. Are we not going to have too many tradesmen? We are not. At present, large-scale or small-scale trade does attract most of our people who want to make a living. But do you think that a peddler who covers a territory with a heavy pack on his back is happy? I think that by means of the seven-hour day we shall be able to make workmen out of all these men; they are such decent, misunderstood, unhappy people, and are perhaps suffering most of all right now. From the very beginning we shall concern ourselves with training them to be workmen. In this we shall be aided by the advancement of the unskilled laborers and their eventual pensioning off. For the pension will consist in something that may seem like paradise to today's peddlers during their disheartened tramping through the villages: a tobacco-shop, a liquor store. I shall get back to this in a moment.

The small businesses will be operated only by women, I think. You can see how this will relieve the pressure for women's rights. Women can easily take care of such businesses in addition to their household chores, even if they are pregnant, and can also supervise their girls and small boys. The bigger boys we shall take, for we can use them all.

But what about dealings in money? After all, that seems to be one of the main problems. At present we are unfortunately a people of stock-market speculators. Is everybody going to rush to the stock-exchange right away? Ah, or are we by any chance not going to have that useful, indispensable institution at all? You may begin to laugh at me. Be patient, gentlemen!

In the first place, I do not believe that our people are crazy about the stock-exchange. I have often had a deep and sympathetic insight into the situation of the little stock-traders. I think they would rather do anything than run to the stock-exchange. A Jew, especially one of small means, is an excellent *pater-familias,* and it is with trepidation that he goes out every day to "grab a percentage," because he can be commercially disgraced, i.e., made incapable of earning a living, in the twinkling of an eye, through some maneouvre of the big boys or some political development that may break suddenly. Then he spends years or even the rest of his life outside the stock-exchange, which is tragic rather than comic. And yet for him there is no other place to go, no other way to earn a living. Even our educated people cannot get in anywhere; what use could be made of these poor people? We, however, are going to use them according to their skill, without any prejudice; after all, they are our own. We shall make new men out of them. Yes, a new life starts for all, with the experience of the past and without the onus of past sins. Out of the present refuse of human society we shall make respectable, happy men, just as beautiful aniline dyes are now made out of factory refuse that once went to waste.

Believe me, these little stock-traders will serve us gratefully and loyally wherever we place them, unless they prefer to become free-lance contractors of jobs and transactions of all kinds. If they want to become small agricultural industrialists, they will get credit in the form of machinery and can make our land arable as leaseholders.

On a larger scale, the same goes for the ordinary stock-holders. They will become manufacturers, building contractors, etc., because they have capital or credit. Impartial observers like ourselves know that a real stock-exchange deal is not child's play, requiring, as it does, the calculation of many factors, powers of observation, quick judgment—in short, many things that can and will be put to far better use. The only thing is that Jews cannot get out of the stock-exchange. In fact, the present political situation forces more and more Jews into it; all our unemployed people of average education must either starve or go to the stock-exchange. On the other hand, the moneyed Jews are driven to pure speculation by the persecution of capital by the Socialists and anti-Semites. They administer their property at the stock-exchange. And the big ones—yourselves, the biggest ones, included—are forced to do likewise. This makes the great fortunes grow frighteningly. At least, that is what everybody thinks, and it probably is so.

Well, we will set all these forces free. We shall channel them our way and have gold mines in our country. I am not speaking of the mines that might be discovered in the new soil over there; that would be a foolish illusion. I am speaking of the certain gold mines, the full extent of which is well known and which we ourselves shall take across with us in the form of labor, capital, and the happy union of both.

By now you will see what I am driving at: the Promised Land is within ourselves! No one has ever looked for it there.

Gentlemen! I am trying very hard not to present things in too tempting a manner. If my words have a beautiful ring, this is due to my subject. But you are certainly not peasants and will not regard this alone as cause for mistrust.

My psychological explanations and predictions why over there our people will not be stock-traders may not satisfy you or my subsequent worldwide audience.

My aim has been to show first the beautiful and the free aspects. These are the front walls of the building. But rest assured that my edifice has steel girders inside.

You see, we are going to close the stock-exchanges right after we have set them up! In other words, we shall institute a stock-exchange monopoly. Yes, all dealings in money will be nationalized. At first I had only the re-education of our people in mind. But the more this plan grew and matured within me, the more the ways in which I found the stock-exchange monopoly right. This will also give us control over the mania for gambling without eradicating sound speculation. Above all, we shall manage our State credits independently of private financiers. Furthermore, we shall get resources for pensioning our higher officials and taking care of their widows and orphans. How does this aspect of it work? Very simply. It involves large, divisible tobacco-shops (*un quart d'agent de change* [a petty stockbroker]). These non-inheritable agencies will be conducted by sworn lessees who are members of a disciplinary association. These licensed agents will guarantee us that their clients are not professional gamblers. That will be hard to establish; it is more of a moral question and we shall have to operate with indefinite standards, like the term "economic ruin" in the Austrian Usury Law.

In a comparable manner, we shall control alcoholism among

our *unskilled** laborers by means of the truck system. Let me here mention the fact that we shall also establish a liquor monopoly. In addition to the profits on the manufacture, this will give us a large number of small retail outlets for pensioners and widows. Small outlets, I say, because as a rule our people are not drinkers. They are not, at present, but physical labor might make them drink; a state must take preventive measures. And this is the place to speak of the tobacco monopoly, the last form of indirect taxation for the time being. If at a later date we need more and bigger sources of revenue, this will have been caused by our needs, i.e., our standard of living. But once we are established we can find whatever forces are required.

The tobacco monopoly has several points in its favor: most Jews are familiar with it from their present locations; it enables us to exact bigger amounts from bigger consumers; it gives us any number of small pensions in the form of tobacco-shops. The last-named will at the same time be the exclusive vending places for newspapers; there they will be available to the public, and to the government, if need be.

This is all I have to say about the stock-exchange monopoly. Of all the fine institutions which we shall create over there, this will probably be the first to be copied by Europe.

Right now, of course, it would be a tremendous hardship if we were barred from the stock-exchanges. Where should the unfortunate Jewish brokers turn? But once we start migrating, this will suddenly be a great boon to the Jews, and at the same time the states will create great resources for themselves and get control of speculation with government credits, as we shall do in our State. Over there we shall offer rich fields to industrious traders and enterprising capitalists. Let the gamblers, the dissolute fellows, stay in Monte Carlo. If they follow us uninvited, we shall tame them, just as we keep mutinous elements among our unskilled laborers in check through our protective troops.

It will be said that we make people unhappy by our measures.

* In English in the original.

I deny this most categorically. A wound that old cannot be healed by moaning and groaning; it has to be *cauterized*. And who will dare deny the moral power of labor? By this I certainly do not mean only manual labor, but brain work as well. The latter undoubtedly includes speculation, provided it is not gambling.

The moral aspects of work have long since been recognized in penal legislation. We have seen them operating in an incomparably nobler fashion, *before* the crime, in the *assistance par le travail*.

Let me briefly tell you a touching story which I came across in an account of the gold fields of Witwatersrand. A man came to the Rand one day, settled down, tried several things, not including gold mining, finally opened an ice factory that prospered, and soon earned general respect for his decency. Years later he was suddenly arrested. It seems that as a banker in Frankfurt he had perpetrated fraud, then had escaped and started a new life here under an assumed name. When he was taken away as a prisoner, the most respected people of Johannesburg turned up at the station and gave him a cordial "Farewell—until we meet again." For he *was* going to return.

There is a lot in this story. First, it says that I am right. And after all, our unfortunate stock-market operators are no criminals. They are conscientious, struggling, decent heads of families. Of course, there are crooks among them. Where aren't there any? In what distinguished office or profession do you *not* find them? How many gamblers are there in the Clubs?!

But even if they were criminals, which they are not, we would still take them along. We shall take the real criminals along as well—after they have served their term, you understand. For in Europe everything must be liquidated in an honorable manner. Then, a new life!

We shall also take along the sick and the aged; do I even have to mention this? The charitable institutions of the Jews will be freely transplanted with the Local Groups. Endowed institutions will remain with their original Local Group over there. The buildings should not be sold, in my opinion, but donated to needy Gentiles in the cities concerned. Over there we shall give the Local Groups credit for this by not charging them for building sites when the land is distributed and giving them special consideration in construction. Also, it shall be credited in the auctioning off of the local community.

I shall speak in a moment about the distribution and auctioning off of the land. I am trying to present everything as succinctly as possible.

Over there we shall from the very beginning put the charitable institutions in a centralized system, and I have already worked it out. If you believe me implicitly, I shall spare you an elaboration of this now.

Private philanthropy must cease, because it is haphazard. Those unable to work will all be provided for by the State and the free Charity Headquarters. Beggars will not be tolerated. Anyone who refuses to choose his own occupation will go to the Workhouse.

You see how we pull some along and let others tag after us, how the third kind is swept along, and the fourth pushed after us.

If the stock-exchange monopoly is instituted after we have left, it will hasten all vacillators after us, overseas, where they may no longer find the best berths.

You see, gentlemen, how cog meshes with cog, how I slowly build a great iron machine out of familiar components that you can touch with your own hands. I shall also show you the coals with which I shall make fire, and the water which I shall turn into steam.

Then there will be a whistle that will mean: Get aboard, or out of the way!

I have already mentioned some of the Jewish State's forms of revenue. It will have still others. Any kind of undertaking that has already been completely investigated, like railroads and insurance of all kinds known up to now, will be nationalized. All Jews who have been serving as officials of such institutions in Europe will freely transfer into the service of our State, receiving positions at least as good and, besides, chances for advancement, etc., which at present a Jew does not have even in a private institution. Certain industries we shall manage ourselves, even at the risk of running them less cheaply than private interests. Mines, particularly, will be operated only by the State, because even with a seven-hour day mine workers should not be subject to an entrepreneur's parsimony. The State will not economize on safety measures. But there is no striking against it. It represents no private interests. On the other hand, the varying difficulty of kinds of work will be compensated for by a scale of pensions. The man who has worked harder will get his tobacco-shop sooner.

The State will collect certain taxes not for its own benefit, but as an informal equalization between poverty and wealth. We cannot remove economic differences. Even if we were visionaries enough to attempt this, they would immediately arise anew. But we *can* establish a moral connection between the joys of some and the sorrows of others. The amusement tax (as in France) will benefit the hospitals. The dowry tax will be used to take care of indigent girls whom men have forgotten to marry because the girls have no money. Many wealthy Jews are doing this sort of thing now, but haphazardly, like everything else. Nor shall this become the prey of chance mendicancy. We shall have no beggars. As for preventing cheating on dowry taxes, I have got that worked out, too.

I have already said that we are going to nationalize all dealing in money, with the exception of the issuing bank. I think the Bank of France is a good model. The stability of the currency can be guaranteed better by a private issuing bank. But its employees resemble state employees anyway.

As for harmonizing the private issuing bank with the State Bank, with all the proper precautions and policies, our financial geniuses, of whom there is no lack, will know more about this than I do.

I am going to concern myself only with fundamentals. The nationalization of the money-exchange will be designed to educate the people in our State, something that will be necessary in the early stages. There will be neither small nor big bankers any more. Those with capital must and will shrewdly invest it in other enterprises. Let the little ones, the hole-and-corner usurers and speculation agents, enter State service. There they will be subject to a sound code of discipline, and they need not be placed in a Ministry, but can also be in branch offices, like manager of Postal Savings, etc.

You are quite aware, gentlemen, that I am not talking nonsense about the state centralization of the money-exchange. And it is also common knowledge where and how the states even now engage in financial deals with themselves, either in the open (savings banks) or under cover, by entering into silent partnership with the issuing bank.

But if that were not so, what would your World House be? I do not believe that our State or any other state will ever have a bigger money-exchange. You know, then, that the large-scale money-exchange not only can stand centralization, but actually thrives on it. By going from one of your windows to the next, I can collect a claim in London and pay a debt in Naples. I can even save myself this little trip, you can take care of it for me. And wherever centralization does not already exist, it is widely sought. For larger financial transactions the banks stand together in groups and form those evil financial cartels which have not yet been recognized in their full harmfulness. And you are right in the midst of everything! *On vous voit trop, messieurs* [One sees too much of you, gentlemen]! I know, of course, that you do not come in uninvited, that people seek you out, that you wait to be asked.

And that is your curse! People can no longer do without you. You are forced to become richer and richer, whether you want to or not. You have lost control of your fortune, you are drifting on this stream of gold and no longer know where you are going!

I don't know whether all governments already realize what an international menace your World House constitutes. Without you no wars can be waged, and if peace is to be concluded, people are all the more dependent on you. For the year 1895 the military expenses of the five Great Powers have been estimated at four billion francs, and their actual peacetime military strength at 2,800,000 men. And these military forces, which are unparalleled in history, you command financially, regardless of the conflicting desires of the nations!

Who has given you the right to do this? What universal human ideal are you serving? And who are you, anyway? A handful of bankers, now more than ever "*Schutzjuden,*" who are occasionally invited to court—with what repugnance you can imagine, if you are not shown it. For you are nowhere given full rights or even regarded as regular citizens. And you who are in a position to tighten the belts of almost three million soldiers, you and your cash-boxes have to be anxiously guarded everywhere, from the people who, to be sure, do not know everything yet.

And your accursed wealth is still growing. Everywhere it increases more rapidly than the national wealth of the countries in which you reside. Therefore this increase takes place only at the expense of the national prosperity, even though you yourselves may be the most decent persons in the world.

For that reason, the Jewish State from the outset will not tolerate your alarming wealth, which would stifle our economic and political freedom. Not even if you go with us! Do you understand that, gentlemen? And how do we intend to keep you from getting richer over there when we should like to make everyone richer? Do we by any chance have special legislation against you in mind? What ingratitude, if you help us, or what nonsense! Gentlemen, if you do not go with us, we shall probably have to outlaw you. We shall not admit you to our country, just as in France the pretenders, all of them scions of famous French families, are barred from the country.

But if you do go with us, we shall enrich you one last time more. And we shall make you big beyond the dreams of the modest founder of your House and even of his proudest grandchildren.

We shall make you richer by tripling your contribution, the billion with which we started. The Jewish State will be given the right to redeem the shares of the *Society* within twenty years at three times their face value. These are the three billions exactly of which I spoke earlier.

We shall make you big, because we shall take our first elected ruler from your House. That is the shining beacon which we shall place atop the finished Eiffel Tower of your fortune. In history it will seem as though that had been the object of the entire edifice.

Just a few words about the Constitution. A principality with an elected head. We shall choose a quiet, modest, sensible man who will not think that he is our master. We shall impose sufficient restrictions on him in our Constitution anyway. For we shall be free men and have no one over us but the Almighty God.

Alas, many of our brethren cannot even imagine in their dreams what it means to be a free man!

We shall not found a hereditary principality. We cannot make ourselves ridiculous in the eyes of the world. It would look like something bought, like some dubious marquisate. In order to prevent for all time subtle pressure from those in power, the second prince will not be a Rothschild, and never will a son be allowed to succeed his father. Any Jew can become our prince, with the exception of the author of this plan. Otherwise the Jews would say that he did everything for his own benefit. And if you examine it closely, even the first Prince Rothschild will not have attained this high position because of his money.

As you will soon see, we are not dependent on your money. But by giving us your contribution you will perform a moral act. You will be subjecting yourself to the National Ideal, helping us to carry out the enormous undertaking without a fight, and sparing the whole civilized world the severest upheavals. For this you shall be rewarded and the world will not deride it.

To make them comprehensible to the people, ideas of this kind must be presented in the simple and moving form of symbols. That is why we shall all be in glittering gala dress when we march to the Temple to crown the Prince. Only one man in our midst will wear the shabby garb of shame of a medieval Jew, including the pointed Jew's hat and the Yellow Badge, and that very man will be our Prince. Only in the Temple shall we put a princely cloak about his shoulders and a crown on his head.

The meaning of this will be: To us you are but a poor Jew; you shall never forget what we have endured and take care not to expose us to fresh dangers. But in the eyes of the world you are our Prince; as such you shall be resplendent and represent us with distinction.

Oh, now you will again think that I am telling you a tale. You are touched and shaken, and yet feel like mocking. Am I speaking of the impossible? In what way is my plan unrealistic? The Temple? I am going to build it wherever I please. Our gala dress? We shall be rich and free enough to wear it. The crowds? Them I shall draw wherever I want. The wondrous garb of the Prince? You must have been moved when I described it, and if you were not, *tant pis pour vous* [so much the worse for you]! Other nations also see old costumes in such festive processions and do not regard them as masquerades, but as meaningful remembrances of the past.

And why do I, who am talking to, and counting on, businessmen, dwell so long on this kind of description?

Because the intangible element of popular enthusiasm, surging like steam out of boiling water, is the power with which I run the great machine!

All right, and now to the as yet unsolved question of what will be done with your fortune if you come with us.

It is extremely simple. Your wealth consists of two parts: of the actual funds, which we shall even increase by two billion (within twenty years the Jewish State will redeem the shares at three times their face value), and of your credit.

The funds you keep. We shall then no longer be afraid of this wealth, great though it is. A large part of it will remain in Europe, but it will no longer be active. Your castles, palaces, all luxury establishments may remain; you can use them for future visits to Europe, when members of your family return on pleasure trips or represent us as diplomats. The natural disintegration of great fortunes will set in: through marriages, ramification of the lineage, and wastefulness. Then, too, over there you will set a good example to the rich by starting beautiful art collections, erecting fine buildings, and making gorgeous gardens. We will subtly entice the intellectually backward to culture. As for the main part of your fortune, the dangerous international power of your credit, we shall take it over for the benefit of our *Society of Jews*.

We shall liquidate the Rothschilds in the same way that we liquidate the smallest shipping agent or shopkeeper. This means that the *Society* will absorb the House of Rothschild.

This, too, will happen in the most natural way in the world. For the time being, all your employees will remain where they are, and you yourselves will remain at the helm everywhere—until such time as you, the present-day Rothschilds, will be used in our State, as directors of our financial system or as other government officials, as governors of provinces or as our diplomatic representatives to foreign powers. Through your connections with the European aristocracy you will be well suited for the diplomatic service. That way you will not need to tear yourselves away from your accustomed surroundings either.

We shall not give you any titles that might sound ridiculous in the beginning. You will simply be the representatives of the Jews in this place or that. Even now you occasionally identify yourselves as representatives of the Jews when, upon the conclusion of a loan, you beg for a bit of protection for the local Jews.

Once the time has come when other nations consider it expedient, and us worthy enough, to send ambassadors to us, we shall gladly return this compliment.

When the other Jews, those of moderate wealth, who are now Consuls-General and the like, join us, we shall make them our representatives in their present localities until such time as we summon them.

We shall recognize the present noblemen among the Jews if they bring proof to our free Office of Nobility by a certain date.

This office will see to it that no overly grotesque nobility is smuggled in. For certain exalted purposes of our policy we need a State nobility, just as we shall have one single decoration (along the lines of the *légion d'honneur* [legion of honor]). This decoration will be called "Jewish honor"! It will consist of a yellow badge, and so we shall make our new honor out of our old disgrace. Our best men, and only they, will be allowed to wear it, which will bring it the respect of the entire world. It will not be available for money. Otherwise it would no longer be a reward for our people whom we shall sometimes ask to give their lives, or who will offer their lives to us. In the hereditary nobility we give the reward after death, that is, we bestow it on the descendants. With our decoration we shall place the reward in the middle of life, and the nation will immediately recognize its oustanding men.

Our sons! Just as I have frequently and tenderly thought of my little boy, who is only 4 years old now, during the drawing up of this plan, you, too, will be thinking of your sons. I wish you numerous and able ones; we shall need all of our boys. Right now the future of your sons is one of your big worries—will you admit this? Will you again make bankers out of them, or loafers, simple-minded sportsmen? They will not be allowed to give any orders anywhere, in the government or in the army; you realize that, don't you? No one will turn the real command over to you in addition to the financial one.

But things will be different in our State. If your sons have the ability, they can become anything, just like any other Jew. But only if they have ability. Nobility and private property will be hereditary in our State, but offices will not be. Otherwise we should be ruined. That must be prevented at all costs.

What will our Constitution be like? It will be neither a monarchic nor a democratic one. I am a staunch advocate of monarchic institutions because they favor a stable policy and the interests of a historically illustrious family, one born and educated to rule—interests that are bound up with the preservation of the state. But our history has been interrupted too long for us to attempt to resume this institution.

I am against democracy because it is extreme in its approval and disapproval, tends to idle parliamentary babble, and produces that base class of men, the professional politicians. Nor are the present-day nations really suited to the democratic form of government; and I believe they will become less and less suited to it. For democracy presupposes a very simple morality, and our morality is becoming ever more complex with the advance of commerce and civilization. *Le ressort d'une démocratie est la vertu* [the concern of a democracy is virtue], said wise Montesquieu. And where will you find this virtue—political virtue, I mean? I have no faith in the political virtue of our people, because we are no different from the rest of modern men and because freedom will at first make our heads swell. Government by referendum does not make sense, in my opinion, because in politics there are no simple questions which can be answered merely by Yes or No. The masses are more prone even than parliaments to be misled by every kind of heresy and lend a willing ear to every ranting demagogue. As you know, the Swiss people, which is famous for its love of freedom and now subsists on its tourist trade, was the first to pass special legislation against the Jews. Neither internal nor external policy can be formulated in popular assembly. I could not even explain the protective tariff or free trade to the people, let alone some currency problem or international treaty, and least of all those sensible principles of popular education which must be our prime concern.

Politics must work from the top down. This does not mean that we shall put anyone in bondage, for we shall let every capable Jew rise, and everyone will want to rise. Can you imagine what a powerful upward surge is bound to move through our people? Every individual will think he is only raising himself, and yet the entire community will be raised. We shall bind this rise in moral forms which will be useful to the State and further the National Ideal.

Therefore I am thinking of an "aristocratic republic," as Montesquieu termed it. This would also be in keeping with the ambitious spirit of our people which has now degenerated into fatuous vanity. Many of the institutions of Venice come to mind, but we shall avoid all the features that caused the ruin of that city. We shall learn from the commercial mistakes of others, just as we shall learn from our own. Our people, to whom we are presenting the new country, will also gratefully accept the new Constitution that we give it. But wherever opposition may appear, we shall break it down. Everywhere we shall try it with friendly persuasion, but if need be we shall push it through by brute force.

I am not going into detail on the public institutions. Take my word for it: I understand the State. We shall also have a grand council of State jurists. We shall impose extensive but firm limits on public opinion, especially in the beginning. You can imagine that I as a journalist am concerned about the freedom and honor of my profession. But we certainly cannot permit our work to be disturbed by obtuse or malicious individuals.

(Here I wish to insert *incidemment* [incidentally] something that will show how easily we can transplant many of our customs. The newspapers which are now being hawked as Jewish sheets— and rightly so, I believe—will have editions over there, like the Paris edition of the *New York Herald*. The news will be exchanged between both sides by cable. After all, we shall remain in contact with our old homelands. Gradually the demand for newspapers will increase, the colonial editions will grow, the Jewish editors will move overseas, leaving the Gentile ones by themselves. Little by little and imperceptibly, the Jewish papers will turn into Gentile papers, until the overseas editions are as independent as the European ones. It is an amusing thought in this serious plan that many a government will be willing to help us for that reason alone.)

Let me just add a few remarks about other public institutions. Someone may think that our lack of a common language would present difficulties. After all, we cannot converse in Hebrew.

Who among us knows enough Hebrew to ask for a railroad ticket in this language? We have no such people. But it is really a very simple matter. Everyone retains his own language. I am a German-speaking Jew from Hungary and can never be anything but a German. At present I am not recognized as a German. But that will come once we are over there. And so let everyone keep his acquired nationality and speak the language which has become the beloved homeland of his thoughts. Switzerland offers visible proof that a federated state of different nationalities can exist.

I believe that German will be our principal language. I draw this conclusion from our most widespread jargon, "Judeo-German." But over there we shall wean ourselves from this ghetto language, too, which used to be the stealthy tongue of prisoners. Our teachers will see to that.

Actually, the only thing by which we still recognize our kinship is the faith of our fathers. Shall we, then, end up by having a theocracy? No! Faith unites us, science makes us free. Therefore we shall permit no theocratic velleities on the part of our clergy to arise. We shall know how to restrict them to their temples, just as we shall restrict our professional soldiers to their barracks. The army and the clergy shall be honored to the extent that their noble functions require and deserve it. But they will have no privileged voice in the State which confers distinction upon them and pays them, otherwise they would cause us trouble externally and internally. Every man will be as free and unrestricted in his belief or unbelief as he is in his nationality. And should it happen later that men of other creeds and other nationalities come to live among us, we shall accord them honorable protection. We have learned tolerance in Europe. I am not saying this sarcastically. Present-day anti-Semitism can only in a very few places be taken for the old religious intolerance. For the most part it is a movement among civilized nations whereby they try to exorcize a ghost from out of their own past.

I believe that by now it must be clear from every aspect: a Jewish State is a world necessity!

And that is why it will come into being—with you, gentlemen, or in opposition to you! Sooner or later it would arise, *par la force des choses* [of necessity], even without this proposal. They cannot throw us into the sea, at least not all of us, nor burn us alive. After all, there are societies for the prevention of cruelty to animals everywhere. What, then? They would finally have to find us some piece of land on the globe—a world ghetto, if you please.

Thus my plan does not invent a need; it only demonstrates one and shows at the same time how things can be accomplished to everyone's satisfaction without upheaval, struggle, or suffering. That is why it is the solution.

We shall found the new Jewish State in a respectable manner. After all, we have in mind our future honor in the eyes of the world.

For that reason all obligations in our old places of residence must be scrupulously fulfilled. We shall grant cheap passage and settlement benefits only to those who produce an official certificate saying "Affairs left in good order." Every private claim originating in the abandoned countries will be heard more readily in the Jewish State than anywhere else. We shall not even wait for reciprocity, but act purely for the sake of our own honor. Thus our claims will later get more consideration from law courts than may now be the case in some places.

It is self-evident, from the foregoing remarks, that we shall extradite the Jewish criminals more readily than any other state, until the time comes when we can enforce our penal code on the same principles as all other civilized nations. For the time being we shall admit Jewish criminals only after they have paid all penalties, but then we shall receive them without any restriction. The criminals among our people shall start a new life, too. The only exception will be made in the case of deserters. Deserters in wartime we shall not let in. If they try to take refuge in our State, we shall arrest them immediately and extradite them. Anyone who remains in his old home until war breaks out must stay there until the war is over, and of course he must fight like any other man who can carry a rifle. But after the war we shall receive them gladly and with great honors, for they will have fought for Jewish honor.

However, they will have to let us take and keep peacetime deserters. Otherwise we shall not be able to start out.

We shall need all hands that are able to work. As it is, we must allow for the loss of half a generation as far as physical labor is concerned. Only in fifteen years, I imagine, will our boys be fully grown and suffice for all the physical work that needs to be done. Until then we shall have to import many products. The atrophied arms of the generation that is already withering are not of much use now. We shall give these people occupations, certainly, but it will be work that is no hardship on them. We shall make them supervisors, mailmen, retailers, etc. We are not going to put them in homes for the aged. These homes are one of the most cruel forms of charity which our fatuous good nature has devised. In a home for the aged an old person dies of shame and grief. Actually, he is buried alive there. But we will leave even those on the lowest level of intelligence the comforting illusion of usefulness till the end of their lives.

In this way we shall seek for all ages, for all walks of life, the physical happiness and moral blessings of work. Thus our people will regain their skill in the land of the seven-hour working day.

Gentlemen! I cannot sketch this plan in concentric circles and straight lines. I must draw it like a map with its zigzag of mountains and waters. This is why I come to speak only now of the event which will be one of the first to take place, the actual occupation of the land.

When peoples migrated in historic times, they let themselves be carried, pulled, propelled by world accident. Like swarms of locusts they settled somewhere in their aimless wanderings. In historic times, after all, people did not know the earth yet.

The new migration of the Jews must take place according to scientific principles.

As recently as some forty years ago, gold digging was carried on in a curiously naive manner. How adventurous things were in California! There a rumor made the desperadoes come running from all over the world; they looted the earth, stole the gold from one another, and then gambled it away in an equally predatory manner. But today! Look at gold digging in present-day Transvaal. Gold mining is no longer run by romantic rogues, but by sober-minded geologists and engineers. Ingenious machines separate the gold from auriferous rock. Little is left to chance.

And so the new Jewish land must be explored and exploited with all modern aids.

As soon as our geographers have decided on the location and the international and private purchase contracts have been concluded, a ship will sail to take possession of the land.

This ship will carry administrative officials, technicians of all kinds, and delegates of the Local Groups.

These pioneers will have three tasks: first, the exact scientific investigation of all natural properties of the land; second, the establishment of a tightly centralized administration; third, the distribution of the land. These three tasks overlap and are to be expanded rationally to fit the purpose which is already sufficiently known.

Only one thing has not been clarified yet, namely, the way in which the land will be occupied according to Local Groups. An indispensable condition will be a variegated climate. We must give our people roughly the same climate to which they are accustomed in their old places of residence. After this general division comes the specific one.

In America the occupation of a newly opened territory still takes place in a rather naive manner. The settlers gather by the border and at the appointed hour rush forward simultaneously and forcibly.

We shall not do it that way. The locations in our provinces will be auctioned off—not for money, but for achievements. It will have been established according to the general configuration of the land which roads, water-regulation systems, bridges, etc., are necessary for commerce. This will be organized by provinces. Within each province the sites of towns will be auctioned off in a similar manner. The Local Groups will take the responsibility for carrying this out in an orderly fashion, and will defray the costs from local assessments. After all, we shall be able to know in advance whether or not they are undertaking too great a sacrifice. The bigger communities will get more elbow-room for their activities. Greater sacrifices will be rewarded by certain concessions. Universities or various technological research institutes and those institutions that do not have to be in the capital will be systematically spread over the country. We do not want to have a hypertrophic capital.

The proper development of what is taken over will be guaranteed us by the interest of the purchaser himself, and, if need be, by the local taxes which we may collect as dues. For, just as we cannot and do not want to abolish differences among individuals, differences among the Local Groups will continue. Everything will fall into place in a natural way; all acquired rights will be protected, all new developments will get sufficient elbow-room.

All these things will have been made clear to our people. Just as we will not take others by surprise or cheat them, we shall not deceive ourselves either.

Everything will be arranged systematically in advance. Even on the ship that sails to occupy the land everyone will know his assignment quite clearly—the scholars, the technicians, the officers and officials, and finally and principally, the authorized representatives of the Local Groups.

But when the new land first comes in sight, our new flag will be raised on the staff. At present we do not have any. I am thinking of a white flag with seven gold stars. The white field signifies our new, clean life, and the seven stars, our desire to start this new life under the banner of labor.

This is the way it can and will be if you go with us, gentlemen. And what if you do not feel like it, if you feel happy enough in your present situation—does that mean that the whole thing will be cancelled by your smile of rejection? It does not!

We would be poor people indeed if we came to you begging for a billion.

If you are not willing, the matter will go to the second level, to the Jews of moderate wealth. We shall send a few copies of the plan to the main centers of Jewish wealth, and bring it to the attention of the medium millionaires. Money-raising will then take a different form. All the medium-sized Jewish banks must be organized into a second, formidable financial power against the top bankers in the name of the National Ideal. The task is to sweep you along or pull you down—and then, across. In the latter case, to be sure, I will have nothing to do with the execution. I will not be a party to money matters.

And yet, for the time being, it will only amount to a money matter, for the billion would have to be deposited in full—there is no starting otherwise—and since this money would be used only gradually, all sorts of banking and loan transactions would be made in the first years. There is also a possibility that in this way the original purpose would gradually be forgotten. The moderately wealthy Jews would have found a new, big business, and the emigration of the Jews would be bogged down.

The notion of raising money in this way is certainly not fantastic—that you know. Several attempts have been made to marshal the Catholic money against you. No one has ever thought that you could also be fought with Jewish money. And this is how you might be beaten.

But what commercial crises all this would produce! How the countries in which these financial battles took place would suffer! How anti-Semitism would necessarily gain ground in the process!

This, then, is not agreeable to me. I am mentioning it only because it lies within the logical development of my thought, because this danger may induce you to go along with us, and because, after all, the Jews of moderate wealth have a right to be given ample notice.

I do not know whether the medium-sized banks will take the matter up. Maybe they will.

In any case, even if those of moderate wealth refuse, this will not finish the matter. No! Then it will begin in earnest, for I shall take it to the Jewish people and the whole world. I shall publish this Address, including all the steps I have taken in the matter and all the reactions that I have received. I know full well to what I should then be exposing myself. People will ridicule me and say that I want to become King of the Jews. They will try to hold me up to contempt and say that I was only interested in making a business deal. Of course, I have never made such a deal, least of all with my pen—but after all, that proves nothing about the future.

Then my peers, the philosophers and artists all over the world, will take me under their protection. For they know that certain words come only to a man who means them sincerely.

And the people will believe me. Not only among the poor Jews, but among all peoples, there will arise a feeling of rage against you who are able to bring this relief to the world and refuse to do so.

I believe that my book will have readers. The people will believe my words—and the governments no less. In the synagogues there will be prayers for the success of this plan—and in the churches as well! The little people and the middle classes and the nobility and the clergy and kings and emperors will warm to the cause. It is a relief from an old pressure under which all have suffered.

No, Messieurs Rothschild, you are not necessary for all that. Do you know who is going to raise the share capital of the *Society of Jews*? The Gentiles!

Perhaps even the poor, very small Jews. For them the billion will be divided into tiny parts. To be sure, in such a case I could not participate in the execution either—not only because it would again be a money matter, but especially because even this money would not be sufficient for the many purposes for which we could have used your world-wide credit.

I do not want to lead the poor people into penury. In this case the migration of the Jews could be accomplished only with the express, definite aid of the governments concerned. People would have to give us a helping hand with everything, procure the requisite and adequate land for us, give us all possible concessions on the transportation—in short, everything that is indispensable for carrying this out soundly.

The governments—by now I am no longer talking to you, gentlemen, but out the window—the governments will soon realize the full scope of what the solution of the Jewish Question will bring them.

Earlier, I spoke about direct and indirect advantages of our exodus. These were only the smallest. Yes, we shall produce considerable fiscal income by moving away. Yes, we shall patronize the railroads, give work to the movers, pay double fees, take care of all our debts, let appropriate numbers of people move into the lucrative positions that we give up, and where the state wishes to take over our industries and institutions, we shall give it the right of first refusal.

These individual voluntary expropriations and nationalizations can and must be something considerable. Yet they are not the most important benefit which the states and their citizens will derive from the emigration of the Jews. The most important benefit is something else. What?

Have you not been thinking all the time: they certainly cannot let us move away with all our money. After all, at present they still have a bit of power over us and can occasionally tighten the leash. Is this, then, the weak point in my system? I think, on the contrary, that it is the strongest.

In the first place, movable property in its most important current form, shares payable to the bearer, can never be regarded as being in the country. These shares can no longer be got at. The Paris commune tried it from below, and we know with what result. No one tries to do it from above. In the second place—and this is the enormous point which everyone must see—we shall free the world's credit system of us, for the moment we move out, the states will nationalize their credit. Through the stock-exchange monopoly, which they will hasten to copy from us, they will get control of the pernicious juggling with the state's credit. Perhaps they will even completely nationalize the money market; otherwise one would have to fear that the civilized peoples will Judaize themselves after we are gone.

We shall be in a position to show how this nationalization can be carried out. Transitional forms are easy to find. The states can found banking organizations which will take over from the *Society of Jews* the incomplete transactions which the *Society* will have taken over from individuals. The *Society* itself can do this organizing for the states and turn over to them those transactions that have been completed. In fact, the whole *Society* can eventually be split in two parts—the neo-Jewish part, which will go to our State, and the old Jewish, i.e., European one, which belongs to the states. The form and scope of the settlement would be a subject for negotiation with the individual governments.

So, you see, we by no means take the world credit-market with us—oh, how happy and strong our national spirit will be once we are rid of it!—rather, by our departure we shall organize the national credit of the states. That will be our greatest gift; it cannot be regarded as an emigration tax, because we shall do it voluntarily. As a matter of fact, in this plan we do everything voluntarily and in keeping with our honor!

Well, what is going to happen with the nations financially less stable? Are they not going to be controlled by the distant Jewish financial power?

Not any more than the others. Our credit will continue to be at their disposal if they seek it—but they will no longer be dependent on us exclusively. The governments will have their own foreign financial policy. They will get together in alliances. There will be a concordance of all political resources.

Whether the governments shall communicate with one another through financial ambassadors, or in a less formal, even a very informal manner, is really only a small detail. The important thing is that internally and externally the State will get control over its finances and will no longer be dependent on international groups and stock cartels. I look at everything through the eyes of the State, for ourselves as well as for others.

The State must exist!

Will there be Jews who will consider me a traitor to the cause of the Jews because I say all this?

I shall immediately enlighten and calm them. I am not representing and defending the bad Jewish cause, but I believe I am performing a service to the good Jewish cause by making these thoughts public.

But their publication will not even harm the selfish and predatory swindlers among the Jews.

For, all this can only be carried out with the free consent of the majority of Jews. It can be done against the will of individuals, even against groups of those now most powerful, but certainly not by the State against all Jews.

The emancipation of the Jews, which I consider just as much a failure on political grounds as I approve of it enthusiastically and gratefully for human reasons, came too late. It was no longer possible to emancipate us by legislation and in our old places of residence.

Nevertheless, the legal equality of the Jews, where it exists, can no longer be abolished. Not only because it would run counter to modern sensibilities—Good Lord, necessity knows no law— but also because that would immediately drive all Jews, poor and rich alike, into the arms of the revolutionary parties.

Therefore, no effective measures can actually be taken against us. And yet, anti-Semitism increases among the nations every day, every hour, and must continue to grow, because the causes have not been and cannot be removed.

The *causa remota* [indirect cause] is the loss of our assimilability which dates from the Middle Ages.

The *causa proxima* [immediate cause] is our overproduction of average minds who cannot sink and cannot rise—that is, cannot do so in a healthy way. At the bottom we are forced into becoming proletarian revolutionaries, constituting the petty officers of all revolutionary parties. And, at the same time, our frightful financial power grows at the top.

That is how it is. That is how things really are. I am not exaggerating and not denying anything. What I am saying is the simple truth.

And this is why my outline contains the solution. Do I hear somebody saying: Well, if such a thing were possible, would it not have been done before?

It was not possible before. It is now. As recently as a hundred or fifty years ago it would have been a fantasy. Today it is all a reality.

You, gentlemen, know best what can be done with money; how rapidly and safely we now speed in huge steamers across formerly uncharted seas. We have built safe railways up into a world of mountains which we previously scaled on foot and with trepidation. A hundred thousand brains are constantly thinking of ways to wrest all Nature's secrets from her. And what one man discovers belongs to the whole world an hour later. It is possible!

And it will happen in a wondrous way: the plain people who do not know these truths as you do, gentlemen, especially the simple souls, will have the greatest belief in me. They have the age-old hope of the Promised Land within them!

And it is real: no fairy tale, no deception! Anyone can find out for himself, for everyone will take across a piece of the Promised Land: one his brain, another his brawn, a third his belongings.

No doubt about it: it is the Promised Land, where it is all right for us to have hooked noses, black or red beards, and bandy legs without being despised for these things alone. Where at last we can live as free men on our own soil and die in peace in our own homeland. Where we, too, can expect honor as a reward for great deeds; where we shall live at peace with all the world, which we shall have freed through our own freedom, enriched by our wealth, and made greater by our greatness.

So that the derisive cry "Jew!" may become an honorable appellation, like "German," "Englishman," "Frenchman"—in short, like the name of any civilized nation. So that by means of our State we can educate our people for tasks which still lie beyond our horizon.

Now it might seem as though this were a long-drawn-out project. I keep speaking of months, years, decades. In the meantime, in a thousand places the Jews are being teased, insulted, scolded, whipped, plundered, and slain.

No, gentlemen, it is the immediate solution. I shall stop anti-Semitism instantly all over the world. It is the making of peace.

For, after we have taken all initial steps with the greatest dispatch and discretion; after we have secured our independence as a State through treaties under public law, and the land through purchases under civil law; after we have acquired cables and boats and made contracts on customs and special rates—in short, after we have done everything that is necessary to carry out our plan inexpensively, we shall make our entire program public.

This will be done in the pages of the *Neue Freie Presse*. For I have a debt of gratitude to this paper to discharge. It sent me to Paris and gave me the means and the opportunity of acquiring much of the knowledge that is now in the service of the cause. Therefore, any literary aspect of my announcement shall be the property of this paper.

On the next morning, a message will fly out into the whole world: Peace!

Peace to the Jews, victory to the Gentiles.

We must make peace because we can no longer fight, because later we should have to surrender under less favorable conditions.

The anti-Semites will have carried the day. Let them have this satisfaction, for we too shall be happy. They will have turned out to be right because they *are* right. They could not have let themselves be subjugated by us in the army, in government, in all of commerce, as thanks for generously having let us out of the ghetto. Let us never forget this magnanimous deed of the civilized nations.

By liberating them from us we shall also relieve them of the atavistic pressure of the Middle Ages which they have been under in the Jewish Question without recognizing it. They are not to blame for the sins of their fathers.

Forgiveness, peace, reconciliation for the whole world. And the relief will come instantly. The middle classes will immediately be drained of our overproduction of average minds which will flow into our first organizations and constitute our first officers, officials, jurists, physicians, and technicians of all kinds.

And so the matter will proceed with dispatch and yet without upheavals. There will be prayers in the synagogues for the success of our wonderful project. But in the churches as well!

The governments will give us their friendly assistance because we relieve them of the danger of a revolution which would start with the Jews—and stop who knows where!

The nations will breathe a sigh of happy relief. But so shall we, we especially! We shall depart as respected friends.

And so we shall move out to the Promised Land, the Land of the Seven Hours, the land which God has promised us in His inscrutable goodness, under the bright banner which we shall fashion for ourselves.

Book Two

With my letter to Bismarck this development of my thought which has been growing in me has logically entered a new stage. I am starting a new book. I don't know how much space the previous notes will occupy; I am not in the mood now to make a clean copy of them.

Today Bismarck has my letter. Will he take me for a gentle fool or a raving one? Will he reply?

Dined with Fürth. I told him of my meeting with Hirsch. I thought he would hear of it in any case, and therefore I wanted to supply some authentic notes on my letters, intended to be passed along. I especially regret that third letter. When shall I break myself of the habit of writing imprudent letters?

Incidentally, Fürth told me that I had judged and treated Hirsch correctly.

He also confirmed my assumption that Hirsch had arranged for the two secretaries to be there as witnesses that my visit actually took place.

Then we went to the circus.

I said: There is one man who would understand my plan (which I did not disclose to Fürth, although he seemed to guess its approximate nature). That is the German Kaiser.

Fürth: Draw up a memorandum for him. Then find a reliable man to transmit it. Perhaps my cousin von Kaiser, the director of the Colonial Office.

I: He is your cousin? Baptized?

Fürth: Yes. He coached Herbert Bismarck for his assessor's examination and in that way became acquainted with the old man who said he could use him if he had himself baptized. Kaiser did it, perhaps partly because he wanted to marry his present wife, a Catholic. First he became State Attorney at Strassburg, then he was promoted and finally appointed director of the Colonial Office. When Bismarck had a falling out with the Kaiser, von Kaiser went over to the latter. He always has access to him.

I: Then he would probably be the right man. But being a convert, will he want to have anything to do with the Jewish cause?

Fürth, with a shrug: Maybe. (After all, F. has also been converted.)

June 26

Today Bismarck's reply is due. It has not come.

I wonder if he has even received my letter. If there are "black cabinets" on either side of the border, the letter will have been opened once or perhaps even twice. The postal censors actually had an invitation in my final remark that I was prepared to receive no answer at all. They could simply have thrown my letter away.

Here is a droll idea: if you want to be sure to get some message into the hands of the government, you only have to put it into such a letter with a conspicuous address.

June 27

No answer from Bismarck. I am already convinced that I shall receive none. I thought of having Feldmann inquire at the *Hamburger Nachrichten* whether Bismarck has received my letter.

But Feldmann would at some later date tell this as an anecdote about me. I no longer care whether Bismarck has received my letter or not. If he has—*tant pis* [too bad].

I am now thinking of Schoen. He could deliver my memorandum to the Kaiser. But come to think of it, isn't Schoen on vacation?

June 27

In the Chamber of Deputies I casually asked Wolff whether Schoen was here. No, he is in Bavaria, on vacation until August 15.

I thought of asking Schoen through Wolff whether he would see me between trains.

Decided later to write Schoen directly. The fewer know about it, the better.

Schoen, by the way, will know me and lend me a willing ear.

Possibly look for some other German diplomat to do this. It will not be hard.

June 27

Addendum to the plan.

Those who die during the passage will not be thrown into the water. This would be a deterrent to immigrants and a ghastly image to the people. Corpses will be safely embalmed and buried on the other side.

June 28

Before I approach Schoen it will be helpful to notify Albert Rothschild. This way, I believe, I shall get back to my original thought in better style. And I shall be covered against the reproach of having acted without, i.e. against, the Jews.

*   *   *

Letter to Albert Rothschild:

Dear Sir:

I shall come to the point without preliminaries.

I have composed a memorandum about the Jewish Question for the German Kaiser. A reliable man (a diplomat) will deliver it to him. It is not a fatuous and querulous complaint. Even if he wanted to, the Kaiser could not do anything against anti-Semitism, as I understand the movement. Rather, my memorandum contains a comprehensive plan for self-help on the part of Jews of all countries. If the Kaiser sends for me after reading my memorandum, I can pursue the matter with him as an independent man because I am not under his political jurisdiction. From the outset there cannot be any doubt that I do not want any favors or special treatment from him or anyone else. And therefore I hope that this alert and vigorous ruler will understand me. My memorandum will bear only my signature and I shall have the exclusive responsibility for it. But since I am taking up the cause of the Jews, I owe them some proof of my good intentions, and for this purpose I need a few reputable and independent persons as references. Note: references, not guarantors or principals. Actually, individuals would not even be entitled to give me an assignment which, incidentally, I do not need.

Would you care to be one of the references? I am having some trouble finding serviceable men. Since I have been concerned with the cause I have already had quite bad experiences. Sometimes I have been utterly fed up. We have such twisted, crushed, money-worshipping people who are therefore booted around even more than they deserve. But even these miserable qualities fill me with pity, in the final analysis; they are products of prolonged pressure.

Let me immediately dispel one doubt that might arise in your mind. My memorandum does not contain even the slightest trace of a violation of duty or of reverence toward our sovereign. I am simply trying to get at anti-Semitism where it originated and still has its center: in Germany. I consider the Jewish Question an extremely serious matter. Anyone who thinks that agitation against the Jews is a passing fad is seriously mistaken. For profound reasons it is bound to get worse and worse, until the inevitable revolution comes.

Some Jews, of course, think that the danger is no longer there when they close their eyes.

Let me recapitulate. My memorandum will be delivered to the Kaiser at the end of July or the beginning of August. In the latter part of July I shall come to Austria. If you would like to know what is in the document, I shall read it to you. We can arrange a meeting for this purpose. I am prepared to come to you for half a day. You will certainly make sure that we are undisturbed. But if you should be traveling at that time, I would like it even better if I could meet you on your travels somewhere—I don't care where.

If you feel no desire to become acquainted with my memorandum, it will be quite sufficient for you to return this letter to me. I shall not regard it as an insult, because I am expressly asking you to.

In any case, I know that I am dealing with a gentleman. And when I now ask you to treat my letter in complete confidence and not tell a soul about the matter, it is just as if I had told it to you verbally and immediately sworn you to secrecy.

It may not be superfluous to remark that no one on my newspaper has any knowledge of the matter. I am doing this alone and independently.

> Respectfully yours,
> Dr. Theodor Herzl,
> 36 rue Cambon.

* * *

June 28

In the Chamber I spoke with the *Communard* Leo Franckel. Fine face, mediocre mind, a sectarian's pride. He boasted of the prisons in which he has "languished."

I explained to him why I am against the democracies.

"So you are a disciple of Nietzsche?" he said.

I: "Not at all. Nietzsche is a madman. But one can only govern aristocratically. In the community I am in favor of the widest autonomy. Parish-pump politics are sufficiently—in fact, best—understood around the parish pump. However, the state and its needs cannot be comprehended by the people."

Franckel: "How are you going to establish this aristocratic government?"

I: "There are all kinds of ways. Here is just one example, from which you need not generalize. The French Academy constitutes an elective aristocracy."

We then spoke about social theories. I said that I was in favor of nationalizing banking, insurance, railroads, and everything that has already been tested, where there no longer is any risk that would justify entrepreneurial profits.

Franckel: "That way everything can be arranged collectivistically."

I: "By no means. The individual must not be done away with."

Here, obviously, is the flaw in the thinking of the Socialists: they say, "everything."

I say: what has been adequately worked out!

June 28

On the Champs Elysées.

Moritz Wahrmann's son rode past. Looks vigorous but bored. Such fellows, with their unused vitality, would be splendid material for us. It would be easy to fill them with enthusiasm for the cause. And how beautiful is my scheme in which such Leo Franckels and young Wahrmanns would find room for their development.

June 28

Champs Elysées.
Poverty: when you wear your winter clothes in summer.

July 4

Albert R's reply, which was due today, has not come. Fortunately I did not degrade myself by excessive courtesy in my letter.

The memorandum to the Kaiser is being given its final form. In this, too, I shall take care to maintain my dignity.

July 4

Now the novel is again very much in my thoughts, because my plan will probably strike everyone as fiction.

When I am at Aussee, I shall request two months' leave without pay and write the novel there in September and October.

July 4

In the novel I shall include everything that I am sorry to have written to Hirsch and that he may have laughingly shown around. My revenge will be a generous one: I am going to make a likeable character out of him. (I do like him, after all.) I shall glorify his stock market coups. He had made them without suspecting that they will benefit the cause which he as yet does not know about. Thus his figure will acquire a vague grandeur. Then there will be a good reversal. The Baron has misunderstood the office of "sovereign." He thought that he was to become not only President of the Company, but also Chief of State. That cannot be. No matter how great his contributions to the cause, he cannot become Chief of State. At that point the hero hits upon an ingenious solution. He says to the Baron when they are about to be recognized under international law: "All right, now both of us will retire. If we want to become part of history, we must do all this unselfishly. Henceforth we shall be merely observers. I shall so arrange it that you are offered the sovereignty—but you must immediately refuse it." The Baron does not see the need for this, but the hero gives him to understand, in no uncertain terms, that this is the way it has to be. And if he did not first pledge himself in writing to reject the honor, he would not even be offered it; in fact, the hero would ruin him completely if he did not comply.

At first the Baron flies into a rage; then he realizes that the hero is right, throws his arms about his neck, and tearfully kisses him.

Then, at the coronation, the two give a symbolic spectacle of selflessness, and the one who has not been truly selfless outdoes the other in manifestations of modesty.

July 5

Strange: While I was writing the above, Hirsch's letter, which I no longer expected, was on its way to me. It arrived last night.

82 Piccadilly, W.
July 3, 1895

Dr. Herzl, Paris.*

I am in receipt of your letter to which this is a somewhat tardy reply. However, an answer was not urgent. When I return to Paris, which, I may add parenthetically, will not be for several months, I shall be delighted to see you, although without any change in the ideas which I have already expressed.

Very sincerely yours,
M. de Hirsch.

My reply to Hirsch:

Paris, July 5, 1895

Dear Sir:

I was greatly annoyed that you did not reply at once to the letter I wrote you after our conversation. That is why I informed you two weeks later that I had given the matter up. But after receiving your letter yesterday I should like to tell you how my decision is to be understood. I shall still try to do something *for* the Jews, but not *with* them. If I ventured to believe that someone would understand my resolute ideas, it was you. From other Jews I can expect even less. The decline of our once-vigorous race is revealed most clearly in our political lethargy. People would deride me or suspect me of making God knows what business deals with the cause. I should have to pass through a swamp of disgust—and I am not ready to make this sacrifice for the Jews. They are incapable of understanding that a man can act out of other motives than money, that a man can refuse to submit to money without being a revolutionary. It follows that the last step, and perhaps even the most effective, that I shall take

* In French in the original.

will be to place the matter before the exalted personage I spoke
to you about. He is said to be an anti-Semite, but this does not
bother me. I have found an approach to him. Somebody is going
to hand him my memorandum. If he then sends for me, the conversation could be interesting. Unless he expressly enjoins secrecy, and if anything at all in the conversation can be passed on,
I shall tell it to you as soon as chance brings us together again. It
is not likely to be in Paris, for I have had my fill of this city and
have prevailed upon the publishers of my newspaper to transfer
me to Vienna. Our conversation would have no value anyway beyond the pleasure of an exchange of ideas. You stick to your views,
and I with equal stubbornness, to mine. You believe that you can
export poor Jews, the way you are doing it. I say that you are
only creating new markets for anti-Semitism. *Nous ne nous com-
prendrons jamais* [we shall never understand each other]. For the
rest I do not regret having made contact with you. I found it
most interesting to make your acquaintance.

One more thing: I should like to clarify something that may
have struck you. I emphasized in every letter that this matter is
not a business to me. *C'est qu'il est horriblement compromettant
d'écrire aux gens riches* [The point is that it is terribly compromising to write to rich people]. I am well aware that a gentleman
carefully guards or destroys the letters written to him in confidence. But the malice of things may bring it about that such a
piece of paper falls into other hands; and if anything worries me
it is the thought that in the course of my efforts I could lose as
much as a shred of my good reputation.

Therefore, keep my memory untarnished.

Respectfully yours,
Dr. Herzl.

July 5

Dined yesterday with little Wolff. He has been called up for
military drill. I listened once again to his tales of the Dragoon-
Guards. He doesn't consider anti-Semitism so bad. The upper-

class Prussians, he says, are not anti-Semites at all; they feel just as superior to the middle-class Gentiles as they do to the Jews. Thus Wolff does not notice that the upper-class people he admires only substitute one kind of contempt for another. He is satisfied to be thrown in the same pot with the middle-class Gentiles and to be despised along with them. He finds it quite natural that he will not get an officer's commission although he got the highest marks on the examinations.

By the way, if there is one thing I should like to be, it is a member of the old Prussian nobility.

July 6

Yesterday with Nordau, over a glass of beer. Also discussed the Jewish question, of course. Never before had I been in such perfect tune with Nordau. Each took the words right out of the other's mouth. I never had such a strong feeling that we belonged together. This has nothing to do with religion. He even said that there was no such thing as a Jewish dogma. But we are of one race. Fürth was also present, and I noticed a certain *gêne* [embarrassment] in his manner. I think he felt ashamed of having had himself baptized when he saw and heard our strong profession of adherence to Judaism. Another point on which Nordau and I agreed was that only anti-Semitism had made Jews of us.

Nordau said: "What is the tragedy of Jewry? That this most conservative of peoples, which yearns to be rooted in some soil, has had no home for the last two thousand years."

We agreed on every point, so that I already thought that the same ideas had led him to the same plan. But he comes to a different conclusion: "The Jews," he says, "will be compelled by anti-Semitism to destroy among all peoples the idea of a fatherland." Or, I secretly thought to myself, to create a fatherland of their own.

Fürth said: "It is not good for the Jews to develop such a strong nationalist feeling within themselves. This will only intensify the persecutions."

July 7, 1895

Why has Hirsch suddenly written me again? I have two explanations for it.

Either Fürth casually mentioned in a letter to him that I was preparing a memorandum for the Kaiser.

Or—and this seems more likely to me—my last letter, in which I wrote "Pull Rothschild with us or pull him down—and then over and across!" really struck home.

He instructed his secretary to write me after exactly two weeks —so that the matter would not appear urgent. Actually, I have been much on his mind.

And if he has any nose for such things he must certainly sense what I am bringing him.

After all, we two are natures such as emerge at the beginning of a new era—he is the *condottiere* of money, I am the *condottiere* of the intellect.

If this man goes along with me, we can really usher in a new era.

July 8

Lunched yesterday with Schiff at Ville d'Avray. We visited Gambetta's house. The most remarkable thing was the death mask. I don't really like Gambetta; he looks as though he were a relative of mine.

Afterwards we went to the restaurant Au bord de l'Etang by the pond. Nine tables were occupied; at three of them I recognized Viennese Jews. That proves something.

Schiff told me that his brother-in-law had been insulted by an anti-Semite on leaving the train at Kitzbühel; as a result of that, so his mother-in-law had written, he was upset and hurt.

And this sort of thing is repeated in a thousand places every day—yet people fail to draw any conclusion from it.

I didn't want to go into the matter further with Schiff, for he doesn't understand me.

No answers either from Hirsch or from Rothschild. Hirsch may be stalling again. But on the part of the other man, it's just bald, vile arrogance. Must be repaid in kind at the first opportunity.

July 9

"If I were a prince or a legislator I would not waste my time telling what ought to be done; I would do it, or keep silent." *

(Rousseau, *Contrat Social*, Book One)

July 9

There is a novel by Ludwig Storch, *The Star of Jacob* (*Der Jakobsstern*), which deals with Sabbatai Zvi.

July 10

Businessmen are best suited for conducting political affairs. But a man seldom gets rich—and wealth is the freedom of businessmen—without having soiled himself.

In order to be able to call on them for political services, nevertheless, some sort of investigation of the way they have made their fortune would have to be instituted, on a voluntary basis. This would have to be done not by jealous peers, but by a political tribunal of honor composed of independent men from all walks of civil life. Often a man in public life finds it necessary, as it were, to permit examination of his books afterwards.

If he does this at the start of his political activity, we shall have, in addition to his business sense, the near-certainty of his decent character. At the same time it will be ascertained what he was worth prior to his public service. If, subsequently, demagogues or intriguers throw suspicion on him, he can proudly point to his financial status.

Of course, I am not thinking of this in terms of a law, but as a gradual moral institution. At first this idea will be carried out by a few reputable businessmen, then it will become more and more firmly established usage, and will finally be embodied in

* In French in the original.

legislation when enough time has elapsed for the young merchants to set this as a goal for themselves.

After about twenty years it can become law.

July 10

I consider money an excellent means of political evaluation, provided the morality of its acquisition can be established. But only then; for otherwise a financial standard would be absurd and repugnant.

Anyone who has earned a lot of money honestly must be a very capable man, a clever speculator, a practical inventor, an industrious, thrifty person—all qualities eminently useful for guiding the state.

Habitual speculation with stock would be grounds for disqualification. On the other hand, occasional stock deals are nothing dishonorable. Naturally, it is hard to draw the line—therefore, a tribunal of honor in each case. The person being investigated must, at any rate, take an oath of manifestation (under penalty of perjury). After all, no one will be forced to become a political figure. That way we shall keep the shady *politicians** off our necks, and politics will become the goal of our cleanest and most capable men.

July 10

Types for my novel, which is to contain real people:

The "dog in the manger" (a village fiddler, a fake aesthete)

Gamel Moishe (extremely likeable)

The "forgotten" girl (include only one, but teach readers to understand them all through her; possibly have someone devise the dowry tax while returning from her funeral. For the excellent girl has missed her "natural calling" and died from it. But what a splendid mother she would have made! I shall call her Pauline!)

And it is to her memory that the novel will be dedicated.

* In English in the original.

July 12

Heinrich's gushing young brother, the musician, will be "trained" to be a ruler in the novel. It is the hero's long-prepared plan to make it up to Heinrich's parents in this way. He chuckles inwardly as he tends this beautiful, useless plant, the visionary and dreamer with his head in the clouds.

July 12

A character for the novel.

A clever swindler (*à la* Schapira, the bank-note splitter) who becomes an honest boy scout after he returns from a European prison.

He fled to the Seven-Hour Land, but his extradition was demanded and he was returned. Before he is deported in the custody of the police, the hero comes to see him in the prison of the port and sets him straight. "You will have to serve your term because of us. But while you are in prison, think about some *honest* schemes that you will put into practice here later."

And the hard-hearted cheat is deeply moved. Before his departure the hero comes up to the handcuffed man and shakes his hand in view of everybody. A commotion. And the swindler quickly bends down and kisses the hero's hand.

In prison on the other side his conduct is excellent, so that he is given time off for good behavior. Then he goes back and becomes an efficient, honest, ingenious businessman.

July 12

For the novel.

Pastimes for the workers after working hours. They make music (Workers' Orchestras).

But the main thing: Jewish National Passion Plays from ancient times (Maccabees) and the Middle Ages. Fear, pity, pride, and adult education in the form of diversion.

Popularization of the amateur theatricals of high society.

This will furnish nice chapters for the novel, comic episodes of the innocent little *cabotinage* [strolling players] in every locality.

Circenses [entertainment] for their own sake.

Teacher-directors will have seen models in the capital.

July 13

Forms of consistency:

(At the rendezvous)

—I have changed my mind and have come.

—But you were going to come.

—Yes, *that* was my first change of mind.

* * *

Letter to Güdemann:

July 15

Dear Doctor Güdemann,

My last letter seems to have made you somewhat annoyed at me, because you did not answer it.

But I hope we shall have an opportunity to have a direct exchange of ideas about this matter which concerns us so closely, and at that time I shall give you an adequate explanation of everything.

The reason I am writing you today is the recent anti-Semitic riots in Vienna. I am very closely following the movement in Austria as well as elsewhere. These are but trifles. Things are going to get worse and more out of control.

Unfortunately, nothing decisive can be done at the moment, although the plan, which has been carefully devised and is mild, prudent, and anything but violent, has been completely worked out. To put it into practice now, that is, with the Jews, would be to jeopardize it. This plan, you see, is a reserve for worse days; please believe me, even if I express myself in such vague terms. You will see and hear about it when we meet in Vienna at the end of the summer.

For the present, I simply would not want this mood of annoyance to take hold of a man whom I respect, and in the midst of this bleak situation in which the Austrian Jews find themselves I should like to hold out to you hope for some relief which we younger, resolute men are preparing for our unfortunate brethren. To be sure, the mean people, the cowards, and those whom their money has made arrogant would be enough to sour one on the noble undertaking; but we must think of the poor and decent Jews. They are in the majority. We are not a chosen people, but not a base one either. This is why I am holding on.

Yours very sincerely,
Herzl.

July 15

Schiff has been here. I asked him what he thought of the anti-Jewish riots outside the Lanner Hall in Vienna.

"The Jews must turn Socialist!" he says obstinately.

In vain I explained to him that this would do even less good in Austria than in Germany. He believes that Hungary, which has a liberal policy toward the Jews, is going to prevent an anti-Jewish reaction in Austria. How wrong he is! In Hungary the Jews are committing the greatest error by buying up the landed estates. The "gentry" who are being ousted from the soil will overnight make themselves the leaders of the people and fall upon the Jews. The liberal government is being kept in power quite artificially by Jewish election funds. The conservative National Party, with Vienna and the army behind it, can overturn everything from one day to the next.

July 16

Dined at Nordau's party yesterday.

It's a lucky thing for me that I've had no social life here. I would have spent myself being scintillating at dinner parties.

For a moment the conversation turned to Baron Hirsch. Nordau said: "With his money I would make myself emperor of South America."

How strange! And that time Schiff had said that I should submit my "crazy" plan to Nordau.

July 16

Novel.

Hero is of the blond type, blue eyes, a piercing look.

His beloved is a Spanish Jewess, slender, dark-haired, highbred. She first sees him as the captain of the ship sailing to occupy the land. He dreams of her in his tent.

July 21

Had a good letter from Güdemann today. I am immediately writing him as follows:

My Dear Friend:

Permit me to address you thus after receiving your letter, which is a joy to me.

I see now that my eyes did not deceive me when I saw in you one of the right people that I need. Now I will give you a little more information about why I recalled my letter. That was done in a terrible fit of demoralization caused by a local friend, the first and only person in whom I have confided my plan so far. When I showed him the letter which I had sent you the day before, he said to me: "Güdemann will think you crazy; he will go to your father right away, and your parents will be unhappy. By doing this you are making yourself either ridiculous or tragic . . ." Only when you know everything that I have in mind —and you will learn it, for I now feel your Jewish, manly heart beating next to mine—will you understand what a severe crisis I went through, after the tremendous birthpangs with which the plan had been born, when my loyal and devoted friend said this to me. I am ready and able to stake my life on the Jewish cause, but I must confine the sacrifice to my person. That would not be the case if people considered me "meshugge [crazy]." It would spoil my parents' last years and ruin my children's future.

Naturally, I did not consider myself crazy just because my

friend, who is a good man but lives in confining circumstances and is not an outstanding intellect, did not understand me. But I had to tell myself: He represents the average educated Jew. He knows me, has confidence in me, respects and loves me; if he feels that way, what must the others say! He showed me how thick the wall is against which I want to beat my head . . . Therefore it can't be done the way I was going to do it. And so I recalled that letter.

But I did not abandon the matter. I thought about other ways of putting the plan into practice.

There are two of them. The first is a memorandum to the Kaiser. An acquaintance of mine offers me a possibility of having this memorandum transmitted to him.

But this acquaintance would not be able to do this before the middle of August. At the end of this month I am going to Aussee where I shall spend my vacation. Perhaps a better way to reach the Kaiser will present itself to me there. I once had some correspondence on a problem of social legislation with the president of the Austrian Chamber of Deputies, Baron Chlumecky. He is in Aussee. If I can explain my plan to him, maybe he will introduce me to Imperial Chancellor Hohenlohe, who can then take me to the Kaiser.

If I don't get to him, there remains to me the last form of implementation: the fictional kind.

I shall tell the Jews didactic fairy-tales which they will understand gradually, in five, ten, or twenty years. I shall put seeds into the earth. That is lovely, apt, and worthy of a poet. Only I fear that by the time the seeds sprout, everyone will have starved.

Yes indeed, it would pain me to have to do this, for my plan is no fantasy.

Now I have your letter. Only when you know everything will you realize how you have guessed my innermost thoughts and I have guessed yours. And, no! We are not isolated cases. All Jews think as we do! I have faith in the Jews, I, who used to be lukewarm and am not a religious man even now! *Les coups que nous recevons nous font une conviction* [the blows we receive give us conviction].

Enough of talking. If you had written me in this vein sooner, we would be one month ahead.

What you write me about Dr. Heinrich Meyer-Cohn makes me long to meet this man immediately. Immediately! It may be in the highest interest of our cause that I get together with you and Meyer-Cohn before I go to the *reshoim*. Could you find out by telegram where he is now, and could the three of us meet somewhere at the end of this week? After your letter and the portrayal you have given me of M.-C., I want very badly to speak with both of you. I suggest some place in Switzerland, such as Zurich. In Austria you and I are too well known. We would run into acquaintances everywhere. At the moment I do not want that.

Zurich is a well-situated central point. After your letter I no longer doubt that you will make the small sacrifice of money and time that this trip will entail. You can tell the head of your congregation—that is, if you must give any reasons for a short absence—that you have to meet Meyer-Cohn in Zurich to give him some important information.

You have already shocked me once—when you did not want to come to Caux right away the time I summoned you in the service of the Jewish cause (!) To be sure, you must have been surprised at first when the author of comedies and writer of feuilletons wanted to speak about serious matters. Do you believe me now? Do you already sense from my every word that I have important, decisive things to say?

I don't need the rich Jews—but I need men! *Donnerwetter* [damn it], they are hard to find! And that was my crisis which my good friend had brought about. For a moment I despaired of the possibility of finding any men among the Jews. The crisis is over now; I had already overcome it before your letter arrived, because every day I pay close attention to the sufferings of our brethren in all countries. I think that such oppression must make men out of even the most degenerate riff-raff. What has been lacking hitherto is a plan. Such a plan has been found!

I am saying this in all humility—believe me. Anyone who thinks of himself in such a matter does not deserve to be engaged in it.

Get Meyer-Cohn to Zurich and go there yourself! I shall leave here on Thursday or Saturday evening and be there the following morning. I authorize you to send this letter to Meyer-Cohn if he hesitates. But if he hesitates, he won't be the person that you have described.

I am taking on the case of Bloch, and you can tell him so. But no one except you and Meyer-Cohn should see this letter.

To get the money for Bloch will be an easy matter. I am acquainted with Hirsch, and if I drop him a line, I am convinced that he will immediately give what is needed. At the moment, to be sure, relations between Hirsch and me are a bit strained, because in my last letter I used some more explicit language than this man, who is accustomed to beggars, parasites, and aristocratic sponges, can stand. Yet there is no doubt but that he will give the required money without thinking twice about it if I ask it for Bloch, because he is already aware that I should not be capable of asking anything for myself. But even without Hirsch, Bloch will be taken care of—you can depend on that. Of course, I only know Bloch's unpleasant side, the evidences of his lack of taste, but the fact that you consider him necessary is enough for me.

Awaiting your acceptance by telegram, I remain, with cordial regards,

Yours sincerely,
Th. Herzl.

July 21

Telegram to Güdemann:

Thanks for kind letter. Wire immediately requesting Meyer-Cohn's whereabouts. We three must definitely meet end of this week, perhaps in Zurich. Please get ready for departure. Details by letter. Regards,

Theodor.

July 22

In the Austrian Beer Hall, Herrschkowitz (Hercovici) came to my table.

I had him describe the situation of the Rumanian Jews to me. Horrible. There are 400,000 in the country; most of the families have been living there for centuries and still have no civil rights. Each person must first apply to the Chamber of Deputies for these rights after he has completed his military service, and his application may be rejected by secret vote.

Since 1867 there have been only two major pogroms. H. was a witness to the one in Galatz. Hundreds of Jews were driven into the Danube by soldiers under the pretext that they were to board Austrian ships. They were not let on board, and so they were drowned. The exact number is not even known.

From time to time the peasants do some looting.

The situation is also bad for the Jews where making a living is concerned. Three per cent of them are artisans, the rest are storekeepers, and the educated men are almost invariably physicians.

The merchants suffer from lack of business. Old firms are collapsing. The bankruptcy lists are full of Jewish names, and, what's more, all Jewish bankruptcies are believed to be fraudulent and the ruined people are locked up. When they get out of jail, they are broken men and go begging.

Many of them emigrate, to Argentina, etc.! But frequently they come back.

(*Parbleu* [Aha]! They haven't got my homeland there yet.)

The Jews in Rumania are a sturdy lot, says H. Fine, fine.

July 22

Pangloss: "the best of all possible worlds!" *

"Let us work without arguing," says Martin, "that's the only way of making life bearable." *

(Voltaire, *Candide*, end of Chapter XXX)

"Very well," says Candide, "but, most of all, let us cultivate our garden." *

(*Ibid.*)

July 22

Note on national psychology.

In the Taverne Royale there are several managers who are actually super-waiters. A clever arrangement! When one of these super-waiters, who does not wear a waiter's jacket, hands a plate to a guest, the latter feels flattered, honored. I have noticed this in my own case. In the same way, our emigrants, too, shall be given "courteous service." Jews are starved for *Koved* [honor], being a despised people; and by catering to it, one can lead them.

July 23

Prophylactic quinine!

Official distribution and administration while standing in line. The quinine must be taken daily in the presence of the health inspectors.

Greatest sanitary precautions in transit and on the other side.

Move very rapidly through fever regions. In such areas, have necessary work on railways, roads, and, later, swamp drainage (Maremma) done by natives who are used to the climate. Otherwise deaths will be puffed up and demoralize the people who, as it is, will be afraid of the floorless water and the unknown. Old prisoners don't like to leave prison. They have to be coaxed and all obstacles inside and outside them have to be cleared away.

* These three sentences are quoted in French by Herzl.

July 23

Blockheads must not be given any explanations!

My grandfather, Haschel Diamant, was a wise man. He used to say: Never give a *kush* [kiss] to a *miesse maad* [homely girl].

Such a warning may seem superfluous, for this would promise no pleasure. But the meaning is this: don't kiss a homely woman out of pity, or because you expect her to be faithful, for she will become presumptuous and then there will be no getting rid of her.

July 23

I have thought of preventing peddling through legal restrictions and police heckling (no voting rights, etc.). Only in the European states would this be something cruel, a pushing into the water like the Galatz pogrom. We, however, will not push a peddler into the water that way, but onto firm ground!

How is this to be attained? Through favoring the big stores (*à la* Louvre, Bon-Marché).

Principle: always destroy harmful elements by favoring their competitors!

The favoring of the Louvre stores will not be unconditional, of course. At the outset the entrepreneur will have to guarantee profit-sharing and old-age benefits as well as education for his employees' children (to the extent that the State has not made provisions for this).

Mass industry as well as mass trade must be handled along patriarchal lines.

The entrepreneur will be the patriarch.

To be considered whether such a stipulation should be specifically embodied in a law; or whether an indirect policy should be pursued in this, too, through honoring the patriarch in various ways.

Laws are easier to circumvent than customs.

Possibly a combination of both: a legal minimum of public

welfare (on account of profiteers and those devoid of a sense of honor) and an indirect policy, *pour encourager les efforts* [to encourage efforts].

July 23

To the bickerers, hatemongers, and grumblers:

In the next twenty years we shall have no time to fight among ourselves. That will come at a later date. For the present, let anyone who feels like fighting and has enough courage do battle against our enemies.

Wranglers should be declared public enemies. We shall deliver them up to the hatred of our people.

July 23

The capital city, our treasure-trove, will be in a location protected by mountains (fortresses on the tops), on a beautiful river, with forests nearby.

Take care that the site is protected from the wind, but not a sun bowl, guarded by mountains, but not too small.

Prevent the hypertrophic development of the capital through a belt of forests which must not be cut down. In addition, decentralization of educational institutions, etc.

July 23

In the process of transplantation, have careful consideration for all local customs.

*Salzstangel,** coffee, beer, customary meat, etc., are not indifferent matters.

Moses forgot to take along the flesh pots of Egypt. We shall remember them.

* Translator's note: A sort of breadstick, strongly flavored with salt and caraway seed.

July 23

The transplantation of the big department stores will immediately supply us with all necessary and not-so-necessary goods, which will make the cities habitable in a very short time.

July 23

Full autonomy for the communities in all parish-pump politics. Let the gabbers play parliament to their heart's content.

But only one Chamber of Deputies which cannot overthrow the government but only deny it particular resources. This will suffice for a public control.

One-third of this Chamber will be named by the ruler upon the recommendation of the government (a life-time appointment, for only nobility and property will be hereditary).

Another third will be elected by the learned academies, the universities, schools of art and technology, chambers of commerce, and trade associations.

The final third will be elected by the community councils (an election commission to examine authorizations), or perhaps by the provinces after a scrutiny of voting lists.

The ruler will name the government. It remains to be considered, however, how the ruler's arbitrariness may be kept in check. For, since the Chamber is not supposed to overthrow the government, a ruler could surround himself with straw men. Perhaps this three-fold composition of the Chamber will suffice to prevent the abuses of the Palais Bourbon, and the Chamber could be given the right to overthrow the government.

To be considered carefully and discussed with state jurists.

July 23

Will the Jews subject themselves to the predetermined Constitution?

Quite simple: whoever wants to be naturalized must take an oath to support this Constitution and submit to the laws. There will be no compulsion to become naturalized.

July 24

A peculiar letter came from Güdemann: he says he cannot travel, on account of a "stomach upset."

Is it possible that I again misunderstood his "good" letter? Could his fighting spirit, the kind that satisfied me, have been due to an indigestible *Pfefferkugel?* *

By the way, he has wired me that I shall receive a letter from him tomorrow. I will wait for that.

July 24

Beer was here.

Had a long discussion with him about "Beerite." It makes possible quick construction, replaces the plaster between bricks, and can even be used for cementing glass bricks, such as are now used in America. Such houses—iron construction, glass bricks— ought to be finished and habitable in two months. "Beerite" dries in two days, yet the houses look impressive faced with this material. "Beerite" will also be used for the statues of public gardens, and soon.

The genuine, monumental things will come later.

Beer also has ideas on the paving of streets.

July 24

I should like to have wood-block paving in the cities. We shall lay out our streets differently from the way the old cities do it. We shall make them hollow to begin with and put the necessary pipes, wires, etc. into the cavity. That way we shall save ourselves the trouble of tearing them up later.

July 24

Beer will come along on the expedition to take the land. On the boat we shall dress for dinner, just as we want to have elegance on the other side as soon as possible.

* A spicy baked dish.

The purpose of this: the Jews shall not get the impression that they are moving out into the desert.

No, *this* migration will take place in the mainstream of culture. We shall remain part of civilization while we are migrating.

After all, we don't want a Boer state, but a Venice.

July 24

In the Constitution, which is to have only the small elasticity of a rubber hose the thickness of an arm, care must be taken that the aristocracy does not degenerate into tyranny and presumption. The hereditary nobility is not our kind of aristocracy. Among us any great person can become an aristocrat. (Money is a good criterion if it has been established that it was acquired honestly.)

Another thing that is to be prevented is a policy of future conquest. New Judea shall reign only by the spirit.

July 25, in the evening

Received another lukewarm letter from Güdemann. I am answering him as follows:

My Dear Friend,

We shall stick to this form of address, if you don't mind. Its advantage, apart from the pleasure and the honor, is that I can tell you my opinion more clearly with all due respect. I shall not dwell on the contradiction between your letters of the 17th and the 23rd of this month. In one letter you are "bold as William Tell." The next time you are exaggeratedly timid. That will not do.

You don't want to "flirt" with me, do you, like a woman who charms and then withdraws?

Where the Jewish cause is concerned I am not to be trifled with.

To be sure, you cannot know what I have in mind.

Why do I not tell you, then? After all, if my idea is a sensible one, that is, simple and comprehensible, I ought to be able to express it in a few sentences. I can, too, dear doctor; I simply don't want to. Because it is not just a matter of the idea itself, i.e., the logical end result which is and must be a universal idea if it is not to be regarded as the isolated thought of a madman or that of a genius, an idea centuries ahead of its time. I am probably not a madman and, alas, certainly not a genius. I am a man of my time who has both feet firmly on the ground; that is why I asked you—if you still recall—to bring a businessman with you to Caux. So it is not simply a question of the conclusion, but of the whole long chain of reasoning. It has taken me many weeks of extremely hard work to get this ethno-psychological, economic, juridical, and historical documentation down on paper. This I cannot crowd into a letter without mutilating it. After all, I want to make myself understood and not the reverse.

My local friend did not understand me. Was it my fault? Who knows? When I asked him, after he had given me his criticism, "Then what is your idea of a remedy?" he replied: "The Jews have to join the Socialist movement!" In my opinion, that would be as nonsensical as Socialism itself. He also thought that the anti-Semites would have to be killed, something that I should consider as unjust as it would be impracticable.

Do you still believe blindly that my friend is right in his attitude toward me?

He still remains my friend, just as you will remain my friend, I hope, even if if you don't understand me—just as all decent Jews are my friends.

But I will have nothing to do with the milksops, the shits, and the s.o.b.'s with or without money.

Please be assured that I greatly appreciate your truly friendly concern about my career. I can set your mind at ease. My career and my ability to provide for my family are not in danger. I think you are not judging my relationship to the *Neue Freie Presse* correctly. I can leave it whenever I please without doing myself harm. It is true that if I then looked for a position nearly as good on another paper, I would be in a bad way. But if I quit my job, I would become the head man on a newspaper, namely my own. That is the situation.

Incidentally, I have nothing of the sort in mind. I am just as amicably devoted to my publishers as they are to me, I hope. I have a deep affection especially for Bacher, although I have had few dealings with him. He is a real man!

To show you how little my plan will put me in opposition to the *N.Fr.Pr.*—its fairy-tale version, which I mentioned to you in my last letter, is to appear in the *N.Fr.Pr.* if the plan cannot be put into operation.

Does this set your mind at rest?

But it is no fairy-tale as yet, and neither you nor Meyer-Cohn can make it one. Nevertheless, I shall gladly confer with you, listen to your objections, and then see what I have to do.

You will evaluate my thoughts and I shall evaluate yours— that is the purpose of our meeting. It can take place wherever you wish—excepting Vienna and vicinity. This I specifically don't want.

Linz would be all right with me. But never have three strangers arrived there at the same time. In that capital of anti-Semitism we would attract too much attention. Wouldn't you rather designate the tourist center Salzburg as the place for our get-together? The difference in time and money is really trifling. Also, this would favor Meyer-Cohn a bit.

That is why I first thought of Zurich.

To be sure, I had another reason for wanting to meet with you two as early as the day after tomorrow. You see, the Jews of Berlin are at present doing something that doesn't please me. I had hoped to convince you and then have Meyer-Cohn take some immediate action. It is certainly tormenting not to be able to do anything about an error which one recognizes as such. But one error, one piece of stupidity, one act of negligence more or less, will not matter in the history of our people's sufferings.

You will have to be the one to extend the invitation to Meyer-Cohn to come to either Linz or Salzburg. I cannot do it. I am not acquainted with him and he may never have heard my name. You are definitely qualified to do it, and I am counting on you to act without delay. Have Bloch give you his address, under whatever pretext. Bloch must not know about our meeting any more than anyone else. This conference must take place in an atmosphere of quiet.

I shall leave here on Saturday evening, and on Monday I shall be at Villa Fuchs, Aussee, Styria.

Don't hesitate, dear doctor. At the very least, you must be curious by now about what I may have to say.

Write to Meyer-Cohn immediately. When I say that I am not acquainted with him, what I mean is that I know nothing about him, don't know what he looks like, etc. Do not consider that odd; knowing a man provides guidance for a correct epistolary style. A letter is the summoning up of a certain will, and for this I need an approximate idea of what the possessor of this will is like, otherwise I grope in the dark and write a confused letter, i.e., one that is not suited to summoning up his will.

When I was preparing my memorandum to the German Kaiser, I very attentively studied various photographs of him, read his speeches critically, thoroughly examined his actions. Have no fear: when I address the memorandum to him, from the first moment I shall so grip him that he will not throw it into the wastepaper basket.

For I am not a babbler and I despise drivellers. Literature, to me, is only a form, a hieroglyphics with large characters, which serves me as these small and ordinary letters flowing from my pen serve me—to express my ideas. When I learned the big writing, the literary kind, I did not know of what use it would be to me, just as I did not know it when I learned how to write as a child. I know it now.

Leave it to ignoramuses and blockheads, then, to distrust a writer. There is no madness in creative writing itself. The important thing is the idea which the big writing puts on paper; if it is sound and clear, the only ridiculous elements will be the doubters. And a man's doubting can even make him a tragic figure, because in delaying or frustrating the relief of his brethren he will also delay or frustrate his own.

To stand by idly and watch when a house is on fire is certainly more insane than to rush up with a modern fire engine. And that is what I want to do.

So immediately write Meyer-Cohn a beautiful letter like the one of the 17th, not of the 23rd. I hope that your indisposition has cleared up nicely by now. Should it be difficult for you at present to write Meyer-Cohn a letter setting forth the necessity for a trip to Salzburg (rather than Linz, as I have said), then send him my letters. Now as before, no one except Meyer-Cohn may read these letters, and he may read them only because I want to tell him everything, just as I have told you.

You ask whether I have childbed fever again. What faulty medical terminology! This fever one only has once, right after giving birth. I had it because I was so terribly overworked, writing down details for weeks from early morning until late at night in addition to my daily work, and then, in a state of exhaustion, putting all these details into an orderly sequence with iron-clad logical conclusions.

Then came the friend who absolutely failed to understand me.

Now all that is finished. The bleeding has been stopped. The uterus has resumed its normal position and its ordinary size. So there is no danger.

And do you know how I got over the attack of doubt? Again, by working; once again I worked hard all day, for the newspaper, as well as doing work of my own.

Farewell! In Aussee I shall soon be expecting an invitation to Salzburg (if worst comes to worst, to Linz) for the fifth, the sixth, or the seventh of August. Fabius delayed in the face of his enemies, but one doesn't play Cunctator toward one's friends.

With cordial regards,

Yours sincerely,
Th. Herzl.

July 26, in the afternoon

Just rode past Hirsch in the street. I am writing him, even though reluctantly. But it may be useful.

Dear Sir:

We just rode past each other in the street. From this I draw the brilliant conclusion that you are in town. I myself am leaving for Austria tomorrow evening. It may be some time before we shall be in the same place again. Would you like to become acquainted with my perfected plan? It goes without saying: without interrupting me again.

On the 6th of August I shall meet in Salzburg with two stalwart Jews, a Viennese and a Berliner. I want to submit to them my memorandum to the *roshe* before I send it off. I shall consult with these older people to see whether some things that could be harmful to the Jews should not be deleted.

If you want to be in on this, write me a line and I shall drop in on you for an hour or so before I leave.

If you don't, don't.

Respectfully yours,
Herzl.

July 27

Hirsch did not reply.

I am writing him the following farewell letter which I may mail in Basel tomorrow:

Dear Sir:

It is part of the Jewish misfortune that you refused to be enlightened.

I saw in you a useful tool for the important cause, *voilà pourquoi j'ai insisté outre mes habitudes* [this is why I insisted beyond my wont].

The legend in circulation about you is obviously false. You engage in the Jewish cause as a sport. Just as you make horses race, you make Jews migrate. And this is what I protest against most sharply. A Jew is not a plaything.

No, no, you are not interested in the cause. *Elle est bien bonne, et j'y ai cru un instant* [It is very nice and I believed it for a minute].

For that reason it was an excellent thing that I wrote you once more from Paris and that you did not honor me with a reply. Now any error is out of the question. Some jackass must have told you that I am only a pleasant dreamer, and you believed it. When men talk about serious business they do not use any polite phrases. Let this serve as an explanation if I have shocked you by the violent way I have expressed myself.

And so I beg to remain

Very respectfully yours,
Dr. Herzl.

July 27

And today I am leaving Paris!
One book of my life is ending.
A new one is beginning.
Of what kind?

July 29

On the way I changed my mind and did not mail the letter to Hirsch. Perhaps the man can still be included in the combination at some later date. I must subordinate my indignation and my self-love to the cause. Besides, they forwarded me a letter from him in which he makes excuses on account of his own departure. He says he would like to continue the discussion about it in late autumn. In late autumn! Finished!

July 29

Zell am See.
The curse must be taken off money.

July 29

Get the soil tilled by renting a farm for half the produce and giving the equipment on credit; after a short period (possibly three years) this rental will become ownership. The debt for the machinery will be liquidated. Later, we shall have a tax on the land. Election of the ruler (for life).

Immediately after the ruler dies (or is rendered incapable by insanity or incompetence), within twenty-four hours each community will choose an elector. These electors must meet at the place of election within the time it takes to reach the capital from the remotest point in the country. The election is to take place in a sort of Versailles, so as to make it independent of public pressure.

The meetings of the legislature will be presided over by the President of the Chamber who will direct all preparations (military, etc.).

The electors will not be deputies, but their votes will count the same as the deputies' in the election of the ruler. Continue balloting around the clock, narrowing it down until one man has a two-thirds majority.

During the interregnum the Prime Minister will be responsible to the President of the Chamber.

Soldiers will be eligible for election only after they have been inactive for at least one year.

July 29

Zell am See.

In a bath-house. The walls full of anti-Semitic inscriptions. Many answered or crossed out by upset Jewish boys.

One reads as follows:

> *O Gott, schick doch den Moses wieder,*
> *Auf dass er seine Stammesbrüder*
> *Wegführe ins gelobte Land.*
> *Ist dann die ganze Judensippe*
> *Erst drinnen in des Meeres Mitte,*
> *Dann, Herr, o mach die Klappe zu*
> *Und alle Christen haben Ruh.*

[O God, won't you send Moses again to lead the members of his tribe away into the Promised Land. Then, when the whole Jewish clan is right in the middle of the sea, O close the lid, Lord, and all Christians will have peace.]

Aussee.

In the last few days a frequent exchange of telegrams with Güdemann.

Meyer-Cohn has been in Vienna. Our rendezvous was supposed to take place at Salzburg within the next few days. Güdemann shows a lot of zeal and willingness. I think I have the right helper in him.

Unfortunately he has not been able to get Meyer-Cohn for our meeting, because he has to go to Posen "on account of a distribution of shares."

I hope that is not the Argentinian one!

I am answering Güdemann as follows:

Dear Friend,

I wouldn't have a sound conception of the stress and strain of real life if I expected that everything will and could go the way I want it to right away.

The only thing that can discourage me is the stupidity, cowardice, and meanness of my fellow Jews. And I want to help even the intellectually and morally deficient ones.

But now, unless my eyes deceive me, I have already found a stalwart ally, although you don't even know what I want. Just have confidence in me, my dear, honored friend! You will see soon enough to what a noble and exalted cause I am summoning you.

When I received your wire yesterday, saying that Meyer-Cohn is not coming and therefore you do not want to come either, I was, to be sure, a bit vexed, although not too much so. My annoyance was directed at the regrettable fact that a helper on whom I had already counted was dropping out.

Then I went out. On the street I overheard people talking about a small, everyday incident: there had just been a scene on the Promenade in which someone had yelled "Dirty Jew." Such a scene apparently occurs in a thousand places in the world every day. You know this as well as I do.

And you can imagine with what scornful bitterness I note this sort of thing, because my closely guarded idea contains the remedy. Nevertheless, this idea will not be got out of me until the right moment which I am awaiting with all necessary coolness and firmness.

However, your letter which arrived today again holds out to me the prospect that we need not give up Meyer-Cohn. Now I make you a new proposal which I ask you to pass on to M.-C. I owe it to my self-respect not to write him before he has written me. For, after all, my last letters to you were indirectly addressed to him too.

You as well as M.-C. are completely on the wrong track if you think that I want to direct a request for protection to the German Kaiser. All misconceptions of this kind are due to the fact that you would like to guess the things that I am minded to tell only orally and with a comprehensive explanation.

Patience! Be patient, but do not tarry, honored friend.

Since M.-C. is ready to counsel with us, but faces obstacles, we must meet him half-way. My suggestion is that we make another rendezvous with him. It could be in Zurich, but need not be. In Munich, Frankfort, as far as I am concerned, any place and any time—but certainly within the next two weeks. You already know what I intend to initiate here in Aussee if I cannot get any Jewish helpers. It will not be my fault if people let me proceed by myself and make mistakes which could have been prevented by consultation. The totality of my plan is right—that is my profound conviction.

I long ago gave up thinking of Salo.

Please send me M.-C.'s article in the *Wochenschrift*. It will be useful for me to try to recognize the make-up of his mind from it.

Expecting to hear from you soon and with cordial regards,

Yours sincerely,
Th. H.

August 4

Spoke with a Viennese lawyer.

He said: "If you don't attend any election rallies you don't notice anything."

The people are especially enraged against the Liberals, he said. They cheer Lueger and Friebeis (the latter is the district councillor who is now replacing the suspended municipal councillor).

I explained to the attorney that if this temporary suspension of the Constitution can be repeated once or twice more without a fight, it will lead to the complete scrapping of the Constitution, with a subsequent change, or, rather, the formation of a new Constitution from which the Jews will be left out.

Then I talked to two physicians from Pest who found it wonderful the way Hungary treated its Jews.

I explained to them the enormous mistake which the Jews of Hungary make by acquiring real estate. They already own more than half the immovable property. In the long run the people cannot possibly put up with such a conquest by the *makk-hetes zsidó* [low class Jew]. Only through a terrorizing force of arms can an identifiable minority, which is alien to the people and not famous historically like the old aristocracy, retain possession of all privileges.

It is common knowledge that only recently the Jews have been the opposite of an honored aristocracy.

The liberal government, which is apparently based on election promises and coalitions, can be swept away by a *coup de main,* and then overnight Hungary will have anti-Semitism in its most virulent form.

August 4

Kohn the cabinet-maker in Aussee!

Last year I was glad when I saw the Jewish wood-carver in the house across the street. I regarded that as the "solution."

This year I have returned. Kohn has enlarged his house, added a wooden veranda, has summer tenants, no longer works himself. In five years he will be the richest man in town and hated for his wealth.

This is how hatred is produced by our intelligence.

August 5

Received a letter lightly tinged with irony from Güdemann. I am answering him:

Dear Friend:

You are, of course, free to regard me as an operetta general. To me your remark proves only that I was right in the first place to consider correspondence as inappropriate. Today, by the way, I am following your advice and writing M.-C. directly, asking him whether he is willing to meet with me in Munich or somewhere else. When the two of us have arranged a get-together, I shall ask you by wire whether you want to participate in it. If you then exclude yourself, I shall regret it, and possibly so will you, later.

M.-C.'s article is a good one. But what use is all the philosophizing? In this matter the watchword is—*primum vivere* [first live]! *deinde* [then], if it is absolutely necessary, *philosophari* [philosophize] is all right with me too.

With kindest regards,

Yours sincerely,
Th. H.

Letter to Doctor Heinrich Meyer-Cohn of August 5:

Dear Sir:

Dr. Güdemann has written me about you and told you about me. I believe you are also acquainted with the letters that I have written him. Therefore I can be brief. Would you like to meet with me somewhere within the next two weeks? I leave it to you to determine the place. It would mean a great deal to me to have Dr. Güdemann participate in our discussion. As I can tell from his letters, it is hard to get him to take a long trip. But he could perhaps be induced to go to Munich. For the present I must ask you to believe that I have really serious things to say. From your willingness to make the sacrifice of a small trip for the Jewish cause I shall recognize that you are the right man in whom to confide my thoughts and plans *avant la lettre* [before writing them down].

What my intentions are I shall tell you only in person, or not at all. Idle chatter in letters is no more in my line than the spoken kind. It would be useless to ask me to give you a hint in advance. I shall only clear up your mistaken notion which Güdemann pointed out to me: I am not considering a request for protection. I am seeking and finding the solution within ourselves. For this I need suitable Jews. If you are one, fine! If you aren't, you aren't!

I have had your article in the *Wochenschrift* sent to me. May I, now that I am addressing you directly, be permitted a judgement? Your article is excellent and sensible—but philosophizing won't lure a pig out of the clover. Fix the time and place, then; take into consideration the fact that we need Güdemann. As soon as I hear from you, I shall communicate with Güdemann by telegram and try to get him there.

With respectful greetings,

Yours sincerely,
Dr. Th. H.

August 6

I am just reading Bloch's *Wochenschrift.*

He is engaging in a theological tussle with the anti-Semites, medieval style, like that rabbi with the Capuchin monk.

". . . that both of them stink!" *

Of course, an out-and-out Jewish paper is needed.

But it would have to be a modern one.

Bloch could be used for Galicia, at any rate. He is acquainted with the local atmosphere and would know how to talk to the people.

* Translator's Note: This is the last line in Heinrich Heine's poem "Disputation."

The miscellaneous news column in his paper is ghastly: There are persecutions like that every week, every day!

August 6

Spoke with old Simon, the president of the Vienna Jewish Community. My words visibly inspired him. Of course I told him only the negative things, and that the rich Jews must be destroyed if they lead lives of avarice, epicureanism, and vanity, while the poor are being persecuted.

August 7

Received a letter from Meyer-Cohn. The letter is a good one. I am wiring him:

Thanks for letter. I wrote you the day before yesterday. Please do your utmost to arrange a meeting soon, anywhere.

Let us communicate about this by telegram.

Regards,
Herzl.

August 10

Yesterday received a letter from Güdemann in which he excuses himself for the ironic tone of his next-to-last letter.

No word from Meyer-Cohn.

I am writing him as follows:

Dear Sir:

I was very pleased with your letter which arrived on August 7. But unfortunately I did not receive the notification which I asked you to send me by telegram. Permit me therefore to tell you one final time what it is all about.

To the extent that I can give information in writing I have already given it to you directly and through Dr. Güdemann indirectly. I should like to submit my plan to Jews of integrity; that means that I am ready to listen to sensible advice concerning the expansion or limitation of my plans. I shall probably not find two men like you and Güdemann so easily. I cannot spend much time looking, either. Certain qualities of character and intellect must be there, and these I may presuppose in you two. But it is not enough that you wish to meet with me; it must be soon, too. It is true, nothing in the Jewish cause, which has been dragged out for so many centuries, would seem to justify my haste, and that might even give you pause. But I have practical reasons for hurrying. Didn't Dr. Güdemann tell you that here in Aussee I want to try to become acquainted with Imperial Chancellor Hohenlohe through Chlumecky, the President of the Austrian Chamber of Deputies, and thus gain access to the Kaiser? And should I find this impossible, I will immediately start on the literary elaboration of my plan.

Upon Güdemann's provisional advice I first wanted, and still want, to confide in you two in all modesty. After all, you have as much at stake in the matter as I, and you are my natural friends and advisors. You must also consider that I would not dare idly to put you to the trouble of a trip. This means that I have serious and important things to say. Do not let me go on alone. I should do so reluctantly, but I should do it finally. Consider that I shall need some time to get the matter rolling with and through Chlumecky, and that I must put the remaining twenty days of my stay in Aussee to the best possible use.

Oblige me by telegraphing me your reply soon. Pick a time and a place for our meeting, with regard for Dr. Güdemann who is not so mobile. It would be downright painful to me if I were disappointed in my expectation of being able to go hand in hand with you.

With respectful greetings,

Yours very sincerely,
Dr. Th. H.

August 10

Talked with Dr. F. of Berlin. He is for baptism. He wants to make the sacrifice for the sake of his son. Tsk, tsk. I explained to him that there are other low-down ways in which one can make it easier for one's son to get ahead.

He will apparently be baptized as soon as his rich father-in-law is dead. The only thing he forgets is that if five thousand like him become baptized, the watchword will simply be changed to "Dirty Converts"!

August 13

In the Kurpark I talked again with old Simon and two other elderly Jews. I outlined all my premises for them, seemingly without premeditation, but naturally not my conclusion. Again I was able to notice that I have the power to stir people. These are only old men, slow-moving and made apathetic by their wealth. And yet I can feel their souls emitting sparks when I strike on them.

The young men, to whom I want to give a whole future, I shall of course carry by storm.

In the afternoon Meyer-Cohn's letter arrived.

He wants to be in Munich on the 17th of this month. I am wiring Güdemann. The difficulty: the 17th is a Saturday. The Rabbi will not be able to come, or can plead official duties if he does not feel like it. However, if he says no, I shall summon him with the greatest urgency—or drop him for good.

August 14

My good Mom likes to tell how Albert Spitzer passed away. One day his housekeeper asked him after dinner, "What shall we cook for tomorrow?"

He replied vigorously, "Rump steak!"

That was his last word. He fell over and died.

In her sovereign way, my Mom derives from this the meaning of a life that ends with a cry of "Rump steak!"

I shall make use of this anecdote in Munich.

August 14

I see only one difficulty in it all: how to get the landlubbers out to sea.

Program for Munich: First I shall tell them the history of my plan, then call on them to differentiate any details which do not appeal to them from the scheme as a whole. I shall advise them in advance of my conclusion and shall explain to them the mistake I made with Hirsch. In presenting the matter to him I proceeded from the State—i.e., I only started, and stopped in time, because I noticed that he was not following me. To these men I shall present it as a business transaction—they must not misunderstand me in the other direction and take me for an "entrepreneur."

Tell them, too, how I want to use a different approach in presenting this same plan to the German Kaiser, stressing the "mounting of the self-[defense?]." *

August 14

Güdemann has wired me his acceptance. He will leave for Munich on Friday morning. He would like me to arrive there at the same time as he, i.e., Friday evening. But I don't want to do this. Meyer-Cohn isn't arriving until Saturday and won't be available for a discussion before Saturday afternoon. I want to avoid talking to Güdemann before that, and so I shall not arrive in Munich until Saturday forenoon. They ought to be together first, wait for me; and Güdemann especially should no longer be tired from the trip, but rested and alert.

The hard part of my presentation will be to lead them over gradually from their accustomed conceptions to mine without their having the feeling that they are losing touch with reality.

Munich, August 18

Actually, I might as well give up keeping this record of daily action, for there is no action.

* Translator's Note: The phrase is incomplete in the original.

I arrived here yesterday morning. In the hotel lobby I ran
into Güdemann who looked fresh and cheerful with his gray
beard and ruddy cheeks.

We went to see Meyer-Cohn who was washing up. From the
very first moment I knew that he was not the right man. A little
Berlin Jew by his outward appearance, and with a spirit to
match. While he finished his toilet, he spun us a long yarn about
"parliamentary" doings in the Berlin Jewish community. Trivi-
alities; but his unassuming manner of presentation makes up
for this.

And just as I found him during that first quarter-hour and described him to Güdemann the moment we left the room, so
M.-C. proved himself to be throughout the day. He has few
convictions, and he clings to them tenaciously, but expresses
them with disarming modesty. He is a mediocre intellect, does
not think that anyone could understand anything better than he
does; however, he believes everyone else, including myself, to be
as capable as he is.

Afterwards, I went to the synagogue, where I was supposed to
meet Güdemann. The services were over when I arrived. Güdemann showed me the interior of the beautiful synagogue. The
shames [beadle] or *shabbes goy,* an elderly man in blue military
tunic, tall and of shrivelling corpulence, bore a great resem-
blance to Bismarck. It was a curious touch to have a Bismarck
figure walking behind us with the keys, while the rabbi was
showing me through the temple. The *goy* [gentile] did not know
that he looked like Bismarck; the rabbi had no idea that he was
doing something symbolic in showing me the beauty of a temple.
I alone was aware of these and other things.

I said nothing that morning concerning the project itself. For
the most part I let Güdemann do the talking; he did not dream
that he would call me "Moses" before the day was over.

We met for luncheon in the Jewish Jochsberger's Restaurant
where I felt very much at home. The proprietor knew Güdemann and set us up in a separate room. Later on he discovered,
with Jewish acumen, that we were conferring about the Jewish

cause, and saw to it that we remained undisturbed. This is the sort of human material we possess in our people. They divine what one would have to hammer into other people's heads. They carry it out with intelligence and devotion.

At table the subject came up quite naturally. Güdemann had already won his way to my heart during the forenoon. More and more I found in him a fine, open-minded, splendid human being. Naturally, our conversation had a theological and philosophical flavor. I incidentally mentioned my views on the Deity. I want to bring up my children with a belief in what might be called the historical God. To me, "God" is a beautiful, dear old word which I want to retain. It is a wonderful abbreviation for conceptions that might be beyond the grasp of a childlike or limited intellect. By "God" I understand the Will to Good! The omnipresent, infinite, omnipotent, eternal Will to Good, which does not immediately prevail everywhere but is always victorious in the end. For which Evil, too, is but a means. How and why, for example, does the Will to Good permit epidemics to exist? Because epidemics cause musty old cities to be torn down and new, bright, healthful cities to come into being, with inhabitants who draw a freer breath.

Thus, anti-Semitism, too, probably contains the divine Will to Good, because it forces us to close ranks, unites us through pressure, and through our unity will make us free.

My conception of God is, after all, Spinozistic and also resembles the natural philosophy of the Monists. But I think of Spinoza's "substance" as something inert, so to speak, and that incomprehensible universal ether of the Monists seems too intangible and too vague to me. But I can conceive of an omnipresent will, for I see it at work in the physical world. I see it as I can see the functioning of a muscle. The world is the body and God is the functioning of it. The ultimate purpose I do not and need not know; for me it is enough that it is something higher than our present condition. This I can again express with old words, and I gladly do so. *Eritis sicut dei, scientes bonum et malum* [Ye shall be as gods, knowing good and evil].

In the course of our table-talk something unexpected happened: Meyer-Cohn revealed himself as an adherent of the idea of Zion. This pleased me very much.

After lunch I brought the manuscript of my Address to the Rothschilds from the hotel and started reading it to them in the empty dining room at Jochsberger's. Unfortunately Meyer-Cohn had made a business appointment for four o'clock so I knew from the outset that I would not be able to finish. The session was not to be resumed until evening. In other respects, too, I was reading under unfavorable conditions.

Meyer-Cohn carped in "parliamentary" fashion at every little detail that bothered him. As a result, I lost my temper for a moment while rebutting these "interpellations."

In spite of this, the effect was considerable. I saw it in Güdemann's shining eyes.

I had to break off at page thirteen because of M.-C.'s engagement. However, Güdemann, the "anti-Zionist," was already won over.

He said: "If you are right, all my views up to now fall to pieces.

"But yet I find myself wishing that you are right. Hitherto I have believed that we are not a nation, that is, more than a nation. I thought that we have the historic mission to be exponents of universalism among the nations and therefore are more than a people identified with a specific area."

I answered: "There is nothing to prevent us from being and remaining the exponents of one humanity on our own home soil as well. To achieve this purpose, we need not actually continue to reside among the nations who hate and despise us. If we wanted to realize this universalist idea of a humanity without boundaries under our present circumstances, we would have to combat the idea of patriotism. However, as far as we can foresee, this idea will prove stronger than we are."

At six o'clock we met again, in my little hotel room. Because there were only two chairs, I sat on my bed and continued my reading. Meyer-Cohn went on carping at the ideas that he considered Utopian. Güdemann was once more carried away. Even then I did not get to the end, but by half past eight the gist of the idea had been unfolded. We were about to leave for supper when Güdemann said: "You remind me of Moses."

I laughingly rejected the thought, and I was completely sincere about it. Now as before I consider the whole thing to be a simple idea, a skillful and rational combination which, to be sure, operates with large masses. Purely as an idea, my plan is not a great thing. "Two times two is four" is, in abstract thought, as great as "two times two trillions is four trillions."

Güdemann further said: "I am quite dazed. I feel like someone who has been asked to come and hear some news, and when he arrives, there is placed before him not a piece of information, but two beautiful big horses."

This simile pleased me greatly, for it made me realize the plastic force of my idea.

Back at Jochsberger's I read the concluding section. The re-installation of a nobility displeased both of them. On the other hand, they saw poetic beauty in the yellow ribbon as a mark of Jewish honor. Accordingly, I shall drop the idea of a nobility.

Güdemann also objected to the final apostrophe, and, naturally, so did Meyer-Cohn.

We came to the conclusion that the Address must not reach the Rothschilds, who are mean, despicable egotists. The idea must be carried straight to the people, and in the form of a novel.

Perhaps, so we thought, the stimulus will take effect and lead to the creation of a great movement.

Of course, I am of the opinion that I would spoil the plan by making it public, but I have to comply. I can't carry it out all by myself. I must believe Güdemann and M.-Cohn when they tell me that the "big Jews" will have nothing to do with it.

I took Güdemann to the station. At parting he said with sober enthusiasm: "Remain as you are! Perhaps you are the one called of God."

We kissed each other good-bye. There was a strange gleam in his beautiful eyes when, from the compartment window, he once more took my hand and gave it a firm squeeze.

August 19, Munich

Novel, Chapter I.

On Christmas Day, 1899, Moritz Frühlingsfeld, the hero, receives a letter from Berlin from Heinrich.

He makes himself comfortable and reads it.

It is the farewell letter written by the suicide.

A profound shock.

Chapter II.

The unwed girl. The ruined stock-trader's family with the father who failed to "provide a husband" for his daughter and tries to make it up to her by a thousand little kindnesses.

This is where Moritz goes to overcome the first shock. He guesses that the forgotten girl loved Heinrich. She will later die, well-bred and silent.

Chapter III.

Departure on the trip to forget; on the advice of his friends (or parents) Moritz must travel in order to "get rid" of the dead man.

He has taken other trips before, but never one like this. He used to have eyes for beautiful women, adventures, and scenery. Now he sees everything with new eyes, through Heinrich's ghost, as it were.

We are in no hurry to die!

This is how the idea comes into being!

August 21

Letter to Meyer-Cohn:

Dear Sir:

I deeply regret not having seen you again before your departure. So I am putting in writing the final conclusion from our meeting, which may not have been in vain. We are obviously antitheses. But I believe that we can pay each other no higher tribute than by admitting this frankly and becoming friends in spite of it. My idea was yours as well. I hope that you will not give it up just because I have demonstrated my way to realize it. That would be an odd outcome.

I believe that we must first and foremost be Jews; only later, "over there," will it be all right for us to split up into aristocrats and democrats. In the first twenty years of our movement, such divisions must be dormant. Later they will probably be useful, representing the free play of forces. In this there will also appear the Will to Good, by which, as you know, I mean "God." The presumption of the aristocrats and the despondency of the democrats can cancel each other out, though amidst struggles. But, above all, we must stick together.

I am setting a good example right away by modestly subordinating my idea to your counsel and that of our honored friend Güdemann.

Should you feel impelled to reply to these lines, which may also be "Utopian," please don't do so before the 22nd of the month. On that date I shall again be at Villa Fuchs, Aussee.

Greetings in friendship from

Yours sincerely,
Dr. Herzl.

Letter to Güdemann:

Dear Friend:

Our great cause, which we discussed in Munich, naturally continues to work in my mind, as it probably does in yours, and perhaps even in that of our third colleague M.-C. To many of the objections I have now found the answers which did not immediately occur to me.

Above all, I can now say why it is no Utopia.

M.-C.'s definition of a Utopia was quite wrong. The hallmark of a Utopia is not the details of the future presented as actualities. Every minister of finance uses estimates for the future in working out his budget, and he uses not only those which he constructs from the average of previous years or from data derived from other times and other countries, but also figures for which there is no precedent, as, for example, when a new tax is introduced. Only someone who has never seen a budget does not know this. But will anyone call a draft of a fiscal law Utopian, even if he knows that it will never be possible to stick to the estimate very closely?

The only valid thing about M.-C.'s objections would be, at most, that I gave too much *graphic* detail. And yet I had omitted from the version which I read to you countless features contained in my draft for it. I explained this in the Address itself by saying repeatedly, "You would otherwise take my plan for a Utopia."

What, then, differentiates a plan from a Utopia? I shall now tell you in precise language: the vitality which is inherent in a plan and not in a Utopia, a vitality which need not be recognizable to everyone and yet may be there.

There have been plenty of Utopias before and after Thomas More, but no rational person ever thought of putting them into practice. They are entertaining, but not stirring.

On the other hand, look at the plan called "The Unification of Germany." Even in St. Paul's Church it seemed only a dream. And yet, from the inscrutable depths of the national psyche there came in response to it an impulse as mysterious and undeniable as life itself.

And out of what was this unification created? Out of ribbons, flags, songs, speeches, and, finally, singular struggles. Do not underestimate Bismarck! He saw that the people and the princes could not be induced to make even small sacrifices for the cause all those songs and orations were about. So he exacted *great* sacrifices from them, forced them to wage wars. And those princes, who could never have been assembled in any German city to elect an emperor, them he led to a small provincial town, where there was a half-forgotten royal castle. And there they did his bidding. A nation drowsy in peacetime jubilantly hailed unification in wartime.

There is no need to attempt a rational explanation for this. It is a fact! So, too, I cannot explain life and its force; I can only state that it exists.

As I noticed in Munich, you think in images. This fact, in addition to others, only endears you to me further. You used an expression in Munich which touched and delighted me. You said,

"I feel like someone who has been called to be given some news, and when he arrives, there is placed before him a pair of beautiful horses."

Why didn't you say, "He is shown a piece of machinery"?

Because you had the impression of something alive!

And that's what it is. In my plan there is life. I shall prove it to you by referring to Hertzka's *Freeland*. I had known this book only from hearsay as a Utopia. After your departure I immediately looked for it in a bookstore. I had forgotten to ask you whether it was also about Jews. And I was worried for that reason. Not for my own sake, as a writer who is afraid of having come too late. (*Peream ego* [Let my ego perish]!) No—rather because then I should have to fear being unable to accomplish anything either, because the plan would already have had currency in the world without success. *Freeland* was not obtainable in Munich, but a more recent publication of Hertzka was: *A Journey to Freeland* (*Eine Reise nach Freiland*, Reclam's Universal Library).

This book gave me sufficient information, too. It is quite an ingenious fantasy, as remote from life as the equatorial mountain on which "Freeland" is located.

You will understand the following comparison:

Freeland is a complicated piece of machinery with many cogs and wheels; but I find in it no proof that it can be set in motion.

As against this, my plan calls for the utilization of a driving force that actually exists.

What is this force? The distress of the Jews!

Who dares deny that this force exists?

Another known quantity is the steam power which is generated by boiling water in a tea-kettle and then lifts the kettle lid. Such a tea-kettle phenomenon are the Zion experiments and a hundred other organized efforts to "combat anti-Semitism."

But I say that this force is strong enough to run a great machine and transport human beings. The machine may have whatever form one pleases.

I am right—although I may not prevail.

But our force grows with the pressure that is exerted upon us. I believe there are already enough sensible people to understand this simple truth.

In Munich I spent the day after your departure with Spitzer, the confidential clerk of the Paris Rothschild. For years I have been asking him, "When are the Rothschilds going to liquidate?"

He had always laughed at this. This time he asked me, "Who told you that this is being planned? Because it is a fact! Only the date is still uncertain."

(You will not breathe a word about this news, if only for our own sake.)

I answered Spitzer: "I know everything that is a logical conclusion from known premises." Naturally, that was all I told him.

Now you will recognize what this means to my plan!

Mere liquidation would be idiotic suicide. I want to utilize the self-destruction of this enormous credit figure for our historic purpose. I want to stay his hand, saying, "Stop! Use your suicide for a world-historic task! And in so doing, get rich again as you never have been before!"

This is complicated in execution, but quite simple in thought.

You said, "It was *narrishkayt* [foolishness] to address that vague letter to Albert Rothschild."

Yes, but how was I to know that he is such a *parakh* [bastard].

Bigger men than this show-off associated with me in Paris. When I visited the Prime Minister or Foreign Minister, he then left his calling card at my place, and things of that sort. When I wrote to the former President of the Republic, Casimir-Périer, he gave me an immediate and courteous reply.

Therefore, the fact that this Jew-boy is vilely arrogant does not prove folly on my part.

For the rest, our agreement still stands. I shall take no further steps without first consulting with you. As a starter I shall discuss with you the manner in which I am to present the matter to Bacher.

After thorough deliberation, I find that Bacher is the necessary man now.

I shall ask him to give me an entire Sunday for the discussion of a highly important matter, and explain everything to him. Then let him decide whether it calls for action or for novel-writing.

If I persuade him to act, he will assemble for us a group of men, himself included, who have enough authority and power to put the plan into effect.

If he thinks it's a novel, it is going to be one.

Of course, for him as well as for everyone to whom I pose the question it is a rather uncomfortably great responsibility.

But to participate in this historic project would be a tremendous honor for anyone. And without risk there is no honor.

You can see the power of my idea from the simple fact that there is no evading it once I have expressed it. By saying Yes or No a man commits himself most heavily.

Do I need to tell you how dear you have become to me in Munich?

You have noticed it, felt it.

With cordial regards,

Yours sincerely,
Herzl.

September 20,
Vienna

Since my last entry a great number of little things have happened which, with a peculiar aversion for writing, I allowed to go by unrecorded. I now intend to add them in a workmanlike fashion, although without the freshness of the actual moment, a freshness I had meant to preserve for a later remembrance when I opened this book.

From Aussee I went to Vienna at the beginning of September. In the course of my very first talk with Bacher, which took place on the day of my arrival, I realized that he would be completely unreceptive to my ideas—in fact, might fight them tooth and nail. Thereupon I immediately gave our conversation a different turn and continued it on a theoretical plane.

Bacher considers the anti-Semitic movement ephemeral, though "disagreeable."

When I called his attention to the fact that all our young intellectuals are being turned into proletarians, he admitted that it was a "calamity," but said that this proletariat would have to struggle through or go under like any other proletariat.

In a somewhat bad mood, I then went to lunch with two of my colleagues, Oppenheim and Dr. Ehrlich. Naturally, the Jewish Question was again our topic of conversation. They grasped my general conception better than Bacher who, as they said, associated mostly with Gentiles—through his wife and her relatives. They also shared my concern about the immediate future.

Afterwards I drove out to Baden where I a number of times met with Güdemann.

He had grown a bit lukewarm since Munich, but I put his enthusiasm back on its feet.

At Güdemann's I once nailed an elderly rabbi named Fleissig against the wall with my arguments. That old gentleman wears his trousers tucked in his boots and a long frock-coat which is a shame-faced caftan; and his thinking, which is narrow in a shrewd way, is equally antiquated. This sort of Jew performs, inside the cage of his world outlook, the thousand-leagued journeys of a squirrel on its wheel.

His sons are well-known chess players. And thus we have countless heads full of shrewdness which is hidebound and expended to no purpose.

I agreed with Güdemann to present the matter to Dr. Ehrlich as a journalist specializing in financial affairs.

One Sunday I went to Vöslau to see Ehrlich, and after I had sworn him to secrecy, I brought him here.

For two hours before and two hours after dinner we sat in a little summer house on which the hot sun beat down, and I read to him the "Address to the Family Council."

The result: He was gripped, shaken, did not consider me crazy at all, and actually had no objections from the point of view of finance and economics. The objections he did make only showed me that he took my outline completely seriously. For example, he said he was against the stock exchange monopoly.

In the end he gave me the positive answer which I had desired and in just the way I had foreseen it.

I asked him to answer yes or no to the question whether Bacher and Benedikt, one or both, might be won over for the cause.

Ehrlich thought not.

Who else in Vienna might be interested in it? Ehrlich didn't know of any outstanding and prominent Jew.

He thinks that the project could cause great danger for the Jews, that is, emigration could give rise to persecution.

But this very apprehension on the part of Ehrlich shows me how right I am in the major points. For, if I can manage to make the problem an acute one, this is the only effective instrument of power at my disposal, and it is a terrifying one. That is why, for the time being, I must not make it into a piece of writing, but treat it as action.

Ehrlich finally asked me to stop, saying that the discussion had been too much of a strain on him.

He said he was my man and was ready to go along with kith and kin.

*   *   *

This is what I told Güdemann the following day. To me Ehrlich's judgment was gratifying and important even though he had thought the immediate realization of my plan through Bacher and Benedikt quite improbable.

Meanwhile, Güdemann had been visited by a Paris member of the *Alliance Israélite*. About this man, Leven by name, Güdemann told me wonderful things; what a concerned and also devoted Jew he was. He was just the man to whom my project ought to be presented; he could then work in Paris for its advancement.

Unfortunately Leven had left town after participating in a session of the Viennese *Alliance Israélite* (which has nothing to do with the one in Paris).

I sent him a telegram in Güdemann's name: "One of my

friends wishes to speak to you on an urgent matter and is ready to follow you to Salzburg."

On the next day came an official wire saying that the addressee could not be located in Salzburg.

We had already forgotten the Leven incident when a week ago Güdemann received a reply from Leven to say that he was expecting Güdemann's friend in Salzburg or Munich.

Güdemann came to see me to the Herzogshof Hotel in a state of great excitement and said that his wife who knew about the matter and was enthusiastic about it was equally excited. She took it as a good omen that today, exactly four weeks after Güdeman's departure, I was going to Munich again and was again stopping at the Hotel Vier Jahreszeiten.

Actually, I was only going as far as Salzburg.

I immediately recognized Leven's exact type: a temperament slow to set in motion, but a well-meaning person; a hater of novelties and a man hardly capable of changing his views or learning afresh. Here my experience with Hirsch repeats itself. Those who have already made experiments with the Jews, Zion and the like, are hard to turn in a new direction.

Leven completely fails to understand the politico-economic aspects of my plan.

His notions of political economy are still quite rudimentary.

He has no idea of how the Jews who emigrated would make a living. He thinks that they are at present living at the expense of the "host nations"—which is a considerable piece of nonsense, easy to reduce *ad absurdum*. After all, economic life is not just a matter of some things that circulate; rather, new goods are produced. I maintain that we produce more than our "hosts," and would produce infinitely more if we were permitted to get rich.

Nevertheless, the talk with Leven was not useless either. He named to me Grand Rabbi Zadoc Kahn of Paris as the next man to turn to.

Zadoc, he said, was an ardent Zionist and shared many of my ideas, which were by no means original ones.

This I liked best of the things Leven said, and I told him:

"But I don't want to be an innovator. The larger the number of people who share my universal idea, the better I shall like it."

Leven thought that especially in Russia I would find many adherents. In Odessa, for example, there had lived a man named Pinsker who had fought for the same cause, namely, the regaining of a Jewish national home. Unfortunately, Pinsker was already dead. His writings are said to be worthwhile. Shall read them as soon as I have time.

Another Jew in England, Colonel Goldsmith, was also an enthusiastic Zionist and had wanted to charter ships for the reconquest of Palestine.

I will keep the Colonel in mind. All this is a confirmation of my thinking. We have the most wonderful human material that can be imagined.

Leven did not listen to a reading of the "Address to the Family Council" in its entirety. When he showed signs of impatience, I stopped reading and presented the matter to him in the form of answers to his objections.

Thus many a detail probably went by the board, but I think I did familiarize him with the main features. Of course, he has absolutely no understanding of the economic part, and in it lies the core of the whole matter.

Still, I believe that I have won him over, too, to the extent that such a refractory personality can be won over to a cause that calls for enthusiasm.

I then traveled back.

* * *

In Vienna, the City Council elections took place on the day before Erev Rosh Hashanah. All the mandates were won by the anti-Semites. The mood among the Jews is one of despair. The Christians have been badly stirred up.

The movement is not really a noisy one. For me, who am used to the clamor of popular agitation in Paris, things are even much too quiet. I find this calm more sinister. Yet one sees looks of hatred everywhere, even if one does not seek them in people's eyes with the watchful fear of a man suffering from a persecution mania.

On election day I was outside the polls in the Leopoldstadt, taking a brief look at some of the hatred and the anger at close range.

Toward evening I went to the Landstrasse district. In front of the polling place a silent, tense crowd. Suddenly Dr. Lueger came out to the square. Enthusiastic cheers; women waved white kerchiefs from the windows. The police held the crowd back. A man next to me said with tender warmth but in a quiet tone of voice: "That is our *Führer* [leader]!"

Actually, these words showed me more than all the declamation and abuse how deeply anti-Semitism is rooted in the hearts of these people.

September 20,
Vienna

Dr. Glogau, Director of the Press Bureau, has just been to see me and has offered me the editorship of a new daily.

"Under certain circumstances I may be willing to accept," I told him.

October 15, Vienna

Various steps forward and backward.

Spoke to Güdemann a few times. I keep finding his ardor cooled and get him steamed up again each time. He cannot be induced to make any effort, being one of the many who will go along when everybody goes. No courage to lead the way.

The negotiations about the newspaper continue. I can accept the editorship only if my independence is assured.

Spoke to Professor Singer who gave me the impression even on his first visit at Baden that he intends to start a daily.

I definitely need a newspaper for the cause.

Singer is ready in principle to start a paper with me. I explained to him the laying of the foundation through advertisements—the cellar, so to speak—as well as the Jewish idea—the tower.

He will go along with the Jewish cause up to a certain point. As for the complete evacuation of the present domiciles, he considers it neither desirable nor possible.

This would be no obstacle to our reaching an understanding.

But he wants a strong opposition paper. That would run counter to my purpose. I wish to be independent but moderate, otherwise the government will give me trouble that may endanger the whole Jewish cause.

Therefore I must not work with Singer either. Incidentally, if I understand him correctly, all he is interested in is a representative's seat from Lower Austria.

October 18

Last night I had a three-hour conversation with Dessauer, the bank director—and won him over.

He thinks it is possible to finance the migration of the Jews through the medium bankers. The Rothschilds cannot be counted on, he says.

He would like to start the *Society* with only four million pounds and keep later issues of shares in reserve. Nor should the entire territory be acquired immediately. He would like to start small.

I said to him: Then I'd rather not do it at all. A gradual infiltration of Jews—no matter where—soon causes anti-Semitism. Then there is bound to come a moment when further immigration is stopped, and thus our entire work will be destroyed.

It is different if we declare our independence from the start. Then the influx of Jews will be greatly desired by the neighboring states whose commerce we shall enrich.

Dessauer finds that it would be "a nice thing" and "good business." I believe all Jews will be quick to recognize that—in that way the State will be founded. D. also thinks it would have to be presented to the Rothschilds only as a business proposition, not as a national idea.

Remarkable: Like everyone else so far, Dessauer too said: "You can count on me, but I doubt that you will find anyone else in Vienna." And yet it makes sense to everyone I tell it to.

I noticed how Dessauer's eyes began to gleam. I arouse enthusiasm in everyone whom I tell about the Jewish cause.

October 19

Spoke with Dessauer once more. In the meantime he had become lukewarm.

Finished.

October 20

Today Benedikt's column "Stock Exchange Week" was excellent, against the big Jews who are unenterprising and narrow-minded. Entirely in my spirit.

Suddenly my decision was made: Win Benedikt for the cause! I went to him right away and immediately plunged *medias in res* [right into it].

He immediately understood me so well that he made a wry face.

While talking we walked as far as Mauer—a three-hours' walking tour over autumnal fields.

I said that I would like best to do it in and with the *Neue Freie Presse*.

He: "You're confronting us with an enormous problem. The entire paper would take on a different complexion. Until now we have been considered as a Jewish paper but have never admitted it. Now we are suddenly supposed to let down all our guards which have been protecting us."

I: "You don't need any more guards. The moment my idea is made public the entire Jewish Question will be solved honestly. After all, we can stay in those places where people are satisfied with our good citizenship and loyalty to the fatherland. Where they don't want us we shall move away. We are saying that we want to be Austrians. In the election the majority of non-Jewish citizens—no, all of them—declare that they do not recognize us as Austro-Germans (Russians, Prussians, Frenchmen, Rumanians, etc.). All right, we shall move away; but over there, too, we shall only be Austrians (Russians, etc.). We shall no more give up our acquired nationalities than we shall give up our acquired property."

He made various objections that were already familiar to me, though on a higher level than those of the Jews with whom I had previously spoken. I had an answer for everything.

He definitely took the matter seriously, certainly didn't consider me crazy, as my first listener, poor Schiff, had done in Paris. He recognized what was old about my plan, i.e., a universal idea, and what was new, i.e., a promise of victory. But he thinks that the governments' immediate reply would be an export prohibition and impediments to emigration. But that is exactly why I am founding the *Society* which will be in a position to negotiate with the governments, offer them compensations, etc.

He said I should make the publishers a proposal as to my ideas about implementing the plan.

I: "It could take two forms. Either you found a smaller paper for me in addition to the *Neue Freie Presse*, in which I may elaborate on my idea. Or you give me a Sunday edition with 'The Solution of the Jewish Question,' by Dr. Theodor Herzl, on the front page. I shall draw excerpts from my outline which will fill six or nine columns. Then the details, questions and answers— for I shall invite all of Jewry to contribute, and it will do so— will appear in a new column, 'The Jewish Question,' which I shall edit.

"Never has a paper contained anything more interesting. The responsibility will be mine alone. You can preface my outline with a disclaimer on the part of the paper."

He: "No, that would be cowardly. If we publish it, we shall accept joint responsibility with you. Your idea is a powerful machine gun, but it could also backfire."

I: "One mustn't be timid. Incidentally, everyone will be able to choose his place: in front of the machine gun, or in back of it." We walked and talked until we were tired. Benedikt is going to let Bacher in on the secret. Then I shall read my Address to the Rothschilds to both of them next week.

Benedikt would like the matter to get into the *Neue Freie Presse* from the outside in some way—perhaps through the fictitious founding of an organization before which I could give this address. I am against it. I need a newspaper for it to begin with—that is, if I cannot do things "aristocratically" through a Rothschild syndicate.

I won't get involved in organizational clap-trap.

* * *

This walk to Mauer was an historic one; I said so to Benedikt on the ride back.

I cannot conceal it from myself that it marked a decisive turning point for me as well. I have set myself in motion. Everything up to now has only been dreams and talk. Action has begun because I shall have the *Neue Freie Presse* either with me or against me.

* * *

I shall be the Parnell of the Jews.

October 27

Today Dr. Glogau was here and an hour later he brought Herr v. Kozmian, Count Badeni's confidential secretary, to see me. They made me a formal offer to take over the editorship of a big new government paper.

In view of my Jewish project I cannot simply decline this offer as I certainly would have done before—prior to the idea! An extremely favorable unexpected chance for the execution of my plan is opening up. Once I am close to Count Badeni, I can confidentially develop my idea to him. After all, it is as friendly to Gentiles as it is to Jews, as fruitful for the conserved and conservative state as it is for the one yet to be founded. I could bring

Count Badeni the *ideé maitresse* [outstanding idea] of his term of government!

Badeni already seems to have a high opinion of me, as I can tell from the hints dropped by Kozmian, a fine old man.

According to Kozmian, Badeni's government by no means wants to be anti-Liberal if it is not forced to be (I take this to mean: if they go along with him), but one never knows. *Il ne s'en ira pas* [he won't abandon them], Kozmian said finally.

I answered: "I could go along with the Count as long as it is compatible with my convictions—*et puis, je m'en irais* [and then I would part company with him]."

We agreed that I should inform the publishers Bacher and Benedikt of the offer the very same day—*tecto et ficto nomine* [under a hidden and disguised name]. For, out of a sense of propriety I do not want to confront them with a *fait accompli*. But I explained to the two people who had made me the offer that I was not making this notification in order to get any compensatory financial advantages for myself.

Glogau did not quite understand what I would really be notifying them of. After all, my notification would make sense only if I wanted to receive financial compensation. But Kozmian understood, or said he did, that I was doing it out of moral considerations.

This is in fact one of my reasons behind which, to be sure, a greater moral consideration is concealed, the consideration for my idea.

And this is how this delicate question of conscience shapes up for me:

I shall prove my gratitude to the publishers of the *Neue Freie Presse* by not simply going to work for Count Badeni (whom I like very much) in order to realize the Jewish idea with his aid. I shall first offer my idea to them, bringing them fame and fortune, as I see it, even at the great risk that I shall thereby carry out my idea more slowly or not at all. If they do not understand me, I shall be free—in fact duty-bound—to break away from them.

Kozmian, Glogau, and I agreed that I should announce my decision within 24 hours.

I immediately drove to Benedikt, who was not at home, and wrote to Bacher requesting an appointment for that evening.

In the afternoon I went to Benedikt and explained to him the matter whose *sine qua non*—the Jewish cause—he is already acquainted with.

He found the situation difficult, complex, and the decision an extremely weighty one for the *Neue Freie Presse*.

I had prefaced my remarks with a few facts which I kept emphasizing strongly, namely, that I did not want any personal advantage for myself, and that I would resolutely decline any financial compensation—a raise in pay or the like—even if I were offered it at this time.

I am conducting the Jewish cause in a completely impersonal manner. It is up to the *Neue Freie Presse* to decide whether or not it wishes to aid me in its realization. I need some authority in the eyes of the world which I want to sweep along with my idea. Out of gratitude to the *Neue Freie Presse*, which made my career possible even though it cannot take full credit for it, I should like best to work with my present friends. But I am conducting the politics of the Jews and cannot let personal considerations induce me to give up my idea.

Benedikt's mind was again working in its full brilliance. "Thinking out loud" and without expecting me to answer him, he discussed the form that the newspaper involved could take. He immediately mentioned the old *Presse* which he had heard was to be reorganized. Then he spoke about the possibility of a "Jewish paper" and of a rival paper of the *Neue Freie Presse* with a large founding capital. In this way he gave me advice without asking me any questions.

In the final analysis, he thought, it was a personal problem. Did I want to continue on my smooth course as a distinguished writer on the *Neue Freie Presse*, easily, comfortably, leaving the office at seven with not a care in the world? Or did I want to ruin my life the way he and Bacher had done—with neither a day nor a night to call my own?

I said: "I am not an easygoing person. I have got twenty more years in which to set the world on fire. I would never do it in order to make money. But I have my idea!"

Benedikt said finally: "Personally, I am in basic agreement with your idea. Whether our paper can be the vehicle for it I cannot decide. I don't dare to. For us your idea is a bombshell. I believe you should first try to found a *société d'études* [study commission] in Paris or in London. We shall give you a leave of absence for that purpose and exert our influence on your behalf. I don't know whether we shall become its journalistic representatives in the foreseeable future or ever, and I doubt if we can promise it to you. Someday there may be serious anti-Semitic riots—murder, killings, plundering; then we may be forced to make use of your idea anyway. In any case, it provides an issue behind which we can jump and thus save ourselves. But do you want us to tell you that we shall do it and thereby mislead you, so that you will reproach us for it later?"

Then I went to Bacher, but he had to leave for the party conference of the United Left. I was only able to tell him in haste that I had an offer and that Benedikt already knew the details. Bacher was, or acted, more disconcerted than Benedikt. We arranged a meeting for tomorrow.

Then I wrote Glogau a line asking him for a twenty-four hours' postponement. They will suspect that I am negotiating for compensation, after all. Painful as this suspicion of money is to me, there is nothing I can do about it.

October 28

A good night's sleep, sleeping on it.

Today is an even bigger day than yesterday. I am facing an enormous decision—and so is the Jewish cause. That also goes for the *Neue Freie Presse.*

They will understand me. *Superos movebo* [I shall move the heavens]!

Actually, the battle of the Jews between me and the powerful Jews has already begun.

At first I thought that I would have to confront the Rothschilds with the dilemma. But I shall have to fight the first battle against the *Neue Freie Presse*.

* * *

In the evening:

The battle has been fought and lost—by whom?

From five to eight p.m. I read the Address to the Rothschilds to Bacher in his apartment.

At least I achieved this: the man who a few weeks ago had refused me *a limine* [outright] now listened to me—and how!

He, the nay-sayer, had changed completely too. He found the idea great and staggering. But he said that he could not make a split-second decision on such an extremely vital question for the newspaper.

He pointed out to me what I would lose if I left the *Neue Freie Presse*.

They really don't need me, but they did create the post of *feuilleton* editor when I did not wish to stay in Paris.

He found my Jewish idea generous—but hardly feasible. The *Neue Freie Presse* would be risking too much. The Jews might not respond to it—and what then?

I pointed out to him that the *Neue Freie Presse* would not be able to evade this problem. Sooner or later it would have to show its colors.

"Well," he said, "for twenty years we didn't print anything about the Social democracy either."

Actually, this was the most remarkable thing he said.

From that moment on it has been clear that I must not expect the *Neue Freie Presse* to do anything for the cause.

What the *Neue Freie Presse* was reproached with as short-sightedness—its prolonged hushing-up of anti-Semitism*—was its policy. I said: "In the end you will not be able to keep silent about

---

* Translator's Note: Probably a slip for "Socialist movement."

this matter any more than you were able to hush up anti-Semitism!"

We were already in the street walking toward the editorial offices when I said that. He muttered, as though talking to himself: "It's a helluva thing."

I answered: "Yes, it's a hell of an idea. There is no escaping from it today. Whether you say Yes or No, you make an awful commitment."

Thereupon he said: "It is a big thing, and I can understand why a decent man would want to risk his life for it. But I doubt if you are going to find many more such Herzls."

The upshot: they cannot bring themselves to take that bold step. I, for my part, cannot allow myself and my idea to be stopped from forging ahead. Therefore, I shall have no other course but to part company with them.

Bacher had found the Address to the R's interesting, rather than exhaustive, a political appeal à la Lassalle. He said he knew that the cause was something enormous and that he might be turning down a lot of success and glory.

*   *   *

October 29

Kozmian and Glogau came to see me first thing in the morning. They congratulated me on my—imminent—decision.

I said that I would first have to speak with Count Badeni before deciding whether to accept the editorship.

*   *   *

In the evening:

Everything in doubt again. I had made the condition that the paper would have to be turned over to me in a year if the publishing company did not wish to run it any longer.

What I had in mind was that I would then have the paper for my Jewish cause unless I had previously succeeded in winning over Count Badeni for my idea—or if I had attained the requisite authority with the big Jews.

But the Press Chief, Privy Councillor Freiberg, won't go along with this. If the paper goes badly, he will claim it for the government.

This would have the additional drawback that I would be dependent on the Press Bureau. But I wish to work with Badeni exclusively, not with his privy councillors. After all, the personal contact with Badeni—i.e., its value to the Jewish cause —is the very reason why I wanted to run the government paper in the first place.

This is what I replied to Kozmian too. If I cannot always deal directly with Badeni if the paper is successful, and keep it for myself if it is unsuccessful, I won't have any part of it.

October 30

In the morning Kozmian came to fetch me for my audience with Badeni.

He asked: "Are we going to Badeni?"

I said: "No—unless my condition is met."

He compromised: "Come along anyway; I shall introduce you to the Prime Minister not as editor-in-chief but only as the former Paris correspondent of the *Neue Freie Presse*."

So we drove to the Ministry. It was my first time in the palace of an Austrian minister. Rooms in a grand style, but bare and cold. On the staircase we made a comparison with the French government palaces.

"*Ça manque de tapis* [there are no carpets]," I said to Kozmian. Through such jests I tried to keep up a good front for the decisive first meeting with a man through whom I want to help the Jews.

We were admitted right after the Excellencies. The other people in the antechamber looked up when they noticed our precedence.

Court air!

Badeni hurried up to meet us, gave me a very lively and vigorous greeting. Evidently a smart, energetic person.

He made me many compliments. He had already heard of the difficulty that had arisen; and since he mentioned the new paper, I spoke about it as well.

I said: "*Ce ne sont pas des considérations pécuniaires qui peuvent me décider à accepter la direction du journal* [It is not financial considerations which can decide me to accept the editorship of the paper]."

We spoke only in French.

Badeni considered it understandable that I did not want to be dependent on his privy councillors. He begged me not to distrust Freiberg, not to let myself be stirred up against him. Of course, there would be no need for me to go to the Press Bureau, but I would send my men *aux informations* [for information]. But if he (Badeni) sent Freiberg or Schill to me, I should not receive them coolly.

This I promised. But I said that I wished to deal only with him directly.

"I think I shall be able to champion your present policies, Your Excellency, and if I go along with you, *je vous serai un partisan resolu et sincere* [I shall be your resolute and sincere supporter]. It may be that from a certain point on I shall not be able to go along any farther; then I shall tell you so candidly and go my way. But if I am still with you by the end of your term of government—which is a long way off, I hope—I shall not leave you then."

Several times I mentioned the end of his government, which visibly disconcerted him, but since he had presumably never heard such talk from any journalist, perhaps not from anyone, this must have given him some respect for me.

Right from the start I wanted him to get the right impression of me: that I was a *partisan* [supporter] and not a *laquai* [lackey], as I had already told Bourgoing in my first interview.

I am conducting the politics of the Jews, today still unrecognized. What I am concluding today is not a semi-official hiring contract—which is what many will, unfortunately, take it for—but an alliance.

Badeni said he thought of our relationship as a permanent one; he would see to it that the publishing company offered me a secure position.

To my expressed desire that I be allowed to call on him at any time, *comme un ambassadeur* [like an ambassador], he said, *"Non seulement je le permets, mais j'y tiens* [I not only permit it, I insist on it]."

We also talked about the conditions under which I would sever my connections with the *Neue Freie Presse*. I made it clear from the start that I always wanted to remember my old friends and would not carry on any injurious polemics against them— unless I was attacked first.

Badeni said he himself hoped that no opposition between us and the *Neue Freie Presse* would arise.

Come to think of it, that was a highly important statement. It means that he wants to govern in cooperation with the German Liberals.

To be sure, he also said several times, *"Je ne ficherai pas le camp* [I shall not quit]."

Thus there was an air of confidence about the whole conversation. While we were talking, my cigar went out a few times. Each time Badeni lit a fresh match for me—a detail which made me think, smiling inwardly: What would the small Jews of my acquaintance, and even the biggest ones, say to that?

Badeni regards the matter as settled.

*   *   *

An hour later I was in the office.

Bacher sent for me: "Well, how does your matter stand?"

"I could still refuse," I answered. But he said nothing more.

Even now I would still prefer it if the *Neue Freie Presse* took up my Jewish idea, now more than ever. I now have access to Badeni; the external advantages I care nothing about; and if I now gained the prestige of the *Neue Freie Presse* for my cause, it would surely be victorious!

In the evening I shall speak with Bacher once more and present the alternatives sharply: I am ready to renounce all the advantages I am offered if you promise me to publicize my solution of the Jewish question within six months. I demand nothing of you, no compensation, no personal advantage!

(It should be noted that they cut my salary when I moved to Vienna and denied me the expected contribution to my moving expenses.)

Benedikt seems to be angry with me; I noticed this when I passed him. He understands the matter completely! Kozmian also told me that Benedikt was furious. Kozmian has this from a third party.

*   *   *

In the afternoon, when I was in the office, Benedikt again had an interview with this third party. In the evening, when Kozmian and I met at the house of Baron Bourgoing, he told me that my superiors are now afraid of my competition. They evidently suspect that in domestic Austrian politics I shall not deviate too far from their point of view.

In the conference at Bourgoing's house I developed the whole plan of the newspaper! I was going to retain all the old staff members of the *Presse*. Among them are two who made base attacks on me in earlier times, I said, "*Je ne peux pas les renvoyer—ce sont mes ennemis personnels* [I cannot dismiss them, they are my personal enemies]." They laughed.

But, at bottom, all evening I longed to remain with the *Neue Freie Presse*. An ingredient in this is obviously my cowardice in the face of the *qu'en dira-t-on* [what will people say], the turned-up noses of those who would probably like to change places with me and will vent their envy in the form of disparagement.

Yet in the conference I gave the best suggestions for the production of a good, lively paper. If, contrary to expectations, I should return to the fold of the *Neue Freie Presse,* these suggestions will have been my payment for the opportunity which this offer has been.

October 31

Kozmian was supposed to send me word today on what Benedikt yesterday told the go-between about me.

By eleven o'clock I had not received anything. It is possible
that the delay of this message is due to some intrigue. I shall get
to the bottom of this. If the *Neue Freie Presse* hatches some plot
to prevent my being hired, this will be the *casus belli* [cause for
war] for me.

Now I am writing to Dr. Bacher:

Dear Dr. Bacher:

With your permission I do not intend to come to the office
today, or as long as the decision is still pending. It is too embar-
rassing a situation for me. For tomorrow you have, in any case,
the *feuilleton* about Heine, unless something more timely arrived
today. On Saturday there is no *feuilleton,* and for Sunday there
probably is a Wittmann piece on hand. The contributions to
date are in good shape.

But if you want to talk to me I shall be at your disposal this
afternoon from 3 to 5 or this evening from 6 to 10. Let me repeat
once more that I shall stay with you if you want me to, at my present salary and in my present position. I am still ready to refuse
all the external advantages offered to me—out of those moral
considerations with which you are acquainted.

Today I can still decline the offer.

With cordial regards,

Yours very sincerely,
Herzl.

November 1

By yesterday evening there was no reply from Bacher. The
thought of making an enemy of the man whom I admire despite
his pig-headedness has been very disagreeable to me and has
grown more unbearable by the hour. Added to this is the possi-

bility that I might not even be helping the Jewish cause with my officiousness.

Out of sorts, I attended a conference at Baron Bourgoing's house where problems of typeface, heading, and newsprint of the new paper were discussed with the manager of the printing plant. I made my best suggestions, but I felt more and more clearly that these were not my kind of people and that I could not work with them.

When I left the conference, I was deeply disquieted inwardly. It occurred to me to seek Güdemann's advice although I had been angry with him for several days. He had "paid his respects" to Count Badeni, as I happened to have found out. He had gone to see Badeni without notifying me, thus actually demonstrating that he did not take me or my leadership seriously. At Badeni's he had tearfully implored him for protection; and finally he had been so overcome by emotion that he asked the Count for permission to bless him.

Nevertheless, I wanted to hear his views. Güdemann was not at home. From there I drove straight to Bacher who had also gone out. But half an hour later I ran into him on a street in the Leopoldstadt. We walked on together and had a heart-to-heart talk.

I told him that giving up his friendship would be unbearable to me.

He was pleased, and, as a friend, he advised me against the newspaper experiment. He said that I had a great future with the *Neue Freie Presse,* but, above all, I would have much more of a chance to implement my idea there than I had through Badeni.

We finally agreed that, if the formation of the *Society* proved impossible, I was to publish a pamphlet which the *Neue Freie Presse* would review.

Besides, he will give me the satisfaction of writing me a letter which I can show to Badeni and in which he declares on his word of honor that I neither demanded nor received financial compensation of any kind for remaining on the staff.

On parting he said to me, "It would have hurt me deeply if you had forsaken us."

November 3

At noon, called on Badeni. This time I had to wait in the antechamber somewhat longer. Gold-braided gentlemen, nervous frock-coated deputations, an old colonel with a petition. Everybody gently clears his throat, draws a deep breath, so as to be in good voice when he faces His Mightiness.

Through it all I had a distinct feeling that I was not made for an antechamber nor for a privy councillor's gold-braided collar.

I was the only civilian there without a frock-coat. Then everybody looked up in astonishment when I was nevertheless admitted ahead of the colonel and the privy councillors who had arrived before me.

The Count again greeted me very amiably: "Well, doctor, what are you bringing me?"

I spoke a few words of regret (actually, it now occurs to me, I did not thank him kindly enough for the honor he had intended for me), and gave him Bacher's letter.

Then we talked politics—the issue of the day: the confirmation of Lueger's election.

Badeni was mildly, almost imperceptibly, put out by my refusal and immediately treated me with caution, as an opponent. Personally, he said, he would be disposed not to confirm Lueger. "I don't like him—most of all, because he is a demagogue. Unfortunately, the Lueger question has been blown up into a difficult problem for me. I wish it had been solved before I took office. It would be helpful if the aura of prestige that surrounds me were not weakened by this sort of thing. As it is, so many indiscretions have already been committed in this affair on all sides that no matter what happens it will appear as though I were yielding to pressure. This is detrimental to my prestige. I cannot decide in the matter all by myself, anyway. I must consult my colleagues; many factors must be taken into consideration, especially the interests of the state and the will of the emperor."

I replied boldly: "I believe Lueger's election as mayor must be validated. If you fail to do it the first time, you can never confirm him again, and if you fail to confirm him the third time, the Dragoons will ride."

The Count smiled: "Oh?!" with a *goguenard* [quizzical] expression. I then substantiated my views and took leave of him. He said: "Whenever you care to come and see me, I shall always be very grateful."

But I suspect that the next time I pay him a call he will not have time for me.

*   *   *

That evening I related the whole affair to Güdemann, who keenly regretted that I had declined the offer. He thought it would have been nice if I had had "the ear of the Prime Minister."

I got angry at his poltroonery and told him: "You are a Jew who is protected—I am a Jew who protects. Obviously you cannot understand me."

I explained to him what an attainment it was that the *Neue Freie Presse* was taking an interest in the cause, even though in a guarded manner, and that I considered this important enough to put aside my own personal interests, which would have been better served in Badeni's employ.

This again seemed to make some sense to him—though for how long I cannot say. I have already wasted too much time on him. It was our last long conversation together. Of a man he has only the beard and the voice. He implored me over and over again to leave the rabbis out of the whole business, for they command no respect.

But what most enraged me against him was his initial refusal to give me a letter of recommendation to Zadoc Kahn in the event that I should go to Paris next week.

Only when I told him that I did not need his introduction and would get along without it did he consent.

This conversation depressed me greatly.

In conclusion I said to him: "It is hopeless. You, to whom I have spoken longest and most frequently about the matter, you keep deserting me. I am sorry to say that you still don't understand what it is all about. We are now standing at Donau-Eschingen, at the first trickle of the river. But I tell you it will yet be the Danube!"

November 5

Yesterday evening some very bad moments. I went to the office again. No one saw anything noteworthy in it—that is, in my rejection of the offer. Rather, I had the feeling that I had lost favor with my colleagues.

It is true that I rejected the government offer on account of the Jewish cause, just as I would have accepted it for that reason.

But what are the prospects of the *Neue Freie Presse*'s assisting me in its implementation? It would be terrible if I had been under an illusion about this and could more easily have gained prestige in the eyes of the Jews in Badeni's employ.

Bacher and Benedikt received me with pronounced cordiality when I appeared in the office. But Benedikt immediately excused himself for lacking the time to discuss the *société d'études*, [study commission] and Bacher only asked when I would supply a *feuilleton* again.

Güdemann gave me something to think about; the project *desinit in piscem* [ends up as a fish tail].* If the *Neue Freie Presse* disposes of my pamphlet with a notice in the "domestic" section, I shall be greatly harmed. I hope they will scrupulously and completely fulfill the promise they have made me. Otherwise I would have to take it as a *casus belli* [cause for war].

*　　　*　　　*

Spoke with Arthur Schnitzler and briefly explained the matter to him.

* Translator's Note: A phrase from Horace's *Ars Poetica*.

When I said: It is a renaissance as a finishing touch to this classical century of inventions in communications—he was enthusiastic. I promised him that he would become the director of our theatre.

*   *   *

Had supper again in the company of Jews at Tonello's.

The same speeches as those of a week ago. The boycotting of theaters praised as a saving device. This petty agitating is degenerating into busybodying clubmanship. Yet to me it is important as a symptom. I am making the acquaintance of some usable agitators: Ruzicka, Billitzer the hatmaker (a crude popular orator), Kopstein, Pollak the wine-merchant, Neumann the attorney, Dr. Kalman, etc.

Funny that they should all regard it as a rather extreme course of action when they go to a minister to complain.

There was also a speech by attorney Ellbogen, the "celebrated orator." He is in favor of founding a "Liberal People's Party" which is presumably supposed to send him to the Chamber of Deputies. He considers the situation of the Jews serious but not hopeless—"otherwise we should have no other course but to proclaim the nationhood of the Jews and to seek a territorial basis." Ellbogen can also be used for agitation.

Dr. Bloch made a clever reply to him, saying that Ellbogen's "Liberals" would be only the Jews all over again. To work with the Socialist Movement would be no help against anti-Semitism. Evidence of this was Germany where despite Marx, Lassalle, and more recently Singer, anti-Semitism had originated and grown strong.

Afterwards I introduced myself to him. He was very pleasantly surprised to find me in that place.

November 5

Today Dr. Ehrlich came to my office at the newspaper and said: "I heard that we have got you back."

I told him the course of events. He made a serious face. He thinks the publishers will not keep their promise.

I started to boil and said: "If they break their word to me, the pillars of this house are going to collapse."

I went to Benedikt right away; later Bacher also came there. I demanded the promised "personal support" which, I said, must consist in a meeting of prominent Jews to take place the following Sunday at Bacher's home or at mine. I would give a speech (my Address to the Rothschilds with the elimination of the Rothschilds from the text), whereupon those assembled would have to place at my disposal their connections in Paris, London, and Berlin. In those places, I shall then found the *"société d'études,"* which does not require one centime as capital, or, rather, get assurances of its founding which must follow immediately upon the publication of my pamphlet.

Benedikt said halfheartedly that he did not know any suitable persons among the big bankers here. But he said he would give me a recommendation to (with pathos) "Privy Councillor of Commerce Goldberger," in Berlin.

I replied: "I have known this Goldberger for eight years, so I don't need your recommendation."

Then he recommended Moritz Leinkauf to me.

I said: "He is my cousin's husband!"

In short, his suggestions were completely worthless or superfluous. I am still loath to believe that he is doing it out of perfidy. That would be monstrous.

Bacher kept silent.

I told them: "I don't need any agitators at the moment. That will come later. At present I need only the interest of the financial circles. But actually I am not dependent on anyone. I am simply notifying the people before I burst the dam."

I think they both sensed the threat. Nevertheless I took Benedikt's advice and immediately drove to Leinkauf with whom I shall have a talk in the afternoon.

*　　*　　*

Spoke with Leinkauf in the afternoon. We sat in the consultation room of the monumental Fruit Exchange.

Leinkauf regretted that I had not asked his advice before declining Badeni's offer. He would have strongly advised me to accept it.

Incidentally, Badeni should be handled with care. Leinkauf told me the following story. When Badeni was still governor of Galicia, a farm crisis broke out in that region. Because of a crop failure the farmers found it impossible to feed their cattle. A farm-aid project was initiated. Supplies of feed were to be bought and distributed among the needy. Badeni came to Vienna, sent for the grain dealer Wetzler (of the firm of Wetzler and Abeles), and invited him to put in a bid. Wetzler did so. Then Badeni sent for him again and said: "I don't believe that you can make this delivery. According to my calculations you would have to charge about thirty per cent more to stay in business."

Wetzler got the point, took his first bid back from the Count, and put in a second one which was that much higher.

This the Count took back with him to Lvov and there the contract was given to some business associates—of whom B. himself is said to have been one—for a price much higher than Wetzler's first bid and somewhat lower than his second one.

Then I spent two hours giving Leinkauf my outline of the Jewish project.

Leinkauf was definitely against it. He thinks the project is not feasible—and very dangerous at the same time. All namby-pamby arguments. I explained to him: Either my pamphlet will cause no reaction; then there is no danger. Or it will have the reaction that I expect; then the matter will be feasible.

*　　*　　*

In the evening I reported to Bacher on this conversation. I said: "Leinkauf cannot understand the matter. He has a land-lubber's mind; but one has to live by the sea in order to comprehend my plan." I showed Leinkauf his own Fruit Exchange and illustrated it this way: The grain trade had its rudimentary focal point in Vienna in the Café Stierböck. You created an organ for the need, the Fruit Exchange on the Schottenring, and then this facility organized the trade and expanded it so greatly that now they have that palatial building on Taborstrasse. For this is how it happens in economic life: first comes the need, then the organ, then the trade. The need must be recognized, the organ must be created—the trade then comes by itself if the need has been a genuine one. Surely, no one will deny that in the case of the Jews there is a need which has grown into dire necessity. The organ will be the *Society*. First the small Study Commission; then, when it has convinced itself that the mood is there, the big one.

That seemed to make sense to Bacher. He promised me to speak with David Gutmann and to tell him of my impending visit. Gutmann was a fanatical Jew, he said, although he did not live by the sea either.

*   *   *

Bacher joked: "The Jews will listen to you more peevishly than the Gentiles. You will become an honorary anti-Semite!"

November 6

A deeply discouraging day. Community Councillor Stern and others came to the office. They are all people who expect salvation to come from the government and who go on bended knee to the ministers. Therefore, they would have believed in me if I had become Badeni's journalistic right-hand man. And so now I have no authority with them.

*   *   *

In the evening I was with Professor Singer and told him everything.

He raised my spirits again, saying I had done the right thing! If I had accepted a semi-official position I would have disgraced myself and the cause.

November 7

Met Dr. Schwitzer in the street and took him into my confidence.

He is against my plan for the loftiest reasons. He does not want nations, but human beings.

I said to him: *"Primum vivere, deinde philosophari* [First live, then philosophize]. Over there I shall build you a splendid ivory tower where you can pursue the loftiest thoughts untroubled by barbarians."

He said that in addition to the misery of the Jews there were many other kinds of misery.

I said: "For the time being I can worry only about my people. Incidentally, with the seven-hour day and other social easements and innovations, we shall give a great example to the world.

"It is a matter of drawing the right conclusions from the wonderful technical achievements of this century. The electric light was not invented in order to illuminate the drawing rooms of a few rich snobs. It was invented so that with its aid we might solve the Jewish Question."

*   *   *

Bacher told me that he had spoken with David Gutmann and prepared him for my visit. I immediately wrote to Gutmann and asked him to set a date.

Gutmann's reply had a comical element. He gave me an appointment for Sunday and signed his letter "Most respectfully yours," which sounds a bit condescending. Unless this complimentary close is indicative of commercial man's lack of refinement, it reveals that the man is not going to understand me. Yet I don't want to be too lazy. Perhaps he will get scared. But I am not likely to stir up the good man who signs himself "Most respectfully yours."

November 9

Spoke with David Gutmann "and Son" yesterday. The old man was a bit condescending at first but I cured him of that by crossing my legs and very nonchalantly leaning back in my armchair. He listened to me with growing seriousness.

The young fellow wanted to joke about "the Jewish State and the Jewish *balmachomes.*" I lit into him: "Don't make any foolish jokes! Anyone who makes such jokes will live to regret it. The jokesters will be stepped on by this movement and crushed underfoot."

Frightened, he stopped his witticisms. His father finally declared that he would have to give such a big matter a lot of thought. He also said that I should speak to the Rothschilds.

At any rate, the big Jews have been informed; this much has been accomplished. Because obviously David Gutmann is going to talk about it to Albert Rothschild and to Hirsch.

Unfortunately I forgot to say how I propose to liquidate Gutmann's coal business.

The mines can either be bought by the Austrian state or acquired by the *Society.* In the latter event the purchase price could consist partly of landed property over there, partly of *Society* shares and cash. A third possibility would be the founding of a "Gutmann Joint-Stock Company" whose stock would be quoted in our State as well. A fourth possibility: continue to operate them in the present way, except that henceforth the owners would be foreigners.

November 10

Spoke yesterday with Güdemann. He gave me the letter of introduction to Zadoc Kahn. I am sending it to Schiff whom I am telling about the great events of the past months. Schiff is to transmit the letter to Zadoc.

*   *   *

Bacher is dampening my spirits again with his objections. To get away from it all, I plan to go to Paris on Wednesday.

*   *   *

Many Jews are foolishly jubilant over the non-confirmation of Lueger's election to the mayoralty. As though Lueger were tantamount to anti-Semitism. I believe, on the contrary, that the movement against the Jews will grow rapidly now.

The force of events will urge what I wanted to bring about by my constructive idea.

Some other anti-Semite will wind up as mayor of Vienna in Lueger's place. Lueger, however, will step up his agitation. All the anti-Semites are already closing their ranks against Badeni. Count Kielmannsegg, the governor of Lower Austria, who is not hostile to the Jews, will probably be overthrown in the near future.

Yesterday there even circulated the anti-Semitic rumor that Count Badeni had resigned. If he stays, the Dragoons are going to ride, as I told him.

They are already yelling in the streets: "Down with Badeni!"

I believe that the non-confirmation of Lueger was a fatal mistake which will cause serious crises. Badeni underestimated the strength of the anti-Semitic current.

Prince Lichtenstein yelled "lie" at the Prime Minister in an open session of Parliament. The anti-Semitic papers talk about Badeni in an insolent tone that is unheard of in Austria.

*   *   *

Wrote to Stiassny, the Construction Councillor. Tomorrow I shall read him my Address to the Jews. He has connections with zealous Jewish political agitators everywhere.

*   *   *

Ferment in Turkey. Should the Oriental question be broached and solved by a partition of Turkey, at the European Congress we could possibly get a piece of neutral land (like Belgium, Switzerland) for ourselves.

*   *   *

Yesterday in our literary section we published a few posthumous letters of Lassalle.

I spoke to Bacher about it after he had tried to tone me down. "What do you suppose Lassalle would be today if he were alive?" I asked.

Bacher grinned: "Probably a Prussian Privy Councillor."

But I said: "He would be the leader of the Jews; of course I don't mean the Lassalle of the age he would be today, but the man with the strength he had then."

November 11

Have been to see Güdemann. He asked me to come to an election meeting intended to raise campaign funds for Bloch's candidacy in Kolomea. I said that I did not wish to appear in public before I had developed my project. I don't want to make a speech if I cannot present the conclusion. But I shall write a letter to Güdemann which he is to read to the meeting. I shall say that I am contributing fifty guilders, although on a number of points I do not approve of Bloch's stand. At a very conservative estimate there are 200 Jews in Vienna who can contribute an equal amount much more easily. Then the campaign money would be raised.

Rabbi Fleissig was at Güdemann's. The latter put his hand on my shoulder and said admiringly: "He is a wonderful fellow!"

Güdemann told me that David Gutmann had blabbed about my plan. I was furious and immediately wrote to Ludwig Gutmann:

Dear Dr. Gutmann:

Because I have had no sign of life from you since our discussion of last Friday, I assume that my plan does not make sense to you two.

By way of precaution, however, I must remind you of something that I may not have stressed sufficiently—namely, that what I told you was strictly confidential. I cannot empower you to tell anyone about it unless you first get my consent in each individual case. A careless treatment of the project could create dangers for the Jews which would necessarily affect you in the most serious way as well.

For this reason I have complete trust in the discretion of two men of honor who do not share my views but know well that they owe me absolute silence.

With kindest regards,

Yours very sincerely,
Dr. Th. Herzl.

*   *   *

I had asked Bloch to meet me at Stiassny's home in the afternoon.

Bloch had hoped that I had come on account of his election campaign. I noticed his disappointment when I only—*excusez du peu!* [is that all?]—read the Solution of the Jewish question. Stiassny was full of enthusiasm.

Bloch left before I had finished reading, saying he had to go home because he was leaving for Kolomea tomorrow. He also had many objections to my plan.

As he left he asked me only to speak with David Gutmann— about money! Nevertheless, I am writing the following letter to Güdemann in support of Bloch's candidacy; it is to be read at the rally:

Dear Dr. Güdemann:

I cannot take part in the discussion because I have to leave town. Dr. Bloch's election seems to me to be necessary. I am saying this with the explicit reservation that my political views differ from those of Dr. Bloch, but he has always been a stalwart champion of the Jewish cause in Parliament. We owe him a debt of gratitude for that, even though we may not be in agreement with him on some, indeed many, points. They can kill us one by one, but if we stick together, never!

I am contributing fifty guilders to the campaign fund. If two hundred Viennese Jews give an equal amount, the essentials will be assured. When I speak of but two hundred Jews of better-than-average means, I am underestimating the financial power of Viennese Jewry as well as overestimating my own. I should prefer doing without the very highest of the high-and-mighty to whom the plight of the Jews evidently still does not come closely enough home.

With respectful greetings,

Yours sincerely,
Dr. Th. H.

Paris, November 16

Conversation with Chief Rabbi Zadoc Kahn. I read the Address to him. On the train to Paris I had already eliminated all references to the Rothschilds from it.

Zadoc Kahn seemed to listen to my two-hour reading with interest.

Afterwards he also professed himself to be a Zionist. But he said that a Frenchman's "patriotism" also had its claims.

Yes, a man has to choose between Zion and France.

Zadoc Kahn is of the breed of *little* Jews. I shall be surprised if I get any serious help from him. Actually, we exchanged only a few words after I had finished reading, because he had to leave for the synagogue. We made an appointment to meet again tomorrow; my Salzburg acquaintance, Leven, is to join us. I don't expect much from the meeting.

Paris, November 17

Talked with Nordau.

His was the second case of understanding me in a flash. The first was Benedikt. But Nordau comprehended me as an adherent, Benedikt, for the time being, as an opponent.

Nordau will, I believe, go with me through thick and thin. He was my easiest conquest and possibly the most valuable to date. He would make a good president of our Academy or Minister of Education.

He recommended me to the *Maccabean Club* of London,

which I first heard mentioned by him. But this club is quite plainly the ideal instrument for my needs: artists, writers, Jewish intellectuals of all kinds compose its membership. The name of the club itself really tells enough. Colonel Goldsmid is said to be a member, also Mocatta, who has likewise been mentioned to me several times.

Nordau is giving me an introduction to the Maccabean, Israel Zangwill, who is a writer.

I asked Nordau to come to London with me. He promised to come later if I needed him.

*   *   *

In the afternoon at Zadoc Kahn's home.

My Salzburg acquaintance, Leven, was there—listless, tepid, and sluggish as he had been in Salzburg. From his objections I could tell that he had not comprehended my plan either on that occasion or on this one.

Later, a few other Jews showed up. I suspect that they had been asked to come by Zadoc: Derenbourg, Feinberg, and a young rabbi who is Zadoc's son-in-law.

One by one I had to trot out all my arguments again. Not a single new note in the discussion.

For the present, the French Jews apparently will not have anything to do with the matter. They are still too well off.

I turned on Leven in no uncertain terms. "I must be very infelicitous in my use of language. For, things which I have explained to you twice are still unintelligible."

When he emphasized his French nationality, I said: "What? Don't you and I belong to the same nation? Why did you wince when Lueger was elected? Why did I suffer when Captain Dreyfus was accused of high treason?"

At parting I said to him: "You and your kind will never go along with me!"

The young rabbi said: "I will go with you!"

Derenbourg, in dismay, kept silent. As a German Jew (Dernburg) he obviously attaches great value to his French nationality.

I explained to them that by founding the Jewish State I would be giving them an even greater possibility of becoming naturalized Frenchmen.

To Feinberg, who seems to be in Hirsch's employ, I said that the existing colonization societies would have to subordinate themselves to our cause.

"Wherever we find opposition," I said, "we shall break it!"

Zadoc said soothingly: "But no one is offering you any opposition yet."

Zadoc's attitude satisfied me completely this time. He even seems to be favorably disposed to my plan.

But I recognized the impression I had made on him most clearly of all when the door opened for a second and an elderly lady—presumably Zadoc's wife—peered in through the crack with curiosity. This moment revealed to me what he must have told people about me.

November 18

In the afternoon with Zadoc Kahn again. His mood had changed. From his remarks I could tell that he had presented my idea to several people and had everywhere met with rebuff.

The French Jews' attitude toward the matter is a hostile one. I didn't expect anything different. They are doing too well here to think of a change.

"All this," I said to Zadoc, "is in my plan. The first families will be the last ones to join with us. Let them only beware of three things: First, lest Jews in other parts of the world find out how enviable the situation of the Jews in France is, for this would bring about a harmful mass influx of Israelites into France. Second, lest they become too brilliant Frenchmen, advance too rapidly in the social scale, acquire too much visible power in the form of wealth or respected positions; in a word, let them take care not to rise in the world. And third, let them completely cease troubling themselves about the Jews of other countries. Such concern would only betray their solidarity to the Christians, but the other Jews would reject them. For these friendly experiments in colonization have not only a genial but also a malign aspect: they are supposed to check or divert the influx of Jews into France. However, anyone who does not declare himself ready to join the migrating Jews has no right to assign them places in various parts of the world. 'Israelite Frenchmen'—if there are such—are therefore no Jews in our eyes and our cause is none of their business."

Later on there came a college professor named Becker, a great chauvinist. *"Il n'est question que d'un grand project* [it's nothing more than a big scheme]," he said as soon as he had entered. It seems that Parisian Jewry has been very busy discussing the matter since my arrival.

This Becker is a typical Jew from the Latin Quarter. A sort of Brunetière translated into Hebrew. He reeks of books and conventional patriotism. With great glibness he started to "refute" me. He also trotted out that satirical anecdote about what things would be like in the Jewish State. Two Jews meet: *"Qu'est-ce que tu fais ici* [What do you do here]?"—*"Je vends des lorgnettes. Et toi* [I sell opera glasses. And you]?"—*"Je vends aussi des lorgnettes* [I sell opera glasses, too]."

To this masterly argument I replied quite calmly: *"Monsieur, ni vous ni moi nous ne vendons des lorgnettes* [Sir, neither you nor I sell opera glasses]."

Afterwards he apologized for having told this joke, and in the further course of the conversation he admitted that the Jewish State would be a great *académie* [academy].

Through questions and answers I familiarized him with the plan and gradually forced him to the wall, using only the arguments from my "Address to the Jews."

His eyes grew bigger and bigger behind his spectacles, and finally he fell completely silent.

November 19

Nordau, so it seems, is completely won over to the cause.
My discussions with him concern reservations of the highest

type. "Are the Jews still anthropologically fit for nationhood?" and the like.

Time will tell.

Nordau thinks that the plan will need three hundred years for its realization.

I believe, thirty—provided that the idea catches on.

Nordau recommends that while in London I should contact *Ha-maggid* and the *Jewish Chronicle*. I am to arrange for my pamphlet to be translated into Yiddish, also into Hebrew, for the Russians.

The campaign's center of gravity is shifted to London.

London, November 21

Visit to Israel Zangwill, the writer. He lives in Kilburn, N. W. A drive in the fog through endless streets. Arrived a bit out of sorts. The house is rather shabby. In his book-lined study Zangwill sits before an enormous writing table with his back to the fireplace. Also close to the fire, his brother, reading. Both give one the impression of shivering southerners who have been cast up on the shores of Ultima Thule. Israel Zangwill is of the long-nosed Negroid type, with very woolly deep-black hair, parted in the middle; his clean-shaven face displays the steely haughtiness of an honest ambitious man who has made his way after bitter struggles. The disorder in his room and on his desk leads me to infer that he is an internalized person. I have not read any of his writings, but I think I know him. He must bestow all the care that is lacking in his outward appearance on his style.

Our conversation is laborious. We speak in French, his command of which is inadequate. I don't even know whether he understands me. Still, we agree on major points. He, too, is in favor of our territorial independence.

However, his point of view is a racial one—which I cannot accept if I so much as look at him and at myself. All I am saying is: We are an historical unit, a nation with anthropological diversities. This also suffices for the Jewish State. No nation has uniformity of race.

We soon get down to practical points. He gives me the names of several suitable men:

Colonel Goldsmid, the painter Solomon, Rabbi Singer, Mocatta, Abrahams, Montefiore, Lucien Wolf, Joseph Jacobs, N.S. Joseph, and, of course, Chief Rabbi Adler.

I shall meet these men next Sunday at the banquet of the Maccabeans and arrange a conference for Monday at which I shall present my plan.

Colonel Goldsmid—for me the most important—is stationed at Cardiff with his regiment.

Zangwill is asking him by telegram to come here. Otherwise I shall have to go to Cardiff to see him.

London, November 22

Rode about all day.

Called on Chief Rabbi Adler. He received me like an old acquaintance. He was in a hurry. Would I come and dine with him tomorrow at his other home in the City. In all haste he counseled me against the Maccabeans, saying they were young people without influence. I would be better advised to speak with Lord Rothschild and others. He gave me an introduction to Sir Samuel Montagu, M.P.

I went to call on Montagu in the City. A busy day at the office. Montague sandwiched me in between two brokers. He invited me to have lunch at his home on Sunday. We could then talk. But he immediately drew my attention to his age, saying that he was no longer fit for any big undertaking.

Then to Rabbi Singer. He, too, was in a hurry; I accompanied him to the beautiful synagogue in Bayswater. A few words about my purpose: I wanted to start a worldwide discussion of the Jewish Question.

He smiled: *"You are ambitious."* *

I said: "That is really the least fantastic aspect of my plan."

He made an appointment with me for Sunday—"to tea."

* In English in the original.

My pet thought about the transitional phase: Am I not like a highclass Jewish "scholar" who travels about and is invited to free meals by rabbis and rich people?

Upon Singer's advice I wrote to Claude Montefiore at Brighton, asking him to come here on Sunday.

Goldsmid has telegraphed Zangwill that he cannot come.

November 23

In the evening with the Chief Rabbi at his other house, in the City. He has two houses, and always stays in the one in the City from Friday to Sunday.

So I drove up to Finsbury Square. I knocked on the door for quite a while. I only heard soft whispering behind it. At length the door opened on a dimly lit hall and I made out a surprising scene: a bevy of young girls who had waited in silence, as though afraid, and now withdrew into the semi-darkness. I thought the Rabbi was holding Sabbath School. He told me afterwards that his daughter was giving a "young girls' tea party," with an amateur show, a musicale, and recitations.

Later on, Mr. Joseph, Adler's brother-in-law, came to dinner to meet me.

Everything British, with old Jewish touches breaking through. Here I had a strong feeling that Jewish ways need not be ludicrous, as they are among us in Austria, where the heart has gone out of our practices.

And so I put on my top hat after the meal, like the others, and listened to the Rabbi's after-dinner blessing.

Of course, I had told the Chief Rabbi, as I had told Zadoc Kahn and Güdemann, that I was not obeying any religious impulse in my project. But I shall certainly honor the faith of my fathers, at least as much as I would honor other faiths.

After dinner we men sat by ourselves, and later on we were joined by Elkan Adler, an attorney and the Chief Rabbi's brother.

I expounded my project.

The Chief Rabbi said that this was the idea of *Daniel Deronda.*

I said: "I wouldn't even want the idea to be a new one. It is 2,000 years old. The only novelty is the method by which I launch the idea and later organize the *Society* and finally the State. That is to say, not I myself, for I shall withdraw from the execution of the project, which must be something impersonal. I am merely creating the instrumentality which is to direct the operation."

Mr. Joseph, a likable, completely anglicized, slow-thinking and prolix old man, an architect by profession, presented the familiar objections. The Jews are not suitable human material; the experience of the Anglo-Russian emigration committees has been distressing; the people are unwilling to work, etc.

I explained to him that this was due to the faultiness of the experiments made thus far. The experiments were bad, the material is good.

The stupid charity, I said, is to blame for everything. Charity must cease, then the *shnorrers* [beggars] will disappear. The existing Jewish relief committees must subordinate themselves to us —or they will be dissolved.

The Chief Rabbi said: "We shall submit your plan to the Anglo-Russian committee, and they will decide whether they will participate in your project."

I replied: "Of course this committee would take up the matter, but I am not submitting it to them. You can't make me yield to majorities. Whoever goes along with me is welcome. I am first turning to notable Jews who have made a name for themselves by their past efforts, but I do not need them. It will only please me if respected people join with me. But I am not dependent on them."

Elkan Adler has been to Palestine, and he would like us to settle in that country. We would have an enormous hinterland over there.

During all this talk, we were drinking a light claret produced in a Zion colony.

Lunched at the home of Sir Samuel Montagu, M.P. A house of English elegance, in grand style. Sir Samuel a splendid old chap, the best Jew I have met thus far. At table he presides over his family—which is actually unfriendly, or merely wellbred— with the air of a good-natured patriarch.

Kosher food, served by three liveried footmen.

After lunch, in the smoking room, I expounded my case. I gradually roused him to enthusiasm. He confessed to me—in confidence—that he felt himself to be more an Israelite than an Englishman. He said he would settle in Palestine with his whole family. He has in mind a Greater Palestine rather than the old one.

He will hear nothing of Argentina.

He is ready to join our committee as soon as one of the Great Powers takes the matter seriously.

I am to send him my pamphlet before its final publication.

* * *

In the evening with the "Maccabeans."

Skimpy dinner, but good reception.

Everyone welcomes me cordially.

The club members include mostly educated Jews. A strapping officer, Captain Nathan, who at one time was supposed to go to Vienna as a military attaché, but was rejected because of his Jewishness.

After dinner Zangwill calls on me with a mildly satirical introduction.

I give my talk extemporaneously and in three parts. The first two in German. Reverend Singer takes notes as I speak and after each part gives an English resumé of what I have said.

The third part I deliver in French.

My speech gets applause. They confer together in undertones and unanimously elect me as an honorary member.

Then follow the objections, which I refute.

The most important of these: English patriotism.

*   *   *

November 25, at Cardiff

With Colonel Goldsmid.

When I arrived at the station I was met by the Colonel, in uniform. Medium height, small black mustache, anglicized Jewish face, with kind, intelligent, dark eyes.

A small dog-cart was waiting outside the station. The Colonel had his horse and rode on it either in front or in back of the wagon. We exchanged a few words as we rode through Cardiff to his house, "The Elms."

He said to me with a cheerful expression: "We shall work for the liberation of Israel."

Then he told me that he was Commandant of Cardiff and the surrounding district, and showed and explained to me the sights of the city.

Mrs. Goldsmid awaited us at "The Elms"—a lean, refined Englishwoman, with her two young daughters, Rahel and Carmel. An English welcome, which makes you feel at once like an old acquaintance.

In the afternoon I read my plan to the Colonel. He doesn't understand much German; the exposition dragged a little.

But he said: *"That is the idea of my life."* *

He cannot undertake leadership in the project, for it is something political, and as an officer he is not allowed to engage in active politics.

But if the movement got started, he said, he would leave the British and enter the Jewish service. Only, instead of "Jews" he would prefer to say "Israelites," because Israel embraces all the tribes.

He showed me the flag of the Hovevei Zion, with the symbols of the twelve tribes. In contrast, I unfurled my white flag with its seven stars.

* In English in the original.

In spite of that, we understood, we understand, each other. He is a wonderful person.

After dinner, while the ladies and the other English colonel in the party were in the drawing room, I went to the smoking room with Goldsmid. And then came the remarkable story.

"I am Daniel Deronda," he said. "I was born a Christian. My father and mother were baptized Jews. When I found out about this, as a young man in India, I decided to return to the ancestral fold. While I was serving as a lieutenant, I went over to Judaism. My family was indignant at this. My present wife was also a Christian of Jewish descent. I eloped with her, and we had a civil marriage in Scotland, to begin with. Then she had to become a Jewess, and we were married in a synagogue. I am an orthodox Jew. This has not done me any harm in England. My children Rahel and Carmel have had a strict religious upbringing and learned Hebrew at an early age."

That, and his tales of South America, sounded like a novel. Because he has worked for Hirsch in Argentina and knows the local conditions, his advice is worth heeding: that only Palestine can be considered.

The pious Christians of England would help us if we went to Palestine. For they expect the coming of the Messiah after the Jews have returned home.

With Goldsmid, I suddenly find myself in another world.

He wants to deliver the Holy Sepulchre to the Christians stone by stone: part of it to Moscow, another part to Rome!

Like Montagu, he too thinks of a Greater Palestine.

A good idea of his is to hit landed property with a graduated tax. Henry George!

*   *   *

The Viennese pianist Rosenthal happened to be in Cardiff. I wrote him to come to "The Elms." He came after his concert.

Rahel and Carmel listened in graceful poses. Truly, another world. In my mind's eye I could already see the aristocratic Jewesses of the coming era. Exquisite creatures with an oriental touch, gentle and dreamy. And as a piece of bric-a-brac there lay on the drawing room table a Torah scroll in a silver case.

November 26, Cardiff

Goodbye to Colonel Goldsmid. I have already taken him to my heart, like a brother.

November 26, London

Evening at the Rev. Singer's.

I had asked Asher Myers of the *Jewish Chronicle,* Dr. Hirsch, the secretary of the Hovevei Zion, and the painter Solomon to meet me there.

The gentlemen were already waiting when I arrived.

The conference degenerated into a theologizing discussion. Asher Myers asked: *"What is your relation to the Bible?"* *

I said: "I am a freethinker, and our principle will be: Let everyone seek salvation in his own way."

Hirsch asked whether I accepted the flag of the Hovevei Zion.

I countered with my national-social flag: white field, seven stars. The Zion flag can serve those who want it as a Temple banner.

In the end I did not succeed in creating the Center I had had in mind. Singer would like to participate, but the intolerant Asher Myers told him: "You can't do that."

Singer thought that the matter must first be submitted to the prominent Jews: Lord Rothschild, Mocatta, Montefiore, etc.

I answered: "You can't make me yield to majorities. This is the cause of the poor Jews, not of the rich ones. The protest of the latter is null, void, and worthless. Nevertheless, I should like to have the project carried out by a committee, because it must be conducted in an impersonal way."

Asher Myers said: "No, you are the man to conduct it. You must be the martyr to this idea. The orthodox Jews will join with you, but consider you a bad Jew. And besides, the Jews will not want to go to Argentina, but to Palestine."

* In English in the original.

He asked me for a resumé of my pamphlet for the *Jewish Chronicle,* and I promised him one.

As I was leaving, Solomon consoled me. He believed that the Study Commission I desired would be created within the Maccabean Club. His brother-in-law Bentwich, he said, was filled with enthusiasm. The club would devote several Sundays in succession to a consideration of my pamphlet.

Good enough.

Paris, November 28

Rev. Singer accompanied me to the Charing Cross station. So as to be able to talk with him a while longer, I left at eleven o'clock instead of ten.

I shall send the pamphlet and the letters to him. For the time being he is my chief representative in London. He does seem to be very devoted to the cause.

He was remarkably attentive during that final hour.

Then a good crossing, but I was ill when I arrived in Paris. Nordau diagnoses it as bronchial catarrh. I must see to it that I get home and finish the pamphlet.

"A prophet must have sound lungs," says Nordau.

"With such a winter coat a man isn't a prophet," I replied in amusement.

Nordau is more reserved now than he was before my departure for London.

He will participate in the project "within the limits of possibility."

*   *   *

By contrast, Beer the sculptor was immediately heart and soul for the idea at my first intimation of it. He came in the evening, when I took my catarrh to bed, and drew up plans: to make the desert arable, import humus soil into Palestine from Africa, plant forests, etc.

Beer will be an excellent helper; I knew it from the start.

Farewell visit to Zadoc Kahn.

November 29

He was very amiable again, saying that he considered my solution the only one, and why didn't I speak with Salomon Reinach. I said that I was too tired now. Actually, I don't expect a thing from the French Jews.

Zadoc said I should send my pamphlet to Edmond Rothschild. I: "Wouldn't dream of it."

*　　　*　　　*

Vienna, December 15

In international dealings there is neither justice nor humaneness. The absence of these two elements—so one could say jestingly—makes the Jewish Question an international one.

December 15

Mimicry on the part of the Jews.

In this we mainly lost our good qualities, because such national mimicry usually produces only bad ones.

December 24

I was just lighting the Christmas tree for my children when Güdemann arrived. He seemed upset by the "Christian" custom. Well, I will not let myself be pressured! But I don't mind if they call it the Hanukah tree—or the winter solstice.

*　　　*　　　*

The Jewish publisher Cronbach in Berlin will not hear of my offer to bring out my pamphlet. He says that it runs counter to his views. I consoled myself when I noticed from the envelope of his letter that he publishes a hairdressers' journal and the like.

Then I wrote to Duncker & Humblot, who will not have anything to do with it, either.

Publish it under my own imprint, then? If the pamphlet sells, I would look like a businessman!

*　　　*　　　*

January 18, 1896

Schidrowitz telegraphed today from London that my preliminary article, "The Solution of the Jewish Question," has appeared in the *Jewish Chronicle*. The first step into the public arena.

January 19

Signed a contract with the publisher Breitenstein.

He was enthusiastic when I read him a few passages from the text which I finished at last after long toil.

I have changed the title—to *Der Judenstaat* [*The Jewish State*].

I now have the sense of relief that comes from the completion of a job.

Success I do not expect.

I am returning calmly to my literary projects. First of all I shall rework the *Ghetto* play.

January 22

The first manifestation of support, from a London book dealer, P. Michaelis, who places at my disposal his "devotion and energy."

January 23

The second is from Rabbi A. Kaminka in Prague, who calls on me to form a national Jewish party in Austria.

I am answering him that for the present I think I ought to refrain from any personal political agitation.

January 25

Dr. Lieben, Secretary of the local Jewish Community, came to the office. I spoke with him in Bacher's room. Lieben has received an inquiry from London as to whether I was the author of that Utopia in the *Jewish Chronicle*. He had replied that he thought not, "for I know him as a sensible person."

In the course of our talk he brought up, one by one, the familiar, basic objections.

When I stated that I was a nationalist Jew, he said: "That's what you make yourself believe."

I did not take any further trouble with him.

January 27

Güdemann has read the first proofs and writes me full of enthusiasm. He believes that the tract will strike like a bombshell and work wonders. Chief Rabbi Adler has written him that he considers the matter impractical and at the same time, dangerous. The Chief Rabbi has too good a position to find my project to his liking. None of these things irritate me.

February 1

The pamphlet is ready in final proofs.

At the office they already have wind of it.

Oppenheim has read the *Jewish Chronicle* article and derides "the Jewish Jules Verne." He sees in it "material" for a humorous weekly *entrefilet* [sketch].

In line with my basic idea about the transitional phase I recognize in him the scoffer in the street who laughs at the prophet or people's spokesman.

I said to him, naturally in a polite tone of voice: "The man who makes jokes about it I shall make jokes about in return— and I can make wicked jokes."

He replied: "The wickedest joke of all is your making the matter public. If that article in the *Chronicle* appears in German, the anti-Semites will raise a hullaballoo over it. Yes, that would suit them just fine."

Another colleague (from the *Economist*) remarked that he and his fiancée had read the *Chronicle* and decided not to join the movement. I disposed of him with a smile.

For the rest, I already see clearly what opposition I shall encounter, and from what quarters. Journalists making fun of the
whole thing are the most immediate danger now. *Il faudra leur
montrer, que j'ai l'épaule terrible* [I will have to show them that
I can be tough too].

This is the way I believe matters will go: If the thing catches
on, they will content themselves with sullen envy.

If the explosion is only an *explosion de rire* [explosion of
laughter], then I shall be marked down for a fool. This is the
sacrifice—apart from the sacrifices which I can only surmise now,
probably much greater ones—that I am quite deliberately making for the Jewish cause. I am being "taken seriously," I have
already been offered the editorship of a newspaper; other offers
of this kind, far better ones even, would again be made. My job
in itself is good enough and would improve every day. I believe that I am endangering my own job—because, in spite of the
pledge Bacher made me that time, I shall probably find myself in
conflict with my editors. It will take a lot of diplomatic skill on
my part to postpone this conflict as long as possible. Even now I
feel that regardless of my able work I am making them uncomfortable. Perhaps things will change if my pamphlet is a success
—the kind that does not result in the "hullaballoo" that Oppenheim talked about. But if I fare badly, I think they will leave me
in the lurch and perhaps compel me, through the nature of their
polemic against my pamphlet, to leave the staff as a matter of
self-respect.

February 2

Bloch, the former deputy in Parliament, came with a letter
from Güdemann and asked me to let him have a few chapters
from my pamphlet for publication in his *Österreichische Wochenschrift*. Güdemann is enthusiastic and writes: "Your colleagues
ought to place wreaths upon your brow."

Bloch seems to have confidence in the cause. I need professional politicians like Bloch. The only thing is that he believes the project to be dependent on the participation of the Rothschilds. I believed that too in the beginning, but I no longer do. Bloch thinks it is out of the question that people will take the whole thing as a joke, and says that I worry too much about this point. Well, I believe that the first impression will determine at least the speed of the development.

February 2

In the afternoon met Güdemann in the Prater. He said: "I was just thinking of you. You have no idea what a great thing you have done."

He was quite enthusiastic and expects an enormous reaction.

Gloomy atmosphere at the office. Talked with Bacher. He has many grave and great misgivings. The chief danger: my saying that we cannot assimilate. The anti-Semites will seize upon this, just as they will in general pick out of my text any "plums" that they can use and keep quoting them. There is something similar in Levysohn's letter which arrived today and in which he announces that he will fight me vigorously. He says that I was right in shifting the ground of the discussion; but this shift works to our disadvantage.

While I was talking to Bacher, Goldbaum came in. Strangely enough—and as I immediately recognized, with malicious intent —he handed me a protest from a would-be contributor to our literary page who complained that a manuscript of his had not received any attention. It was just as if he wanted to weaken further my position on the staff, which he already considered shaken.

His conversation, too, was full of barbed allusions. He spoke about the Bulgarian Prince Ferdinand and Count Goluchowski who was about to be deposed because his innovations were causing embarrassment and he constituted a menace.

When we were leaving he handed me the page proofs of my pamphlet which had been loaned to him and said: "You have moved me but not convinced me."

After these cordial-sounding words I was ready to believe that in my nervousness I had misinterpreted his behavior in Bacher's room.

But when I came home I saw that in two places he had not even cut the pages of my pamphlet.

Once more, before leaving, I went to Bacher's room. Benedikt came in and made as if to go out again when he saw me. I asked him whether he had read my pamphlet. He replied: "I cannot dwell on trifling fault-finding here and there in the text. One has to take the whole thing or leave it alone."

His voice dropped when he spoke the words "leave it alone." That was all. Still, a downright dramatic touch. Storm clouds hovered over this brief conversation. We had understood each other—and, as though nothing serious or momentous were under discussion, we passed on to indifferent matters, spoke about the Easter number, to which Lemaître was to be requested to contribute an article, and the like.

February 3
At night.

I have sized up Benedikt correctly. This evening he came to my room and asked—*he* asked *me!*—if he could have a talk with me. He wanted to discuss the matter with me "not as the *Neue Freie Presse,* but as an individual." I was to take no decisive action before our talk, nothing that could not later be undone.

I said: "I shall not bring the pamphlet out before then, but I cannot stop the printing of it. Later changes would entail expense."

He answered: "Money can take care of that."

I don't know if I understood him correctly. Does he want to offer me money to desist from publication?

In any case, my answer tomorrow or the next day—whenever this momentous encounter takes place—is determined in advance. I shall, I must tell him: My honor is pledged. Even if I wanted to, I could no longer backtrack. My idea has been expressed in the *Jewish Chronicle* article. It no longer belongs to me. If I kept silent, if I withheld the pamphlet which I have promised publicly, it would appear that I had sold myself to the rich Jews who oppose my plan.—I shall go along with small alterations that he may desire, but make him pay the printing costs involved. Such payment must *in eventum* [for the future] furnish the proof that I may need some day.

But how right I was when I told my parents this afternoon that I was already in the thick of the fight.

Yes, I believe that the hardest battle is now taking place. There is in it an almost pantomimic silence, a dramatic climax with little talk, but every word is a tragic action.

The *Neue Freie Presse* is wrestling with me, the boss with his employee. He has all the strength of his superior position; I have justice on my side.

If I am driven into a corner, there is one utmost concession I can make: waive my claim to the promised article, which was to be my entire compensation for declining that editorship.

February 3

Was at the printing office and talked with the managers, the Hollinek brothers. Both are presumably anti-Semites. They greeted me with sincere cordiality. They liked my pamphlet. One of them said: It was necessary that a man stand up and undertake the task of mediation.

February 4

Lay awake for hours during the night, reflecting about the situation at the *Neue Freie Presse*. There is no doubt that I am in the thick of the battle. Bacher said yesterday: "You are burning your bridges behind you!"

When I speak with Benedikt I must make him understand what faces them if they do not keep their promise to me.

If he forces me to leave the paper, I must immediately have another paper at my disposal. If worst comes to worst, I shall write another pamphlet telling dispassionately of all happenings.

In this campaign I have long been prepared for the first battle. I only marched straight ahead. Suddenly, a small skirmish that does not look like anything. Just a few shots back and forth.

And yet I already know that the big battle, perhaps the decisive one, has begun.

I must remain hard and firm, agree to no procrastination, accept no more promises. Ehrlich's words are in my mind: "They will not keep their promise to you."

I am staking a lot, my entire position—but so is the *Neue Freie Presse!*

February 4

My publisher Breitenstein wants to have a first printing of only 3,000 copies. He has no confidence as yet in its commercial success!

February 4

Showdown discussion with Benedikt.

He said: (1) No individual has the right to take upon himself the tremendous moral responsibility of setting this avalanche in motion and endangering so many interests. (2) We shall no longer have our present fatherland and not yet have the Jewish State. (3) The pamphlet is not yet ripe for publication.

He said there was a personal danger for myself in that I was risking my established prestige. By doing this I was also harming the paper, for among its assets was my literary reputation. Furthermore, I was in direct opposition to several principles of the *Neue Freie Presse*. He wants me to refrain from publication.

I answered: "My honor is pledged. I have already published the idea in the *Jewish Chronicle*. It no longer belongs to me, but to the Jews. If I kept silent now, I would endanger my reputation all the more."

He begged me to think it over once more. At least I should postpone the publication for a few months. He himself would help me do the necessary re-writing. I asked: "When?"

He answered: "In the summer—when I take my vacation."

I merely laughed to myself.

He threatened me in no uncertain terms, although he expressly conceded my right to publish the pamphlet. He forcefully warned me "as a friend," "as an experienced journalist." He "strongly advised," he "urgently desired." He said: "You are really not an Austrian at all, but a Hungarian."

I replied: "I am an Austrian citizen."

He told me some tale, dragged in by the ears, with the point that it was his habit to "swing with my fists when something gets too much for me to take."

He mentioned in passing that he had many young friends in literary circles (which implied the threat that I could easily be replaced as literary editor).

He tickled my vanity: "It is not a matter of indifference if Dr. Theodor Herzl publishes such a piece of writing. You are one of our most outstanding collaborators, an integral part of the *Neue Freie Presse*. If you do publish the pamphlet, at least you should not put your name to it."

I said: "That would be cowardice, and, what's more, needless cowardice."

In the end, he asked me to think it over for another 24 hours. Presumably I am supposed to be racked by deep psychic struggles.

*　　*　　*

In the evening I went to Bloch and then took him along to Güdemann. I told them everything.

At first Güdemann believed that I wanted his consent to retreat, and consequently counseled me to do what two excellent men like Bacher and Benedikt advised me.

But I put my problem on the right plane. Desisting from publication was out of the question, I said. I am not a little boy who backs out of something at the last moment. I shall follow this through. I said it was only a question of the following. Bloch wants to publish in his weekly a translation of my article in the

Jewish Chronicle. I gave him the original manuscript and he had it set in type. I cannot step on Benedikt's toes, must not supply him with the *casus belli* [cause for war] which he would welcome. I do not want, then, to create a *fait accompli* in Vienna before I am acquainted with all his reservations.

Therefore I am withdrawing my manuscript from Bloch—of course, I could not prevent him from printing the translation of my article which Professor Kaufmann has sent him.

This is how we finally left things. Bloch is going to return my manuscript but will publish Kaufmann's translation on his own.

Now, however, Güdemann said that I was right in not retreating. Finally, he went so far as to remark that Benedikt was behaving like a rather petty businessman. When they were afraid that I might found a rival newspaper, they promised to support my pamphlet; now, they actually want to stop me from publishing it.

February 5

Saw Benedikt, but had no talk with him—i.e., we spoke only about ordinary political affairs of the day.

In the evening Bacher came to my room, was very affable, but talked about all sorts of other things.

He was waiting for me to bring up the subject of the pamphlet. But all I talked about was contemporary French literature.

February 6

Alexander Scharf called on me. He had heard from Bloch that I had written a magnificent pamphlet. He would like to get it ahead of the dailies, because his weekly, published on Monday, takes a long time to produce. I was unable to give him permission to reprint anything from it, in view of what was happening at the office.

But we got to talking, and I answered his objections with arguments from the pamphlet. For the objections he made were only the expected ones.

After the first half hour, he compared me to Hertzka, the author of *Freeland,* and reminded me of the story about the lunatic in the asylum who said: "Look at that poor fool; he thinks he's the emperor of Russia, when *I* am."

After another half hour, he compared me to Christ.

He said I was the second Christ who would do the Jews grievous harm.

Amused, I rejected both comparisons, and said: "I am, quite simply, a modern and, at the same time, natural and unaffected person. I am doing the whole thing without any nonsense or fanciful gestures. I can even contemplate with equanimity the possibility that my enterprise will come to nothing."

He: "This merely shows me that you are a *hokhem* [clever person]. At first people will certainly make a laughing-stock of you. The Jewish-owned papers will call you the Mahdi of the Pelikangasse."

"Just let them," I laughed.

Finally he said: "If I didn't know that you can't be bought, and if I were Rothschild, I would offer you five million to suppress the pamphlet. Or I would assassinate you. For you will do the Jews terrible harm.

"Incidentally, I shall read your pamphlet with care; and if you convince me, I shall honestly acknowledge that I am on your side."

I lent him the pamphlet on his word of honor that he would not publish anything from it without my authorization.

Then I tried to make him understand that my tract was not a danger to the Jews, but a boon. I used the simile of a U-tube. Relief for all Jewry begins with an outward flow. In the arm marked "Jewish State," the level gradually rises, while it sinks in the arm representing the places where Jews now reside. No one is ruined; on the contrary, the foundations of new wealth are laid. And through the progressive improvement of the standing of the Jews who emigrate, the situation of those who remain behind improves.

*　　*　　*

In the evening I met Dessauer, the bank director, and strolled with him through the wintry, snow-covered Stadtpark.

Dessauer sees no danger but only benefits in my publication. He thinks that a new and better tone will be introduced into the Jewish Question. Nor does he see any danger to the *Neue Freie Presse* from my tract. He thinks it odd of the *Neue Freie Presse* to believe that it is not regarded as a Jewish paper. For the rest, its publishers should not even take a stand themselves, but simply have my pamphlet reviewed by some Heidelberg professor.

Then we spoke of future developments. Dessauer had a nice idea. He said it would be interesting to see the Jewish State a hundred or two hundred years from now. To see what had come out of my idea. He thinks it quite as likely that the Jewish State will come into being during our lifetime as that it will not be established until decades after our death. In fifty years' time, he believes, the Jewish State will already be in existence. He thinks it will be a great state, for, as the case of England proves, the strength of a state does not depend on the number of its citizens, but on their intelligence.

We did a bit of dreaming about the future achievements of the Jewish people for the welfare of mankind.

* * *

February 7

Bloch's weekly is out and the issue does not contain the Kaufmann translation. At the same time there comes a letter from Bloch in which he excuses himself for not publishing it by saying that he found the translation unsatisfactory; he preferred waiting another week in order to be able to publish my original.

Actually, he has left me in the lurch. He is evidently afraid of the *Neue Freie Presse*.

That, too, is all right with me. This, like everything else so far, just goes to show again that I have no support whatever, that I have to do everything myself.

And Scharf told me yesterday that Bloch had boasted of having assisted me in the writing of the pamphlet.

And yet every line, every word, is my own work.

February 8

In the Diet of Lower Austria, Deputy von Pacher yesterday demanded that anyone who is demonstrably of Jewish ancestry might be deprived of his civic rights.

* * *

My good friend, the Rev. Singer, writes me from London that my scheme has scarcely been discussed in public, but in all the more lively fashion in private. He himself has spoken of it from the pulpit. But on the whole, it still does not come closely enough home to English Jews, for anti-Semitism there is not calamitous.

* * *

In the Berlin monthly *Zion* there is a friendly review of my *Chronicle* article from the pen of Dr. J. Holzmann. However, he is against a language federalism.

I am writing him that we should not conjure up any differences among ourselves at this time, but save wrangling for later.

February 9

Met Bloch who told me that in response to my article reproduced in *Zion* a delegation of students had called on me while I was out. They also wished to invite me to Güdemann's lecture in the *Lesehalle*. I went there with Bloch. On the way he told me that Scharf had been to Güdemann to request G. to prevail upon me as well as my father not to publish my treatise. Scharf also said that the community would hold it very much against Güdemann if he failed to dissuade me.

I said: "I shall give Güdemann a letter to the effect that he made every effort to dissuade me from my purpose."

This only goes to show again that no one helps me, in fact, that everyone tries to hinder me—the very people who will undoubtedly claim later, if success comes, that they were my collaborators.

As for those who tremble for their possessions—Scharf owns several houses in Vienna—I shall simply tell them this: "If you want to cover yourselves against possible losses, simply subscribe for shares in the *Jewish Company*. What you lose here through the moving out of your Jewish tenants, you will gain over there by their moving in. The U-tube! By the same amount that you sink here, you will rise there. And besides, you can have the same houses again on the other side. The *Company* will build them for you."

*   *   *

In the *Jüdische Akademische Lesehalle* I was greeted with enthusiasm. When the chairman welcomed the guests, my name received the longest and most tempestuous applause—which, if my eyes did not deceive me, may have piqued one or another among the guests of honor.

After Güdemann's lecture, a few of the young people came up to me, and I spoke extemporaneously for an hour. There were some hundred of them—many erect figures, all eyes sparkling with intelligence. They stood crowded together and listened with mounting enthusiasm. A great success—as I had expected. I had long ago pictured the entire scene just as it happened. As I drove away, they stood in the street and shouted after me through the night a loud, many-voiced "*Prosit* [Cheers]!"

February 9

One of the students in my audience yesterday, Carl Pollak, came to see me, because he had to "give vent to my enthusiasm."

He said that right after my speech a few people who had hitherto been lukewarm declared that they would get behind the national idea.

February 10

Read today the pamphlet entitled *Auto-Emancipation* which Bloch gave me.

An astounding correspondence in the critical part, a great similarity in the constructive one.

A pity that I did not read this work before my own pamphlet was printed. On the other hand, it is a good thing that I didn't know it—or perhaps I would have abandoned my own undertaking.

At the first opportunity I shall speak about it in public, and possibly write an article about it in *Zion*.

February 14

Days of excitement, full of palpitations and shortness of breath.

Talked with Ludassy today. The *Wiener Allgemeine Zeitung* should lead it off. After a quarter of an hour he got the point. He asked: "Shall I review it as a friend or a critic? In the latter case, I may draw blood."

To which I said: "*Hanc veniam damus petimusque vicissim* [we pardon and ask for pardon in turn]." Whoever whacks me, I shall whack in return. *Je ne me laisserai pas faire* [I won't stand for it]. I'll fight hard. But those who go with me will all become famous figures in history."

He said: "I will go with you."

*　　*　　*

My 500 copies came this evening. When I had the bundle carted to my room, I was terribly shaken. This package of pamphlets constitutes the decision in tangible form. My life may now take a new turn.

Then I went to the office. I recalled the fisherman on the "*Seewiesen*" at the Alt-Aussee Lake who said: "The most remarkable thing is a man's never giving up hope."

February 15

My good papa comes and tells me that the pamphlet is already on display in Breitenstein's window.

Will there be a fight at the office today?

*   *   *

Spoke again with Ludassy. He is already dropping off. He has changed his mind. He "must write the way my readers want it." There was "a difference between what a writer of *feuilletons* says and what an editorial writer says."

When I replied that I believed the masses would share my views, he remarked: "I shall always be able to wheel round."

That's all right, too.

Afterwards went to see Szeps. He seemed to understand the matter, but he too has nothing but misgivings. "A newspaper must not be original," he said. "Newspapers cannot propagate new ideas."

He wants to think it over.

Meanwhile, the pamphlet has appeared in the bookstores. For me, the die is cast.

February 15

At this point my good father is my only standby. All those with whom I have conferred on the subject up to now are cautiously keeping in the background, watching events, biding their time. At my side I feel no one but my dear old dad. He stands firm as a rock.

Oppenheim made some jokes last night at the office. He wants to have my pamphlet bound. "If you are *meshugge* [crazy], have yourself bound," he said, after I had given him a copy at his own request.

I must be prepared for this sort of thing. The grown-up street urchins will be on my heels. But a man who is to carry the day in thirty years has to be considered crazy for the first two weeks.

At the Stock Exchange, too, there is supposed to have been a lot of discussion of the pamphlet yesterday. If anything, the mood seems to be hostile to me.

February 16

Dr. S. R. Landau came to see me. I believe I have in him a devoted and capable supporter.

He seems to be an ardent enthusiast, with the main fault of that type of person: intolerant zeal.

But a good, stalwart man. Properly controlled, such energies can work wonders.

February 17

Not a single local paper has expressed itself yet. Still, the pamphlet begins to be a known quantity. Acquaintances ask me: "Is that pamphlet people are talking about by you? Is it a joke or something meant to be serious?"

I answer: "Deadly serious! Of course, anyone who undertakes a thing of this kind must expect that at first the street urchins will run after him. And there is such a thing as grown-up street urchins."

February 18

If nothing happens at the office today, I shall send the following letter to Badeni:

Your Excellency:

When I last had the honor of being received by you, I took the egregious liberty of steering the conversation to the pending problem of the day.

That happened to be—at the end of October—the Lueger question. I noticed your consternation, Excellency, when I said: If you do not confirm his election, you will be endorsing Jew-hatred as a whole.

The reason I said that was the pamphlet which I herewith beg to put in Your Excellency's hands and which was already finished at that time. I wanted to impress myself on your memory by a little short-term prophecy, so that you might later read my political treatise with some attention.

This pamphlet will presumably cause a certain commotion: laughter, outcries, wails, abuse, misunderstanding, stupidities, baseness.

I face all these things with the utmost composure. *Les chiens aboient—la caravane passe* [The dogs bark, the caravan passes].

But I would want Your Excellency to read my political treatise, which is of great practical interest to you, before it is distorted by wild discussion. To read it with your own unprejudiced eyes. You will then notice that I have only touched lightly upon many matters that are of the highest importance . . . (interrupted).

February 18, evening

At noon the university lecturer Feilbogen called on me at the office and said he had to talk to me about the pamphlet—"It is the most significant thing that Zionist literature has produced to date," etc.—paeans of praise.

In the afternoon he came to my house and opened the conversation by asking whether my pamphlet was meant to be taken seriously or whether it was not a satirical presentation of Zionism.

I was quite taken aback and answered: "I am too old for such Alcibiadic jests."

Then, for hours on end, he split hairs, harping on this, carping on that.

I was so sickened by it all that I was unable to go on writing the letter to Badeni, and, in fact, didn't feel like doing anything any more.

In the evening, however, I heard at the office that the *Deutsche Zeitung* (anti-Semitic) is going to publish an editorial on the subject tomorrow. Presumably abuse. But important in any case, because of the attitude the other papers will take in reply.

Now I again feel like writing to Badeni.

*   *   *

(Continuation of letter to Badeni).

Every state has a rightful claim on its Jews—what is to become of these claims? This is one of the many politically delicate points which I barely touched upon in my tract. I am prepared to give Your Excellency quite detailed and perhaps satisfactory explanations on this as well as all other points.

I believe the Jewish State to be a world necessity—and that is why it will come into being.

Anyone who issues such a call will, first of all, have the street urchins running after him with amusement—and there are also grown-up street urchins. As for the masses, they will look up and perhaps join in the laughter, but in any case they will not understand immediately. And part of the masses is a certain section of the press, on both sides, which has an ear cocked for the confused babble of the public and allows itself to be led by everybody and his brother, instead of leading them.

These words of yours, Excellency, caused me at that time to consider your offer which I later had to decline so regretfully when an appeal to my sense of gratitude was made. I would have wanted you first to get to know me as a dependable person through closer association, and at some later date I should have liked to be able to point to this way out from the calamitous situation of the Jews. Today's editorial in the *Deutsche Zeitung* is quite naive and self-contradictory; the writer simply fails to understand my pamphlet, because he does not understand the conditions of modern life. What I am proposing is actually no more than the *regulation* of the Jewish Question, and certainly not the emigration of all the Jews. Least of all can and will it entail the economic weakening of the countries which are at present anti-Semitic.

However, through the same door which I am trying to push open for the poor masses of Jews, a Christian statesman who seizes the idea aright will enter world history. I will not even emphasize the fact that immediate, direct political advantages are also bound up with it.

Should Your Excellency wish to become acquainted with all

these trains of thought, on which my pamphlet is silent, I beg you to summon me to a secret audience—perhaps some evening or other.

No one would ever learn of our conversation through me.

I am Your Excellency's most respectful and obedient servant,

Dr. Th. Herzl

(Mailed on the evening of February 19).

* * *

February 19

Old Heit, a dealer in textiles and property owner on the Franz-Josefsquai, was here and invited me to attend a lecture at the hitherto anti-Zionist "Union."

He said that up to half an hour before reading my pamphlet he had thought it quite impossible that he could ever get interested in a thing of this sort. But I had converted him completely, and he was prepared to sell his real estate, even at a loss, and go overseas.

February 20

Wilhelm of the *Fremdenblatt* informs me in a "humorous" letter that I am rumored to have become "*meshugge* [crazy]." Is that true, he asks.

February 21

Yesterday a students' party at the *Kadimah*. The students gave me a great ovation. I had to make a speech, and the speech was temperate—and mediocre. I didn't want to arouse any beery enthusiasm, urged them to study hard, and warned them against unhealthy fanaticism. We might never get to Zion, so we must strive for a Zion within us.

Attorney Ellbogen came from another meeting and told us that Dr. Feilbogen had made an excellent speech there in *support* of my idea.

Dr. Landau proposed to me the founding of a weekly paper for the movement. That suits me, and I shall look into it. This weekly will become my organ. Landau had another good idea. Newlinsky, the publisher of the *Correspondance de l'Est,* is a friend of the Sultan's. He might be able to procure for us a status of sovereignty—for *baksheesh* [gratuity].

I am also thinking of Kozmian. I shall send Landau to him and try to interest him in the matter.

February 23

At the Concordia Club yesterday Government Councillor Hahn from the Correspondence Bureau tried to make fun of me: "What do you want to be in your Jewish State? Prime Minister or President of the Chamber of Deputies?"

I answered: "Anyone who undertakes the sort of thing I am undertaking must naturally be prepared that at first the street urchins will be on his heels."

Whereupon he crept away sadly.

* * *

At the Volkstheater I spoke with many journalists. My pamphlet is the talk of the town. Some people smile or laugh at me, but in general, the earnest tone of conviction about my treatise appears to have made an impression.

Hermann Bahr told me he was going to write against me, because people cannot do without the Jews. *Pas mal* [not bad]!

February 23

Dr. Landau was here. I asked him to speak to Kozmian so that I might personally discuss the matter with him. Landau thinks that I neglected agriculture in the Jewish State. The answer is simply that we shall have agricultural cooperative societies and agricultural small industrialists, both with credit for machinery from the *Jewish Company.*

We then got on the subject of the language. Landau, like many

Zionists, is in favor of Hebrew. I think the main language must gain acceptance without constraint. If we found a neo-Hebrew state it will be only a New Greece. But if we do not close ourselves off in a linguistic ghetto, the whole world will be ours.

In Vienna they are making jokes about me.

Julius Bauer says: "It's all right with me if we go to Palestine. But I want a republic with a Grand Herzl* at its head."

February 26

In the *Westungarischer Grenzbote* there is an editorial on my book by the anti-Semitic deputy Simonyi. He refers to me in a chivalrous manner.

February 27

The *Daily Chronicle* publishes interviews with the painter Holman Hunt and Sir Samuel Montagu about *The Jewish State*.

Holman Hunt claims priority on the idea, because he had written a letter to an English Jew before my article appeared in the *Jewish Chronicle*.

Montagu thinks that one might offer the Sultan two million pounds for Palestine.

* * *

Neumann of the *Fremdenblatt* writes me that in financial circles the most extravagant praise and blame are being heaped on my book. I knew that it would leave no one indifferent.

* * *

Kosmian came to the office to see Bacher. I ran into him in the anteroom. Landau had called on him. But even before that he had heard about my pamphlet—possibly from Badeni. Kosmian said: "*Il parait que c'est très excentrique* [It seems that it is very eccentric]." I replied: "*C'est un dérivatif* [That's irrelevant]."

* Translator's Note: *Grossherzl,* a pun on *Grossherzog,* the German word for "Grand Duke."

February 28

Yesterday's election to the Vienna City Council again proves me right. Since September the anti-Semitic vote has again increased enormously. Big majorities everywhere, even in the "strongholds" of liberalism: the Innere Stadt and the Leopoldstadt.

Our editorial today is quite resigned.

* * *

Received from Nordau an enthusiastic letter which fills me with pride. He thinks that my *Jewish State* is a "great accomplishment," a "revelation."

March 1

Ludassy attacks me in the *Wiener Allgemeine Zeitung*. "Zionism is madness born of desperation. Away with such chimeras!"

One of his staff humorists makes a little derisive quip about the "Maccabees of Flight."

* * *

In the *Zeit* Professor Gomperz makes an attack on Zionism, using as a "point of departure" my book—which he says he has not read.

The Zionists Birnbaum, Jacob Kohn, and Landau paid me a joint visit and wrangled among themselves.

Kohn is against Landau, *Kadimah* against *Gamalah*.

Birnbaum wants the agitation to be confined to scholarly weeklies, Landau wants to agitate everywhere, Kohn only in Vienna.

It is downright disheartening to observe their rank hostility toward one another.

Birnbaum is unmistakably jealous of me. What the baser sort of Jews express in vulgar or sneering language, namely, that I am out for personal gain, is what I catch in the intimations of this cultured, refined person.

The predicted rancor, from within and from without, is already here.

I regard Birnbaum as envious, vain, and dogmatic. I hear he had already turned away from Zionism and gone over to Socialism when my appearance led him back to Zion again.

* * *

March 2

Hermann Bahr came to see me. He tells me that the Jews of the higher intellectual circles, who in Old Vienna formed the literary salons, the circle around Bauernfeld, and the Grillparzer cult, are horrified at me.

That was to be expected.

* * *

One Professor Schneidewin in Hamlin writes me that my *Jewish State* has convinced him that the solution he had presented in a pamphlet was wrong. At the same time he sends me this 162-page booklet which embodies the standpoint of the "better" anti-Semites.

March 3

A fashion-goods dealer at Semlin, S. Waizenkorn, writes me that all the Semlin Jews are ready to emigrate, bag and baggage, as soon as the *Jewish Company* is founded.

March 4

My warmest adherent so far is—the Pressburg anti-Semite Ivan von Simonyi, who bombards me with flattering editorials and sends me two copies of each.

* * *

Dr. Birnbaum today wrote me a letter in which he bemoans his financial straits. I gave him twenty guilders, which I record

here, because I am certain that he is hostile to me and will grow
more so.*

In conversation with me, he disparaged Landau. In the evening, at the meeting called by Landau, he made a socialistic
speech, and from Landau's report I gather that it contained a
barb against a discussion of my pamphlet, which was on the
agenda.

These are rather discouraging observations.

Landau further writes that Birnbaum wants to become the
Socialist leader in Palestine. We haven't got the country yet, and
they already want to tear it apart.

March 6

The vilest attack so far has appeared in the *Münchner Allgemeine Zeitung,* by A. Bettelheim. He calls my tract "the founding prospectus of a Jewish Switzerland." The contents are reproduced by splicing heterogeneous quotations together.

March 7

Bacher is charming to me now. This is attracting attention in
the office and apparently makes people well disposed toward me.

*   *   *

In the Berlin *Allgemeine Israelitische Wochenschrift,* Klausner
(of the *Börsen-Courier*) pounces on me and "pans" my book
roughly in the foul-mouthed tone of Berlin theater hyenas turning thumbs down on a premiere performance.

The editor of this weekly invites me to answer as sharply as I
please. I am not going to answer at all.

March 7

The local Zionists want to stage rallies in support of my tract.

* Translator's Note: This last sentence was crossed out by Herzl.

310 THE COMPLETE DIARIES OF THEODOR HERZL

The Berlin association "Young Israel" invites me to give a public lecture before a big audience. Rejected this, as well as similar invitations.

March 10

The newspaper *Ha-am* in Kolomea places itself at my disposal.

An enthusiastic letter from Dr. Bierer, Sofia. The Chief Rabbi there considers me the Messiah. This Passover, a lecture on my publication will be given in Bulgarian and Spanish before a large audience.

*　　*　　*

The Rev. William H. Hechler, chaplain to the British Embassy in Vienna, called on me.

A likeable, sensitive man with the long grey beard of a prophet. He waxed enthusiastic over my solution. He, too, regards my movement as a "prophetic crisis"—one he foretold two years ago. For he had calculated in accordance with a prophecy dating from Omar's reign (637-638) that after 42 prophetical months, that is, 1260 years, Palestine would be restored to the Jews. This would make it 1897-1898.

When he had read my book, he immediately hurried to Ambassador Monson and told him: the fore-ordained movement is here!

Hechler declares my movement to be a "Biblical" one, even though I proceed rationally in all points.

He wants to place my tract in the hands of some German princes. He used to be a tutor in the household of the Grand Duke of Baden, he knows the German Kaiser and thinks he can get me an audience.

March 14

Great excitement at the University of Vienna.

The "Aryan" duelling associations have decided that they will no longer give satisfaction to Jews with any weapon, on the grounds that all Jews are devoid of honor and are cowards.

My young friend Pollak and another Jew have challenged two anti-Semites who happen to be reserve officers; and when they refused to fight, the two Jews reported the matter to the General Command. There they were referred to the District Command.

A great deal depends on this decision—namely, the future position of Jews in the Austrian army.

I got Benedikt, whose son is now at the University, and Bacher, all steamed up about the matter.

March 15

Benedikt publishes in the *Economist* a peremptory appeal to the rich not to let the Jewish battle be fought out by the poor and the young alone.

With the exception of my conclusion, Benedikt stands in this article completely on the ground of my political treatise.

March 16

Yesterday, Sunday afternoon, I visited the Rev. Hechler. Next to Colonel Goldsmid, he is the most unusual person I have met in this movement so far. He lives on the fourth floor; his windows overlook the Schillerplatz. Even while I was going up the stairs I heard the sound of an organ. The room which I entered was lined with books on every side, floor to ceiling.

Nothing but Bibles.

A window of the very bright room was open, letting in the cool spring air, and Mr. Hechler showed me his Biblical treasures. Then he spread out before me his chart of comparative history, and finally a map of Palestine. It is a large military staff map in four sheets which, when laid out, covered the entire floor.

"We have prepared the ground for you!" Hechler said triumphantly.

He showed me where, according to his calculations, our new Temple must be located: in Bethel! Because that is the center of the country. He also showed me models of the ancient Temple: "We have prepared the ground for you."

At this point we were interrupted by the visit of two English ladies to whom he also showed his Bibles, souvenirs, maps, etc.

After the boring interruption he sang and played for me on the organ a Zionist song of his composition. From the woman who gives me English lessons I had heard that Hechler was a hypocrite.* But I take him for a naive visionary with a collector's quirks. However, there is something charming about his naive enthusiasm, and I particularly felt it when he sang his song to me.

Afterwards we came to the heart of the matter. I told him: I have got to establish direct contact, a contact that is discernible on the outside, with a responsible or non-responsible statesman —that is, with a minister of state or a prince. Then the Jews will believe in me, then they will follow me. The most suitable man would be the German Kaiser. I must be given help if I am to carry out the task. Up to now I have had nothing but obstacles to combat, and they have been sapping my strength.

Hechler immediately declared that he was ready to go to Berlin and speak with the Court Chaplain as well as with Prince Günther and Prince Heinrich. Would I be willing to give him the travel expenses?

Of course I promised them to him at once. They will come to a few hundred guilders, certainly a considerable sacrifice in my circumstances. But I am willing to risk it on the prospect of speaking with the Kaiser.

At the same time I fully realize that Hechler, whom I don't know yet, may only be a penniless clergyman who likes to travel, and that he may come back with the word: it was impossible to get to the Kaiser.

But even if he is granted an audience, I have no idea of how he will strike these princely families. Actually, here is a major enigma in my path. My previous experience tells me that highly

---

* Translator's Note: One of the occasional puns in the *Diaries*. The German word for "hypocrite" is "Heuchler."

placed persons do not reason any more broadly or see any more clearly than do the rest of us. It is therefore quite as likely that the German princes will laugh at this old tutor for his collector's quirks as that they will go along with his naive fancies. The question now is this: when he comes to Berlin, will they pat him on the shoulder ironically and say, "Hechler, old man, don't let the Jew get you all steamed up?" Or will he stir them? In any case, I shall take the precaution of impressing upon him that he must not say he "came at Herzl's behest."

He is an improbable figure when looked at through the quizzical eyes of a Viennese Jewish journalist. But I have to imagine that those who are antithetical to us in every way view him quite differently. So I am sending him to Berlin with the mental reservation that I am not his dupe if he merely wants to take a trip at my expense.

To be sure, I think I detect from certain signs that he is a believer in the prophets. He said, for example, "I have only one scruple: namely, that we must not contribute anything to the fulfilment of the prophecy. But even this scruple is dispelled, for you began your work without me and would complete it without me."

On the other hand, if he only faked these signs which have made me believe in him, he will all the more be a fine instrument for my purposes.

He considers our departure for Jerusalem to be quite imminent, and showed me the coat pocket in which he will carry his big map of Palestine when we shall be riding around the Holy Land together. That was his most ingenuous and most convincing touch yesterday.

* * *

In the evening I heard from Leo, my wife's brother-in-law, all the snide gossip current among the Jews of his circle, who cannot understand "why he has undertaken this thing in view of his position, and without needing to."

I answered him with a few words which Professor Leon Kellner said to me the other day: "There are Jews who live on Jewry, and those who live for Jewry."

Which will not prevent these same Jews who now make sport of my Quixotism from calling me, in envy, a shrewd speculator afterwards, when success has come.

This people must be educated—and by our example.

* * *

In Vienna people are saying that the students' conflict over satisfaction may be attributed to my pamphlet.

* * *

An editorial in last Thursday's issue of the *Norddeutsche Allgemeine Zeitung* about my pamphlet caused a stir here, and of course a much greater one in Berlin, I imagine.

March 17

Yesterday Heinrich Steiner, the editor of the *Wiener Mode*, came to see me. He impresses me as a good, capable, resolute man with definite convictions. He offered me his services. I gave him my ideas about how the necessary publicity should be organized in the beginning. I told him to buy the *Wiener Allgemeine Zeitung* or Szeps' *Tageblatt* and turn it into a Zionist paper; I would assist him behind the scenes. In this way I could immediately give our first associates in Vienna (Landau, Birnbaum, J. Kohn, etc.) their earliest rewards by procuring good positions for them.

I spent two hours and a half talking to Steiner, and when I spoke some powerful closing words to him on the street, he answered in a voice choked with emotion: "What I am feeling now is a lot for me."

March 17

Letter to Martin Fürth, Secretary of the Prince in Sofia:

Dear Friend:

I have to write you again even before I have your reply to my letter. By wiring for the Congress catalogue (which goes off to you today), you brought yourself to my attention at the exact moment when I discovered a bit of meanness which you could advise or help me in combating.

The perfidy with which certain Jews in Vienna attack me because of my pamphlet defies description. At first they tried to make me out a madman. After this lovely expedient had failed and the attitude of respected "Christian" papers—notably an editorial in the *Norddeutsche Allgemeine Zeitung*—forced people to take me and my plan quite seriously, there were other dirty tricks. Yesterday I was informed that the following lie was disseminated from a certain journalistic nest where the shabbiest among my opponents are based: They say that I published my pamphlet only "in order to get even with Baron Hirsch for rejecting (my) application for the post of general manager of his Jewish colonies."

At the same time someone told me that this lie was supplied to the journalistic nest by a person close to the local *Alliance Israélite*.

I would be very pleased if someone had the courage to publish this slander in a tangible form, because then I could take a few of those rascals by the ears and pin them down. Unfortunately I shall have to wait some time for that, because at present they are giving me the "silent treatment" in Vienna. The result of this silence is that my project is being discussed steadily and excitedly among *all* classes and circles in Vienna. But this also gives the vulgarities of my opponents underground publicity, and I have to think about a remedy.

What do you think? Can this mendacious statement be traceable to the circle around Baron Hirsch? If the answer is yes, what person do you consider capable of it? Hirsch himself I regard as a ruthless man but not one who will strike any low blows. Maybe you could provoke him into making a declaration in which he gives the true state of affairs, namely, that I did not apply to him for anything, but, using the same arguments that are contained in my pamphlet, merely tried to convince him in an interview and in several letters that his efforts to date have been misguided.

He could make such a declaration in a few lines in a letter addressed to you. You will know best in what way you can ask him to do this. If he is the grandiosely constructed fellow that I take him to be, although I now have no use for him and may later pit myself against him sharply, he will *loyalement* [loyally] confirm the truth immediately if you write him a few lines about my righteous indignation.

As for the little curs that are now yelping at me, I shall break their necks with kicks. *J'ai fait du chemin* [I have made some headway] since we discussed the Jewish Question around the *Cirque d'Été*. It won't be long before you will hear something very, very surprising. But one must keep one's mouth tight shut about a *bonne surprise* [good surprise]. That is what I am doing.

Please let me know quickly to what extent I can count on you, for you can imagine that I am not going to take this rotten attack lying down. If this method does not work, another will.

With cordial regards,

Yours sincerely,
Th. Herzl.

March 17

Dr. Beck, my parents' old family physician, has examined me and diagnosed a heart ailment caused by excitement.

He cannot understand why I concern myself with the Jewish cause, and among the Jews he associates with, no one understands it either.

March 26

Breitenstein the publisher tells me that Güdemann has declined to give a lecture on my *Jewish State*. My standpoint, he says, is political, whereas his is religious. From his point of view he must disapprove of my attempts to anticipate Providence.

In other words: he does not dare; he no longer finds it opportune; he is afraid of the rich Jews who are against it.

Earlier he was supposed to write an article about the subject in Bloch's *Wochenschrift*.

* * *

The "Sion" society of Sofia sends me an enthusiastic resolution in which I am proclaimed the Leader.

Met Dessauer the bank director in the street. He is ready to finance the newspaper I need. I require a million guilders for the paper. With this paper I shall subdue the other sheets and the refractory Jews of high finance.

But Dessauer has his moods. A week from now he will plead some fatigue or other. In any case, my next step must be to put our publicity campaign on a sound foundation.

March 29

Seder of the Jewish student association Unitas. Friedmann, a lecturer at the University, explained the history of this festival which, after all, is our most beautiful and most meaningful one. I sat next to him. Later he spoke briefly with me in private, reminded me of Sabbatai Zvi, "who enchanted all people," and winked in a way that seemed to say that I ought to become such a Sabbatai. Or did he mean that I already was one?

March 30

My strange adherent, the Pressburg anti-Semite Ivan von Simonyi, came to see me. A sexagenarian, a mercurial, loquacious man with an astonishing amount of sympathy for the Jews. His conversation is a mixture of the sensible and the nonsensical; he believes in the ritual murder lie, but along with it has the brightest, most modern ideas. Loves me!

April 3

The three Marmorek brothers announce their adherence to my movement with a certain flourish of solemnity. The Parisian Marmorek, of the Pasteur Institute, called on me at the office with his younger brother, the lawyer, in order to declare "in our own name and in that of our brother, the architect" that they are joining in with me and are enthusiastic about it.

April 5

Dr. Schnirer and Dr. Kokesch, of the Vienna "Zion" society, brought me a resolution to the effect that I should continue my work confident of the Zionists' support. Schnirer wants to have an appeal circulated among Jewish intellectuals all over the world. A committee of 15-20 people is to be formed here, each of whom is to send the appeal to three or four of his friends in other cities. In this way thousands of signatures are to be collected. This would give me a substantial backing.

April 7

During the last few days, several conferences with Steiner and Dessauer for the purpose of financing the needed daily paper. A wretched job.

April 9

Dr. Beer-Hofmann has the following idea for an "initial institution": a great medical school, to which all Asia will stream and where, at the same time, the improvement of sanitation in the Orient will be developed. He also has a design for a monumental fountain: Moses Striking Water from the Rock.

April 10

A "free-lance scholar" by the name of Carl Bleicher called on me. At first I took him for a *shnorrer* [beggar] who was out for modest donations for a book. But he would not accept anything from me and placed himself at my disposal as a propagandist. I am recording this because it is a sign of the way the poor have been moved. This old man, who lives on donations of guilders and ten-kreuzer pieces, opened his purse, showed me what he had, and refused my donation. This is the most important difference between my effectiveness and that of Baron Hirsch. They beg from him but do not love him. I am loved by the beggars. That is why I am stronger.

April 13

Dr. Alfred Stern, the "liberal" Community Councillor, came to see me in the office today and unmistakably tried to get closer to me. He said it was nice that someone was championing the Jewish cause and speaking the way I was speaking. I said to him: "Join us and I shall guarantee you popularity. Make this public declaration: I, Alfred Stern, whom you have known as a quiet person, am joining the Zionist movement!—That will have a great effect. Hundreds will follow your example."

He replied: "I think so too. Personally, I would have no objections. But I would be taking on the responsibility for hundreds and thousands."

I countered: "Our party will soon relieve you of this responsibility. When you run for office again, the organized Zionists will come to your election rallies."

This gave him pause for a bit.

April 14

The English clergyman Hechler came to me in the afternoon in a state of great excitement. He had been to the *Burg*, where the German Kaiser arrived today, and spoke to Dryander, the General Superintendent, and another gentleman from the Kaiser's retinue. He strolled through the city with them for two hours and told them the contents of my pamphlet, which greatly surprised them.

He told them the time had come *"to fulfill prophecy."* *

* In English in the original.

Now he wants me to join him tomorrow morning on a trip to Karlsruhe to see the Grand Duke; this is where the German Kaiser is going tomorrow evening. We would beat him there by half a day. It was Hechler's idea to call on the Grand Duke first thing, tell him what it was all about, and say that he had brought me to Karlsruhe against my will, so that I might give the gentlemen further information.

I declined to go along, because it would make me look like an adventurer. If then Their Highnesses did not feel inclined to admit me, I would be standing in the street in an undignified posture. I told him to go there by himself, and if they wanted to speak to me, I would immediately follow a wired invitation.

Hechler asked me for my photograph in order to show it to the gentlemen; he apparently thinks that they would picture me as a "shabby Jew." I promised to give him a photo tomorrow. Strange that I should just have had my picture taken—something that had not occurred to me in years—for my father's birthday today.

Then I went to the opera, sat in a box diagonally across from the imperial box, and all evening studied the motions of the German Kaiser. He sat there stiffly, sometimes bent affably to our Emperor, laughed heartily a number of times, and in general was not unconcerned about the impression he was making on the audience. At one time he explained something to our Emperor and underlined it with firm, vigorous, small gestures with his right hand, while his left hand rested permanently on the hilt of his sword.

I came home at eleven o'clock. Hechler had been sitting in the hall for an hour waiting for me. He wants to leave for Karlsruhe at seven in the morning.

He sat with me until half-past twelve making gentle conversation. His refrain: *fulfill prophecy!**

He firmly believes in it.

---

* In English in the original.

April 15

Hechler left as scheduled this morning. I went to his place to inquire about it; that is how improbable it still seemed to me, despite everything.

April 15

In the evening, at the offices of the *Wiener Mode* with Steiner and Colbert. The latter is well qualified to secure the financial backing for my newspaper. He outlined a clever plan which involves the expansion of his present enterprise by adding a paper factory and by incorporating the paper which I am to direct with limited liability.

April 16

Hechler wires me from Karlsruhe:

Everyone enthusiastic. Must stay through Sunday. Please hold yourself in readiness. Hechler.

April 17

The invitation to come to Karlsruhe has not arrived yet. I am beginning to believe that Hechler is creating illusions for himself.

April 17

The most stalwart people so far have been the Zionists in Sofia. Today there arrived a resolution which was passed in the synagogue of Sofia under the chairmanship of the Grand Rabbi. Six hundred signatures. Enthusiastic words.

April 18

From two sources I hear that Privy Councillor Baron Erb, a former Section Head in the Ministry of the Interior, is greatly interested in *The Jewish State* and would like to have a talk with me.

*   *   *

Agliardi, the Papal Nuncio, spoke with my colleague Münz some time ago and told him he was prepared to receive me. Unfortunately I did not go to him right away. Now he has been called to Rome by the Pope and is supposed to represent him at the coronation of the Czar. If I had spoken with the Nuncio and won him over, the matter would immediately have been brought before the Pope and the Czar; their consent is necessary because of the Holy Sepulchre.

* * *

No word from Hechler. I now explain it to myself this way: with his telegram Hechler wanted to let me down easy about the failure of his mission. But since, in any case, he will have brought my pamphlet to the attention of the Grand Duke and perhaps even to that of the Kaiser, his travelling expenses are worth it to me. I shall give them to him without making a face, because that way I shall make all the more certain of his good services in the future.

April 18

Hechler wires from Karlsruhe:

Second conversation with H. M. and H. R. H.* yesterday excellent. Must wait some more. Hechler.

April 21

Heard nothing more from Hechler. Meanwhile the Kaiser has left Karlsruhe and gone to Coburg.

Wrote to Nordau and gave him the diplomatic assignment of putting out feelers toward Hirsch. If Hirsch hands over a few million, we can give the project a tremendous resonance and can spread some of the money around for *baksheesh* [gratuities] in Turkey.

---

* Translator's Note: The initials stand for His Majesty (i.e. the German Kaiser) and His Royal Highness (i.e. the Grand Duke of Baden).

April 21, afternoon

I began the letter to Nordau yesterday and finished it today.
Between yesterday and today Baron Hirsch died on an estate
in Hungary.

I learned of it an hour after I had mailed the letter to Nordau.
So I had to recall this letter by telegram. But what a strange
coincidence. The pamphlet has been finished for months. I gave
it to everyone except Hirsch. The moment I decide to do so,
he dies. His participation could have helped our cause to success
tremendously fast.

In any case, his death is a loss to the Jewish cause. Among the
rich Jews he was the only one who wanted to do something big
for the poor. Perhaps I did not know how to handle him properly.
Perhaps I ought to have written that letter to Nordau two weeks
ago.

It seems to me as though our cause has grown poorer this day.
For I still kept thinking of winning Hirsch over to the plan.

*   *   *

Hechler telegraphs from Karlsruhe:

Third conversation yesterday. Fourth today, four o'clock. Hard
work to make my wish prevail. Nevertheless, all goes well. Hechler Zirkel 2.

April 21, at night

I had intended to go to Pest tomorrow morning. Late this evening I received Hechler's call to come to Karlsruhe.

A curious day. Hirsch dies, and I make contact with princes.

Now begins a new book of the Jewish cause. After my return
I shall add Hechler's last two telegrams to this full notebook.

Book Three

Begun April 22, 1896
On the way to Karlsruhe

April 22

A sunny Spring day. Today at seven I wanted to take the boat to Pest. And now I am sitting in a compartment of the Orient Express, going to Karlsruhe.

I am writing these pages in pencil and in shaky handwriting directly into the diary which I am holding on my knees, because later I shall probably have no time to make a clean copy. If I did not have a chance to do this when the Jewish cause was only in its beginnings, what will it be like in the future when we pass from the dream into the reality! For now it may be presumed that every day there will be interesting events, even if I should never get to the point of founding the State.

The fact that the Grand Duke has sent for me is the plainest evidence that he—and consequently also the Kaiser, who was with him three days ago—takes the matter seriously. And this fact is the most momentous, the most improbable. If it is true, it will affect the world like a thunder-clap and will be the "success" which Bierer is praying for in Sofia.

* * *

A delightful day, a lovely one. A flush of green on the beckoning meadows. On a wooden hill the trees are divided, giving the appearance of a broad hair-parting. Through them one can see as a delicate background the pale Spring sky—and at this moment my thoughts turn to the dead Baron Hirsch.

The living are right. I am right—as long as I am alive.

The Jews have lost Hirsch, but they have me.

And after me they will have someone else. Progress must go on.

A Vienna morning paper said in its obituary today: Hirsch was unable to help the poor because he was rich. This was the general idea—and it is right. I am tackling the same task differently, and, I believe, better and more forcefully, because I am not using money but an idea.

* * *

Before my departure I received another telegram from Hechler:

Cannot possibly remain here till Saturday. Conference with H. R. H. set for Thursday for both of us. Must I really return with mission half accomplished? . . . I must leave tomorrow if you cannot come by Thursday noon. Hechler.

He had interpreted my yesterday's message that I was leaving for Pest as a reply to his second telegram of yesterday, which it was not. It is a good thing that he thought it necessary to urge me again. But today, beaming with joy, he will report to the Grand Duke that I am coming after all.

* * *

I really don't know much about the Grand Duke: only that he is an old man and was a friend of Friedrich. At present he seems to have Wilhelm's ear, too. Therefore, a great deal depends on this conference and on the impression I make upon him.

Yet I must not become dizzy on these heights. I shall think of death and be earnest.

I shall be cool, calm, firm, modest but determined, and speak the same way.

April 23, Karlsruhe

I arrived here at eleven last night. Hechler met me at the station and took me to the Hotel Germania, which had been "recommended by the Grand Duke."

We sat in the dining-room for an hour. I drank Bavarian beer, Hechler milk.

He told me what had happened. The Grand Duke had received him immediately upon his arrival, but first wanted to wait for his privy-councillor's report on my *Jewish State*.

Hechler showed the Grand Duke the "prophetic tables" which seemed to make an impression.

When the Kaiser arrived, the Grand Duke immediately informed him of the matter. Hechler was invited to the reception, and to the surprise of the court-assembly the Kaiser addressed him with the jocular words: "Hechler, I hear you want to become a minister of the Jewish State."

Contrary to etiquette, Hechler replied in English, whereupon the Kaiser continued in English: "Isn't Rothschild behind this?"

Naturally, Hechler answered in the negative. And with that the "conversation" seems to have been at an end.

So far, then, the results have been rather meager.

On the other hand, Hechler had better luck with the Grand Duke. There he was received a number of times. The Grand Duke spoke of the late Prince Ludwig, whose tutor Hechler had been, and wept freely. Hechler comforted him and read him a psalm in which Zion is mentioned.

Then the Grand Duke was open to further conversation. His main misgiving was that his action might be misinterpreted if he went along with my plan. People would assume that he wanted to drive the Jews out of his country. Also, my status as a journalist gave him pause. Hechler guaranteed that nothing would get into the papers.

At that point the Grand Duke asked what he could actually do for the cause.

Hechler said: "It was Your Royal Highness who, first among the German princes at Versailles, proclaimed King Wilhelm emperor. What if you were to participate in the second great founding of a state in this century, too! For the Jews will become a *grande nation* [great nation]."

This made an impression on the Grand Duke, and he consented to Hechler's calling me here, in order that I might expound the matter to him.

I am to come to a private audience at four o'clock this afternoon.

I accompanied Hechler to his quarters through the clean, deserted streets of this nice capital. Now and then, night owls, coming from a tavern, raised a loud and cheerful shout.

A pleasant provincialism revealed itself to my eyes in these night scenes and in Hechler's stories. The sentinel in front of the castle gate listened complacently while Hechler told me where the apartments of the Grand Duke and of the Grand Duchess were located and where he himself had once lived. Nostalgically he pointed to the elegant windows. I accompanied him to his door. He is staying in one of the outlying court buildings.

* * *

My task this afternoon will be to get the Grand Duke to recommend me to the Kaiser for an audience, and also to interest the Grand Duke of Hesse, the Czar's father-in-law, in the cause. Then the latter might talk about it in St. Petersburg, when he attends the coronation of the Czar.

* * *

Walked and rode about with Hechler. We viewed the mausoleum of Prince Ludwig, which is just being completed. With a solemn beauty this red sandstone chapel stands in the charming hunting forest next to the Wolfsgraben, where young Ludwig used to play.

I had Hechler give me details about the grand-ducal family, so as to know with whom I would be talking.

I also took a good look at the photographs of the Grand Duke which are displayed in the shop windows. Looks like a well-meaning, commonplace person.

Hechler told me further that the Grand Duke had seemed concerned lest the departure of the Jews might also involve an enormous exodus of money.

I shall accordingly reassure him on this point.

* * *

Hechler related how Napoleon I came to Karlsruhe one day and forced the Margrave Karl to marry his step-daughter on the spot—otherwise his days as a ruler would be over. The margrave complied and in return was made a grand duke.

* * *

The lay-out of the city of Karlsruhe is enchanting. Everything radiates from the castle. Behind the castle, a park and beautiful forests. In front, the peaceful town.

April 23

Lunched with Hechler. He had brought his decorations along and was more excited than I was. I did not change my clothes until after lunch, half an hour before the audience. Hechler asked me if I did not want to wear tails. I said no, for too formal an attire on such an occasion can also be tactless. The Grand Duke wishes to speak with me, as it were, *incognito*. So I wore my trusty Prince Albert. Externals increase in importance the higher one climbs, for everything becomes symbolic.

The rainy morning had turned into a delightful afternoon when we came out of the hotel. It was only twenty minutes to four o'clock, so we were able to stroll about a bit.

In good spirits I said to Hechler: "Remember this fine day, the lovely Spring skies over Karlsruhe! Perhaps a year from today we shall be in Jerusalem." Hechler said he planned to ask the Grand Duke to accompany the Kaiser when the latter went to Jerusalem next year for the consecration of the church. I should also be present then, and he, Hechler, would like to go along as a technical adviser to the Grand Duke.

I said: "When I go to Jerusalem, I will take you with me."

Although we only had a few more steps to go, we took a cab and drove up in front of the castle in style. We went up the little ramp, something that struck me as a touch of special refinement about our visit. It was the first time I had driven up before a princely castle. I tried not to let myself be overawed by the soldiers on guard. The door-keeper treated Hechler like an old friend. We were led into the first waiting-room. It was the Adjutants' Hall. And this did take my breath away. For here the regimental flags stand in magnificent rank and file. Encased in leather, they rest solemn and silent; they are the flags of 1870-1871. On the wall between the flag-stands is a painting of a mili-

332 THE COMPLETE DIARIES OF THEODOR HERZL

tary review: the Grand Duke parading the troops before Kaiser Wilhelm I. One might say that only now did I realize where I was.

I tried to divert myself from becoming excessively impressed by taking an inventory, like a reporter: furniture upholstered in green velvet; the brown, curved wooden legs of the chairs trimmed with gilt beading; photographs of the three German emperors.

Fortunately, Hechler chattered without a break, too. He told me about the first time he was in this hall when as a young fellow he brought a petition to retain an Inspector of Secondary Schools who was to be dismissed. At that time an adjutant had come up to him and said: "Don't be afraid! The Grand Duke is only a man like ourselves."

I thought to myself, smiling inwardly, "That's good to know, anyway."

Then the Gentleman of the Bed-Chamber appeared and invited us to step into the next salon. The Grand Duke was taking a little stroll among his pheasants and would come shortly.

This second salon is rococo. Red silk damask tapestries, the arm-chairs covered with the same material. Large photographs of the German emperors. On the wall, oil portraits of a former grand duke and his wife.

Hechler continued to bolster my spirits by his prattle. If he did this intentionally, it was very discreet.

He had, in general, prepared me in a most tactful manner. For instance, he had remarked on our way to the castle that I must unglove my right hand, in case the Duke offered me his hand to shake.

Insertion: At lunch I had told him that the Vienna Nuncio, Agliardi, had sent me word (through Dr. Münz) that he wanted to have a talk with me. I told him this so that he might induce the British ambassador, Monson, to speak with me. Hechler immediately warned me against Agliardi and Rome. He bade me be careful. Meanwhile I thought to myself: just let them be jealous of one another, Englishmen and Russians, Protestants and Catholics. Let them contend over me—that way our cause will be furthered.

While we were sitting in the red salon, Hechler told me about the deceased Grand Duke whose portrait hung on the wall: he was reputed to be of dubious parentage. At least that is what the house of Bavaria had asserted. Bavaria wanted to drive out the reigning family of Baden and had a secret agreement with Austria. Austria had promised the Palatinate to Bavaria and secretly paid her two millions a year, up to 1866. And then, in order to justify the claims upon Baden, the Caspar Hauser myth was started in Bavaria. I listened to Hechler's story absent-mindedly. I don't even know if I am reproducing it correctly now.

It only pleased me to hear of these egotistic wranglings among the great, because it made me feel a bit superior in the purity of my own movement and gave me more self-assurance.

Suddenly the door from the study opened, and there entered an old general who looked robust but not obese—the Grand Duke. We jumped up from our arm-chairs. I made two bows. The Grand Duke shook hands with Hechler—but did not avail himself of my fittingly bared right hand. He motioned to us to follow him. I went in last and closed the door behind me. I have no idea how the study looked, for I had to keep my eyes on the Grand Duke, either speaking or listening, all the time. He is seventy years of age, but looks six to eight years younger.

Three arm-chairs were in readiness. The one I got faced directly against the light. The arm-rests were not far enough apart to let a man drop his arms by his side. These arm-chairs may be very comfortable for relaxing, leaning back, and propping one's forearms on the rests. But since it would not have been proper for me to lean back, I sat for two and a half hours in a strained position, which may also have affected my manner of delivery.

At first I spoke self-consciously. I felt constrained to speak in an undertone, which eliminated the usual self-intoxication of speech. In response to the first polite questions about what kind of a trip I had had and where I lived, I told him what my profession was and also mentioned my former position in Paris.

The Grand Duke said: "I take the *Neue Freie Presse*." He inquired about Paris. I described the parliamentary crisis and particularly the present Bourgeois cabinet.

After a few minutes he interrupted me: "But we were going to talk about other things."

Whereupon I came right to the point and asked him to interrupt me with queries wherever my exposition was not clear enough.

So I unfolded the entire subject. Unfortunately I had to concentrate so much while I was speaking that I was not able to observe well. Hechler said afterwards that the conversation should have been taken down stenographically. He thought I had spoken quite well and had found some felicitous expressions.

All I know is that the Grand Duke kept looking straight into my eyes with his beautiful blue eyes and calm, fine face, that he listened to me with great benevolence; and when he himself spoke, he did so with ineffable modesty. After exerting my entire brain power for two hours and a half, I was so exhausted that I can no longer remember the exact course of the conversation.

In any case, the Grand Duke took my proposed formation of a state quite seriously from the beginning.

His chief misgiving was that if he supported the cause, people would misinterpret this as anti-Semitism on his part.

I explained to him that only those Jews shall go who want to.

Since the Jews of Baden are happy under his liberal reign, they will not emigrate, and rightly so. In the course of his conversation I reverted several times more, and from different angles, to his friendliness toward the Jews and used it in various ways as an argument. If he supported our cause, I said, it would no longer be possible to regard it as something hostile to the Jews. Moreover, it was our duty, as leaders of the Jews, to make clear to the people that the establishment of the Jewish State would constitute an act of goodwill and not of persecution.

Further I said: "If Your Royal Highness' benevolent attitude toward the Jews became known, your duchy would get such an influx of Jews that it would be highly calamitous."

He smiled.

(Continued on the train, returning home, on April 24)

"Quite generally," I said, "it is part of the Jews' misfortune that their well-wishers don't dare to concern themselves with them at all. During their long martyrdom they have grown so sensitive that one can't even touch them."

The Grand Duke then reformulated the same thought. He said he was afraid of offending his Jewish subjects if he publicly endorsed my plan. To be sure, it was common knowledge how he had felt about the Jews up to now, but people would probably misunderstand him anyway and believe that he had simply changed his mind. He said he had never had reason to complain about his Jewish citizens. "For twenty-five years a Jew was my Minister of Finance," he said, "and he always did his duty to my satisfaction. He governed well. He has adhered to your religion to this day. But even here in Baden conditions are no longer what they used to be. A Jew named Bielefeld, with whom I was working on a literary project, advised me himself to omit his name from the publication, because nowadays this might cause trouble. We have had other difficulties caused by anti-Semitism, especially in the judiciary. We have Jews at all levels of legal life, and this has caused certain difficulties.

"And yet the Jews have many good qualities. I have yet to see a drunken Jew. They are sober-minded and thrifty; they always know how to shift for themselves. A cattle dealer, out on the road all day, will still keep away from the taverns—in fact, he eats nothing from early morning until he gets home at night. In addition to frugality there is also great intelligence, which, to be sure, sometimes applies itself to fraud. But, on the other hand, if one looks at the blockheads who allow themselves to be outwitted like this, one can't help saying, 'it serves the fools right.'

"At all events, you will have very intelligent human material for the founding of your state.

"But how do you imagine the practical implementation will go?"

I then presented the entire plan, which he had actually known only in Hechler's version—that is, in its "prophetic" aspects, which, of course, I don't have much to do with.

The Grand Duke thought that the governments could take a closer interest in the matter only if they liked the looks of the *Society of Jews.*

Naturally I advocated the opposite course. Some princes should manifest their favorable disposition; this would enable the *Society of Jews* to act with more authority from the outset. And authority was necessary if such a big movement was to be carried out in an orderly way. For even during the migration the Jews would stand in need of education and discipline.

(Continued in Munich, April 25)

The Grand Duke mentioned the degradation which, according to newspaper reports, existed among the Russian Jews who had emigrated to London.

I said: "In order to bring this under control, we need a strong authority. This is precisely why it is indispensable that we be recognized by the Great Powers at the start."

The Grand Duke said: Actually, Germany cannot very well take the initiative in this. In the first place, she is not interested in the question to the same great extent as, for example, Austria. In that country, of course, there are great anti-Semitic problems, due to Lueger. Germany has no excessive number of Jews. Their departure would not even be welcomed by the economists.

I then explained how only the *trop plein* [surplus] was to be drained off; how movable property can never be considered as tied to any particular country; and how, after this solution of the Jewish Question, it will have to come back all the more. I said that at present such capital was creating trouble for the domestic economy by stimulating industry in remote lands with cheap labor. There is no need to bring the Chinese to Europe; factories are being built for them *out there.* In this way, after agriculture has been imperiled by America, industry is being threatened by the Far East.

To offset this, my movement wants to help on two fronts: through draining off the surplus Jewish proletariat, and through keeping international capital under control.

The German Jews cannot but welcome the movement. It will divert the influx of Jews from Eastern Europe away from them.

The Grand Duke repeatedly punctuated my observations with a murmured "I wish it were so."

He then half turned to Hechler:

"I suppose that cooperation between England and Germany is not very likely. Relations between the two are, unfortunately, badly disturbed at present. Would England go along?"

I said: "Our English Jews will have to see to that."

The Grand Duke said, somewhat ill-humoredly: "If they can manage that . . ."

I said: "If it were known that the Grand Duke of Baden took an interest in the matter, this would make a profound impression."

He cried: "That is not true. My position is not great enough. Ah, if the German Kaiser or the King of Belgium did it!"

I persisted: "Oh, but if an experienced prince, one who helped to fashion the German Empire, one to whom the German Kaiser turns for counsel, endorses this new enterprise, it will make a great impression. Your Royal Highness is the Kaiser's adviser."

He smiled: "I advise him, but he does what he pleases."

I: "I would make an effort to explain the merits of the matter to the Kaiser, too. If he consented to receive me, it would remain as secret as our present conversation."

The Grand Duke: "I think you ought to create the *Society of Jews* first. Then we shall see whether one can have any dealings with it."

I: "Then there will already be more heads than one. The primary steps, the first rising bubbles, would presumably still have to be my work."

The Grand Duke: "In any case, the project can succeed only if few people know about it. Public discussion immediately distorts everything."

Hechler now came to my aid: "Would not Your Royal Highness permit Dr. Herzl to tell a few trustworthy men in England that the Grand Duke of Baden takes an interest in the matter?"

The Grand Duke assented to this, with the repeated stipulation that the matter might be discussed only outside the borders of his country. Then he asked me whether I had taken any steps yet with the Sultan.

Thinking of Newlinsky, I said that someone had already offered to speak with the Sultan.

At that point I set forth the advantages which the project would bring to the Orient. If Turkey were partitioned in the foreseeable future, an *état tampon* [buffer state] could be created in Palestine. However, we could contribute a great deal toward the preservation of Turkey. We could straighten out the Sultan's finances once and for all, in return for this territory which is not of great value to him.

The Grand Duke wondered if it would not be better first to send a few hundred thousand Jews to Palestine, and then raise the question.

I said with determination: "I am against that. It would be sneaking them in. The Jews would then have to confront the Sultan as insurgents. But I want to do everything open and above-board, fully within the law."

At first he looked at me in surprise when I spoke so forcefully; then he nodded approval.

Next I expatiated on the general advantages of the Jewish State for Europe. We would restore to health the plague-spot of the Orient. We would build railroads into Asia—the highway of the civilized peoples. And this highway would then not be in the hands of any one Great Power.

The Grand Duke said: "That would also solve the Egyptian

question. England clings to Egypt only because she must protect her passage to India there. Actually, Egypt costs more than it is worth."

Hechler said: "Could Russia have designs on Palestine?"

The Grand Duke said: "I don't think so. For a long time to come, Russia will have her hands full in the Far East."

I asked: "Does Your Royal Highness consider it possible that I shall be received by the Czar?"

He said: "According to the latest reports, the Czar is accessible to no one. He receives only his ministers when necessary, and no one else. However, one might try in Hesse to place your book in his hands. I believe that the Czar is not hostile to the Jews, but he must take the mood of the Russian people into account. An autocrat by no means always rules autocratically."

I asked the Grand Duke for permission to write him from time to time, and he graciously consented. What modesty and plain-dealing, all around! I felt inwardly ashamed at having wished to reduce him to the commonplace before I had even spoken with him. He is of a grand, noble naturalness. I no longer recall at what points in the conversation he discussed parliamentarianism, the standard working day, and other things.

He deplored the decline of parliamentary government and said he was "a genuine constitutional ruler." The legislative process is getting worse and worse. Many laws are being passed that are worthless.

A propos of my seven-hour working day with overtime, he spoke about experiments that have been made with the standard working day in Switzerland. The workers themselves are not satisfied with it.

To illustrate the psychology of the worker, I told him an incident from *Tom Sawyer* by Mark Twain, how one Sunday afternoon Tom has to whitewash his father's fence as a punishment, and how he turns this to profit. Tom does not say to his chums, "I *have* to," but "I am *allowed* to whitewash the fence." Then they all importune him to let them help him.

The Grand Duke smiled: "Very pretty."

He then told me about the hatred people have for anything new: how someone wanted to establish a useful credit-bank in Baden and how this proved impossible, because hidebound private interests put up a fight against it. When relating or explaining something, he repeatedly used the expression "You will agree with me," or something similar. With all his dignity he has a chivalric modesty.

When Hechler took the floor afterwards and discoursed on the imminent fulfilment of the prophecy, the Grand Duke listened silently, magnificently, and full of faith, with a strikingly peaceful look in his fine, steady eyes.

Finally he said something that he had said several times before: "I should like to see it come about. I believe it will be a blessing for many human beings."

An addition just occurred to me.

I had spoken of the communications I had received from Semlin and Great-Becskerek, where a number of families want to start out right away.

To this he said: "That is a sad sign of the conditions there."

I also told him about the beggar who refused to take anything from me, and that I had concluded from this incident that I had found a path straight to the heart of the poor. He nodded.

Against parliamentarizing I said: "I cannot have such high esteem for the Word. In the beginning was the Deed." * To this he also nodded.

Now that I think back to it, I feel that I have won him over.

After two hours and a half, which were exhausting for him as well, for he often held his head when I was discussing some difficult point—after two and a half hours he terminated the audience. This time he shook my hand and even held it for quite some time, while he spoke kind words of farewell: he hoped that I would reach my goal, etc.

Together with Hechler I went past the lackeys and guards who wondered at the length of the audience.

* Translator's Note: A paraphrase of a quotation from Goethe's *Faust*, Part I.

I was slightly intoxicated with the success of our conference. I could only say to Hechler, "He is a wonderful person!"

And so he is.

However, as a contribution to the psychology of the visitor, I did take note of this slight intoxication following an audience.

The fear that comes before an audience is later balanced by the intoxication that comes after the audience.

The more naturally and simply the giver of an audience behaves, the greater will be the intoxication of the man who was overawed at first.

I still had time for a walk in the castle park, while Hechler packed his things.

There was a lovely evening mood in the park. A few quiet strollers, boys walking on stilts in the moat. Loud singing of birds in the rejuvenated tree-tops. The clear light of evening, peace, the cloudless mood of Spring.

* * *

Later I accompanied Hechler, who was on his way to Basel, to the station. He was very pleased with the result; the next day he was going to send a telegram from Basel to the "Prophetic Assembly" in London, saying that he had spoken with two sovereigns about the Jewish State, whose realization he considered imminent.

I asked him not to send such a telegram, because the Grand Duke might not approve of it.

Now I regret having kept him from sending it. It would have caused a sensation in England, and the Grand Duke would not even have been mentioned.

April 26, Vienna

When I boarded the Orient Express at Munich yesterday at noon, Hechler was on it. From Basel he had gone to Karlsruhe again and there boarded the Orient Express. "I will pay the difference in fares out of my own pocket," he said.

Naturally I wouldn't hear of it. The whole trip shall be at my expense. In my present circumstances this is a bit of a sacrifice, to be sure.

We had a comfortable trip. In the compartment he unfolded his maps of Palestine and instructed me for hours on end. The northern frontier ought to be the mountains facing Cappadocia; the southern, the Suez Canal. The slogan to be circulated: The Palestine of David and Solomon!

Then he left me to myself, and I drafted my letter to the Grand Duke. Later Hechler found fault with some things. His criticisms are excellent, although it is then that his anti-Semitism occasionally comes through. Self-confidence on the part of a Jew seems insolence to him. When it was getting dark, he even treated me to a downright anti-Semitic story. He had once put a Jew up at his home, and by way of thanks the Jew had robbed him. A Talmudic scholar, to whom he told his troubles, answered him with a comparison of flowers and nations, saying the rose was the English, the lily the French etc., the fat thistle on the dung-heap the Jewish flower.

I disposed of him rather drily: "If you take a hundred Jews and a hundred Gentiles into your house, you will have more bad experiences with Gentiles than with Jews."

This man Hechler is, at all events, a peculiar and complex person. There is much pedantry, exaggerated humility, pious eye-rolling about him—but he also gives me excellent advice full of unmistakably genuine good will. He is at once clever and mystical, cunning and naive. In his dealings with me so far, he has supported me almost miraculously.

His counsel and his precepts have been excellent to date, and unless it turns out later, somehow or other, that he is a double-dealer, I would want the Jews to show him a full measure of gratitude.

*　　　*　　　*

Letter to the Grand Duke of Baden:

Your Royal Highness:

Upon my return home I feel impelled to express to you my respectful thanks for your kind reception in Karlsruhe.

The thought that I was sitting across from one of the co-founders of the German Empire, the friend and adviser to three emperors, made me self-conscious. Yet the cause must not suffer from the weakness of its representative, and I beg Your Royal Highness' permission to put a few points in even sharper focus than I may have done orally.

The Jewish Question is probably not so burning a problem in present-day Germany as it is in Austria, Russia, Rumania, etc. But this very respite, which cannot possibly be of long duration, may make it appear desirable to tackle the solution of the problem. The state's authority cannot yield before the clamor of irresponsible street-corner politicians. However, if this authority is not being hard-pressed, it can support a beneficial project all the more readily.

For it is our hope that a stream of happiness will flow from our project for many people, and not only for the Jews by any means.

If it is God's will that we return to our historic fatherland, we should like to do so as representatives of Western civilization, and bring cleanliness, order, and the well-distilled customs of the Occident to this plague-ridden, blighted corner of the Orient. We shall have to do this so as to be able to exist there, and this obligation will educate our people to the extent that they need it.

The details are outlined in my work *The Jewish State*. On pages 16, 77, 78f. there is information about how economic damage to the countries that will be abandoned can and must be prevented.

There is, incidentally, no thought of a complete evacuation. Those Jews who have been, or still can be, assimilated, will re-

344 THE COMPLETE DIARIES OF THEODOR HERZL

main. The emigration will be voluntary, and the Jews, who will have been informed in good time, will not regard it as an expulsion but as an act of mercy on the part of their sovereigns.

But our movement will have two results—and this is something that I barely hinted at in my pamphlet, which is intended as the basis for public discussion; I should like to direct Your Royal Highness' especial attention to these two effects: our weakening of the revolutionary parties and our breaking of the international financial power. If we find support, these will be not merely presumptuous words.

If Your Royal Highness should feel impelled to place my plan before His Imperial Majesty, I most humbly ask you to emphasize these points.

I beg Your Royal Highness to accept the expression of my respectful devotion.

Dr. Theodor Herzl,
Vienna IX,
Pelikangasse 16,
April 26

Budapest, May 3

Dionys Rosenfeld, editor of the *Osmanische Post* of Constantinople, called on me here.

He offered his services as an intermediary. He claims to be on good terms with Izzet Bey, the Sultan's favorite. I told him in a few words what it was all about. We shall bestow enormous benefits upon Turkey and confer big gifts upon the intermediaries, if we obtain Palestine. This means nothing less than its cession as an independent country. In return we shall thoroughly straighten out Turkey's finances.

We shall acquire the lands belonging to the Sultan under civil law—although in that country there probably is not such a marked contrast between sovereignty and private property.

Rosenfeld says the moment is very propitious, for Turkey is in serious financial straits. However, he believes that sovereignty would not be relinquished—at best, a status like that of Bulgaria. This I reject outright.

Rosenfeld wants to hurry up and go home; he believes he can procure for me the necessary audience with the Sultan for the end of May. *Vederemo* [We shall see].

I declared that in any case I would come to Constantinople only if Izzet Bey expressly assured me of the audience with the Sultan in advance.

May 7, Vienna

Kozmian published a very flattering article about *The Jewish State* in the Lvov official gazette, the *Gazeta Lwowska*.

Today I paid him a visit in order to thank him and to resume the threads of our association. I found him still in bed.

Sitting on the edge of his bed, I described to him the situation into which Badeni has got himself by capitulating to Lueger. He will either have to continue collaborating with the anti-Semites and thus incur the insidious hatred of the Jews, or he will again seek contact with the Jews, and then the anti-Semites, heartened by their success, will quickly overthrow him.

He can no longer lean on the decaying Liberal Party in the next House of Deputies. He will seek and find more conservative helpers. That will net him the full hatred of the remaining liberals. Then the only way out will be to court the Zionist movement and thus create a split among the Jewish opposition.

Kozmian intends to talk to Badeni about this.

May 7, evening

Newlinsky came to see me after I had telephoned him.

In a few words I brought him *au courant* [up to date]. He told me he had read my pamphlet before his last trip to Constantinople and discussed it with the Sultan. The latter had declared that he could never part with Jerusalem. The Mosque of Omar must always remain in the possession of Islam.

"We could get around that difficulty," I said. "We shall extraterritorialize Jerusalem, which will then belong to nobody and yet to everybody—the holy place which will become the joint possession of all believers. The great *condominium* of culture and morality."

Newlinsky thought that the Sultan would sooner give us Anatolia. Money was no consideration to him; he had absolutely no understanding of its value—something that may frequently be observed among rulers. But there was another way of winning the Sultan over: through supporting him in the Armenian situation.

Newlinsky is even now on a confidential mission on behalf of the Sultan to the Armenian Committees in Brussels, Paris, and London. He is to induce them to submit to the Sultan, whereupon the latter will "voluntarily" grant them the reforms which he refuses to accord under pressure of the Great Powers.

Newlinsky now asked me to procure for him the support of the Jews in the Armenian situation; in return he would tell the Sultan that Jewish influence had rendered him this service. The Sultan would show his appreciation of this.

This idea immediately struck me as excellent, but I told him that we shall not give our aid away free, i.e., give it only in return for positive counter-services to the Jewish cause.

At this, Newlinsky proposed that no more than an armistice be obtained from the Armenians. The Armenian Committees were preparing to strike some time in July. They ought to be persuaded to wait for a month. We would use that period for negotiations with the Sultan. Since Newlinsky himself is becoming an interested party to the Jewish cause, he wants to drag out the Armenian matter profitably, so that one cause may promote the other.

I said: "The Jewish cause will bring you greater returns than the Armenian. I have nothing to do with money matters, to be sure, but I shall give you a recommendation to our wealthy men."

Newlinsky, whose close acquaintance with the Sultan is common knowledge, claims that with this approach we shall be able to succeed. But on no account should official diplomatic circles intervene; in fact, it would be better if they put difficulties in our way. Then the Sultan would do what we desire out of spite.

* * *

In the evening I had my wife's cousin explain Turkey's financial situation to me.

As I see things now, the financial plan will have to consist in our eliminating the European Control Commission and taking the payment of interest under our Jewish auspices, so that the Sultan will be relieved of this humiliating control and can raise new loans *ad libitum* [at will].

* * *

Today I also wrote to the Sculptor Moïse Ezechiel at Rome. He is said to be a Zionist and well acquainted with Cardinal Hohenlohe.

May 8

The Hassid Ahron Marcus of Podgorze again writes me a fine letter in which he holds out the possibility that the three million Hassidim of Poland will join my movement.

I am answering him that the participation of the orthodox will be most welcome—but no theocracy will be created.

May 10

Newlinsky came to say goodbye before leaving for Brussels.

He will in any case work on the Sultan in our behalf, and even if we do not bring about a settlement of the Armenian matter, he will tell him that we helped him.

He is relying upon the generosity of the Jews, in case he achieves anything for us.

He tells me that Kozmian said about me that I reminded him of one of the great Jews whom Renan writes about, but that my effort was Utopian.

May 11

Nordau writes that he has tried to establish contact with Edmond Rothschild through Zadoc Kahn. However, Rothschild was a proponent of infiltration.

I am writing to Nordau about the Armenians and requesting his support.

*   *   *

Talked with Hechler and asked him to notify Ambassador Monson that a semi-official agent of the Sultan has set out for Brussels and London in order to conciliate the Armenians. Monson should inform Salisbury. For Salisbury this would be a great and effortless diplomatic success.

May 12

Hechler was here. The news was very welcome to Ambassador Monson, because England desires peace in Armenia. I advised that Salisbury be induced to renew his conciliatory pronouncements.

May 12

Great things need no solid foundation. An apple must be put on a table so that it will not fall. The earth floats in mid-air.

Similarly, I may be able to found and stabilize the Jewish State without any firm support.

The secret lies in motion. (I believe that somewhere in this area of thought lies the invention of the dirigible airship. Weight overcome by motion; and not the ship but its motion is to be steered.)

May 13

Letter to Newlinsky at London:

Dear Sir:*

I have done some work for you and hope that you will see the results of it. In particular, I have had Lord Salisbury aproached,

* In French in the original.

and it seems to me that we may expect a favorable attitude in that quarter. As regards my co-religionists, I have already got them going, in Paris as well as in London. But among my friends there are some who raise a rather serious objection. They say that we run the risk of doing the King of Prussia's work and that once the pacification is achieved, we shall quickly be forgotten. One of our most influential friends, who is absolutely opposed to this intervention, thinks that the dissolution of this great force would be more advantageous for us.

However, as I told you then and there, I am of the contrary opinion that it is to our well-considered interest to move in the direction you indicated. I want to preserve and strengthen the present powers which will soon realize that they are dealing with friends.

For the rest, at the first evidence of good will accorded to our cause, the objectors will rally to my side.

Please write me if there is any important news. I wish you the fullest success.

With kindest regards,

Yours sincerely,
Th. H.

May 13

Nordau telegraphs: "No!"

This means that he will have nothing to do with the Armenian affair. Whether he has had enough all around I do not know, but I am anxiously awaiting his next letter.

May 14

S. Klatschko, who is taking care of the Russian translation, was here.

When, in the course of our conversation, he told me that he used to be a Nihilist, I asked him whether he knew the Armenian Committees.

He does! The leader at Tiflis, Alawerdoff, is the fiancé of a lady who lives in Klatschko's house; and Klatschko has a connection with the London chief, Nikoladze, through the Russian Zaikowski.

I asked him to write to Zaikowski that I have learned the Sultan desires a reconciliation and has dispatched a negotiator for that purpose. The Armenians may confidently deal with him. I consider the peace offer a genuine one, but naturally can answer for the negotiator only to the extent of what I have learned from him. But the Armenians wouldn't be risking anything. If after their honorable submission the Sultan still does not grant the reforms within the stipulated period of time, they can openly declare that they have been cheated and make the entire negotiations public. Klatschko promised to write to London immediately to this effect.

May 14

Received at last a long-awaited letter from the Rev. Singer. I was beginning to think he had dropped off, like Güdemann and others who had gone with me for a distance.

He writes that Montagu wants to avoid public notice, for several reasons; but Montagu has given a copy of my book to Gladstone. Should Gladstone express an opinion, his words will be given *retentissement* [reverberation] in the press.

I am answering Singer by informing him for Montagu's benefit that I do not wish to address an "appeal" to the Sultan (which would be a typically English notion), but will negotiate with him secretly and possibly summon Montagu to Constantinople so that he may support me.

I also wrote to Goldsmid and to Solomon that I am planning to come to London in July to make a big speech (probably at the Maccabeans) about the results achieved to date. Singer had thought that I should hold a big meeting "with an admission fee." But this I reject. I do not address paying audiences. Although, for all I know, this may be the usual thing in England.

May 15

Letter to Newlinsky:

Dear Sir:*

I have just received your telegram. The day before yesterday I wrote you at the Berkeley Hotel, Piccadilly; please claim my letter there.

I shall briefly repeat its contents. I have had the ground prepared for you with Lord S., and I have asked my friends to make contact also with the heads of the Armenian movement. In London, I believe Mr. Nikoladze is the man to talk to. One of my friends has also undertaken to take steps with the head of the Russian Committees** at Tiflis.

You will have to overcome the mistrust of the Armenians. Their leaders will believe that we want to compromise them by a fruitless submission which will cripple the entire movement. Actually, on the basis of information which I received last night, we could get them to conclude an armistice without any detrimental effects.

The Tiflis leader may come to Vienna, and then I shall see him.

With kindest regards,

Yours sincerely,
Herzl.

May 15

Second letter.

Dear Sir:***

I have made a mistake. The head of the movement in London is Avetis Nazarbek, and he directs the paper "Hutschak." Someone will contact him.

Best regards,
H.

* In French in the original.
** Translator's Note: Probably a slip of the pen for Armenian Committees.
*** In French in the original.

May 16

Had a good letter from Nordau which makes up for the "No" telegram that had shaken me a bit.

After he had written me that letter, he talked with Edmond Rothschild yesterday afternoon. Zadoc Kahn took him to the Rue Laffitte.

That Rothschild should have this distinguished man of letters brought to his office rather than his home is somewhat snobbish and recalls my rendez-vous with the coal-Gutmanns.*

May 18

Nordau reports that he went with Zadoc to Edmond Rothschild. The "audience" lasted 63 minutes, out of which Rothschild spoke 53, and Nordau "with difficulty and rudeness" only ten.

Rothschild will hear nothing whatever of the matter; he does not believe that anything can be accomplished with the Sultan, and at any rate will not cooperate. He considers what I am doing dangerous, because I am rendering the patriotism of the Jews suspect, as well as injurious—namely, to his Palestinian colonies.

Accordingly, we shall pass over him and on to the order of the day.

After this, there is something comical about today's dispatches from Paris, which report street demonstrations against the Jews and in particular the Rothschilds. In front of the same house on the Rue Laffitte where on Friday E. R. had rejected my friend Nordau, the mob cried on Sunday: "Down with the Jews!"

May 19

Agliardi the Nuncio sent me word yesterday through our colleague Münz that he would receive me today, at ten a.m. sharp.

At ten I entered the Nuncio's quarters, on the "Am Hof" square, looking around furtively, like a man entering a house of ill repute. I must record this feeling here, because it was the most noteworthy one.

* Translator's Note: "Kohlengutmännern"; Herzl puns on their name.

Anyone who saw me enter there could easily have misunderstood my errand.

The nunciature is a musty, chill, old, run-down little palace. No stately servants, and on the staircase a shabby carpet.

My card was quickly handed to the Nuncio; he quickly had me shown in and just as quickly came to the point.

He made the one reservation that this must not be an "interview!" Naturally, I promised him this.

Then I briefly presented him the proposal, which he knew only in general outline.

I spoke in French, but was not really in good form today, although not in the least self-conscious. It seems that I am beginning to lose my self-consciousness.

Agliardi listened in fine style. He is tall, slim, well-bred, and stiff—come to think of it, exactly the way I had pictured a papal diplomat. His grey hair is sparse; while talking he frequently adjusts his violet skull-cap. His nose is fine, large, and aquiline. His eyes are searching.

He interpolated some questions in bad French. Was I keeping the difficulties in mind? In what way was the government of this new "kingdom" to be established and how would the Great Powers be induced to recognize it? Would the Jewish "grand-seigneurs"—Rothschild and others—contribute money for this purpose? And the like.

I said: We do not want a kingdom, but an aristocratic republic. We need only the consent of the Great Powers, and in particular that of His Holiness the Pope; then we shall establish ourselves, with Jerusalem extraterritorialized. We shall straighten out the Sultan's finances.

Agliardi smiled: "He will be very pleased at that. So you propose to exclude Jerusalem, Bethlehem and Nazareth, and presumably set up the capital more to the north?"

"Yes," I said.

He thought it was doubtful whether the Great Powers would give their consent, particularly Russia. Nor did he believe that this was the solution of the Jewish Question.

"Let us assume," he said, "that you will be able to withdraw 30,000 of the 130,000 Jews in Vienna. 100,000 would still remain. Suppose only 50,000 remained in Vienna. They would continue to cause anti-Semitism—the mild sort of persecution that we are witnessing now. How do matters stand with us in Italy? We have perhaps 10,000 Jews in the entire country. 5-6000 of these are in Rome, a few thousand in Leghorn and Mantua, the rest scattered about. Now then, these 10,000, or let us say, 20,000 Jews, out of a total population of 30 millions, give rise to the same complaints as do the Jews here. People say that they dominate the stock exchange, the newspapers, and so on.

"It seems, my good man, that you Jews possess a particular energy which we lack, a special gift from God—"

At that moment the servant knocked on the door.

"*Avanti* [Come in]!" called the Nuncio.

The servant announced: "*Sua Excellenza l'Ambasciatore di Francia* [His Excellency the Ambassador of France]!"

The Nuncio rose and asked me to come back another time. In the ante-chamber waited Lozé, the French ambassador.

Result of the conversation: I believe Rome will be against us, because she does not see in the Jewish State the solution of the Jewish Question and perhaps even fears it.

May 21

Sylvia d'Avigdor reports from London that Samuel Montagu gave her translation of my *Jewish State* to Gladstone and that he then commented favorably on it in a letter.

Whit-Sunday

Tomorrow it will be a year since I started the movement by my visit to Hirsch. If during the coming year I make proportionate progress, as from the zero point at that time to today's achievements, then we shall be *leshonoh haboh birusholayim* [Next year in Jerusalem].

*   *   *

Attorney Bodenheimer of Cologne invites me to come to Berlin to attend the Convention of German Zionists at the end of June. I am answering him, *inter alia* [among other things]:

"I have grateful admiration for what the Zionists have done up to now, but I am fundamentally opposed to infiltration. If infiltration is allowed to proceed, it will increase the value of land and it will become harder and harder for us to buy it. The idea of a declaration of independence "as soon as we are strong enough over there" I consider to be impracticable, because the Great Powers would certainly not recognize it, even if the Porte had weakened enough. My program, on the other hand, is to halt infiltration and to concentrate all energies on the acquisition of Palestine under international law. This requires diplomatic negotiations, which I have already begun, and a publicity campaign on the very largest scale."

Whit-Sunday

Newlinsky wires and writes from London that he is unable to accomplish anything; he wants me to recommend him to Lawson of the *Daily Telegram* and support him with "the Prime Minister who doesn't want to do anything."

I am wiring him a recommendation to Lucien Wolf of the *Daily Graphic* and will try later to send Hechler to Monson.

To Newlinsky I am writing: "*La chose a eté mal emmanché et surtout trop tard* [The whole thing has been started badly and, above all, too late]." I told him to come back; I would take matters in hand.

Whit-Sunday

Two fellows from the *Kadimah,* Schalit and Neuberger, called on me. At the University the assimilationists seem to be gaining the upper hand again. At the *Lesehalle* no one wants to hear about Zionism. They also told me that a proposal was afoot to recruit a volunteer battalion of one or two thousand men and to attempt a landing at Jaffa. Even if some might have to give up their lives in the attempt, Europe would start paying attention to the aspirations of the Jews.

I advised them against this fine Garibaldian idea, because these thousand men, unlike the men of Marsala, would not find a nationally-prepared population awaiting them. The landing would be suppressed within twenty-four hours, like a schoolboys' prank.

May 26

Newlinsky wires: "*S veut pas recevoir. Faites possible* [S(alis-bury) refuses to receive. Do what you can]."

I am answering him:

Advise return home as soon as possible. May procure admission to S. end of June myself. Let us go to your principal* first.

*　　*　　*

Letter to Rev. Singer (reply):

Dear Friend:

I am not writing to Sir S. Montagu directly because I cannot express myself well in English, and clarity is important. Therefore I ask you to trouble yourself again and explain the matter to him incisively. None of us knows how much longer he is going to live—I did not tell Baron Hirsch this when I had an important conversation with him a year ago yesterday, although I thought it to myself. Today this man, who had so much feeling for the Jews, is dead, and all he accomplished was philanthropy—that is, things for the *shnorrers* [beggars]. When he could have done something for the nation!

Have a serious talk with Montagu, for our cause is an exalted and serious one. In him I see a suitable force for part of the task. No material sacrifices of any kind are being asked of him; he need not give a penny.

* Translator's Note: The reference is to the Turkish Sultan.

If he does not want to participate, we shall simply have to get along without him.

I am sorry that the beginning of July should again be an unfavorable time. But I cannot leave here before the middle of June and I want to go to Constantinople first. However, should my trip there have to be postponed for any reason, I will come to London first. You will be notified of this in ample time, so that the evening with the Maccabeans can perhaps be scheduled for the twenty-first of June.

If I go to Constantinople, and for the time being this must be kept a closely-guarded secret, I shall give you sufficient notice of this as well, so that you may prevail upon those members of your *Community** whose presence, when I get there, will be desirable, to stay in London until July 5.

In that case we would meet with the Maccabeans on that date.

In a previous letter I asked you to give me the names of some persons whom we could elect to the *Society of Jews*. This *Society* is to consist of a large Committee on which we shall put distinguished Jews—Englishmen, for the most part—and of an Executive Committee. On the latter I should like to have you, Goldsmid, Montagu, Nordau, etc.

Please let me have an early reply on this last point.

With cordial regards,

> Yours sincerely,
> Herzl.

> May 29

Our colleague Schütz visited Count Leo Tolstoy on his estate near Moscow and wrote a *feuilleton* about it.

At the same time he sent me a postcard informing me that Tolstoy mentioned my pamphlet. But all the *feuilleton* says is that with reference to the Jewish Question Tolstoy expressed opposition to the Jewish State. This is the first time that *The Jewish State* has been mentioned in the *Neue Freie Presse*—without my name being given and without anyone being able

---

* In English in the original.

to understand what is actually meant. At this moment, the principle of dead silence becomes downright comical.

May 31

Already a split among the young Zionists. Already symptoms of the ingratitude which I expect. A student called on me and told me how the Jewish-National organizations are wrangling among themselves; then he made veiled but comprehensible allusions that he and possibly others as well consider my amiability toward the young people as play-acting.

I was highly indignant and immediately gave him a piece of my mind. If they sour me on my efforts, I shall simply give them up; and if I notice ingratitude—of course, not on the part of individuals, who are a *quantité negligeable* [negligible quantity], but from the masses—I shall withdraw completely.

*   *   *

Similarly as with the students, however, a certain dissatisfaction with my results already seems to be astir among the adult Zionists. I hear that "counter-currents" are being formed—so soon! I am told that Dr. Jacob Kohn wants to establish a "bloc" that is supposed to take an active part in Austrian domestic politics, i.e., have seats on the Municipal Council, the Diet, and the *Reichsrat*. It is obvious to whom these will go.

I received another invitation from Dr. Bodenheimer to come to the Berlin Zionist Convention. At the same time, he sent me the "Principles" of the Cologne Zionists which I fully subscribe to—with the exception of infiltration, which I should like to see stopped. I wrote Bodenheimer that if I were prevented from going to Berlin he should initiate resolutions there for use at our London meeting on July 5. Also, a delegation should be sent to London and arrive two or three days ahead of time, so that we might agree on a plan of action. For the Berlin Zionists I also made a brief sketch of the composition of the *Society*, which is to include the Grand Committee and the Executive Committee. Both committees, composed mainly of Englishmen, are to be reinforced by coöpted members from other countries.

* * *

Rosenfeld writes from Constantinople that his contact wants to know what financial forces are behind me, because he would be risking his head if the negotiations broke down. Since Rosenfeld made his debut in Budapest by asking me to advance him some money, I shall have no further dealings with him for the time being. Incidentally, there is good news from Newlinsky in London. I think I can gather from his brief letters that he has confidence in the cause. If this is so—and I shall find out when he returns—we shall apparently go to Constantinople the middle of June.

* * *

Received an interesting letter from Klatschko about the steps he has taken with the Armenians in London. His informant writes from Harrow that he has spoken with Nazarbek, who distrusts the Sultan but thanks the "leader of the Jewish movement" for his kind sentiments.

* * *

Klatschko's letter, like Nordau's about his conversation with Edmond R., will have to be inserted in this notebook according to their dates.

June 1

My yesterday's *feuilleton*, "The Dirigible Airship," was quite generally taken as an allegory on the Jewish State.

* * *

Today the London news services carry Gladstone's letter to Montagu about my *Jewish State*. In our office this news item was handled like a hot coal. The editor for British affairs, Vincenti,

360 THE COMPLETE DIARIES OF THEODOR HERZL

sent it to the city editor, Oppenheim, who cautiously left it alone. Thereupon I simply took the bull by the horns and showed the dispatch to Benedikt, who was especially pleased with me today on editorial grounds.

"Are you going to run this?" I asked him in the hallway when he was just about to leave. He read the item attentively and said: "Yes."

"Should someone write a few lines of introduction?" I asked.

"No," he said. "Simply run it under the caption 'Gladstone on Anti-Semitism,' quite casually, as though we had already written about it. Also send for the novel which Gladstone mentions; but when you write about it, you mustn't discuss your Jewish State."

"Have I ever given you any trouble?" I asked gently.

*   *   *

And so, on June 2, 1896, the skimpy item which I am pasting in at this point was the first to appear in the newspaper on which I have worked for years. But I should be very much mistaken if it did not produce a great effect. For the other papers, which have been thinking that a deep rift exists between the publishers and myself, will take this as an important sign of reconciliation; and the readers of the *Neue Freie Presse* will start talking about the Jewish State.

Gladstone on Anti-Semitism:

Gladstone has addressed the following letter to Sir Samuel Montagu, M.P., who had sent him Dr. Theodor Herzl's pamphlet *The Jewish State:* "The subject of the publication which you were good enough to send me is highly interesting. For the outsider it is not easy to form a judgment regarding it, nor perhaps pertinent, having formed a judgment, to express it. It surprises me, however, to see how far-reaching is the distress among the Jews. I am, of course, strongly opposed to anti-Semitism. In a curious and arresting novel, *The Limb,* you will find a rather unusual treatment of Judaism."

June 5

Nordau writes that he would not at any price sign an appeal for money unless it also included the names of well-known millionaires. He apparently does not want to join the Executive Committee either—only the big showcase and honorary committee of the *Society*.

I am answering him that I, too, would not be naive and unsophisticated enough to sign an appeal for money which was not above suspicion. But I have made sufficient financial sacrifices, considering my means, and henceforth must leave it to the Jewish people to decide whether they want to do anything for themselves, and if so, what.

June 6

Newlinsky has been in town for three days and has not shown his face. Has he swung away? I am writing him:

Je compte partir le 15 juin. Êtes-vous avec moi? Mille amitiés, votre devoué [I count on leaving on June 15th. Are you with me? Kindest regards, yours sincerely]

Herzl

June 7

Newlinsky came to see me today while I was in Baden. Question is, is he still with me or has he lost confidence in the cause—if indeed he ever had any?

June 8

I called today on Newlinsky who gives me the impression of having cooled. He said the present moment was not propitious for the trip to Constantinople; the Sultan thought of nothing but the Cretan riots, etc.

Perhaps everything he said to me before his trip to London was said only that I might support him there. Now he backs out and says he cannot come to Constantinople uninvited.

June 9

Newlinsky spent an hour and a half with me this morning. I had a showdown talk with him, in the course of which I tried to instil in him confidence in our cause again. Obviously his courage has gone out of him in London, and also here. I worked on him very forcefully. I spoke in a strong, determined, imperious voice. I paraded our resources before him, I advised him to serve us while he could derive great benefits from it—that is, early, at the beginning of our operations.

He told me that in journalistic circles, and consequently in financial and government circles as well, my project was regarded as Utopian. The director of the *Länderbank* had declared it a fantasy, our editor Benedikt, madness. All the journalists were laughing at it.

I answered him: *"D'ici un an toute cette racaille me lêchera les bottes* [A year from now this whole rabble will be licking my boots]."

He thought I should not go to Constantinople at present, for no one there now had his mind on anything but the Cretan rebellion.

I said that if he did not want to join me I would go alone— although I have no such intention. For, official recommendations, provided I get them in the first place, will hardly procure me a private audience. And whether Rosenfeld, who wants to take me to Izzet, is reliable seems more than doubtful to me.

Newlinski described his English impressions. People there believe in the impending downfall of Turkey. No English prime minister can dare to declare his support of the Sultan because he would have public opinion against him. There is some thought of making the Bulgarian Prince Ferdinand, because he is a Coburg, heir to the Turkish empire. If this is no *diceria* [rumor], it is most interesting. Newlinsky thinks the only salvation for the Sultan would be to make an alliance with the Young Turks—who for their part are on good terms with the Macedonians, Cretans, Armenians, etc.—and to carry out the reforms with their help. He said he had given this advice to the Sultan in a report. Now I said he should add to this program the fact that he was bringing the Sultan the means to carry this out, in the form of Jewish aid. Let the Sultan give us that piece of land, and in return we shall set his house in order, straighten out his finances, and influence public opinion all over the world in his favor.

Newlinsky skeptically referred to the attitude the Vienna papers were taking toward me. To this I replied that if I wanted to, I could make them all tractable, without exception, by starting rival papers.

I told him that the Zionists' declaration addressed to me had already been signed by three thousand holders of doctor's degrees —a fact I had learned on Sunday from my cousin Löbl.

He left me, I believe, shaken and half re-won. I urged him to write the Sultan immediately and get himself summoned. This he promised to do.

*   *   *

In the Delegation at Budapest, Goluchowski today made a speech full of serious warnings to Turkey. Thereupon I am writing to Newlinsky:

Dear Sir:*
The Budapest speech gives you an excellent opportunity of renewing your no less excellent advice at Constantinople. Be energetic and highlight all the advantages which we would be able to confer.

If you decide to travel with me, I certainly hope that you will give me the honor and pleasure of making that trip as my guest.

With kindest regards,

Yours sincerely,
Th. Herzl.

In the afternoon at Hechler's home I met the English Bishop Wilkinson, a clever, slim old man with white whiskers and dark,

* In French in the original.

intelligent eyes. The Bishop had already read my pamphlet and thought it was "rather a business." * I said categorically: *"I don't make businesses. I am a literary man."* ** Whereupon the Bishop declared that he had not meant this as an insult. On the contrary, he regarded the matter as a practical one. Even though it might start as a business, it might become something great. After all, England's Indian empire had also come into being unconsciously. In the end he blessed me and invoked God's blessing on the project.

June 15

At night on the train, having boarded the Orient Express in Vienna, alone.

Newlinsky won't get on until 2 a.m., at Budapest.

I shall now hastily add here the events of the past week, during which I was so overworked that unfortunately I didn't have a chance to capture my impressions when they were still fresh in my mind.

After his return from London, Newlinsky was in no mood to go to Constantinople with me.

He resisted in several forthright conversations; he was evidently under the influence of adverse comment on the cause from my own group. *Par ricochet* [in a roundabout way] I learned from a few of them that he had made inquiries about me.

I finally won him over by showing my determination to go to Constantinople by myself. This might have made him concerned lest others reap the great benefits which he has in prospect if he supports me.

On Friday, after a lengthy conversation, we agreed that we would each sleep on the question of leaving on June 15 for Constantinople: I, as to whether I would go ahead with the matter without him, i.e., with the aid of my "other Constantinople connections"—he, whether to participate.

* In English in the original.
** Translator's Note: In English in the original. Herzl obviously misunderstood the Bishop's use of the word "business."

On Saturday I went to see him again. I really no longer expected anything and had practically abandoned the dubious expedition. He asked me with subtle watchfulness: *"Eh bien, partez-vous* [All right, are you leaving]?"

I guessed what was hidden in this question, and answered firmly:

"Je pars [I am]."

Since he now realized that I would go in any case, even without him, he said he was ready to go with me, and even begged me "to take along no further introductions." *Bon* [Good].

Yesterday we got together again and made the final arrangements for our departure. He said he would go on ahead to Pest this afternoon and catch the Orient Express during the night.

His questions, for which I was really not prepared, then led us to the financial plan. It had been quite a while since I had occupied myself with the details, and some of them I had yet to look into.

Unprepared as I was, I merely told him that we imagined we would give twenty million pounds in return for Palestine. (Montagu offered only two million in the *Daily Chronicle*.)

Afterwards I went to Baden and telephoned Reichenfeld, my wife's cousin, to come out the same evening in order to give me some information.

He came to Baden at nine o'clock, and I asked him to brief me on the Turkish national debt. While he was explaining to me the status of the *dette publique* [public debt], I worked out the financial scheme.

We spend twenty million Turkish pounds to straighten out the Turkish finances. Of that sum we give two millions in exchange for Palestine, this amount being based on the capitalization of its present revenue of eighty thousand Turkish pounds per annum. With the remaining 18 millions we free Turkey from the European Control Commission. The bond-holders of Classes A, B, C, and D will be induced by direct privileges we shall grant them —increased rate of interest, extension of the amortization period, etc.—to agree to the abolition of the Commission.

Reichenfeld was surprised at this plan which I immediately elaborated with all details and foreseeable eventualities, and he asked me what financier had worked it out. I wrapped myself in mysterious silence.

Today I brought Newlinsky his ticket for Constantinople. The expedition is costing me quite a bit. Newlinsky also asked me to take along some fruit for the Turkish court. He has even made out an order which I was supposed to have filled at the Hotel Sacher: strawberries, peaches, grapes, asparagus—all imported from France. The basket cost seventy guilders—and yet luckily there were only half the quantity of grapes to be had, only six peaches instead of twenty-four, and only one bunch of asparagus. I took all there was. *Ultra posse nemo tenetur* [no one can be required to do more].

My poor Hechler was less demanding when we travelled together.

June 17

On the Orient Express, six o'clock in the morning, outside Eski-Baba.

Yesterday's portion of the trip was extremely interesting. When Newlinsky got on at Budapest at 2 A.M., he told me that several pashas were on the train—particularly Ziad Pasha, head of the Turkish delegation at the Moscow coronation.

Later yesterday morning Newlinsky introduced me to Ziad, Karatheodory, and Tewfik Pasha, the Ambassador at Belgrade. Afterwards he briefed Ziad Pasha, the most important of these Excellencies, on the purpose of my trip to Constantinople. Ziad immediately became interested in the matter, and we only awaited the moment when we should be alone in order to let him in further on the secret.

Ziad Pasha is a small, elegant, graceful, Parisianized Turk, who despite his small stature knows how to give himself an air of due respect. There is a serious and bold look in his dark eyes;

his features are fine and sharp, his nose curved, and the short, pointed beard as well as his thick hair are black and on the verge of turning grey.

Karatheodory is white-bearded, fat, smart, full of fun, speaks a brilliant French; reads, when not chatting, a new History of Russia; tells wonders about the riches of the Moscow coronation— and at train stations he doesn't think twice about eating the native fruits and washing them down with the local water.

Tewfik is a young pasha, speaks of the *Neue Freie Presse* with admiration, quotes passages from old editorials.

In the afternoon, when Karatheodory had left the smoking-room of the dining car and only Ziad, Newlinsky, and I were there, I set forth my plan to Ziad who listened earnestly and intently.

He said: "I can see that you speak without ulterior motives." (For I had declared that we wished to acquire Palestine as a completely independent country, and if we could not get it as such, we would go to Argentina.)

"You come right out with your idea," said Ziad, "but I must tell you that no one is likely even to have *pourparlers* [parleys] with you if you demand an independent Palestine. The benefits in money and press support which you promise us are very great, and I would say that your proposal is a very favorable one; but it is against our principles to sell any territory."

I replied: "That has occurred in history countless times."

Newlinsky interjected that only recently England had relinquished Heligoland to Germany.

Ziad persisted: "Under no circumstances will you get Palestine as an independent country; maybe as a vassal state."

I replied that this would be a bit of hypocrisy from the start, for, after all, vassals constantly think of nothing but how to become independent as soon as possible.

The conversation went on until we got to Zaribrod. There the Bulgarian minister, Natchowitch, was waiting for Newlinsky, having come to meet him there.

I in turn was met by a delegation of Sofia Zionists. I had tele-graphed them the day before yesterday that I would be passing through.

The two gentlemen asked me how my Zionist work was coming along. I told them as much as I could. Then I had to leave them in order to eat with Newlinsky and Natchowitch in the dining car. Natchowitch made a special point of requesting that on the occasion of his next resignation from office the *Neue Freie Presse* refrain from devoting any flattering post-mortem to him, because otherwise he would be regarded as too much of an Austrian favorite in Bulgaria, which is at present Russophile; this would hamper his activities in behalf of Austria.

In Sofia a touching scene awaited me. Beside the track on which our train pulled in there was a crowd of people—who had come on my account. I had completely forgotten that I was actu-ally responsible for this myself.

There were men, women, and children, Sephardim, Ashkena-zim, mere boys and old men with white beards. At their head stood Dr. Ruben Bierer. A boy handed me a wreath of roses and carnations—Bierer made a speech in German. Then Caleb read off a French speech, and in conclusion he kissed my hand, despite my resistance. In this and subsequent addresses I was hailed in extravagant terms as Leader, as the Heart of Israel, etc. I think I stood there completely dumbfounded, and the passengers on the Orient Express stared at the odd spectacle in astonishment.

Afterwards I stood on the carriage steps a while longer and surveyed the crowd. The most varied types. An old man with a fur cap looked like my grandfather, Simon Herzl.

I kissed Bierer farewell. They all pressed about me to shake my hand. People cried "*leshonoh haboh birusholayim* [Next year in Jerusalem]." The train started moving. Hat-waving, emo-tion. I myself was quite touched, particularly by the story of a Rumanian who had told me his troubles. After completing his military service he had been obliged to emigrate, because he was denied his civil rights.

Newlinsky and Ziad were less struck with the demonstration

than I had expected them to be. Or were they not showing how much they had been impressed? Newlinsky, for his part, had been met by the Bulgarian church dignitary Gregory, to whom he had likewise telegraphed his arrival in advance—possibly so that I might take note of his (N's) reputation in Bulgaria.

*   *   *

In the evening Newlinsky and I sat by ourselves in the dining car, and I outlined for him the financial plan based on the 20 million pounds—of which two millions would be earmarked as an immediate advance for the cession of Palestine, and 18 millions for the freeing of the Turkish government from the Control Commission.

Newlinsky objected violently. He said he had already told Ziad that I was proposing the liberation from the Control Commission in the following form:

One third we pay in cash. For the second third we take the responsibility (or rather, if we become a vassal state, this third is credited against our tribute). On the remaining third we pay interest from the revenues taken away from the present Commission and assigned to us.

Newlinsky thinks we could not possibly dare to offer the Sultan 20 million pounds for the land of Palestine. That was its mere commercial value, so to speak; but we would have to pay a *pretium affectionis* [premium]. However, we could perhaps stipulate several additional concessions and thus facilitate our payments—e.g., an electric-power monopoly for all of Turkey, etc. But this triple division, he said, must definitely be maintained.

*   *   *

I have slept on this and think that Newlinsky is right. I can even derive a fresh advantage from this turn in the affair. I can, and shall, say in Constantinople that the conditions must remain absolutely secret because I have to familiarize my Committee with everything first. In this way I shall prevent the possibility of Montagu or E. Rothschild making protests against my proposals.

But if I come to London strengthened by my conversation with the Sultan, I shall carry through whatever I wish.

If necessary, I shall establish contact with Barnato.

*   *   *

Bierer told me at Sofia that Edmond Rothschild sent his representative to Constantinople a few days ago in order to offer the Sultan money for permission to continue the colonization.

Might this be a chess move against me?

June 18, Constantinople

Newlinsky is extremely valuable to our cause. His skill and devotion are beyond all praise. He will have to be given a very extraordinary reward.

We arrived in Constantinople yesterday afternoon. At the station we were met by Baron B. Popper of Vienna as well as by two local journalists who are at Newlinsky's disposal. The pashas who had been on the same train and had put on their formal attire even before our arrival, so as to be able to go to the Sultan right away, were met by a crowd of people.

We drove through this astonishingly beautiful, dirty city. Dazzling sunshine, colorful poverty, dilapidated buildings. From a window of the Hotel Royal our view extends over the Golden Horn. The houses on the slopes are situated among greenery, and it looks like grass growing between stones—as if nature were slowly recapturing this crumbling city.

*   *   *

Newlinsky has a fine reputation and much influence here. He is on the same good terms with many prominent Turks as he is with our traveling companions, Ziad and Karatheodory.

As soon as he had changed his clothes, he drove to Yildiz Kiosk. I accompanied him in the carriage. The street life is strangely poverty-ridden and gay. The latticed harem-like windows present a charming mystery. Behind them, disappointment presumably awaits the intruder.

A wonderful view of the Bosporus from the white palace of Dolma Bagjeh!

* * *

After Newlinsky got out at Yildiz, I rode and strolled by myself through the bumpy streets of Pera and down to the old bridge.

* * *

Newlinsky returned late and in a bad humor. Izzet Bey, the First Secretary of the Sultan, had displayed a bluntly negative attitude toward our project. "Too many commissions are being promised in this matter!" he said; and Newlinsky thinks that the man who has already taken some preliminary steps here has gone about it clumsily. We will have to make amends for this, and it may not be easy.

Another difficulty: the Sultan apparently is ill. Newlinsky was not received. What ails the Sultan cannot be learned. Baron Popper heard from his sister that Dr. Nothnagel of Vienna was asked whether he could come here. It would be a terrible *contretemps* [mishap] if this were to wreck my audience.

* * *

After dinner we went to the open-air concert hall of Pera where a visiting Italian light-opera company was performing. During the first intermission we ran into Djawid (or Djewid) Bey, the son of the present Grand Vizier. I was introduced and immediately plunged *medias in res* [into the midst of things]. We sat on a garden bench, the operetta tunes sounded distantly from the arena stage as I acquainted the still youthful State Councillor with the project.

His objections were: the status of the Holy Places. Jerusalem, he said, must definitely remain under Turkish administration. It would run counter to the most sacred feelings of the people if

Jerusalem were ceded. I promised a far-reaching extra-territoriality. The Holy Places of the civilized world must belong to no one, but to everyone. In the end, I believe, we shall have to agree to Jerusalem's remaining in its present status.

Djawid Bey further inquired what the relationship between the Jewish State and Turkey would be. Much like Ziad's question about vassalage.

I said that I would see complete success only in independence, but we would at any rate discuss a status like that of Egypt or Bulgaria, that is, a tributary relationship.

Finally, Djawid asked about the form of the future government.

"An aristocratic republic," I said.

Djawid protested vigorously: "Just don't mention the word 'republic' to the Sultan! People here are frightened to death of it. They are afraid that this revolutionary form of government will spread from one province to another like a contagion."

I explained to him in a few words that I had in mind a form of government like that of Venice.

At length I begged him to be present at the audience which his father, Khalil Rifat Pasha, the Grand Vizier, is to grant me.

The young Excellency promised me this, and he wishes to help us with advice and action in other ways, too. In reply to his question concerning the proposals which I planned to make, I said that I could communicate the details only to the Sultan.

June 18

Newlinsky told me today that Russia has gained the upper hand in Yildiz Kiosk. The position of Turkey was not considered to be in danger as long as the friendship with Russia lasted. Izzet, he said, was leaning toward Russia. Whatever I told the Grand Vizier would be submitted to Russia.

Therefore we agreed that I would speak with Yakovlev, the influential dragoman of the Russian Embassy, before I went to see the Grand Vizier.

I immediately wrote to Yakovlev asking him for an appointment, which he promptly gave me for one o'clock. Evidently their attention has already been drawn to my arrival by the newspapers and by gossip in diplomatic circles.

June 19

Yesterday was a hectic day—with an unfavorable ending.

My first call was on the Russian dragoman Yakovlev. He lives in the consulate at Pera. A building run down in Turkish fashion. In the courtyard, Kavasses and seedy-looking servants. An unkempt maid received my card and took it to Yakovlev, who was still at table, to judge from the clatter of dishes in the adjoining room. Yakovlev had some cigarettes brought out to me. Ten minutes later he appeared—gaunt, tall, dark-haired, with a narrow face, a scraggly beard, and small, slit-like eyes.

His manner was likeable.

I briefly told him the purpose of my visit, but in order to prepare him for the shock, I took the precaution of speaking at first only of colonization. I asked him to take note of the fact that I was calling at the Russian Embassy before talking with the Turkish government. I said it was my intention and hope to obtain an introduction to the Czar through a member of the latter's family (by whom I meant the Prince of Wales, but without naming him).

By way of reply Yakovlev gave me an account of his experiences when he was Consul at Jerusalem. The Jews he met there inspired him with little sympathy, although he treated them benevolently and, if they were Russians, accorded them all the privileges of Russian citizens. He said they behaved deceitfully toward the Consulate, tried to evade the consular taxes they owed, and claimed to be Turks or Russians, whichever suited their convenience.

To this I remarked that considering the persecutions to which my people had been subjected for many centuries, it was no wonder if they displayed moral defects. He agreed.

Then I went into my plan more deeply, saying that it was not

a matter of colonization on a small but on a large scale. We
wanted the territory as an autonomous one.

He listened with growing attention and sympathy, and thought
it was a great, fine, humanitarian plan.

I said: "*Je crois que cette idée doit être sympathique à tous
les honnêtes gens* [I believe this idea ought to appeal to all decent
people]."

In conclusion he remarked that the project would require
many decades. I would probably not live to see its fruition, but
he wished me every success and was glad to have made my acquaintance. He wished me strength and good health to carry out
the task, and then I took my leave.

As we were saying good-bye he advised me to call on the local
Russian *chargé d'affaires,* and he accompanied me to the stairway.
Then, as though to make amends for his previous disparaging remarks, he said: "You have among your people perhaps twenty
per cent who are not much good ethically, but that is what one
finds among other peoples, too."

"Yes," I said, "but in our case they are counted double, so that
one could believe it was forty per cent."

*   *   *

From Yakovlev I drove to the Sublime Porte, where I had already been announced. My dragoman sat on the coach box next
to the red-fezzed coachman.

A drive through winding, filthy streets to Stambul. The Sublime Porte is a decaying, old, dirty, imposing building, hum-
ming with the most remarkable activity. The soldiers on guard
duty stand on small pedestals in the entrance halls.

Poor devils squat on the ground. Countless officials and servants run up and down.

My first call was on His Excellency, Khair Eddin Bey, Secre-
tary-General to the Grand Vizier. I am writing down by ear the
names of all the functionaries. I don't know whether correctly.
I learned only today that the son of the Grand Vizier is not
named Djawid, but Djewad Bey.

Khair Eddin is a man of about thirty years, nice looking, with smooth, pale cheeks, a handsome black beard, and prominent ears. At every word he gives a smile that is friendly and astonished at the same time. After a few minutes we were called to the Grand Vizier. We crossed a vestibule and several ante-chambers. In a large salon, with his back to the wall, was His Highness, the Grand Vizier, Khalil Rifat Pasha. He rose at my entrance and gave me his hand. He is a tall, stooped old man with a white beard and a wrinkled, withered face. On the desk in front of him lay two sets of religious beads.

He sat down and motioned me to an armchair next to him; facing us, beyond the large desk, Khair Eddin took a seat as interpreter.

After handing me a cigarette, the Grand Vizier inquired about my arrival, the traveling weather, the probable duration of my stay.

Then he paid a few compliments to the *Neue Freie Presse*.

Khair Eddin translated the banalities with amiable seriousness, I replied with other *salaams*: the *N. Fr. Pr.* had always had friendly sentiments toward Turkey and would always be happy when it could report something favorable about the Empire. At times, perhaps, we were insufficiently informed about the facts; but we desired nothing better than always to report the truth.

The Grand Vizier wanted me to know that our correspondent could call at any time and he would be told everything.

I thanked him for this assurance.

Then I had the interpreter ask His Highness whether he knew the purpose of my trip.

"No," came back his reply, and as he spoke his half-closed eyes kept glancing downward at the edge of the table or at his large hands which were toying with the beads.

So I presented my proposal to Khair Eddin to have it conveyed to the Grand Vizier.

The Grand Vizier listened imperturbably. He asked questions such as this: "Palestine is large. What part of it do you have in mind?"

I had the interpreter answer: "That will have to be weighed against the benefits we offer. For more land we shall make greater sacrifices."

His Highness inquired about the terms.

I begged pardon for not going into detail. I said I could state the scope of our proposals only to His Majesty. Should they be accepted in principle, Sir Samuel Montagu would submit our financial program.

Khalil Rifat Pasha made long pauses during the conversation, while he ticked off his beads between his fingers, one by one, as though he had to take time for reflection between every word.

I was left with the impression that he is not only averse to this project, but actually distrusts it.

During our conversation there was a constant stream of officials and servants, bowing low, bringing messages and documents, and then backing out of the room.

Following the appearance of another solemn old man, Khalil Rifat had the interpreter indicate to me that the conference was at an end. He half rose and gave me his hand.

In the ante-chamber I asked Khair Eddin, who had a friendly smile on his face, whether the Grand Vizier had taken it amiss that I had kept silent on the terms for the present.

"No," said the smiler, "he is a philosopher and can only be pleased that you fulfill your obligations as he fulfills his. It is quite all right with him if you establish direct contact with his exalted master."

Khair Eddin also showed me a magnificent view of the Bosporus and the distant Dolma Bagjeh; then he gave my hand a long and cheerful squeeze.

*   *   *

Down many corridors, past guards, servants, idlers, and officials, I was taken to the Foreign Office and to Nuri Bey.

He is a russet-haired, elegant, intelligent, cultured Armenian who has lived in Paris for a long time and is quite Parisianized. A few foreign diplomats came and went. The talk happened to be about two women who had fallen into the hands of brigands somewhere and were to be released in return for ransom. An attaché of some embassy begged Nuri Bey to defer all non-urgent matters because he didn't want to tackle anything new before going on his vacation. One could tell that absolutely nothing seemed urgent to him.

When we were alone, I told Nuri Bey what I wanted. His eyes lit up. He got the point right away.

"*C'est superbe* [That's splendid]," he said when I told him— as I had told the Grand Vizier previously—that we wanted to liberate Turkey from the Debt Control Commission. Then there would be the means to carry out all the needed reorganization. Nuri was delighted and sold on it. But he had grave doubts regarding the Holy Places. Who is to administer them? "That can be arranged," I remarked; "just consider that we are the sole purchasers of an article that is worthless to everyone else and unproductive—and purchasers at a stiff price."

Thereupon Nuri Bey took me to Davout Efendi, who is a Jew, but also First Dragoman and thus the Foreign Minister's right-hand man, regarded as the most influential person in the Foreign Office.

I recognized his high position by the low *salaams* of those who enter. The officials deposit the documents at his feet, so that he always has to stoop and therefore is less comfortably served. He works seated in an armchair, with no table in front of him, and as he writes he holds the paper in his hand unsupported.

He is a tall, fat man with a short, grey beard. His eyeglasses are perched on a curved, fleshy nose in front of bulging eyes.

He understood me at once. But he was visibly afraid. He saw the tremendous benefits to Turkey, but as a Jew he must impose the utmost reserve upon himself.

There would be enormous difficulties, he said; in fact, he thought the matter impracticable. Soon he was speaking to me like a brother, with earnestness and concern. He said I should have someone else introduce me to the Foreign Minister, but he accompanied this refusal with an amiable glance that begged my forgiveness. I am supposed to come and see him again before my departure.

The Jews are doing well in Turkey, he said, and they are good, loyal patriots.

As though by way of illustrating this, when he walked with me through an outer corridor, the two guards on the pedestals presented arms to him, clattering and rattling.

I also saw Nishan Efendi, the Chief of the Press Bureau, in his little office where a few editors were manufacturing the public opinion of Turkey out of European newspaper reports.

Nishan complained about the editorials in the *N. Fr. Pr.* and about Goluchowski's latest speech.

*   *   *

In the evening Newlinsky returned from Yildiz Kiosk with a long face and bad news.

He ordered only half a bottle of champagne—*en signe de deuil* [as a sign of mourning]—and told me in two words: "Nothing doing. The great lord won't hear of it!"

I took the blow stout-heartedly.

"The Sultan said: 'If Mr. Herzl is as much your friend as you are mine, then advise him not to take another step in this matter. I cannot sell even a foot of land, for it does not belong to me, but to my people. My people have won this empire by fighting for it with their blood and have fertilized it with their blood. We will again cover it with our blood before we allow it to be wrested away from us. The men of two of my regiments from Syria and Palestine let themselves be killed one by one at Plevna. Not one of them yielded; they all gave their lives on that battlefield. The Turkish Empire belongs not to me, but to the Turkish people. I cannot give away any part of it. Let the Jews save their billions. When my Empire is partitioned, they may get Palestine for nothing. But only our corpse will be divided. I will not agree to vivisection.' "

Then they spoke of other things. Newlinsky advised him to let the young Turks participate in the government.

The Sultan said ironically: "A constitution, then? As far as I know, Poland's constitution did not keep your fatherland from being partitioned."

* * *

I was touched and shaken by the truly lofty words of the Sultan, although for the time being they dashed all my hopes. There is a tragic beauty in this fatalism which will bear death and dismemberment, yet will fight to the last breath, even if only through passive resistance.

June 19

Newlinsky showed himself pleasantly surprised at my not betraying my disappointment through a fit of depression. I immediately tried to think of other moves, and I hit upon the following, which I asked Newlinsky to take care of: We will endeavor to give the Sultan's circle "proof of our devotion" right from the start.

Newlinsky was to do his utmost through Izzet Bey and directly to get the Sultan to receive me after all. I want to *planter un jalon* [drive in a stake] at least. I will present our proposal to the Sultan, *tout en m'inclinant respectueusement devant sa volonté* [while respectfully bowing to his wishes]. He should know that whenever he sees fit to fall back on this resource, the Jews will be ready to place their financial power at his disposal for the straightening out of Turkey's finances.

June 19

The *selamlik*, Friday.

On this sunny day we drove out to Yildiz Kiosk. *En route,* troops in full-dress uniform. The Bosporus gleamed.

At Yildiz, in front of the guest pavilion, we were received by two adjutants of the Sultan in gala uniform. Within less than an hour the most magnificent images rushed past us: The white Yildiz Mosque in the sunlight; over on the other side, the blue

Bosporus; in the distance, the islands in a haze. Troops came marching up. Sturdy, sinewy, sun-tanned fellows, full of energy, "hardship-defying," splendid battalions. On the right, cavalry regiments came riding down the hill, their red pennants aflutter. In front of us, up the hill, zouaves with their green-and-red turbans were marching along at a smart goose-step. The buglers held their horns to their lips, ready to blow.

Pashas in gala uniform came driving or riding toward us.

Worshippers in the most colorful costumes were filing into the fore-court of the mosque.

A riot of color. Each moment brought fresh gorgeous hues.

Small boys in officers' uniforms, the sons of pashas, made their appearance with droll *grandezza* [grandeur].

At last came the Court. First, the Sultan's sons and other princes. They mounted their horses at the foot of the Yildiz hill and there in imposing line-up awaited the appearance of the Caliph. Among the ranks of the princes were two grey-bearded officers, their military tutors.

The Chief Eunuch, a large, fat *castratus*, moved past majestically.

Three closed royal equipages with heavily veiled ladies of the harem.

Next a double line of palace officers came down the hill at a ceremonious pace. And then the Sultan's carriage, a half-closed landau with outriders, flanked by a thick, walking hedge of guards and officers.

In the carriage sat the Sultan; facing him, Ghazi Osman Pasha.

From the minaret, a muezzin called to prayer in a clear voice. Between calls, military music.

The troops hailed the Caliph with two loud shouts.

He is a slight, sickly man with a large hooked nose and a medium-sized beard which looks as though it had been dyed brown. He gave the Turkish salute with a flourish close to his mouth.

As he passed the terrace on which we were standing, he sharply stared at Newlinsky and me.

Then he drove in behind the railings of the mosque, left the carriage at the protruding angle of the left wing, and slowly ascended the steps.

Cheering. He saluted again and entered the mosque toward which all the soldiers of his guard now turned their faces.

The service lasted about twenty minutes. In the courtyard of the mosque the pilgrims spread out prayer rugs and knelt or crouched on them.

The soldiers in the burning sun were given water.

After his devotions, the Sultan reappeared and boarded an open two-horse carriage, which he drove himself.

In the courtyard, a low-bowing lane of pashas and generals.

The princes mounted their horses again.

When the Sultan passed us the second time, he stared at me (whom he could identify at Newlinsky's side) with a steely look.

A bustle of officers scurrying up the hill behind the carriage.

Then this picture of fairy-tale splendor faded away.

* * *

After the *selamlik* I saw the whirling dervishes in the mosque on the Rue de Pera.

One little boy among the old gaunt "fanatics," with their apathetic yet sly look, who perform the solemn, grotesque dance routine.

Homespun music, snuffled prayers, a walk-around like a sort of *chaine anglaise* in a quadrille, with low bows; then the dizzy, senseless whirling. After throwing off their colored cloaks, they continue in white garments *à la Loïe Fuller,* the left palm turned toward the ground, the right turned up.

* * *

In the afternoon, at the Sweet Waters of Europe with Margueritte, the favorite of the Grand Vizier.

Margueritte offered me his services. He claims he can get anything he pleases from the Grand Vizier. He said he would shortly receive a concession for the oil-wells of Alexandretta. He told me the story of Baron Popper's abortive loan. The latter had wanted to handle the loan of three million Turkish pounds which was later made by the Ottoman Bank. He had already concluded everything and enlisted the interest of Izzet, Tahsin, the Sheik of the Palace, and a few other people. The Grand Vizier accepts no gifts, but P. was going to present the Vizier's wife with a necklace or something like that.

The embassies abroad were instructed to support Popper. Then it turned out that the bank whose representative P. claimed to be stated that it did not know him.

That created ill-will against him here—*parbleu!*—without, however, compromising him permanently. Margueritte said that Popper was now competing for the Alexandretta-Damascus railroad concession, which would draw off the Asiatic traffic from the Suez Canal.

Margueritte further informed me that late last night Newlinsky had sent him a request in my name—without having informed me of it—to drop the matter which I had presented to him.

Margueritte promised me to interest Djewad Bey, the Grand Vizier's son, in my cause.

With Djewad, he said, it was possible to "speak openly."

June 20

Each morning at breakfast we hold a council of war in our parlor with its long green damask sofa. Today I proposed to Newlinsky that we hold out the prospect of an initial transaction to the people at the Palace and the Porte. I would try to induce them to take a small loan of one or two million, since in my opinion this would not compromise our future plan. The money would be thrown into a bottomless well, but with it we would gain a firm footing and become popular.

I begged Newlinsky to do everything possible to get the Sultan to receive me. If I return home without an audience, with a "No," people will take everything for a dream.

At present, of course, no one dares mention me to the Sultan, after the formal refusal which he gave Newlinsky in the presence of Münir Pasha, Izzet Bey, etc.

Izzet Bey, however, advises the following: the Jews should acquire some other territory and then offer it to Turkey as a trade (with additional payment).

I immediately thought of Cyprus.

Izzet's idea is good, and it shows that he is thinking with us and for us.

He declines a personal share in it. But he has his family in Arabia, numbering—1500, for whom something would have to be done.

June 21

Yesterday afternoon I saw Nuri Bey again, just after Newlinski had left him. I waited for Newlinski in the carriage outside the Sublime Porte. A hot afternoon.

After an hour Newlinski appeared. He had discussed our matter with the Grand Vizier and Nuri Bey. The Grand Vizier is against it, Nuri Bey all fire and flame for it.

Nuri Bey received me very cordially. Then he took me from the room, in which there were visitors, to a private room next door and there spoke to me quite openly. He said he was completely on our side, but unfortunately the large number of wooden heads here must be taken into account.

He acted a bit coquettish about his European education and intelligence and said complacently: "Among these blind people I am a one-eyed man."

He really is of a much higher intelligence than most of the others.

This is what he advises: The Jews ought to buy up the Turkish issues and put their own people on the Commission of *Bondholders.** This Commission, according to him, has great influence and steps in whenever there is a crisis.

He has also communicated this idea to Newlinski, as I found out later. Newlinski opposed it immediately, because this would make the Jews just as detested here as the Commission is at present.

* In English in the original.

Newlinski even tempers my singing of Nuri's praises by re-marking: "It would be proof of his intelligence if he were giving this advice only to compromise the Jewish cause."

Nuri promised me his fullest support, particularly if we pro-ceeded against the Ottoman Bank, which is here held responsi-ble for the financial troubles.

* * *

Then with Davout Efendi, in my view the most irreproach-able of the functionaries I have met thus far. I am proud of the fact that he is a Jew. The Sultan has no more loyal official. At heart he is with us, but he must be careful not to show it.

He considers it possible that we shall reach our goal one day, when Turkey *"sera dans la dèche, et si vous dorez la pilule* [is completely broke, and if you sugar-coat the pill]"—that is, es-tablish our State as a vassal state.

He promised me to be on hand when I visit Tewfik, the For-eign Minister, today. Only, it must appear as if we did not know each other.

* * *

Last evening Newlinski informed me that Izzet Bey would receive me today.

June 21

I am writing Davout Efendi that for the time being he should not speak with his Minister about the matter. The moment is not auspicious.

* * *

Yesterday the Sultan told Newlinski that he would not receive me as a journalist, because following Bacher's interview, the *N. Fr. Pr.* had made a violent personal attack on him.

Yesterday morning I drove with Newlinski to Yildiz Kiosk in order to see Izzet Bey. It had been agreed in advance that the conversation must consist only of polite nothings.

At half-past nine we were driving along the familiar route, which is bordered by colorful scenes of the poverty-stricken life in the Orient, past the Dolma Bagjeh, where the blue Bosporus lies shimmering, and up the hill to Yildiz.

We entered the palace courtyard where repair work on the buildings is going on.

Izzet Bey happened to be standing in the courtyard. We greeted him and went to the building where his office is located. It looks rather shabby. The individual offices look like beach cabins. Even the room of Izzet Bey, the all-powerful, is small and paltry. Izzet's desk, a smaller one for his secretary, a few armchairs, and a curtained four-poster (in case he has to spend the night there on continuous duty): that is all. But a window faces the wide, laughing beauty of the Bosporus, overlooking the white minarets of the *selamlik* mosque as far as the hazy Princes Islands.

Another man waiting for Izzet Bey was a Jewish jeweller who had brought a silver pendulum-clock ordered by the Sultan. This clock is a reward for the army doctor who, a few days previously, had operated on the Sultan's boil.

Izzet Bey came in and, after I had been introduced to him, took care of the jeweller.

Izzet Bey is a man in his forties, of medium height and slight build. His wrinkled, tired, but intelligent face is almost ugly. Large nose, sparse, semi-long, dark beard, intelligent eyes.

I spoke the prearranged banalities. I did not wish to leave without having made the acquaintance of one of the most outstanding men of this great country. I should be very pleased if I succeeded, through my newspaper, in imparting to others the favorable impressions I was carrying away from Constantinople. I planned to write a series of articles about the political circles of Turkey, and would be glad if I could be of some use.

Izzet Bey smiled at all this very affably and was "delighted to have made your acquaintance" when, after a quarter of an hour, I took leave of him.

Newlinski had forewarned me that all the servants must be given *baksheesh*. Izzet's servant in the second-floor corridor took two mejidiyes, the servant on the ground floor, who had held my cane, one mejidiye. But at the Yildiz exit the thing became comical. There stood two gatekeepers. As I reached into my pocket, both held out their hands, side by side, and I deliberately delayed the donation for a few seconds in order to spin out my enjoyment of the symbolic spectacle of these baksheeshites at the court gate. Each got a mejidiye.

Then we drove along the Bosporus out toward Bebek, past daydreaming harem-castles. The sun was burning hot, but a gentle breeze came from the Bosporus.

Only then did Newlinski tell me what he had accomplished the day before (Saturday) at the Porte and the Palace. He had felt constrained to keep this from me so that I might not make even the slightest unintentional allusion to it in my conversation with Izzet.

The Grand Vizier, he said, was opposed to the proposal I had made. (Margueritte, the Grand Vizier's confidant, had told me the contrary. Who was lying? Could it be that the Grand Vizier was only giving Newlinski diplomatic double-talk because he wanted to keep me guessing?

Newlinski begged the Grand Vizier, even though he was opposed to it himself, at least not to say anything about it to the Sultan. For the Grand Vizier is not supposed to know that the Sultan is against it. Everybody here has the servile habit of confirming the Sultan in whatever he already desires, and of boldly opposing whatever he is already against.

At Yildiz Kiosk, according to what Newlinski observed on Saturday, the disposition toward me had improved somewhat. The Sultan at least permitted Newlinski to speak of me. Newlinski had told the Sultan on Saturday that I had thought his first refusal sublime and had admired it greatly. He said I was a friend of Turkey and wished to be of service to the Sultan. The Sultan ought to receive me.

The Caliph declined to do this. He could not and would not receive me as a journalist after the experience he had had with Bacher and the *N. Fr. Pr.* A few months after Bacher's audience our paper had published the most malicious attack on his person that had ever appeared in the press—including the English and Armenian papers. The Sultan complained about this to the Austrian ambassador, Calice, and expressly regretted that the latter had introduced Bacher to him.

On the other hand, he could and would receive me as a friend —after I had rendered him a service. The service he asks of me is this: For one thing, I am to influence the European press (in London, Paris, Berlin, and Vienna) to handle the Armenian question in a spirit more friendly to the Turks; for another, I am to induce the Armenian leaders directly to submit to him, whereupon he will make all sorts of concessions to them.

In his talk with Newlinski the Sultan used a poetic locution: "To me all my peoples are like children I might have had by different wives. They are my children, all of them; and even though they have differences of opinion among themselves— with me they can have none."

I immediately told Newlinski that I was ready *à me mettre en campagne* [to start my campaign]. Let them give me a pragmatic presentation of the Armenian situation: which persons in London are to be brought round, what newspapers to be won over, etc. Of course, my efforts would be greatly facilitated if the Sultan were to receive me.

Newlinski said: "He will receive you afterwards and confer a high decoration on you."

I answered: "I don't need a decoration. All I want now is an audience with him. *Planter le premier jalon* [drive in the first stake]—that is our only task now."

We carried on this conversation in the garden café at Babek on the Bosporus. We were sitting under the shade of a tree, in the great noon-day heat.

*   *   *

Afterwards we rode up the hill to Madame Gropler, a remarkable, dear old invalid lady. Hers is a Polish emigrant's house where for the last forty years all exiled politicians, every itinerant artist and diplomat *en rupture d'ennui officiel* [escaping from difficulties with the government] have been in and out.

A Polish violinist, the nephew of our hostess, played to us after the meal. There also appeared His Excellency Reshid Bey, son of the famous Reshid Pasha and grandson of Fuad Pasha.

Reshid is a fat, intelligent man, still young, who used to be attached to the embassy in Vienna. His two little boys, whom he had brought along, speak German and sweetly sang German songs for us.

After lunch Newlinski had spoken about my project with Reshid, who is in the Sultan's good graces. Reshid's reaction to it was sympathetic; and when, before leaving, I stood with him on the terrace for a few minutes, he promised me his support.

* * *

In the afternoon I attended a training session of the fire brigade, to which Count Széchényi, an easy-going old gentleman, who here holds the rank of a pasha, had invited me very urgently.

The firemen are fine, sturdy specimens from Anatolia. It is easy to understand that the master of such troops, which don't need to get any pay and yet gladly serve, will not soon, if ever, regard his situation as lost.

Unfortunately, the great worries caused by my political efforts have made me half blind to the beauty of the place, the wonders of its history, and the colorfulness of the figures that are constantly before my eyes. At the firemen's exhibition, too, there were groups of people by the side of the road on the slopes of the hill, women squatting about in their mysterious garb, and much else that ordinarily would have been a feast for my eyes.

* * *

In the dilapidated graveyards, tombstones many centuries old on which people sit or hang out their clotheslines.

In the evening, Newlinski returned from Yildiz Kiosk tired and upset. Bad news had come in from various parts of the Empire. Bloodshed in Crete; the Druse (in the Lebanon?) have exterminated an entire battalion of regulars, i.e., killed them off one by one; and recently Armenians broke in across the Russian border and massacred three hundred Mohammedans.

The Sultan would like to make peace with the Armenians at any cost. He takes a gloomy view of the future and said to Newlinski: "*C'est une croisade déguisée contre la Turquie* [It is a crusade in disguise against Turkey]."

This magnanimous, melancholy prince of decline reminds me of Boabdil el Chico whom Heine wrote about.*

The hill of Yildiz is perhaps the "mountain of the last Caliph's sigh." *

After sundown I sailed up the Bosporus on a small yacht, in the direction of Büyükdere.

The veils of evening slowly draped themselves around the beautiful, white, proud castles where the harem wives dwell, the widows of former sultans and the widows of the present one. For he does not live with them.

June 22

Newlinski, whose diplomatic acumen and finesse I admire more and more, thinks that first of all I ought to have some position in the palace from which I personally—without using anyone as a go-between, for it might look as though he were bought—could keep reiterating the proposal of the Jews.

That is an excellent idea.

Every hour I press Newlinski to get me that audience with the Sultan, so that my London friends may believe that I was here.

If the Sultan had said yes, he need not have received me. I would have left town and got things started.

Since he is saying no, it is indispensable that he receive me, so that my friends may realize *que tout n'est pas rompu* [that all is not lost yet].

* Translator's Note: *Cf.* Heine's poem, *Der Mohrenkönig.*

June 23

Nothing much happened yesterday. Také Margueritte spoke to the Grand Vizier and told him that I wanted to do him the service of interviewing him. Khalil Rifat Pasha sent me word that he would receive me.

I thereupon wired Benedikt that I was going to talk general politics with the Grand Vizier and would telegraph the whole interview, but on condition that the editorial comment would acknowledge the amiability with which I was received here.

Benedikt wired back: "Shall do everything you wish."

That was what I expected.

* * *

Newlinski is an uncommonly interesting man to whom people in Vienna are doing a grave injustice. The better I get to know him, the more his character appeals to me. If he had had enough money, he would have become one of the finest *grand-seigneurs* and a diplomat with a name in world history. He is a warped man, but very sensitive and full of noble impulses. He is an unhappy Pole and often says: "Since I cannot shape the policy of my nation, I don't care a rap for anything. I go on artist's tours in politics, like a piano virtuoso—that is all."

It is hard not to be touched by this noble Polish melancholia. He is much more cultivated than most aristocrats; he has a feeling for art and a sense of tact. I intended to use him only as an instrument, and I have come to the point where I esteem and love him. He is obliging but proud, crafty and yet sincere, too, and his unmistakable gentlemanly qualities are detrimental to his reputation only because he moves among the bourgeoisie. He is the most interesting figure I have had to deal with since I have carried on the Jewish cause.

June 24

Yesterday I had that interview with the Grand Vizier for the *N. Fr. Pr.* It lasted an hour and a half. Haireddin Bey again was the smiling interpreter. He said cheerfully: "It was nothing—just a couple of hundred dead."

I sat by the window in the sunshine and sweated while I wrote on my knees. The sunlight fell on the paper, too, and blinded me. It was very tiring.

An Oriental touch: As we were crossing the bridge over the Golden Horn, a beggar boy kept pestering me even after I had given him something. I asked Také Margueritte to get him to leave me in peace. He simply spat in the poor boy's face.

Half an hour later we were at the hotel. Newlinski was writing, and suddenly he said to Také in a gruff tone of voice: "*Sonnez* [ring]."

And Také obediently rang. The beggar boy was avenged.

Newlinski, to whom I had related the scene at the bridge, later mocked Také further by saying: "*Ici on reçoit des crachats, et on les rend* [Here one is spat on, and one spits on others]."

* * *

Newlinski spent the whole afternoon yesterday with Izzet and Nuri Bey at the palace. I am reported to have made a most favorable impression on both of them. Izzet said that I was an "*inspiré* [inspired man]," which is the highest praise among the Moslems, and Nuri called me an *homme hors ligne* [a swell person].

* * *

Of course, the main thing, my reception by the Sultan, has proved unattainable.

It is, at any rate, a tremendous thing; because Széchényi Pasha, for example, at whose house we had lunch yesterday, has not spoken with the Sultan in ten years, although he never misses a *selamlik* and will shortly be promoted by the Sultan to the rank of marshal.

Yesterday the Sultan sent me word that I should not leave to-day; he would probably have something to say to me before my departure. This is a success—though an uncertain one.

Yesterday I telegraphed the *N. Fr. Pr.* a rather long *entrefilet* [notice], presenting the local, undeniably critical situation in a manner friendly to the government.

Then, in the afternoon, I sailed on a small yacht to Büyükdere, to see the Austrian ambassador, Baron Calice.

He received me more graciously than he probably would have if I had turned to him in the first place.

Calice is a well-preserved man in his late sixties. Bald head, large nose, moustache, a rather grand manner, not inconsiderable loquacity. From time to time in his stream of words he suddenly remembers what an exalted person he really is—*et alors il se reprend* [and then he checks himself].

We sat in the beautiful big salon of the embassy's summer residence at Büyükdere. Through the large windows one's eyes lovingly embrace the rosy and blue beauty of the Bosporus.

Calice expounded to me in detail his understanding of the situation. He spoke approximately in the style of the diplomats in Gregor Samarow's novels. He "presented the situation on a chess board." Anyone who knew the game, he said, looking up meaningfully, would understand the importance of this piece or that.

Russia's influence was great because of her geographical position. England had lost her position here, because the Turks saw that she did not force the issue of the Dardanelles, not even after her threat. On the other hand, the Bosporus was open to Russia. Added to that was the present complexion of Bulgaria which has become Russianized.

As for Turkey's position, Calice considers it rather serious—but the vitality of this Empire has already been demonstrated so often that it will perhaps continue to exist. Of course . . . the many rebellions, the lack of finances, etc. He hopes that Turkey will find a way out again, but he is not sure. He presents the Armenian question in a way fundamentally different from that of the Turks who always falsify the facts. Now, of course, they don't want any foreign intervention, they are going to do everything themselves, reforms, etc. But once the emergency is past, they no longer think of that.

There could be no question of a *croisade déguisée* [crusade in disguise], rather of a "crusade of the crescent," for the Turks were persecuting the Christians.

Austria, he said, was, as always, observing a policy of preserving Turkey. He praised my proposal for friendly counsel which Goluchowski was to give the Armenians as a patriotic one.

On the whole, a barren conversation.

Later we dined at Petala's on the shore of the Bosporus. A wonderful evening by the sea.

We sailed back to Constantinople in the moonlight. An ineffably delightful night.

Také Margueritte was drunk.

June 25

Sent off the Grand Vizier interview to Vienna today, by a passenger on the Orient Express.

In the evening Newlinski came from the Palace where, it appears, people are already very favorably disposed toward me. They are taking to the Jewish idea.

Right now they seem to be in a very bad fix in regard to money. However, the matter would have to be presented in some other form. *Sauver les apparences* [Save face]!

Izzet (through whom, of course, the Sultan speaks) or the Sultan (through whom Izzet speaks) would be willing enough to yield Palestine if the proper formula could be found for the transaction. Precisely because things are going badly for them they must not sell any land, Newlinski reports; but he observes that my idea is making good progress.

In a few months' time, the people in Yildiz Kiosk will perhaps be ripe for it. *L'idée les travaille visiblement* [it is plain to see that the idea agitates them].

Nuri Bey, too, is very sympathetic toward our cause. Today he said that we should endeavor to win over the Czar.

*　　*　　*

Bad news again today from Anatolia.

New massacres at Van.

June 26

Another *selamlik*. Exactly the same spectacle as a week ago.

Newlinski says he is convinced that the Turks are willing to give us Palestine. He says it is just like when a man has a hunch that a woman is willing to surrender; in such a situation one may not even be able to say as yet what this hunch is based on.

"I say she's a whore—I don't know why; I just feel sure," he said in his broken Polish-German.

*　　*　　*

After the *selamlik* I drove to Therapia, while Newlinski was received by the Sultan.

In the evening, after my return, he gave me an account of his audience.

The Sultan began to speak about me of his own accord. He expressed his thanks for the article I had telegraphed to the *N. Fr. Pr.*

Then he brought up the subject of Palestine. To begin with, he reproached Newlinski for having submitted the matter in a thoughtless way. As someone acquainted with the local situation, Newlinski should have known that Palestine could never be given up in the proposed form of a purchase. But according to what he—the Sultan—had heard, Mr. Herzl's friends were thinking of a possible exchange.

This idea of an exchange, which originated with Izzet Bey, seems to have been presented by Izzet to the Sultan as coming from us. Izzet also was the interpreter at Newlinski's audience today.

Newlinski did not know immediately what to say to this, and referred the Sultan to the information which I would be able to give. He said it was my most ardent desire to be received by His Majesty.

To that the Sultan replied: "I shall see. In any case, I shall receive Mr. Herzl—sooner or later."

Newlinski pointed out that I have to speak with my friends in London early in July. The Sultan repeated: "I shall see."

It is possible, then, that I shall be received after all.

The Sultan then made Newlinski a further and rather surprising disclosure: he had already been sounded out by a Great Power as to his attitude toward my proposal.

Which Great Power that was Newlinski was unable to ask.

(Here I must make a parenthetical remark on my own behalf: I have already accomplished a thing or two after all, if my plan, which quite a few people have called crazy, is already the subject of diplomatic steps among the Great Powers. Poor Friedrich Schiff! Poor Moritz Benedikt!)

The Sultan then asked: "Do the Jews have to have Palestine at all costs? Couldn't they settle in some other province?"

Newlinski answered: "Palestine is their cradle; that is where they wish to return."

The Sultan rejoined: "But Palestine is the cradle of other religions as well."

Thereupon Newlinski said:

"If the Jews cannot get Palestine, they will simply have to go to Argentina."

Following this the Sultan continued talking about me with Izzet in Turkish. Newlinski caught only the repeated recurrence of my name. Izzet seems to have spoken about me in friendly terms.

Then the Sultan put another question to Newlinski: "How many Jews are there in Salonica?"

Newlinski didn't know. Neither do I.

Does he perhaps want to let us have the region around Salonica?

Next the Sultan discussed the general situation. He said that the day before yesterday the Powers had made an unjust joint protest against the Van atrocities, when it was actually the Moslems who had been massacred by the Armenians at Van.

He also spoke about the financial situation which is anything but rosy.

Newlinski concludes: "It's a whore!"

June 27

Newlinski tells me stories of Yildiz Kiosk. Dreams play a great part there. There is Lufti Aga, the Sultan's chamberlain and a great dreamer. Lufti Aga is around the Sultan all day, waits on him personally, has great influence. If Lufti Aga says: I have dreamed such and such, it makes an impression on the Sultan. If Lufti Aga were to say one day: I dreamt that the Jews are coming to Palestine, this would be worth more than the "steps" taken by the entire diplomatic corps.

It sounds like a fairy-tale, but I have absolute confidence in Newlinski.

When the reconciliation with the Prince of Bulgaria took place, Lufti Aga's dreams played a great part. He does not dream gratis. The Prince of Bulgaria didn't immediately understand why this chamberlain should receive a gift of 20,000 francs. But Ferdinand owed his appointment as a *mushir* to a dream.

* * *

Diplomatic gossip.

I had told Calice that Széchényi Pasha would probably go to Vienna with a holograph letter from the Sultan. Calice gave a superior smile and said: "*C'est de la menue monnaie* [That's small change]."

However, at yesterday's *selamlik* he stepped up to Széchényi and said: "I am told by Dr. Herzl that you are to get a mission to our Emperor"—when I had told him this only in confidence.

Széchényi, who had already seen himself as a *mushir* (marshal), as a reward for putting out Constantinopolitan conflagrations over many years, is quite beside himself now. He is afraid of losing his leave, his mushirship, and his "mission," because Calice will be jealous and work against it.

* * *

Idea for London.

I must make the matter palatable to the English lords of finance in the following form:

"Convinced that the Jewish Question can be solved only territorially, we are forming a *Society* for the acquisition of an autonomous country for those Jews who cannot assimilate in their present places of residence."

This formula will unite Zionists and assimilationists. Both Edmond R. and Lord Rothschild can subscribe to it.

June 27

Nuri Bey, the most intelligent mind in the Foreign Office, and very popular with the Sultan, has, it appears, made a favorable report to the Sultan on my proposal. Nuri Bey is all for my idea. Perhaps the noticeable change in the Sultan's attitude can be traced back to Nuri's report.

Izzet Bey was a bit annoyed—but not at me—because Nuri had made this report behind his back.

Incidentally, Izzet and Nuri are friends.

June 28

Yesterday morning, as the ultimate insight of my wisdom, I said to Newlinski with reluctance and secret shame:

"If the Sultan won't receive me, he should at least give me a visible token that, after listening to my proposal and rejecting it, he still wants to remain *en coquetterie* [on flirting terms] with me. A high decoration would be suitable for that. But I implore

398 THE COMPLETE DIARIES OF THEODOR HERZL

you not to take me for a decoration hunter. I have never given a hoot for decorations, and I don't give a hoot now. But for my people in London I badly need a sign of favor from the Sultan."

Newlinski immediately wrote this to Izzet Bey; but no reply came in the course of the day.

Instead, in the afternoon there came a message from the Master of Ceremonies, Munir Pasha, informing me that today I would be shown the Sultan's castles and treasures by an adjutant.

At that moment there arose a slight ill feeling between Newlinski and me.

I said I was a bit disappointed. Thereupon Newlinski made a point of emphasizing the honor of this invitation. But I said: "*Je ne suis pas assez fabricant de chocolat pour être touché jusqu'aux larmes par cette faveur* [I am not enough of a chocolate manufacturer to be moved to tears by this favor]."

Newlinski disagreed with this, a bit irritated, saying that he himself was very receptive to such attentions and grateful for them.

However, in the course of the evening, I tried to erase this disagreeable impression.

Later the Greek Constantinides called, an obsequious journalist for whom Newlinski obtained a decoration today.

The sycophantic Greek wore his brand-new ribbon in his buttonhole and kissed Newlinski's hand.

For my benefit, Newlinski evinced a perceptible satisfaction.

*　　*　　*

Tonight we are leaving for Sofia.
This trip is costing me about three thousand francs.
The *fonds perdu* [irrecoverable expenses] are increasing.

June 28

At the *Jardins des Petits Champs* at Pera, which is situated in an old Turkish cemetery, a visiting Italian light-opera company is performing. The star is the singer Morosini—pretty, graceful, dissolute, Newlinski had repeatedly spoken of asking her to supper. It never worked out. He calls her *"la Morosina."* Of these ten days during which we manipulated a bit of world history—for this very attempt to found a Jewish State will live in the memories of men, even if the plan remains a dream—of these colorful and serious days the name of *la Morosina* will surely stick in our memory, precisely because it remained only a word. Every day Newlinski would tell his henchmen, the fat Danusso, the comical Roumanian Také Margueritte, and the fawning Greek Constantinides: *"Invitez-moi la Morosina* [Invite la Morosina for me]."

There was something inimitably grand-seignorial about it.

I loved the view over the Golden Horn from our hotel windows. Whistler-like dusk and nights aglow with lights, wonderful rosy morning mists; the thick violet and grey-blue splendor of the evening vapors. The big ships disappearing in the fog and then emerging again. On moonlit nights, light powdery veils. Today it is sunny. The heights over there—Eyub, I believe—stretch between two sheets of blue. Above, the delicate sky; below, the oily waters on which the silver strokes of oars flash.

* * *

One can understand the greed with which the whole world eyes Constantinople.

Everyone wants it—and this is the best guarantee for the continued existence of Turkey.

None of the pirates will let any of the others enjoy this beauty—and so perhaps it will remain unplundered.

June 29, Sofia

Yesterday afternoon, accompanied by the Sultan's adjutant, I saw the treasures of Eski Serai and the Bosporus palaces of Dolma Bagjeh and Beylerbey.

The adjutant spoke little French, but had enormous respect

for me; to each question he replied, *"Oui, Monsieur* [Yes, Sir],"
and then switched to Excellency: *"Oui, mon Excellence* [Yes,
Your Excellency]!"

The castles are magnificent.

The baths at Beylerbey, a sultry Oriental dream.

The Sultan's caique, in which we traveled, was rowed by eight
of the Caliph's sturdy boatmen; the helmsman, squatting cross-
legged in the stern, wore a frock-coat.

* * *

When I got back to the Hotel Royal from this hot but beautiful trip, Newlinski, who was writing letters in his underwear,
said to me: "He sends you that!" and handed me a box containing the Commander's Cross of the Mejidiye Order.

* * *

We then took our leave of the *edundi exercitus* [eating army]
Danusso, Margueritte, and Constantinides, and left by rail.

On the train Newlinski related the following:

"The Sultan told me he would have given you a decoration
even if I hadn't asked for it. But he could not receive you on this
visit, because your plan hadn't remained secret and several persons had even made reports about it—namely, the Grand Vizier,
Nuri Bey, Davout Efendi, and Djawid Bey. Under such circumstances the audience would no longer have had an intimate character; and since the Sultan is obliged to reject your proposal in
its present form, he did not care to talk about it at all. But he
did tell me: 'The Jews are intelligent; they will find some acceptable formula.' From this we may gather that the Sultan merely
wants to *sauver les apparences* [save face], and I believe that in
the end he will accept. He seems to have in mind some form of
trade; in any case, in diplomatic dealings one must not discuss
the heart of the matter too plainly. Often people negotiate for
a long time and dodge the main issue. Izzet Bey seems to be
working for you; that is the impression I have.

"The Grand Vizier submitted an unfavorable report, saying

that he did not regard the plan as seriously meant, but as fantasy. Nuri Bey also made a report and only stressed those aspects that militate against it, although in our presence he acted so cordially. Nuri Bey had probably learned that the Grand Vizier would oppose the plan, and he wanted to be on the safe side. But it will be easy to win him over again as soon as the wind veers. The most intelligent report was written by Davout Efendi. He gave a clear analysis of the whole plan and added that as a Jew he could counsel neither for nor against it. Djawid Bey, the son of the Grand Vizier, in his report categorically declared himself in favor of the plan, but on the stupid grounds that the Jews were such good subjects of His Majesty that one could only welcome the immigration of more of them.

"The Sultan takes this last view and mentioned a report by the Governor of Salonica to the effect that the Salonican Jews emigrated as soon as they had got some money. I explained this to the Sultan by saying that, after all, the Jews had no real home and that it was precisely a matter of obtaining a *foyer* [home] for them.

"The Sultan now expects you to help him in the Armenian matter. Moreover, he wishes you to procure for him a loan based on a lien on the revenue from the light-houses. For that purpose he is sending you the contract with Collas. The revenue is 45,000 Turkish pounds annually. The loan is supposed to amount to two million pounds."

*　　*　　*

We were on our way to Sofia. *En route* we discussed the next steps. Bismarck is to be interested in the cause. Newlinski has connections with him as well as with the Roman Curia which, after all, we must also approach.

*　　*　　*

On the train Newlinski again told me a lot of stories about court, diplomatic, and government circles. I have long since felt intuitively that the great of the earth are composed only of the respect we have for them. Every little anecdote confirms me in this assumption. E.g., what Newlinski tells me about Petrow, the Bulgarian Minister of War. To this man the Sultan once promised a horse, and because it has not materialized so far, Petrow is quite furious. Every week he writes to the Bulgarian envoy at Stambul: "Where is my horse?"

And he declares he will not give orders to shoot at the Macedonian rebels, because he has not received the horse.

When Prince Ferdinand was visiting the Sultan, the latter distributed gifts among the Bulgarian ministers. They compared the boxes etc., and were incensed when one present had less value than another.

June 30

At the station in Sofia I was met by two gentlemen from the Zionist Society, who had been informed by telephone from Philippopolis that I was just passing through there.

Sensation in the city; hats and caps were thrown in the air everywhere. I had to request that there be no welcoming parade.

At the Zionist Society, speeches. Afterwards I had to go to the synagogue, where hundreds were awaiting me.

I warned against demonstrations and advised calm behavior so as not to arouse popular passions against the Jews.

After I had spoken in German and French, my words were repeated in Bulgarian and Spaniolic.

I stood on the altar platform. When I was not quite sure how to face the congregation without turning my back to the Holy of Holies, someone cried: "It's all right for you to turn your back to the Ark, you are holier than the Torah."

Several wanted to kiss my hand.

*   *   *

In the evening, dined with Minister Natchevitch. I mentioned the grievance of the local Jews, whose synagogue grounds are to be expropriated. On this site the synagogue has stood for 500 years.

The liberated Bulgarians are more intolerant than the Turks were.

Natchevitch promised to take care of the matter favorably.

July 1

Baden-bei-Wien, at my parents' house.

Even the last day on the train with Newlinski was full of stimulation. He is a rare, unusual person of great gifts.

He had the following idea. It ought to be suggested to the Sultan that he take charge of the Zionist movement and proclaim to the Jews that he would throw Palestine open to them as a principality, under his suzerainty, with its own laws, army, etc. In return, the Jews would have to pay a tribute of about a million pounds each year. This tribute could then be immediately mortgaged against a loan (which we would raise).

I consider this idea excellent. I had thought of something similar in Constantinople, but didn't speak about it. For that is an acceptable proposition, and up to now I was allowed only to make unacceptable ones, because I am not sure whether the Londoners won't leave me in the lurch at the last moment.

Now I am taking this proposal to London where I am already expected with some impatience.

Newlinski proposes further that Bismarck be interested in the Jewish cause through his friend Sidney Whitman. Whitman is to be called from London to meet Newlinski at Carlsbad, and from there go to Friedrichsruh. All this at my expense. Whitman will be doing Newlinski a friendly turn, of course, but we shall have to reimburse him *largement* [generously] for his expenses.

Bismarck should then write the Sultan a letter containing the proposal which Newlinski made on the train. The Sultan will receive me, issue the call to the Jews, which I will spread all over the world—and the thing is done.

Newlinski says: *"Si vous arrivez a pacifier les Arméniens, si vous faites l'emprunt de 2 millions de livres sur les phares, et si nous avons la lettre de Bismarck—nous enlevons la chose en huit jours* [If you succeed in pacifying the Armenians, if you make a loan of two million pounds on the light-houses, and if we have Bismarck's letter—we will carry the thing off in a week]!"

* * *

We took cordial leave of each other in Vienna. I promised Newlinski my friendship for life.

If it is through him that we obtain Palestine, we shall give him a fine estate in Galicia as an honorific recompense.

July 2

Last night I spoke with the Armenian Alawerdow in my parents' apartment. Mr. Klatschko served as interpreter.

I offered the Armenians my services as a conciliator. Alawerdow did not dare to speak out, because he is a Russian and afraid of his government. Also, he didn't seem to trust me. We finally agreed that he will announce me in London as a friend of the Armenians and act as a pacifier in his circle.

* * *

I spoke with Reichenfeld of the Union Bank about the two-million loan. He wasn't sure; one would have to see, ask questions, talk it over. I refused to make further inquiries.

* * *

Hechler telegraphed me from Karlsruhe yesterday that an audience had been promised. Therefore I am leaving for Karlsruhe today in order to obtain a conference with the Kaiser through the Grand Duke.

July 2

On the Orient Express, on the way to Karlsruhe.

All these days I have forgotten to note down a splendid message which Bismarck sent to the Sultan via Whitman-Newlinski.

The Sultan had sent Bismarck via Newlinski-Whitman a wired request for advice on his present difficulties. Bismarck replied: "*Fermeté, pas se laisser intimider, et loyauté éclairée aux traités* [Firmness, a refusal to be intimidated, and enlightened loyalty to treaties]."

Loyauté éclairée is absolutely delightful.

* * *

Newlinski said a number of times: "When I hear Bismarck talking about politics, I feel like a musician who is listening to Rubinstein's playing."

* * *

At the station this morning I was a bit upset by Schnirer, the president of the Vienna Zionist Association, whom, like Landau, I had asked to see me before my departure.

When I outlined the favorable results of Constantinople, and especially when I mentioned the decoration, his face darkened.

I immediately took the opportunity to tell him that I wanted to induce Edmond Rothschild to join the movement by resigning my leadership. For, I said, there are *Yids* and there are *Jews*. The *Yids* will be in no mood to support the cause, for fear of thereby lending me personally a helping hand.

July 3

On the train, bound for Brussels.

Yesterday Hechler met me at the station in Karlsruhe. The Grand Duke had gone to Freiburg and requested me to join him there, that is, at St. Blasien.

Since I don't need the Grand Duke at the moment, I had Hechler wire him that I was pressed for time, being expected in London, and could I have permission to report to him on my way back. The Sultan, I added, appeared to be well disposed toward our project.

July 5, London

Once again in London. This time *fine weather,** and everything enchanting.

The approach, incidentally, was bad. On the crossing from Ostend to Dover we ran into some ugly waves. I had wished for bad weather in order to test my will-power. Sure enough, one by one all the passengers had got sea-sick by the time we approached Dover. I, too, had a slight touch of faintness, and I don't know how my psychological experiment would have turned out if the thing had lasted a quarter of an hour longer.

I arrived here a bit depressed and found other depressing things awaiting me.

Goldsmid excused himself. He can't get away from Cardiff tomorrow on account of a batallion inspection.

Montagu invited me by letter to come and see him—but he said he had to leave in the evening (yesterday). I wrote him I could not come immediately, but begged him to sacrifice his Sunday for me, because I had brought along from Constantinople the *presque-certitude* [near certainty] that we would regain Palestine. Despite this, Sir Samuel Montagu went away and merely gave me an appointment for tomorrow at his office. I don't know whether I shall even go there. I am preparing myself for his complete elimination from my plan, although this is certain to do me harm in Constantinople where I have already mentioned his name.

The Rev. Singer came to see me in the evening. I stirred him up a bit. In fact, I shall first have to light a fire under everybody here.

*   *   *

This morning was better. I put the finishing touches on my speech for the Maccabeans and in the course of the forenoon sent it to Sylvie d'Avigdor, bit by bit, to be translated.

* In English in the original.

*   *   *

Lucien Wolf of the *Daily Graphic* came to interview me.

During the past few days all the local papers have started to make a noise.

Singer said yesterday that I should ask Lord Rothschild for an interview. I rejected this as something beneath my dignity. Singer said: "Lord Rothschild is a 'patron.' A patron has been defined by an English writer as follows: 'One who looks with unconcern on a man struggling for life in the water, and when he has reached ground, encumbers him with help.' *

When you have triumphed in the Jewish cause, he will invite you—together with other lions—to dinner."

I said: "So a dinner at Rothschild's is the victor's prize! *Moi, je m'en fous* [Me, I don't give a damn about it], if you know that expression."

So today, hearing about the stir that is starting in the newspapers, I am asking myself with amusement whether this is already enough for that Rothschild invitation.

Then I went to see our correspondent, Schidrowitz. If I cannot have the *superos* [top men] of Jewish finance for the lighthouse loan which the Sultan desires, I shall move Acheron.

I promised Schidrowitz a commission for procuring this loan. But even if *he* made money on it, I said, the truth must be made known at all times and to everybody—namely, that I am not making anything on these transactions and am carrying them out only as *entrée en matière* [means of entry] in order to do the Sultan a favor with a view to the Jewish cause.

July 5

At noon, Lucien Wolf of the *Daily Graphic* came to interview me, after an interview with Zangwill, concerning me, had already appeared in today's *Sunday Times*.

During lunch, Wolf took notes for his story.

In the afternoon there came Claude Montefiore and Frederic Mocatta of the Anglo-Jewish Association. I had requested Monte-

* Translator's Note: Dr. Samuel Johnson in a letter to Lord Chesterfield (1755).

fiore to postpone the meeting of their Executive Committee, as it conflicted with tomorrow's Maccabean banquet. I said I wanted to consolidate all the Jewish committees into a single big organization; and lest anyone believe that I wanted to promote myself in this way, I offered, in return for the acceptance of my simply formulated program, to resign the leadership of the movement.

I stated the program as follows:

"The *Society of Jews* sets itself the task of acquiring, under international law, a territory for those Jews who are unable to assimilate."

The gentlemen asked for time to think this over, and I naturally acceded. However, I said that I did not want to take into the *Society* the *associations* as such, but simply the outstanding individuals.

It was an exhausting battle of words. Mocatta, who had not read my book, brought up all the old arguments.

Montefiore said with gravity that I was demanding a revolution in all the ideas he had held up to now.

July 6

Finished the speech for the Maccabeans *tant bien que mal* [after a fashion], tired as I am.

I wrote to Montefiore and Mocatta that I accepted the proposal, advanced in the course of yesterday's discussion, to make the *Society of Jews,* in the beginning, a *société d'études* [study commission].

(To such a body I would not, of course, make available the connections I have already acquired. My resources for action I would give only to a committee geared for action.)

*   *   *

A few hours later Mocatta answered that he considered the whole plan unacceptable, and the Jewish State neither possible nor desirable.

The funny part of it is that I had not even sent for Mocatta, but only for Montefiore. Mocatta came along with Montefiore as Antonin Proust once went along with Spuller to call on Casimir-Périer, when the latter had been asked to form a cabinet. Casimir-Périer thereupon took Proust as well into the cabinet, because he had happened along.

Mocatta impressed me somewhat like an officious second at a duel.

Schidrowitz came in order to worm out of me what the loan to the Sultan was to be based on.

Because I am afraid that he would peddle it around as a "deal" and offer it to every Tom, Dick, and Harry, thus compromising me in Constantinople, I didn't tell him anything. It is true, it would be excellent for the project if I could make the light-house loan through bankers of the second rank, through the Africanders like Barnato, etc., because I could control them better than the Rothschilds, Montagus, etc. But I cannot risk letting myself be compromised by Schidrowitz's business treatment. I'd rather not have the loan raised at all.

July 7

Last evening, the Maccabean Dinner.

I hadn't been able to get Miss d'Avigdor's translation type-written until yesterday afternoon.

At five o'clock I received the clean copy and read it through with the Rev. Singer's aid. I learned English, as it were, an hour before the meeting. I jotted down the pronunciation of the words between the lines.

The banquet had a very festive character. To the toast proposed by Chairman Singer I replied in German and in French, which caused Zangwill to say jokingly that I was like the new periodical *Cosmopolis,* which appears in German, French, and English.

Afterwards we moved to the auditorium, and I courageously read off my speech.

It was a very great success. There followed a debate with the old arguments which I rebutted with the familiar material. With the exception of two almost impolite people—the political economist Levy or Leve, and a Russian whose name I did not catch—even the opponents spoke respectfully.

L. Wolf moved the appointment of a study commission, to be composed of Maccabeans and others, for an examination of my proposal.

This elicited a debate, which only once again strengthened my antipathy to organizational claptrap.

July 7

Colonel Goldsmid telegraphed he would be here on Thursday.

* * *

Schidrowitz telegraphs he cannot undertake the transaction the way I proposed it.

* * *

Nordau wrote yesterday about Zadoc Kahn's visit. Zadoc came to complain because—as he and Edmond Rothschild surmise—due to my publication the Turkish authorities in Palestine are giving the recent arrivals among the colonists a hard time and have even destroyed the latest colony.

At the same time, Nordau, in a manner indicative of his cooling, excused himself for his absence from today's Maccabean dinner.

I immediately telegraphed Zadoc Kahn:* Have just arrived from Constantinople. Your apprehensions unjustified. Sultan displayed much good will. If subordinates commit acts of brutality I am authorized to complain directly to him. Give details Hotel Albemarle.

Herzl.

To Newlinski I wired:

Lighthouse and Armenian affairs effectively launched. But everything hopeless if it proves true that Turkish authorities

* In French in the original.

in Palestine are forcibly deporting newly arrived colonists. Please inquire Constantinople immediately. Report results here. Regards, Theodor.

July 8

I am already very tired.

Yesterday I got the Armenian matter started with Lucien Wolf. I asked him to initiate a little press campaign for the cooling of tempers in the Armenian question.

* * *

Then I drove to the House of Commons to see Montagu.

The Gothic stone carvings and the activity in the waiting hall interested me greatly.

At the sight of these imposing parliamentary trappings—after all, externals have a dramatic effect—I experienced a touch of dizziness such as I had felt that time in the ante-chamber of the Grand Duke of Baden. At the same time I began to understand why the English Jews should cling to a country in which they can enter this house as masters.

Montagu appeared and led me into a charming little conference room with Gothic windows which looked out on a Gothic courtyard.

I recounted for him the practical results, from the Grand Duke to the Sultan.

He was greatly surprised and soon regained his enthusiasm. A splendid old fellow.

His first and foremost misgiving was that the Sultan, once he had been paid the Jewish tribute-loan, would kick the Jewish immigrants around.

The violent sound of a bell signal summoned Montagu to a vote on the tea tax. During his ten minutes' absence, the solution of this difficulty occurred to me.

We accept a tribute of one million pounds, on which a loan of 20 millions is to be raised. We pay the tribute and the loan in instalments.

For the first years, 100,000 pounds tribute, and a loan of two millions on that. Gradually, as the immigration proceeds, the tribute increases together with new portions of the Jewish loan based on it, until the entire amount is paid up and there are so many Jews in Palestine, accompanied by Jewish military power, that one need no longer fear that the Turks will attempt to get a stranglehold on them.

I then drove with Montagu to his house. On the way he told me that we must try to win over Edmond Rothschild without fail.

Further, he told me in confidence, yesterday evening, that the Hirsch Foundation had at its disposal a "liquid" sum, the actual amount of which no one had any idea of. It is ten million pounds sterling.

If we win over the Hirsch Association for our plan and obtain something like five million pounds, this could assure the tribute for the first few years of immigration.

*   *   *

A Jewish mass meeting is to be called for me here on Sunday. Montagu, in whose constituency—the East End—the meeting is to take place, thinks it would be premature to address this gathering.

I am still reserving my decision on this. *Flectere si nequeo superos Acheronta movebo* [If I cannot bend the powers above, I will move the lower world].

July 8

Received a letter of thanks from Zadoc Kahn, which I am answering as follows:

Reverend Grand Rabbi:*

I am making an immediate *démarche*—if the word does not seem to you too diplomatic and *"puissant"*—to Constantinople.

* In French in the original.

I shall let you know the result, maybe in person, next week in Paris.

My plan, scornfully referred to as a dream, has been taking on the shape of reality for some time.

I have already achieved astonishing results—astonishing even to me. It is imperative that Edmond Rothschild be with us. In order to obtain his assistance, I am offering to withdraw completely from the leadership of the movement, in order to dispel any suspicion of personal ambition. Let him accept my program and undertake to continue the work that is already started, and I shall give my word of honor to occupy myself with the matter only as a soldier in the ranks.

Together with Sir Samuel Montagu and Colonel Goldsmid I shall endeavor to find the form in which we could offer Edmond Rothschild the presidency of the *Society of Jews*—and later some other title.

All this is absolutely confidential—and important, believe me. I shall supply you with proof of this. Please prepare Rothschild.

Very sincerely yours,
Herzl.

July 9

I slept on this letter to Zadoc Kahn and then didn't send it off. As Newlinski says, "Let 'em simmer!"

Yesterday I spoke with Alfred Cohen and asked him to get me an introduction to Salisbury through Lord Rothschild. I said I wanted to do Lord Salisbury's policy the favor of settling the Armenian question and thus restoring the lost English influence in Constantinople.

Alfred Cohen is a pleasant, intelligent gentleman. He took down a sort of protocol in which the facts are set down elegantly and clearly for Lord Rothschild. He plans to discuss it with Rothschild while riding horseback today.

414 THE COMPLETE DIARIES OF THEODOR HERZL

Goldsmid is here.

After luncheon we talked in his smoking room which is half in the basement. His house in Princes Square is a bit quaint. The Goldsmid-d'Avigdors are one of the best Jewish families, and the house contains beautiful mementoes.

Goldsmid seemed cooler than he did that time in Cardiff— or was I more easily satisfied in the early days?

Nevertheless, I stirred him up with an account of my results up to date. But what he liked best of all, unless I am mistaken, was my word that I would withdraw from the leadership of the movement if Edmond Rothschild joined it. By this I want to show the latter that I do not care about my personal leadership. Goldsmid pointed out that he could not play any prominent part as long as he was *on full pay.** Incompatibility, etc. Still, I could see that he agreed in principle.

I requested him to introduce me to Arthur Cohen, Queen's Counsel, as the latter is a friend of the Duke of Argyll, who is important on the Armenian Committee.

I also asked him to get the Prince of Wales to give me an introduction to the Czar.

July 10

Paid the publisher David Nutt 19 pounds and a few shillings for the English edition. He has sold only 160 copies.

Had to send 300 francs to Paris, too, a few days ago, to Nordau, for the French translation.

July 11

The Russian journalist Rapoport (from *Novosti*) came to interview me.

As we talked it turned out that he has connections with the Armenian Committees, particularly with Nazarbek, the leader of the Hindjakists. Rapoport indicated to me that he suspected the

* In English in the original.

Armenian revolutionaries were being supported with money by the English government.

I asked him to put me in touch with Nazarbek. I want to make it clear to this revolutionary that the Armenians should now make their peace with the Sultan, without prejudice to their later claims when Turkey is partitioned.

* * *

Wrote to Newlinski, telling him that Montagu and Goldsmid agree to the idea of a vassal state. I also outlined for him the plan of a graduated immigration loan, beginning with a tribute of 100,000 pounds sterling—that is, a loan of two millions as earnest—and rising up to a million annually—which would bring the total loan to 20 millions.

Also informed him of the steps I have taken in the Armenian affair to date.

Luncheon at Montagu's. Also present were Colonel Goldsmid and a Polish Jew, Landau, who lives here. The latter has an aggressively sharp mind, but seems to have influence in local Jewish circles and also is a member of the Hirsch Committee.

After the meal, a short practical debate. I explained to the three what the record is so far, and that we want to induce Bismarck to write to the Sultan and launch the idea of vassal status.

Montagu laid down three conditions for his public adhesion:

1) The consent of the Great Powers.
2) That the Hirsch Fund give us its liquid capital, that is, ten million pounds.
3) That a Rothschild, which means Edmond, join the Committee.

Landau proposed the formation of a secret committee which would come out into the open as soon as the matter were assured.

Goldsmid said, pointing to me: *"He is more than any committee."* *

He pledged himself to write a letter of recommendation to Edmond Rothschild.

* In English in the original.

All three voiced apprehension with regard to tomorrow's East End meeting. They said it was premature and meant incitement of the masses.

I said that I did not want a demagogic movement, but if worst came to worst—if the aristocrats proved too aristocratic—I would set the masses in motion, too.

July 12

Last night at the Rev. Singer's. Lucien Wolf and Solomon also present. The discussion dragged pitifully and kept repeating itself.

The greatest zeal for organization and ability was displayed by the painter Solomon. Lucien Wolf would have liked to "learn details about the Sultan," but he is a very fine young fellow, too. Rev. Singer is not sure whether he would not weaken his position if he participated in the *Society of Jews*.

Finally we did agree to form an *enquiring or watching committee**—namely, from among those Maccabeans who last Monday had spoken in favor of my plan.

The name of the committee should not be *"Society of Jews"*— Rev. Singer said this name was *"colourless"* *—but a name that would in some way express a relationship to Palestine.

All these people, no matter how decent and likeable they may be, by their vacillation make me the leader!

July 13

Letter to the Grand Duke of Baden:

Your Royal Highness:

Unfortunately I was not fated to make use of your kind permission to come to St. Blasien when I arrived at Karlsruhe after Your Royal Highness had departed. Meetings which had been arranged for months were awaiting me here in London.

Now, however, I could report on important developments in the Jewish cause in which Your Royal Highness is taking such a gracious interest. Notable advances in Constantinople as well

---

* In English in the original.

as here in London may be registered. Tomorrow I am leaving for Paris, and from there I plan to go to Austria at the end of the week. May I now again ask for the great favor of being received by Your Royal Highness on Monday the 20th or Tuesday the 21st of this month for the purpose of rendering my report to you? If you will kindly state the place where I am to make my appearance, your answer will reach me at Paris, Hotel Castille, rue Cambon.

Permit me, Your Royal Highness, this expression of my respectful devotion.

Dr. Theodor Herzl.

July 13

Yesterday noon I went to Westbourne Park Chapel with an introduction from Rev. Singer to hear the "non-conformist" preacher Dr. Clifford. I listened to the soporific last part of his sermon in which with passionate gestures and in an oratorical voice he served up hoary platitudes.

The audience was hypnotized—mass psychology—and afterwards the collection plate went around.

On the way out I spoke with Clifford and told him that I had come for the reconciliation of the Armenians.

He sent me to Mr. Atkin.

Then I took the Underground to Shepherd's Bush to see the Armenian revolutionary, Nazarbek. When I arrived at his house, he had just left for the Underground with Georg Brandes.

The house is noisy, second-rate, middle-class elegance, and from time to time wild Armenian faces appear in the crack of the door. They are refugees who find shelter here.

The Russian Rapoport had introduced me. Together with him and Mme. Nazarbek I waited in the living-room for the man of the house. I said that I had not had my lunch yet, whereupon the woman with an unfriendly expression had a piece of meat brought out to me.

Nazarbek came home. The head of a genius, the way they are

fixed up in the Quartier Latin. Black, tangled serpentine locks, black beard, pale face.

He mistrusts the Sultan and would like to have guarantees before he submits. His political ideas are confused, his acquaintance with the European situation downright childish. He said: Austria is building fortifications on the Black Sea!

And, as it seems, his word is obeyed by the poor people in Armenia who are being massacred. He lives in London, not uncomfortably.

I asked whether he knew who was finally benefitting from all this unrest, Russia or England?

He replied that he did not care; he was revolting only against the Turks.

The woman kept interrupting us, speaking in Armenian and evidently against me. She has a wicked look; and who knows how much she is to blame for the bloodshed. Or is it the evil look of the frightened, the persecuted?

I promised I would try to get the Sultan to stop the massacres and new arrests, as a token of his good will. But he would hardly release the prisoners in advance, as Nazarbek desired. I explained to him in vain that, after all, the revolutionaries could watch the course of the peace negotiations without disarming, with their guns at their feet.

* * *

In the evening, my mass meeting in the East End, at the Workingmen's Club.

Posters in English and Yiddish on the walls; the Yiddish text stated erroneously that I had spoken with the Sultan.

The workingmen's clubhouse was full. People crowded into every corner. A stage served as the platform from which I spoke extemporaneously. I had merely jotted down a few catchwords on a piece of paper. I talked for an hour in the frightful heat. Great success.

Succeeding speakers eulogized me. One of them, Ish-Kishor,

compared me to Moses, Columbus, etc. The chairman, Chief Rabbi Gaster, made a fiery speech.

Finally, I thanked them with a few words in which I protested against their effusiveness.

Great jubilation, hat-waving, hurrahs that followed me out into the street.

Now it really depends only on myself whether I shall become the leader of the masses; but I don't want to be, if in some way I can buy the Rothschilds at the price of my resignation from the movement.

* * *

In the East End propaganda committees are springing up spontaneously. Program: The Jewish State!

Party leaders: Rabbinowicz, Ish-Kishor, de Haas, and others—fine, enthusiastic people!

July 14

Last night I did the most stupid or the most clever thing I have yet done in this matter.

The Hovevei Zion Society had invited me to their "Headquarters Tent." This is being held out in the East End, at the Spanish synagogue at Bevis Marks. I came late; the discussion had been going on for an hour and a half

(Continued at Folkestone, July 15)

and I had been its subject before my arrival—as young de Haas, who had been waiting for me at the gateway, informed me. The Hovevei Zion want to offer to join in with me if I pledge myself not to attack them again.

My entrance was greeted with friendly drumming on the tables, and as usual I was given the place of honor. On the other side of Chairman Prag sat Goldsmid, looking a bit gloomy.

They read lengthy reports about a settlement which is to be founded and is to cost I don't know how many hundreds of pounds: so-and-so-many oxen, so-and-so-many horses, seeds, timber, etc.

The question was asked whether the colonists were protected, and it was answered in the negative.

I tied onto that when my project came up for discussion. I said I wanted only the kind of colonization that we could protect with our own Jewish army. I had to oppose infiltration. I would not interfere with the efforts of the Zionist societies, but Edmond Rothschild's sport must cease at all costs. Let him subordinate himself to the national cause and then I would not only be prepared to give him the highest position, but also pay for his assumption of leadership with my own resignation.

A storm ensued.

Dr. Hirsch spoke against me at great length.

Rabbinowicz, my friend from the East End, declared that no Hovev Zion could ever come out in opposition to Edmond Rothschild. He hoped that Jewish history would not have to record any strife between Edmond Rothschild and myself.

Ish-Kishor asked Colonel Goldsmid up to what point a Hovev could go along with me unofficially.

Goldsmid gave an evasive answer, saying that naturally he could dictate no one's actions outside the Hovevei Zion.

I got up and said:

"I shall formulate Mr. Ish-Kishor's question more precisely. He means: does the Colonel regard my secret steps to be in any way practical and to be taken seriously?"

The Colonel said haltingly: "Well * . . . if Dr. Herzl—I mean, if the people to whom he spoke—if they are not acting in bad faith, then Dr. Herzl has already achieved a remarkable result."

I then declared that I could not abandon my stand on infiltration even if I thereby lost the support of all the Hovevei Zion societies, which are now under a central organization.

Thereupon the chairman, Mr. Prag, adjourned the meeting with a dry, curt "Good-bye, Dr. Herzl!" *

Goldsmid drew me aside and told me that in the afternoon, at the Queen's garden-party, he had not been able to get to the

* In English in the original.

Prince of Wales and therefore had been unable to do anything in the matter of an introduction.

Accordingly, now as previously, it will be left for me to do everything by myself.

In the street I immediately took Rabbinowicz by the arm and said: "Organize the East End for me!"

Then I drove with Herbert Bentwich, who is devoted to me, to the House of Parliament, where I wanted to speak with Stevenson about the Armenian problem.

Bentwich called my attention to my mistake: I had been too brusque; I should not have told the Headquarters Tent that they had bungled things, but should have praised their ideas and past achievements as exemplary.

He was right. And yet I immediately had the feeling that in addition to having been frank, my attitude could have been wise, despite its momentary bad effect.

Folkestone, July 15

As I was packing my things at the hotel yesterday morning, I was surprised by a visit from Ish-Kishor. He is the poor Russian-Jewish teacher whose speech in the Jewish jargon at the East End meeting had moved me deeply and carried away the other listeners.

As I sat on the platform of the workingmen's stage on Sunday I experienced strange sensations. I saw and heard my legend being born. The people are sentimental; the masses do not see clearly. I believe that even now they no longer have a clear image of me. A light fog is beginning to rise around me, and it may perhaps become the cloud in which I shall walk.

But even if they no longer see my features distinctly, still they divine that I mean very well by them, and that I am the man of the little people.

Of course, they would probably show the same affection to some clever deceiver and impostor as they do to me, in whom they are not deceived.

This is perhaps the most interesting thing I am recording in these notebooks—the way my legend is being born.

And while I was listening, on that people's tribunal, to the emphatic words and the cheering of my adherents, I inwardly resolved quite firmly to become ever worthier of their trust and their affection.

* * *

Ish-Kishor, then, came yesterday to offer me the formation of an organization which would recognize me as its head. A hundred men would join together in the East End, recruit comrades in all countries, and carry on agitation for the Jewish State.

This I accepted; and when de Haas, who wishes to be my *"honorary secretary,"* * came, I proposed that they name this association *The Knights of Palestine.** However, I said that I would have to remain outside its ranks, because I must not belong to any propagandizing organization.

* * *

De Haas understood my position and explained it to Ish-Kishor: I intended to unite the poor in order to put pressure on the lukewarm and hesitant rich.

When I went to Montagu later to ask him to get the Armenian matter rolling for me with Stevenson, the Vice-President of the Anglo-Armenian Committees, I could tell from his at-your-service manner the effect of my success in the East End.

* * *

I am satisfied with the result of my trip to London.

The conditional promise of Montagu and Goldsmid to join in with us if Edmond Rothschild and the Hirsch Fund participate and the Sultan enters into positive negotiations, suffices me for the present.

* In English in the original.

July 16, Boulogne-sur-mer

Nevertheless, it should not be forgotten that both Montagu and Goldsmid declined to preside at the East End meeting. Nor did either of them attend the banquet of the Maccabean Club.

But I need them—consequently———

July 17

In Paris again.

It was in one of the rooms I am now occupying at the Hotel Castille that I wrote *The Jewish State* (in the form of the Address to the Rothschilds).

Telegrams from Newlinski were waiting for me.

One of them reads:*

Sidney Whitman has just arrived, wants to undertake mission. How much can I offer him in addition to traveling expenses? Kind regards, Newlinski.

The second one:*

Special request: buy two sets of mantel clocks, two silver candlesticks, first quality, half a meter or more in height, massive, renaissance style, one Oriental or Moorish style, each two or three thousand francs cash. I need them urgently for His Majesty himself. Unobtainable here. In any case, come see me at Carlsbad. Prince of no use at moment.

Newlinski

The third:

Would be good if you came to discuss everything again. Day after tomorrow Whitman returning from Herbert.** Reply about sets, have to wire Constantinople whether obtainable. Regards, Newlinski.

* * *

That business with the mantel sets I don't quite understand. Why am I to get them, of all things? In any case, I am in no

* In French in the original.
** From here on in French in the original.

position to pay for them out of my pocket. I wired back he should indicate whether I should suggest to my friends that they make the Sultan a present of two sumptuous sets. If not, to whom should it be sent C.O.D. I told him that I could not spare Whitman any more than his expenses. But if he participated, our future gratitude would be all the greater.

* * *

Talked with Bernard Lazare. Excellent type of a fine, clever French Jew.

* * *

Nordau has fresh scruples: it would be an internal Russo-Jewish affair, etc.

I told him, as well as Lazare, that I intend to purchase the enrollment of Edmond Rothschild and the Hirsch Fund by my own withdrawal. This seemed the right thing to both of them.

July 18

Nordau said yesterday: "The story goes that they entered into conversations with you in Constantinople. Didn't the people ask, whom are we talking to? who has the money?"

I said: "I have made the connection, that is all. I had a right to make reference to Montagu. And, incidentally, this is where my tremendous risk lay. Montagu had merely declared to me, in absolute privacy, his conditional willingness to join in with me. I ran the risk of his telling me, on my return: that was only smoking-room talk, not serious. However, he has stuck to his word even now; and so today I am covered."

* * *

Yesterday afternoon the likeable Bernard Lazare brought me Mr. Meyerson of the Agence Havas and of the local Zionist associations.

Nordau and the sculptor Beer joined us later. This gathering of intellectually notable men in my own room and on my own ground once again gave me a distinct feeling of what enormous progress my idea has made.

Meyerson raised many, all too many, objections, particularly with regard to the ability of Jews to become farmers.

I finally begged him: *"Ne me faites donc pas tant de misères. Nous ne pouvous pas prevoir l'avenir. Marchons, et nous verrons* [Don't make me mountains with your mole hills. We can't foresee the future. Let us go forward and we shall see]."

That mollified him. He took it upon himself to go to Edmond Rothschild and tell him that I was prepared to call on him. I did not hide from the gentlemen the fact that this was one of the greatest sacrifices I was making for the Jewish cause. For Edmond Rothschild's treatment of Nordau has soured me on him. As for Albert Rothschild's *parcheschkat* toward me in Vienna, I kept silent about that.

I asked Meyerson to formulate my standpoint clearly: I am demanding the unification of all Zionist groups, particularly of the Hirsch Fund and of Edmond Rothschild. The latter need declare his adherence only conditionally. When I have completed the diplomatic side of the whole matter, the gentlemen designated by me are to take over its direction. For my part, I shall give my word of honor to abstain from assuming the leadership of the masses. I do not want a demagogic movement, although in case of need I am prepared to create one. The consequences, to be sure, could be serious.

But if my program is accepted, I shall withdraw completely from the leadership of the movement.

* * *

In the evening, had some beer with Schiff. I reminded him of last year. He said: Well, so perhaps I was wrong.

Actually, he is still quite obdurate and uncomprehending.

July 18

Telegram from St. Blasien, dated July 17:

Grand Duke unable to receive you at time stated. Requests you to present matter in writing.

Secret Cabinet.

July 19

Yesterday I delivered the "Address to the Rothschilds."

Thus everything I proposed to do comes to pass, even though at another time and in another way, and the goal will undoubtedly be attained, although I myself shall hardly live to see it.

Yesterday morning I visited Leven in his *appartement de bourgeois cossu* [upper-middle class apartment]. Leven treats the Jewish question rather nonchalantly. He's not badly off. While we were talking, Meyerson was announced. He had come from "Baron Edmond" to invite Leven and me to a conference at which he was also going to be present. Time: one-thirty p.m.

At half past one I was in the rue Laffitte. The attendant took my card and ushered me into the first waiting room, for general visitors who have business with this banking house. A few minutes later I was shown into another wood-panelled reception room where Meyerson was already waiting and where he prepared me for the fact that the Baron was a human being like ourselves.

I was not surprised at this piece of information.

After we had been waiting for about ten minutes, a door opened and Leven came in, followed by a tall, slim man in his forties. I had thought he was much older. He looks like an aging youth, his movements are quick and yet shy, and he has a light-brown beard on the verge of turning grey, a long nose, and an offensively large mouth. He wore a red necktie and a white waistcoat which flapped about his thin body.

I asked him to what extent he was acquainted with my plan, whereupon he began to spout: he had heard about me as a new

Bernard l'hermite—and lost himself all over the map in a refutation of my program, of which he had no exact knowledge.

After five minutes I interrupted him, saying: "You don't know what it is all about. Let me explain it to you first."

He stopped in bewilderment.

I began: "A colony is a little state, a state is a big colony. You want to build a small state, I, a big colony."

And once again, as so many times previously, I unfolded the entire plan. He listened at times with surprise; at a few points I read admiration in his eyes.

However, he has no faith in the promises of the Turks. And even if he did believe in them, he still would not engage in such an undertaking. He thinks it would be impossible to keep the influx of the masses into Palestine under control. The first to arrive would be 150,000 *shnorrers* [beggars] who would have to be fed. He didn't feel equal to it, but perhaps I would be. He could not undertake such a responsibility. There might be mishaps.

"Are there none now?" I interjected. "Isn't anti-Semitism a permanent mishap with loss of honor, life, and property?"

The adherence of the Londoners is not enough for him. Sir S. Montagu wanted to stand behind him, that he could well understand. But as for Colonel Goldsmid, in a letter he had just received Goldsmid had represented my undertaking as downright dangerous.

This news staggered me greatly. I should never have expected this from Goldsmid. If he is against me, why didn't he tell me so with military candor, why did he leave me confident and on that Hovevei Zion evening expressly assure me of his sympathy in my undertaking, provided that I was not being led astray in Constantinople?

Colonel Goldsmid will no longer be counted upon.

Mr. Leven nodded pleasantly to every word "the Baron" said; Meyerson, too, agreed with everything.

After two hours of this battle of words, I picked up my umbrella from the floor and rose:

"By way of concluding this conversation, which has been a serious one and which we have not carried on for our entertainment, I say to you: By what do I recognize the power of an idea? By the fact that a man commits himself when he says Yes and commits himself also when he says No."

The Baron made a very uncomfortable face, indeed, an angry one.

I added: "You were the keystone of the entire combination. If you refuse, everything I have fashioned so far will fall to pieces. I shall then be obliged to do it in a different way. I shall start a mass agitation, and that way it will be even harder to keep the masses under control. I was going to turn the direction of the whole project over to you, the philanthropic Zionist, and withdraw. Once the affair with the Sultan had been straightened out, you could have made public or kept secret as much of it as you pleased. The regulation of mass immigration is a matter for the government. If, e.g., a "run" were to set in, unfavorable reports about housing or the employment situation could be published, which would slow down the torrent. All these are details of administration. You think that it would be a misfortune to operate with such masses. Reflect whether the misfortune will not be greater if I am forced to set the masses in motion by unplanned agitation.

"This is precisely what I wanted to avoid. I have shown my good intentions, and that I am no *intransigeant entêté* [obstinate cuss]. You are not willing—I have done my share."

Then I took my leave. We both declared that we were delighted to have made each other's acquaintance, and then I left.

Rothschild detained the other two by their coat buttons; I think, he had asked them there for his protection, in case I turned out to be an anarchist.

A half-hour later Meyerson came to my hotel with a sweet-and-sour expression. Was he under unofficial orders from the Baron when he advised me to start on a small scale, and obtain small concessions in Turkey for Edm. R.'s colonies? Then, he said, the Baron might gradually show himself more favorably disposed toward my plans.

General impression: Edmond is a decent, good-natured, fainthearted man, who absolutely fails to understand the matter and would like to stop it, the way a coward tries to stop necessary surgery. I believe he is now aghast at having got himself involved with Palestine, and perhaps he will run to Alphonse and say: "You were right; I should have gone in for racing horses rather than resettling Jews."

And the fate of many millions is to hang on such men!

*   *   *

To Newlinski I telegraphed:

Edmond R. is making difficulties which are threatening to have repercussions in London. He first wanted small concessions for which he would presumably offer small counter-services.

July 20, Paris

Addendum to Rothschild conversation.

Actually, I have noted down very little on the preceding pages about this talk which was one of the most important I have had.

I had to combat feelings of listlessness yesterday. When I think how easy and obvious the whole thing will appear to people once it is accomplished and against what idiotic obstacles I get sick fighting and wearing myself out——

Among other things, Edmond R. said, piqued: "I didn't need you to come along and tell me that we now have machines at our disposal."

I answered: "I had no intention of instructing you."

At another point in the conversation he said:

"*Et qu'est-ce que vous me demandez* [and what do you want me to do]?"

I answered brusquely: "*Pardon, vous ne m'avez pas compris. Je ne vous demande rien du tout. Je vous invite seulement de donner votre adhésion sous condition* [I beg your pardon, you did not understand me. I want nothing at all from you. I am inviting you only to give your conditional adherence]."

Leven and Meyerson, as I said, quite agreed with him.

Ils abondaient dans le sens indiqué par lui [they echoed whatever line he took], they obligingly provided him with arguments. When Edmond said that there would be no curbing the masses, Meyerson said darkly: "Yes, just like what happened on the Chodinko plain."

Leven even had the presumption to declare that up till now I had not achieved anything.

Twice Edmond R. said: *"Il ne faut pas avoir les yeux plus gros que le ventre* [one mustn't have eyes bigger than one's stomach]." That, I believe, is the extent of his philosophical insight.

July 20, Paris

I am writing de Haas in London that they should begin to organize the masses. This will be the reply to the Chodinko argument.

July 21

On the train past Jaxtzell, on the way to Carlsbad where Newlinski has urgently summoned me.

Another addendum to the Rothschild conversation:

I mentioned the fact that I was being aided by three people whose traveling expenses I was paying: a diplomat (Newlinski), a journalist (Sidney Whitman), and an English clergyman (Hechler). I did not give him their names. I said that the clergyman was not expecting any reward but that if success comes we would have to buy the diplomat a fine estate and give the journalist some decent compensation. When I said this, Rothschild gave Leven a very sly look which was intended to mean "Aha!"

July 21

Talked with Nordau and Beer yesterday and told them the answer I had found to Rothschild's objection: the organization of our masses, without delay. Our people will be organized before their departure, and not merely upon their arrival. No one will be allowed to enter without a certificate of departure.

Nordau expressed his complete agreement with me and even wishes to join the Paris Committee, as I put it, "as Chief of the Movement in France." He demurred a little against the title "Chief," but accepted the post.

*　　*　　*

In the afternoon I spoke in the club rooms of the Russian Jewish students, out in the Gobelins quarter. B. Lazare was present, also three Jewish female students from Russia. The room was packed. I made the speech with which I am familiar by now, but was not in good form.

I spoke with forbearance of the moneyed Jews who are in no hurry, and concluded with the words: *"Je ne vous dis pas encore: marchons—je dis seulement: la jeunesse, debout!* [I am not saying to you as yet, 'Forward march!' All I am saying is, 'Youth, to your feet!]"

I called on them to start organizing the cadres.

*　　*　　*

Et nous voilà repartis de Paris [And here we are, leaving Paris again].

Never has this charming city so enchanted me as on this parting-day.

When shall I see Paris again?

of our ranks, with no delay. Our people will be organized before their departure, and not merely upon their arrival. No one will be allowed to enter within a certificated departure.

Nordau requested his complete agreement with me and even wishes to join the Paris Committee, as I put it, "as Chief of the Movement in France." He demurred a little against the title "Chief," but accepted the post.

In the afternoon I spoke in the club rooms of the Russian Jewish students, out in the Odeons quarter. Besides there were present also three Jewish female students from Russia. The room was packed. I made the speech with which I am familiar by now, but was not in good form.

I spoke with forbearance of the monied Jews who are in no hurry, and concluded with the words: "Je ne vous dis pas encore: maintenant—je dis seulement: la jeunesse, debout! [I am not saying to you as yet, 'Forward march!' All I am saying is, 'Youth, to your feet!'"

I relied on them to start organizing the ladies.

Et nous nous reverrons dès Paris! And here we are, leaving Paris again.

Never has this charming city so enchanted me as on this particular day.

When shall I see Paris again?